FLASH FOCUS

POLITICAL PARTIES

VOLUME 2

an imprint of

www.scholastic.com/librarypublishing

© 2005 by Lakeside Publishing Group.
This library edition first published by Scholastic Library Publishing.

Set ISBN 0-7172-5935-8
Volume ISBN 0-7172-5938-2

Library of Congress Cataloging-in-Publication Data
Flash focus
    p. cm.
  Includes bibliographical references and index.
  Contents: Vol. 1. Presidential elections, 1788–2000 – v. 2. Political
Parties – v. 3. The Supreme Court – v. 4. Equal rights under law.
  ISBN 0-7172-5935-8 (set : alk. paper)
    1. United States--Politics and government--Juvenile literature. I.
Grolier (Firm)

JK40.F58 2004
320.473--dc22

2004042417

All rights reserved. Except for use in a review, no part of this book may
be reproduced, stored in a retrieval system, or transmitted in any form,
or by any means, electronic, mechanical photocopying, recording, or
otherwise, without prior permission of Scholastic Library Publishing.

For information, address the publisher:
Scholastic Library Publishing,
Old Sherman Turnpike, Danbury, Connecticut 06816

Printed and bound in Thailand.

Contents

How to Use This Book 1

The Roles of Political Parties 3
Parties and Paying for Election Campaigns 6
Federalist Party, 1794–1816 9
    Biography: Alexander Hamilton
Democratic-Republican Party (Antifederalists), 1796–1826 13
    Biography: Thomas Jefferson
Democratic Party, 1828–60 17
    Biography: Andrew Jackson
National Republican Party, 1828–32 21
Anti-Masonic Party, 1827–36 23
    Biography: William Wirt
Whig Party, 1834–56 27
    The Cotton Whigs
Locofocos, 1835–48 32
Liberty Party, 1840–48 34
    Biography: James G. Birney
Law and Order Party of Rhode Island, 1841–51 38
    Biography: Thomas Dorr
Free Soil Party, 1848–54 42
    The Wilmot Proviso
American (Know-Nothing) Party, 1849–57 46
Constitutional Union Party, 1860 50
Southern Democratic Party, 1860 52
Republican Party, 1854–76 55
    The Union Party
    Biography: Charles Sumner
Democratic Party, 1860–76 61
    The Copperheads
    Biography: William Tweed
Prohibition Party, 1869– 66
    Biography: John Bidwell
Liberal Republican Party, 1872 69
Equal Rights Party, 1872–88 72
Republican Party, 1876–1900 75
    Biography: Mark Hanna
    Silver Republicans
Democratic Party, 1876–1900 80
    Biography: Adlai Stevenson
Workingmen's Party of California, 1877–80 85
    Biography: Denis Kearney
Greenback Party, 1874–1940 88
    Biography: James Weaver
National Silver Party, 1880–1904 92
Socialist Labor Party, 1874–1976 95
    Biography: Daniel DeLeon

People's Party (Populists), 1891–1908 98
    Biography: Charles Macune
Social Democratic Party, 1897 102
    Biography: Victor Berger
Republican Party, 1900–32 105
    Biography: Henry Cabot Lodge
Democatic Party, 1900–32 111
    Biography: James Curley
    Biography: Thomas Pendergast
Socialist Party, 1901– 116
    Biography: Norman Thomas
Progressive ("Bull Moose") Party, 1912–16 121
    Biography: Hiram Johnson
Farmer-Labor Party, 1918–44 125
    Biography: Floyd B. Olsen
Communist Party, 1919– 128
    Biography: Earl Browder
Progressive Party, 1924 132
    Biography: Roberrt La Follette
Republican Party, 1932–68 135
    Biography: Robert Taft
Democratic Party, 1932–68 141
    Biography: Richard Daley
Union Party, 1936–39 149
    Biography: William Lemke
American Labor Party, 1936–56 152
    Biography: Fiorello La Guardia
America First Party, 1943–47 155
    Biography: Gerald L.K. Smith
Liberal Party, 1944– 157
    Biography: David Dubinsky
Progressive Party, 1948–52 160
    Biography: Henry Wallace
Democratic Party, 1968–2004 163
    Biography: Terry McAuliffe
Republican Party, 1968–2004 169
    Biography: Karl Rove
National Socialist White People's Party, 1967– 176
    Biography: George Lincoln Rockwell
American Independent Party, 1968; American Party, 1972 179
    Biography: George C. Wallace
La Raza Unida Party, 1970–81 183
    Biography: José Gutiérrez
Libertarian Party, 1971– 187
    Biography: Harry Browne
Green Party, 1989– 190
    Biography: Ralph Nader
Natural Law Party, 1992– 193
    Biography: John Hagelin
Reform Party, 1992– 196
    Biography: Pat Buchanan

Set Index 199

Introduction

How to Use This Book

This book presents portraits of a variety of political parties that have shaped America from the years just after the Constitution was adopted in 1789 to the present. Many institutions of government have remained remarkably constant throughout this period—the presidency, Congress, and Supreme Court, for example, all function in largely the same forms as envisioned by the authors of the Constitution. But political parties, existing outside the confines of the Constitution, have been a constantly changing swirl of ideas and personalities, both absorbing and reflecting the dramatic changes in the United States. Over time, the country has evolved from an agricultural nation of about four million people, most of them farmers of British or African ancestry, nestled along the Atlantic seaboard to an industrial nation of about 288 million people with ancestors from every continent except Antarctica, spread from the Atlantic to the Pacific and beyond, a global military power with a very small portion of its population living on farms.

As the nation changed, so did its political parties. Individual parties, such as the Democratic-Republicans of Thomas Jefferson (see p. 10), evolved into the Democratic Party (see pp. 13, 17, 61, 80, 111, 141, 163). Over decades, the Democrats went from being the party of small southern landowners to being the party of northern industrial workers who owned no property—even while not abandoning its original constituency. Other parties, such as the Whigs (see p. 24), rose to power, then faded away when they failed to bridge differences between quarreling factions.

This volume presents brief portraits of the most significant political parties, as well as smaller parties. The party portraits include an overview of the party's origins, its principal positions on issues of the day, and its successes (or failures) in achieving political influence. Also included are short biographies of personalities who played important roles in their respective parties and excerpts from party platforms or other key documents that provide a sampling of each party's positions on the issues. (A complete collection of political party platforms is available on the Web at The American Presidency Project at the University of California at Santa Barbara: *http://www.presidency.ucsb.edu/site/docs/platforms.php.*)

Parties are arranged in general chronological order, based on date of founding. In the case of the Democratic and Republican Parties, which have existed longer than any others and have unique roles in American political life, the portraits have been divided into separate articles, each covering distinctive eras.

The Roles of Political Parties

Nowhere in the Constitution are political parties mentioned. Nevertheless, it is difficult to imagine American democracy—or, indeed, any democratic government—working without them. Political parties play a vital role in organizing candidates for office and organizing voters to support them.

The term "political party" encompasses a range of organizations and functions within the American political system. People often speak of the "two-party system," referring to the fact that for much of American history there have been two main parties competing for power at the federal level, running candidates for the presidency and for Congress. This volume also covers dozens of "third parties" that never stood the least chance of electing a president.

What Is a Political Party?

At first glance, the definition of a political party seems simple: a group of people with similar ideas about government who coordinate their activities to elect candidates to office. This is the definition seen in action every four years during presidential elections, when the Democrats and the Republicans hold national conventions, nominate candidates, and coordinate battles in the "blue states" and "red states" (named after television graphics depicting which party's candidate won a particular state's electoral votes; for no particular reason, states won by Republicans were colored red, and those won by the Democrats were colored blue). Political parties play a key role in collecting contributions from interested individuals and organizations to pay for advertising meant to persuade voters to choose their candidate, as well as organizing activities on a local level on election day to "get out the vote," i.e., encourage sympathetic voters to go to their polling place and vote.

The Democrats and Republicans, and some smaller third parties, like the Green Party (see p. 190), also nominate candidates for the House of Representatives and Senate and for state legislative offices, which leads to parties' second role: passing legislation. During each session of Congress, laws are passed that cover a broad range of topics, ranging from passing a budget for the military to paying for prescription drugs for senior citizens, to regulating international trade. Many laws are hundreds of pages long and depend on a degree of expert knowledge that no single individual can possibly hope to achieve. Thus, legislators depend on the opinions of like-minded individuals—other members of the same party—to make recommendations on whether to vote for or against a particular law. In the legislative branch, whether on the federal level or within states, political parties function as broad alliances. As with any alliance, not all members of a party will agree on all subjects, and within the Congress, Republicans and Democrats do not always vote along straight party lines. Rather, regional groups of, say, Democrats will sometimes vote with regional groups of Republicans for a particular piece of legislation. Nevertheless, parties play an important role in bringing order to a legislative process that could easily disintegrate into chaos.

Principal versus Practicality

Passing legislation usually involves making compromises. A legislator who would like to spend $100 million to fund a favorite project will be willing to cut the amount to $80 million as the price of getting enough votes to pass the measure at all. The principle here is: something is better than nothing. Commentators often condemn the willingness to compromise as a sign of lacking firm beliefs in principles—typical of being a "politician." In practice, however, if democratically elected legislators constantly stood firm on their ideas, nothing would get accomplished, social problems would go unsolved, and voters would end up being unhappy.

The ability to negotiate compromises takes many forms. One form is mentioned above: settling for a portion of what is wanted rather than gaining nothing at all. Another form takes the form of "you scratch my back, I'll scratch yours." A legislator agrees to support a measure important to one region or group of voters in exchange for getting support for another measure important to his region or constituents. Sometimes, the terms of vote swaps are simple; other times, they are much more complicated. In the years before the Civil War, for example, northern Democrats agreed to vote for the Fugitive Slave Law (obligating officials in nonslave states to seize and return runaway slaves to their southern owners) as a means of satisfying southern Democrats who were thinking of splitting off from the United States (as eventually happened). When compromises end up violating basic beliefs, the result can be splitting a political party (or inspiring formation of a new one) and losing influence.

Evolution over Time

The contemporary Democratic Party traces its beginnings to the Democratic-Republican Party of Thomas Jefferson (see Vol. 1, p. 13), which took form as early as the election of 1796 (see Vol. 1, p. 9) under the name Antifederalists (see p. 13). In the beginning, the Democratic-Republicans were the party of independent farmers, particularly in the South, who distrusted the central government and were primarily concerned with preserving their individual freedoms against government incursions. The industrial revolution was still decades away. By 1936, the Democratic Party had evolved into the party of industrial workers living in the urban North, while also speaking for drought-stricken farmers in the West (see p. 141). If there is a common thread linking Jefferson's Democratic-Republicans and twenty-first century Democrats, it is representing the interests of individuals of modest means against the interests of wealth (which in Jefferson's time was represented largely by merchants and bankers). Over the past two centuries, however, the Democratic Party has taken on many different forms as politicians jockeyed for power and influence in government.

The same evolution has marked the Republican Party since its founding in 1854 (see p. 55). Originally, Republicans were focused almost entirely on stopping the spread of slavery into western territories that had not yet become states, and on opposing the principle of "nullification," or the idea that states could refuse to observe federal laws that did not suit them. The Republicans then became dominant in the Union during the Civil War and later evolved into the heirs of the Whig Party (see p. 27) as the party of business interests. For Republicans in the nineteenth century, as well as in the twenty-first, policies that help businesses grow and prosper are seen to be in the interests of all the people, since a prosperous economy benefits everyone, business owners and employees alike.

Although American politics has been dominated by the same two parties, Democratic and Republican, since 1860, other major parties have also come into power and faded from the scene. The Federalists (see p. 9) competed with the Democratic-Republicans from the mid-1790s until about 1814; the Whig Party emerged in the 1830s as a modified form of the Federalists backing business interests and government support for the economic infrastructure (roads and canals at the time) to boost economic growth, only to disappear in the 1850s when its northern and southern wings were torn apart over the issue of slavery.

Third Parties

While Democrats and Republicans are often willing to compromise on particular issues in order to achieve their broad philosophical aims, other parties have emerged along much narrower principles. For example, the Prohibition Party (see p. 66) emerged in the nineteenth century with a particular goal in mind: prohibiting the sale of alcohol. The party eventually achieved its aim (in the form of the Eighteenth Amendment), though not by electing a president or a majority in Congress. Another example of a narrowly based third party was the National Silver Party (see p. 92), dedicated to using silver, as well as gold, as the basis for money. Both of these parties focused on a specific solution to the problem of economic difficulties and social suffering by their constituencies (working people in the case of the Prohibitionists, struggling western farmers in the case of the National Silver Party).

In other cases, parties have arisen in the United States based on political philosophies, sometimes imported from Europe. Such was the case with a variety of parties dedicated to socialism—the idea that democratic control should extend to the economy as well as to government. Within this broad concept have existed a variety of specific ideas, ranging from control over the economy exerted by democratically elected government (see Social Democratic Party, p. 102), to advocating revolution, violent if necessary, to seize private property (capital) for the benefit of everyone rather than just a small group of wealthy owners (Communist Party, see p. 128).

In most cases, one or the other major party has absorbed ideas and programs from third parties, thereby robbing the smaller group of its unique appeal—and its political support. In many instances, this has been the manner in which third parties have effectively been absorbed into one of the major parties, and the American "two-party system" has survived.

Geography, Economics, Ideology

In broad terms, political parties are organized in three ways: by geography, by economic interests, and by ideology. These three divisions are by no means mutually exclusive; to the contrary, geography and economic interests often coincide, only to be divided by ideology.

For example, in the 1850s, the Democratic Party (see p. 17) was dominated by the southern farmers who owned large cotton and tobacco plantations worked by slaves. To keep the loyalty of this key constituency, the Democratic Party supported slavery, which was an economic issue in the South but an ideological and moral issue in the North. Opposition to slavery on principle became the preserve of the Liberty Party (see p. 34) and eventually of the Republican Party. For the Free Soil Party, also (see p. 42), the issue of slavery was economic, but from a different viewpoint. The Free Soil Party did not challenge slavery in the South, but it did oppose the spread of slavery into western territories in order to prevent slave labor from competing with free white settlers.

For over a century, the Republican Party managed to capture the White House and a majority in Congress without carrying a single state of the former Confederate States of America.

Some parties have evolved on the state level, such as the Law and Order Party in Rhode Island (see p. 38), the Farmer-Labor Party in Minnesota (see p. 125), and the Liberal Party in New York (see p. 157). These state parties succeeded in gaining power within a single state, but never spread elsewhere. They nevertheless had the potential of playing a national role by affecting the electoral college vote in presidential elections, and by influencing policies of national parties seeking to capture the loyalty of their adherents.

It is tempting, and not entirely misleading, to see broad economic issues at the heart of the differences between the major parties, with Democrats broadly presenting themselves as representatives of working people and Republicans as representatives of the business sector. But that division ignores important sets of issues that are not economic in nature. Social issues have long played an important part in party loyalty. Such issues range from political rights for minorities, to women's right to abortion, to government regulation of individual behavior (the use of drugs, for example; see Libertarian Party, p. 187). Social issues often cut across economic or class lines and across regional lines, serving to unite voters whose economic interests might be widely divergent or even antithetical. When these issues involve deeply held religious beliefs, as they often have, they can be compelling to some voters. Examples of religion playing a key role range from the anti-Catholic, anti-immigrant sentiments of the Know-Nothing Party (see p. 46) to arguments over reciting prayers or including religious symbols in public buildings and public schools.

Given that such a wide variety of topics and issues become embroiled in the process of choosing a government, it is no wonder that the beliefs and actions of political parties fail to fit into neat, consistent categories of ideology, geography, or economics. They are, rather, part of the complex swirl of human affairs known as politics.

Parties and Paying for Election Campaigns

Running for political office has always been expensive, and one important role of political parties has been to help raise funds for campaigns, as well as to organize volunteers to do the work of publicizing a candidate's positions on issues and persuading voters to go to the polls on election day.

As early as 1757, when George Washington (see Vol. 1, p. 6) was running for the Virginia House of Burgesses (colonial legislature), he was expected to provide "the customary means of winning votes," which included rum punch, wine, and beer for voters. In 1832, President Andrew Jackson (see Vol. 1, p. 37) complained that "it is to be regretted that the rich and powerful too often bend the acts of government to their selfish purposes" at the expense of "the humble members of society."

Political parties and political "machines" were extensively used in the nineteenth and twentieth centuries to funnel money from wealthy contributors, either as individuals or as stockholders in industrial corporations, to help pay for campaigning. Around the turn of the twentieth century, political parties often "assessed" corporations for a percentage of their profits in the form of contributions. Whether or not direct links could be established between such donations and subsequent acts by elected officials, the appearance of impropriety undercut the basic premise of democracy: that free citizens each possess an equal voice, one vote, in choosing representatives in office.

Early Attempts at Reform

Although the importance of personal wealth has long been an issue in American politics (as Andrew Jackson observed), smaller contributions have also played an important role. In 1838, a committee of the House of Representatives discovered that the Democratic Party had required federal Customs employees to pay a percentage of their salaries to the party. Whigs (see p. 27) proposed legislation to bar any federal employee from paying money to advance the election of any public official, but the legislation died without being passed, and the practice of collecting contributions from government workers continued until after the Civil War.

The Naval Appropriations Bill of 1867 barred government officials and employees from soliciting contributions from workers at navy shipyards. In 1883, the Civil Service Reform Act extended the ban to cover all federal civil service workers, ending a practice in which government employees were expected to make campaign contributions in order to keep their jobs.

In 1883, the Pendleton Civil Service Act created a new class of federal employees who earned their positions by passing competitive examinations, rather than being appointed as a political favor. The 1883 law also banned soliciting contribu-

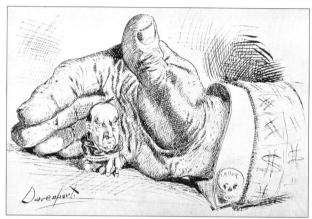

This 1896 cartoon depicts Republican presidential candidate William McKinley as tied up and sitting under the thumb of Mark Hanna, his campaign manager and fund raiser. Hanna was widely considered to be the link between the Republicans and major corporate interests. He devised a system whereby corporations contributed a percentage of their profits to the Republicans, a system that motivated efforts at campaign finance reform in the first decade of the twentieth century.

tions from civil service workers, consequently reducing the importance of government employee contributions in financing campaigns. One result was to shift the burden to corporate interests that had major stakes in government policy.

Corporations, Parties, and Campaigns

Over the next two decades, corporate contributions rose dramatically and became the mainstay of party financing. Mark Hanna (see p. 76), a key campaign advisor to President William McKinley (see Vol. 1, p. 106), developed a system of collecting contributions from corporations based on their profits. Hanna's system underscored not only the ways that parties acted to finance elections, but also the role of private interests in influencing parties. In addition, expenditures on federal campaigns soared. McKinley's two presidential campaigns in 1896 and 1900, for example, spent at least $3 million each, twice the amount spent by Benjamin Harrison's presidential campaign in 1888. Corporate contributions became favorite subjects of progressives and muckraking journalists, who charged that such contributions amounted to buying the government.

During the 1904 presidential election, the Democratic nominee, Judge Alton Parker (see Vol. 1, p. 115), accused Republican Theodore Roosevelt (see Vol. 1, p. 114) of soliciting contributions from some of the nation's wealthiest businessmen, and of promising to consult them afterwards on some government policies. Stung by the criticism, Roosevelt sent a message to Congress in 1905 (just a month after his elec-

Under the spoils system, government workers were expected to contribute part of their salaries to the party in power. Government employees were an important source of funding for political parties in the nineteenth century, and the practice was the first target of campaign finance reform. This 1889 cartoon depicts President Benjamin Harrison, wearing a top hat, grinding out contributions and jobs for Republicans after four years of Democrat Grover Cleveland in the White House.

tion) in which he declared that "there is no enemy of free government more dangerous and none so insidious as the corruption of the electorate.... I recommend the enactment of a law directed against bribery and corruption in Federal elections." A year later, Roosevelt proposed that "all contributions by corporations to any political committee or for any political purpose should be forbidden by law." Roosevelt's proposal did not, however, extend to individuals who owned or operated corporations. Roosevelt also called for public financing of federal candidates via their political parties. Finally in 1907, under growing public pressure, Congress passed the Tillman Act to prohibit corporations and nationally chartered banks from making direct financial contributions to federal candidates. But the act did not include strong enforcement tools and proved largely ineffective.

The 1910 Federal Corrupt Practices Act required candidates for the House of Representatives to disclose their spending for office; this requirement was extended to Senate candidates in 1911. The bill also established limits on spending, but like earlier legislation, the law lacked a means of verifying or enforcing its provisions and proved to be ineffective. The 1910 act was revised in 1925; the revised law served as the basic law governing federal campaign financing for nearly half a century, until 1971. But because Congress was given the power to enforce the law, it was usually ignored.

PACs and Unions

In 1940, the Hatch Act set a $5,000 annual limit on contributions by an individual to a federal candidate or political committee (but did not prevent people from contributing to several committees, each of which could work for the same candidate) and extended regulations to cover primary elections. Individuals and companies working for the federal government were banned from contributing to federal candidates. The ban on business or bank contributions was extended to labor unions under the Smith-Connally Act of 1943, reflecting in part a sharp increase in union political activities after 1936.

The Smith-Connally Act gave rise to the first political action committee (PAC), organized in 1944 by the Congress of Industrial Organizations to support the reelection of President Franklin Roosevelt (see Vol. 1, p. 141). PACs skirted the law since they were funded by voluntary contributions from individuals—initially, union members—rather than from the union itself. Later, PACs emerged as an important, and controversial, way of amplifying the small contributions of individuals to make their voices heard in federal elections.

In 1947, the Taft-Hartley Act included a permanent ban on contributions to federal candidates by unions, corporations, or federally chartered banks and extended the ban to primary elections as well as general elections.

Although the 1925 Corrupt Practices Act called on the clerk of the House of Representatives to collect campaign finance reports, the first clerk to actually do so was W. Pat Jennings, a former congressman, who began collecting the reports in 1967. His reports revealed a number of violators, but the Justice Department ignored these.

Federal Election Campaign Act

The biggest step forward in regulating campaign contributions came in 1971 with passage of the Federal Election Campaign Act (FECA) that repealed the previous Corrupt Practices Act and substituted a complex framework to regulate financing of federal elections, including primaries, runoffs, general elections, and conventions. The act covered a broad range of topics, including full disclosure of spending, limits on spending for media advertising, and limits on contributions from candidates and their families. The act also allowed both unions and corporations to solicit voluntary contributions from union members, employees, and stockholders to finance PACS, and allowed unions and corporations to pay for the overhead in operating PACs. A companion law, the 1971 Revenue Act, created a fund for presidential candidates starting in 1976, financed by check-off boxes on federal tax returns to contribute $1 to the fund. The act also allowed individuals to deduct $50 from their taxes for contributions to political campaigns (a provision eliminated in 1978), or a $12.50 tax credit (raised to $50 in 1978 and eliminated in 1986).

After the Watergate scandal of 1974, which forced President Richard Nixon (see Vol. 1, p. 174) to resign, the FECA Amendments provided full public financing for presidential elections and matching funds for primary campaigns, as well as for nominating conventions. Accepting these funds was voluntary and required candidates to observe a set of limitations on private fund raising, including a limit of $1,000 per individual for a single candidate and a limit of $5,000 for PAC contributions to a single candidate. Total individual contributions were limited to $25,000 a year. Candidates were also limited in the amount of their own money they could spend. The law created the Federal Election Commission (FEC) to administer the law.

The limits imposed in 1974 were challenged in court in a suit filed by Republican Senator James Buckley of New York and former Minnesota Democratic Senator Eugene McCarthy against Francis Valeo, secretary of the Senate (see *Buckley v. Valeo*, Vol. 3, p. 164). Buckley and McCarthy argued that the limits imposed on campaign spending violated the constitution's guarantee of free speech. The Supreme Court upheld the law's disclosure requirements, limits on individual contributions, and provisions for voluntary public funding, but the justices ruled that limits on a candidate's personal campaign spending were unconstitutional (unless a candidate accepted public funding, in which case a candidate was voluntarily accepting a limit in exchange for the public funds) and also struck down limits on "independent" spending not coordinated with a candidate or a candidate's election committees.

After Buckley v. Valeo, amendments to campaign finance laws limited individual contributions to national political parties to $20,000 a year and to a PAC to $5,000 a year (but did not limit the number of PACs to which an individual could contribute). Three years later, in 1979, further amendments allowed state and local parties to promote federal candidates by spending unlimited amounts on signs, bumper stickers, and other materials used by volunteers.

McCain-Feingold

Continuing controversy over campaign financing, and the role of wealthy contributors and corporations, led to passage of the McCain-Feingold Bill (named for Republican Senator John McCain and Democratic Senator Russell Feingold) that focused on "soft money," or contributions to promote "issues" often clearly associated with specific candidates rather than to candidates directly. Despite strong and persistent opposition to the bill from some Republicans, the bill was finally passed as the Bipartisan Campaign Reform Act in 2002, six years after it was first proposed. President George Bush (see Vol. 1, p. 205) signed the law in March.

The main thrust of the new law was to limit undesignated contributions to political parties ("soft money") and advertising on "issues" rather than candidates. The law specifically limits contributions related to federal candidates and political parties, but leaves largely unregulated certain tax-exempt groups operating under the terms of section 527 of the Internal Revenue Service code. These so-called "527 committees" became the subject of controversy in the 2004 election when they began running television advertisements attacking both President Bush and his Democratic challenger, Senator John Kerry of Massachusetts. Under the new campaign finance law, these committees were intended to be wholly unconnected to political parties or campaign committees. Nevertheless, early in the 2004 campaign, such committees on both sides attracted criticism and claims that they were, in fact, controlled or directed by the candidates.

More Information

▶ Dwyre, Diana and Victoria A. Farrar-Myers. *Legislative Labyrinth: Congress and Campaign Finance Reform*. Washington: Congressional Quarterly Press, 2001.

▶ Mutch, Robert E. *Campaigns, Congress, and Courts: The Making of Federal Campaign Finance Law*. New York: Praeger, 1988.

▶ Sorauf, Frank J. *Money in American Elections*. Glenview, IL: Scott, Foresman, 1988.

▶ Thayer, George. *Who Shakes the Money Tree?* New York: Simon and Schuster, 1973.

On the Web

▶ Campaign Finance History, The Hoover Institution. *http://www.campaignfinancesite.org/history/financing.html*.

▶ Corrado, Anthony. "Money and Politics: A History of Federal Campaign Finance Law." The New Campaign Finance Sourcebook. The Brookings Institution. *http://www.brookings.edu/gs/cf/newsourcebk.htm*.

▶ The Federal Election Campaign Laws: A Short History. Federal Election Commission. *http://www.fec.gov/info/appfour.htm*.

Federalist Party, 1796–1816

FlashFocus: Federalist Party

Origins
The Federalists were one of the first two political parties. They represented the Founding Fathers who favored a strong central government under the newly adopted Constitution. The intellectual leader of the Federalists was Alexander Hamilton, who, with John Adams, generally supported a strong federal government, even if that power came at the expense of the states.

Issues
Strong federal government. Federalists advocated a strong central government in the aftermath of the failed Articles of Confederation, which had created a weak central government.
Bank of the United States. Hamilton proposed the bank to provide a national currency and to help relieve the nation from debts incurred in the Revolutionary War. The bank was chartered in 1791 for 20 years; a second charter eventually followed. Federalists believed a national banking institution would stimulate commerce and industry, especially in urban areas, and that it was important that the government have an influence on trade. Opponents of the bank argued that the establishment of the institution was illegal since it was not mentioned in the Constitution.
Foreign policy and trade. Federalists were neutral toward the French Revolution, but generally preferred to establish trade relations with England despite the significant assistance France lent to the colonies in the Revolutionary War (when the French government was a monarchy). Federalists also advocated a light tariff on imports that would encourage domestic economic growth.
Opposition to the War of 1812. Federalist opposition to the war with England proved highly unpopular and helped lead to the party's demise.
National defense. Federalists believed in a strong national navy and army to protect American interests.

Impact
George Washington was a great unifying force during the first eight years of the federal government under the Constitution, but members of his cabinet were already divided in their opinions on the nature of the new government. Supporters of a strong central government, the Federalists backed John Adams for president in 1796 and controlled the first six Congresses. Adams was the only Federalist elected to the White House. The death of Hamilton in 1804 left Federalists without a strong advocate, and the party's policies, which favored interests of commerce and industry over agriculture, became increasingly unpopular. Federalists opposed both the Louisiana Purchase and the War of 1812, and after the election of 1812 the party was no longer a factor in national politics.

See also: Democratic-Republican Party, p. 13; National Republican Party, p. 21; Whig Party, p. 27.

After the Constitution was ratified and a new federal government started operating in 1789, there were no political parties. But a distinct group of leaders associated with Treasury Secretary Alexander Hamilton (see p. 10) was widely recognized as "Federalists"—men who believed that the new central government should take precedence over individual state governments. On the other side were followers of Thomas Jefferson (see Vol. 1, p. 13), who believed in the supremacy of the state governments over the central government—men who became known as Antifederalists and were later called Democratic-Republicans (see p. 13).

Origin and Philosophy of the Federalist Party

The Federalist Party originated not as a political party in the modern sense, but as an outgrowth of a policy debate. Nor should the Federalists be confused with the coalition of advocates known by the same name who promoted ratification of the Constitution in a series of essays known as *The Federalist Papers.* Proponents of the new Constitution included Thomas Jefferson and James Madison (see Vol. 1, p. 20), both of whom were leaders of the Democratic-Republicans, having split with Alexander Hamilton and other members of the cabinet of President George Washington (see Vol. 1, p. 6) over new issues facing the United States.

Although Federalists saw themselves as the government itself, rather than a political party, they were not blind to the need for public support of their policies. In 1795, the House of Representatives was evenly divided over the issue of federal funding for the Jay Treaty (a treaty with Britain resolving outstanding issues left from the Revolutionary War and addressing newer issues related to trade). Federalist leaders responded by creating a Federalist caucus in Congress designed to persuade other Federalist members to coordinate their votes. The Federalists also organized a petition campaign directed at particular congressional districts where representatives were vulnerable to public opinion. By the end of the 1790s, the Federalists were responding to challenges by working together to sway public opinion in town meetings and through local party committees.

Nevertheless, opposition to Federalist positions took hold both in public opinion and in the Congress. A particular target of opponents was Hamilton. He proposed establishing a national bank, arguing that the nation's full faith and credit should be established by committing the Treasury to fully pay the federal debt. Hamilton expressed confidence in commerce and industry, which alienated Jefferson and those who favored a focus on agrarian society.

Another divisive issue was the French Revolution, the subsequent war between Britain and France, and a treaty with Britain negotiated by Supreme Court Chief Justice John Jay

FlashFocus: Alexander Hamilton

Born: January 11, 1757, Nevis, West Indies
Died: July 12, 1804. New York, New York
Political career: Alexander Hamilton was one of the most influential Founding Fathers, the politicians who shaped the United States in its infancy. Ineligible to be president because he was born in the West Indies, Hamilton played a major role in shaping a strong federal government and organizing the new country's financial system. He was both the philosophical and practical leader of the Federalist Party which emerged during the first decade of government under Presidents George Washington and John Adams.

Hamilton was educated in New York City and attended what is now Columbia University. During the American Revolution, Hamilton commanded artillery, served as aide-de-camp (general assistant) to General George Washington, and commanded an infantry regiment that helped seize Yorktown in the final battle of the Revolutionary War. Hamilton earned the rank of major general.

After the war, Hamilton practiced law and served in the New York legislature. He made a major contribution as a delegate to the convention in Philadelphia in 1787, where the constitution was drafted. Hamilton was a leading proponent of establishing a strong central government. After the convention, Hamilton actively campaigned for the ratification of the constitution, principally by contributing essays to the *Federalist Papers*.

Washington named Hamilton to be his first secretary of the Treasury. As a member of the cabinet, Hamilton actively promoted the creation of the navy and urged that the federal government should take over debts from the Revolution, including states' debts. In this he was opposed by Thomas Jefferson and James Madison. Hamilton also proposed excise taxes and a charter for the Bank of the United States, and stressed American neutrality in the French Revolutionary War.

After Hamilton resigned from the cabinet in 1795, he remained close to Washington and drafted significant portions of Washington's Farewell Address.

Hamilton was at the forefront of the growing division along factional lines in American politics which pitted Hamilton against Jefferson. Hamilton and his allies were identified with the Federalist Party, which advocated Hamilton's proposals for strong government. Hamilton became disenchanted with fellow Federalist John Adams during Adams's presidency, leading to a split among the Federalists that allowed Jefferson and his Democratic-Republican Party to defeat Adams in the election of 1800 and begin a long domination of the national government.

In 1804, Vice President Aaron Burr, who was running for governor of New York, challenged Hamilton to a gun duel over remarks that Burr judged to be insulting. Hamilton was fatally wounded in the fight and died on July 12, 1804.

(see Vol. 3, p. 2). Many politicians felt the treaty was one-sided in favor of Britain. Although Washington reluctantly supported the treaty, opponents drummed up widespread opposition. Jefferson accused the Federalists of trying to transfer responsibility for formulating the country's commercial policy from the House of Representatives to the Federalist-controlled Senate. Federalists organized petition drives and rallies in support of the treaty. The dispute over Jay's Treaty was a key element in the emergence of the Federalists as a political party.

In Washington's farewell address upon leaving the presidency, he warned against the dangers of party factionalism. John Adams (see Vol. 1, p. 10), who had served as Washington's vice president, was elected president in 1796 (see Vol. 1, p. 9). Unlike the election of Washington in 1789 (see Vol. 1, p. 5) and again in 1792 (see Vol. 1, p. 7), the 1796 election was a genuine contest that pitted Adams, a Federalist, against Thomas Jefferson, the Democratic-Republican.

Beyond the Constitution

The issue of the relative influence of the federal government vis-ávis the individual states was a somewhat abstract debate. As the party in power under Adams, and as the opposition under Jefferson, the specific policies advocated by the Federalists began to cast the party in a slightly different light. Federalist policies came to be viewed as favoring the wealthy merchant and manufacturing class, rather than small farmers or urban workers. The term Federalist began to take on a slightly aristocratic tone, and the party seemed to favor policies that would restrict the exercise of democratic power by the common man.

The Federalists themselves began to experience internal disagreement when Adams and his supporters passed the Alien and Sedition Acts in 1798. Supposedly a protection against "dangerous" immigrants and insurgents, the laws authorized the president to deport any aliens considered dangerous and made it a crime to publish criticism against the federal government. The Naturalization Act increased from five years to 14 the period before immigrants could become citizens.

The acts were a rather obvious political ploy to prevent immigrants from becoming citizens and voting for the Democratic-Republicans, who enjoyed the support of immigrants. The new laws were widely unpopular and backfired on the Federalists. All of the acts were repealed or expired by 1802, at which time Federalists had begun to wither in electoral contests.

End of the Federalists

Adams's policy, under which the United States engaged France in an undeclared naval war, turned away many Federalists in the Hamiltonian wing of the party. Hamilton urged his supporters to vote for Timothy Pickering, rather than Adams, for president in 1800. Jefferson was elected to the White House, denying Adams a second term. After both Jefferson and his vice presidential candidate, Aaron Burr, won

73 electoral votes, resulting in a deadlock, it was Federalist leader Hamilton who arranged to break a subsequent tie in the House of Representatives, resulting in Jefferson being named president (see Vol. 1, p. 12).

After losing the White House in 1800, Federalists recognized the need to build a stronger organization on the state level and to form strategic plans for national and local campaigns. The Federalists' strength was concentrated almost entirely in New England, and the party gained a reputation as a regional grouping. This reputation was solidified in 1803 when the Federalists opposed Jefferson's purchase of France's remaining North American possessions, known as the Louisiana Purchase, on grounds of cost.

The Federalists revived briefly in 1807, after Jefferson ordered a trade embargo against both France and Britain in an effort to avoid being drawn into the war between the two European powers. The embargo was highly unpopular in port cities throughout the nation. Despite the controversy, the Federalist candidate for president in 1808, Charles Pinckney (see Vol. 1, p. 19), lost to the Democratic-Republican, James Madison.

Four years later, Federalist opposition to the War of 1812 sealed its fate. The Federalists opposed the cost of what it termed "Mr. Madison's War." Opposition was especially strong in New England, where state legislatures refused to send their militias into federal service. Some Federalists, like Pinckney and John Lowell, went so far as to support a separate peace between New England and Britain. In 1814, the Massachusetts legislature called for a conference of representatives from all of New England, called the Hartford Convention. The meeting, held in secret at Hartford, Connecticut, was presided over by George Cabot of Massachusetts, a moderate Federalist. The convention issued a final report highly critical of President Madison's prosecution of the war and proposed several constitutional amendments to correct perceived advantages the Constitution gave to the South. It seemed the party that had once advocated the strength of the central government had turned in favor of states' rights.

The Hartford Convention cost the Federalist Party its remaining prestige, which it never regained, especially when the War of 1812 ended with American success. Federalists presented candidates in only three states in 1816 and did not formally endorse a candidate for president.

Political Philosophy

The early political parties did not draft formal platforms; these did not come until the Anti-Masonic Party (see p. 23) held the first political convention in 1831 and adopted a written platform. One example of how the Federalists viewed the key issue of federal powers versus state powers came in a resolution passed by the Massachusetts state senate in February 1799, responding to a resolution passed by the Virginia legislature the previous year. The Virginia Resolution of 1798 was passed in response to the Alien and Sedition Acts of 1798 and

An anonymous drawing around year 1800 depicted Democratic-Republican Thomas Jefferson kneeling at the "Altar of Gallic Despotism," a symbol of the French revolution that Federalists opposed and Jefferson had supported. The letter labeled "To Mazzei" refers to a letter by Jefferson to an Italian friend that described the American people as democratic but the government as despotic.

declared that individual states ought to be able to declare an act of the federal Congress unconstitutional. In response, Massachusetts passed its own resolution. Excerpts from the Massachusetts resolution follow:

The legislature of Massachusetts, having taken into serious consideration the resolutions of the state of Virginia…relative to certain supposed infractions of the Constitution of the United States, by the government thereof; and being convinced that the Federal Constitution is calculated to promote the happiness, prosperity, and safety, of the people of these United States…feel it necessary to make any professions of their attachment to it, or of their firm determination to support it against every aggression, foreign or domestic…

But they deem it their duty solemnly to declare that, while they hold sacred the principle, that consent of the people is the only pure source of just and legitimate power, they cannot admit the right of the state legislatures to denounce the administration of that government to which the people themselves, by a solemn compact, have exclusively committed their national concerns…That this legislature are persuaded that the decision of all cases in law and equity arising under the Constitution of the United States, and the construction of all laws made in pursuance thereof, are exclusively vested by the people in the judicial courts of the United States…

But, should the respectable state of Virginia persist in the assumption of the right to declare the acts of the national government unconstitutional, and should she oppose successfully her force and will to those of the nation, the Constitution would be reduced to a mere cipher, to the form and pageantry of authority, without the energy of power; every act of the federal government which thwarted the views or checked the ambitious projects of a particular state, or of its leading and influential members, would be the object of opposition and remonstrance; while the people, convulsed and confused by the conflict between two hostile jurisdictions, enjoying the protection of neither, would be wearied into a submission to some bold leader, who would establish himself on the ruins of both.

The legislature of Massachusetts, although they do not themselves claim the right, nor admit the authority of any of the state governments, to decide upon the constitutionality of acts of the federal government, still, lest their silence should be construed into disapprobation, or at best into a doubt as to the constitutionality of the acts referred to by the state of Virginia; and as the General Assembly of Virginia has called for an expression of their sentiments, - do explicitly declare, that they consider the acts of Congress, commonly called "the Alien and Sedition Acts," not only constitutional, but expedient and necessary…

The act complained of is no abridgment of the freedom of either. The genuine liberty of speech and the press is the liberty to utter and publish the truth; but the constitutional right of the citizen to utter and publish the truth is not to be confounded with the licentiousness, in speaking and writing, that is employed in propagating falsehood and slander. This freedom of the press has been explicitly secured by most, if not all the state constitutions…

By the Constitution, the legislative, executive, and judicial departments of government are ordained and established; and general enumerated powers vested in them respectively, including those which are prohibited to the several states…The government is not only empowered, but it is made their duty, to repel invasions and suppress insurrections; to guaranty to the several states a republican form of government; to protect each state against invasion, and, when applied to, against domestic violence…Whenever, therefore, it becomes necessary to effect any of the objects designated, it is perfectly consonant to all just rules of construction to infer that the usual means and powers necessary to the attainment of that object are also granted…

This construction of the Constitution, and of the existing law of the land, as well as the act complained of, the legislature of Massachusetts most deliberately and firmly believe, results from a just and full view of the several parts of the Constitution; and they consider that act to be wise and necessary, as an audacious and unprincipled spirit of falsehood and abuse had been too long unremittingly exerted for the purpose of perverting the public opinion, and threatened to undermine and destroy the whole fabric of government.

More Information

- Bailyn, Bernard. *The Federalist Papers.* Washington, D.C.: Library of Congress, 1998.
- Ball, Lea. *The Federalist-Anti-Federalist Debate Over States' Rights.* New York: Rosen Publishing Group, 2004.
- Brookhiser, Richard. *Alexander Hamilton, American.* New York: Free Press, 1999.
- Epstein, David F. *The Political Theory of the Federalist.* Chicago: University of Chicago Press, 1984.
- Livermore, Shaw. *The Twilight of Federalism: The Disintegration of the Federalist Party, 1815–1830.* New York: Gordian Press, 1972.
- Millican, Edward. *One United People: The Federalist Papers and the National Idea.* Lexington: University of Kentucky Press, 1990.
- Ostrom, Vincent. *The Meaning of American Federalism: Constituting a Self-Governing Society.* San Francisco: ICS Press, 1991.
- Schlesinger, Arthur. *History of U.S. Political Parties.* New York: Chelsea House, 1973.
- Wills, Garry. *Explaining America: The Federalist.* New York: Penguin Books, 2001.

On the Web

- Federalist Party. *http://gi.grolier.com/presidents/aae/side/fedparty.html.*
- The Hartford Convention. *http://civilwar.bluegrass.net/secessioncrisis/hartfordconvention.html.*

Democratic-Republican Party (Antifederalists), 1796–1826

Flash Focus: Democratic-Republican Party

Origins

The Democratic-Republican Party began as a faction called Antifederalists who opposed Alexander Hamilton and the idea of a powerful central government. Thomas Jefferson and James Madison were the most prominent Democratic-Republican leaders and were regarded as the founders of the party. The party's initial power was based in the agrarian south, along with some support among northern business interests. This support eventually spread to the nation at large, resulting in the Era of Good Feeling during which the Democratic-Republicans were effectively the only political party during terms of President James Monroe (1817–1825).

Issues

Role of the federal government. The Democratic-Republican Party believed in a limited central government. Jefferson and Madison had lobbied to add the Bill of Rights to the Constitution to protect both state governments and individuals from an overreaching federal government.

National Bank and commerce. The Democratic-Republican ideal was a society of independent farmers, large and small. The party opposed Hamilton's national bank which was at the center of the Federalist vision of government in the service of building a national economy with emphasis on trade and industry.

Foreign affairs. Democratic-Republicans favored minimizing dependence on trade with Great Britain. Jefferson particularly hoped to build a positive relationship with France, and Democratic-Republicans were sympathetic to the French Revolution. After France and Britain came into armed conflict in the 1790s, Democratic-Republicans tilted toward France, even while favoring American neutrality in the conflict.

Personal liberty. For the Democratic-Republicans, the Bill of Rights was an important highlight of the Constitution. The party of Jefferson and Madison emphasized the importance of personal and political liberties of the individual—a philosophy that conflicted sharply with the Alien and Sedition Acts passed in 1798 under Federalist John Adams.

Impact

From 1801 until 1829, the president of the United States was an avowed Democratic-Republican—Jefferson, Madison, James Monroe, and John Quincy Adams were all elected president on the Democratic-Republican ticket. The electoral victory of John Quincy Adams over Andrew Jackson in the House of Representatives caused an irreparable split in the party between Jackson's Democrats and Adams's new National Republicans in the election of 1828. Jackson's Democrats claimed the mantle of the Democratic-Republicans and controlled the White House for 12 more years, until 1841.

The sense of national political unity created by the American Revolution was already starting to wear thin by the time of the convention assembled in Philadelphia in 1787 to draft a new constitution. Some delegates to the convention, especially those from New York and New England, envisioned a much stronger central government capable of dealing with a range of social and political problems, particularly in the area of finance. Other delegates, led by Virginians, remained skeptical of a strong central government. Their model was an agrarian society in which state governments would continue to hold the greatest power with the central government assigned only those areas, such as foreign relations, that were beyond the natural limits of state governments.

The Democratic-Republican Party began as a loose alliance of political leaders who opposed the efforts by the Federalists (see p. 9) to institute a stronger federal government at the expense of the states. They constituted a political faction, emerging during the 1790s under the name Antifederalists, that opposed many of the policies proposed by Treasury Secretary Alexander Hamilton (see p. 10) and President John Adams (see Vol. 1, p. 10).

Origin of the Democratic-Republicans

The Democratic-Republican Party was spearheaded by Thomas Jefferson (see p. 15 and Vol.1, p. 13) and James Madison (see Vol. 1, p. 20). Although not organized as a party until 1794, the philosophy of the Democratic-Republicans had its roots in the earliest debates over the Constitution. Under their original name, "Antifederalists," Democratic-Republicans insisted on a relatively weak central government that would retain most government power for the states and delegate only a few tasks to the newly formed federal government. At the root of the differences between the Democratic-Republicans and the Federalists were two issues: the best way to preserve individual liberties and the best way to build economic wealth.

Democratic-Republicans tended to view the Constitution adopted in 1789 as a threat to individual liberties. In their view, the Constitution created an overpowering central government with a presidency that contained too much power for one individual. Democratic-Republicans likened the presidency to the monarchy that the young nation had just shed in the Revolution. They were not antigovernment; rather, they believed that limited government would best suit the liberty of citizens. Madison and Jefferson led the move to adopt the first 10 amendments to the Constitution—the Bill of Rights—specifically designed to protect a range of individual rights such as free speech, free assembly, a free press, and the right to trial by jury and freedom from self-incrimination. The Bill of

Rights reserves for the states (or "for the people") any powers not specifically granted to the federal government.

For Democratic-Republicans, the backbone of the new republic was the independent farmer—of whom Jefferson himself was an example—who wanted to be left alone to till the land without interference from the government. In practice, many such farmers owned large estates in the South and used slaves to work the land. Federalists, on the other hand, saw commerce and industry as the key to the nation's economic future and thought the government should be an active partner in encouraging economic growth. This translated into policies such as encouraging foreign trade and, most important, establishing a unified national economy by founding a national bank that could issue a single national currency, help finance debts incurred during the Revolution, and otherwise benefit businesses.

In foreign affairs, the Democratic-Republicans, led by Jefferson as secretary of state under George Washington (see Vol. 1, p. 6), were intrigued by the French Revolution of 1789 that overthrew the monarch and established a republic. The Federalists, on the other hand, favored trade with Britain and policies that would encourage British lenders to issue credit for growing American businesses.

Democratic-Republican View of Government

Coupled with their disputes over domestic policies, the gap between Jefferson and Hamilton brought to light two fundamentally different views of republican government. It was around this division that the country's first two political parties formed. These parties were perhaps better called factions than parties in the modern sense since neither the Democratic-Republicans nor the Federalists held conventions, published written platforms, or even had presidential "tickets" in the modern sense.

This limited concept of parties was illustrated in the presidential election of 1796, when Jefferson came in second to John Adams in electoral college votes (see Vol. 1, p. 9). This made Jefferson the vice president under Adams, a Federalist. (At the time, the presidential candidate finishing second in electoral votes became vice president, without regard for party affiliation.) Jefferson initially hoped to work with Adams, continuing the nonpartisan spirit established by George Washington's first two administrations (see Vol. 1, pp. 5-8). But differences of opinion over how the United States should deal with the war between Britain and France resulted in an increasingly partisan atmosphere. Jefferson and the Democratic-Republicans wanted the United States to remain neutral, while Adams and the Federalists favored an alignment with Britain and against France's revolutionary republican government. With the threat of war looming, Federalists in Congress passed the Alien and Sedition Acts in 1798, which Jefferson and the Democratic-Republicans viewed as an effort to silence their party by strengthening the power of the federal government and giving it authority to punish citizens thought to be disloyal to the United States. Drawing on increasing public perception that these acts were unconstitutional, Jefferson and Madison took action.

Madison and Jefferson respectively wrote the Virginia and Kentucky resolutions in 1788 that were passed by those states' legislatures and invoked the authority of the states to declare the Alien and Sedition Acts unconstitutional—in other words, asserting the states' rights to overrule federal laws. While drawing attention to the constitutional questions raised by the Virginia and Kentucky resolutions, Jefferson and Madison also demonstrated a peaceful method—passage of resolutions by state legislatures—by which public opinion could be shaped. The Democratic-Republicans succeeded in building broad opposition to the Alien and Sedition Acts throughout the nation, with the result that in 1800 Jefferson defeated Adams's bid for reelection (see Vol. 1, p. 12). Jefferson became the third president, and Democratic-Republicans captured a majority in Congress.

Era of Good Feeling

The Democratic-Republican Party dominated national elections for the next 24 years. Jefferson was reelected in 1804 (see Vol. 1, p 16), followed by Madison in 1808 (see Vol. 1, p. 19) and 1812 (see Vol. 1, p. 22), James Monroe in 1816 (see Vol. 1, p. 26) and 1820 (see Vol. 1, p. 29), and John Quincy Adams in 1824 (see Vol. 1, p. 32). The party also maintained healthy majorities in both houses of Congress. The Federalists gradually faded and sealed their fate by opposing the War of 1812 against Britain, which proved widely popular among the people. The height of Democratic-Republican electoral strength came when Monroe was elected president in 1820 with all but one vote in the electoral college, giving rise to the term Era of Good Feeling to describe a time when partisanship virtually disappeared.

The election of 1824 ended the Era of Good Feeling. With four Democratic-Republicans competing for the presidency, Andrew Jackson (see Vol. 1, p. 37) won a plurality (but not a

---

REPUBLICANS

Turn out, turn out and save your Country from ruin !

From an *Emperor*—from a *King*—from the iron grasp of a *British Tory Faction*—an unprincipled banditti of British speculators. The hireling tools and emissaries of his majesty king George the 3d have thronged our city and diffused the poison of principles among us.

DOWN WITH THE TORIES, DOWN WITH THE BRITISH FACTION,

Before they have it in their power to enslave you, and reduce your families to distress by heavy taxation. Republicans want no Tribute-liars—they want no ship Ocean-liars—they want no Rufus King's for Lords —they want no Varick to lord it over them—they want no Jones for senator, who fought with the British against the Americans in time of the war.—But they want in their places such men as

Jefferson & Clinton,

who fought their Country's Battles in the year '76

This poster encouraged voters to support the Democratic-Republican candidates in 1792. The Democratic-Republicans opposed the Federalist policies of a strong central government with ties to Britain, favoring instead a smaller central government with ties to France.

majority) of the popular vote, sending the election to the House of Representatives. There, a deal between Adams and Henry Clay of Kentucky (see Vol. 1, p. 41), the third-place candidate in popular votes, resulted in Adams's election as president in the House of Representatives. In the next election, Jackson's supporters, appropriating the first half of the Democratic-Republican name by calling themselves Democrats (see p. 17), defeated Adams's supporters who campaigned under the other half of the old name, calling themselves National Republicans (see p. 21).

The Democratic-Republican Party of Jefferson was no more, although Jackson's Democrats—and Democrats to the present day—claimed to be the true heirs of Jefferson as the party of frontier farmers and the common man. Subsequently, in 1834 the Whig Party (see p. 27) emerged with the pro-business stance associated with the Federalists. In the 1830s, this translated into support for a national bank (which had been an issue between Jefferson and Hamilton), government financing of roads and canals, and tariffs on imports to help protect domestic businesses.

Virginia Resolution, 1788

In 1798, in response to passage of the Alien and Sedition Acts, James Madison and Thomas Jefferson wrote two resolutions that were passed by the state legislatures of Virginia and Kentucky. The resolutions challenged the legitimacy of the Alien and Sedition Acts and asserted that the states had the right to declare acts of the federal government to be unconstitutional. The resolutions provide a snapshot of the antifederalist philosophy of the Democratic-Republicans, just as an answering resolution from the Massachusetts legislature (see p. 11) provides an insight into federalist thinking. The Virginia Resolution, written by Madison with collaboration by Jefferson:

> RESOLVED, That the General Assembly of Virginia, doth unequivocally express a firm resolution to maintain and defend the Constitution of the United States, and the Constitution of this State, against every aggression either foreign or domestic, and that they will support the government of the United States in all measures warranted by the former.
>
> That this assembly most solemnly declares a warm attachment to the Union of the States, to maintain which it pledges all its powers; and that for this end, it is their duty to watch over and oppose every infraction of those principles which constitute the only basis of that Union, because a faithful observance of them, can alone secure its existence and the public happiness.
>
> That this Assembly doth explicitly and peremptorily declare, that it views the powers of the federal government, as resulting from the compact, to which the states are parties; as limited by the plain sense and intention of the instrument constituting the compact; as no further valid that they are authorized by the grants enumerated in that compact; and that in case of a deliberate, palpable, and dangerous exercise of other powers, not granted by the

FlashFocus: Thomas Jefferson

Born: April 13, 1743, Shadwell, Virginia
Died: July 4, 1826, Monticello, Virginia
Political Career: Author, *Declaration of Independence,* 1776; governor of Virginia, 1779-81; diplomat to France, 1785–89; secretary of state, 1789–93; vice president, 1797–1801; president 1801–09.

Thomas Jefferson was the intellectual godfather, along with James Madison, of the Democratic-Republican Party. During the 1790s, Jefferson led the political faction known as the Antifederalists who opposed plans by Treasury Secretary Alexander Hamilton, leader of the Federalists, for a strong, activist federal government. After President George Washington retired in 1797, the competing factions took shape as the Democratic-Republicans led by Jefferson and the Federalists led by Hamilton.

Jefferson summarized his concept of government in the Declaration of Independence: *"We hold these truths to be self-evident, that all men are created equal, that they are endowed by their Creator with certain unalienable Rights, that among these are Life, Liberty and the pursuit of Happiness. —**That to secure these rights, Governments are instituted among Men, deriving their just powers from the consent of the governed...**"*(emphasis added). For Jefferson, government's duty was to protect the rights of all citizens, common man and aristocrat alike.

On his return from France, filled with enthusiasm for the French Revolution, Jefferson led the drive to adopt the Bill of Rights (first 10 amendments to the Constitution) that enumerated the rights of citizens and specifically declared (in the Tenth Amendment) that "powers not delegated to the United States by the Constitution, nor prohibited by it to the states, are reserved to the states respectively, or to the people."

Jefferson and his fellow Democratic-Republicans thought state governments were more likely to protect the rights of individuals than a faraway central government. Jefferson's views were widely shared in the South by other "gentlemen farmers"—a form of American aristocracy that often depended on slaves to work their farms.

In 1798, the Federalists pushed through the Alien and Sedition Acts that provided, among other things, for jailing people who published criticism of the government in times of crisis. Jefferson responded by authoring a resolution passed by the Kentucky legislature in November 1798, declaring that states were "not united on the principle of unlimited submission to their general government; but that, by a compact under the style and title of a Constitution for the United States, and of amendments thereto, they constituted [created] a general government for special purposes—delegated to that government certain definite powers, reserving, each State to itself, the residuary mass of right to their own self-government; and that whensoever the general government assumes undelegated powers, its acts are unauthoritative, void, and of no force...."

The rights of states and the limited powers of the federal government, as articulated by Jefferson in the Kentucky Resolution of 1798, became a *de facto* platform for the Democratic-Republican party and its successor, the Democratic Party, for well over a century.

said compact, the states who are parties thereto, have the right, and are in duty bound, to interpose for arresting the progress of the evil, and for maintaining within their respective limits, the authorities, rights and liberties appertaining to them.

That the General Assembly doth also express its deep regret, that a spirit has in sundry instances, been manifested by the federal government, to enlarge its powers by forced constructions of the constitutional charter which defines them; and that implications have appeared of a design to expound certain general phrases (which having been copied from the very limited grant of power, in the former articles of confederation were the less liable to be misconstrued) so as to destroy the meaning and effect, of the particular enumeration which necessarily explains and limits the general phrases; and so as to consolidate the states by degrees, into one sovereignty, the obvious tendency and inevitable consequence of which would be, to transform the present republican system of the United States, into an absolute, or at best a mixed monarchy.

That the General Assembly doth particularly protest against the palpable and alarming infractions of the Constitution, in the two late cases of the "Alien and Sedition Acts" passed at the last session of Congress; the first of which exercises a power nowhere delegated to the federal government, and which by uniting legislative and judicial powers to those of executive, subverts the general principles of free government; as well as the particular organization, and positive provisions of the federal constitution; and the other of which acts, exercises in like manner, a power not delegated by the constitution, but on the contrary, expressly and positively forbidden by one of the amendments thereto; a power, which more than any other, ought to produce universal alarm, because it is leveled against that right of freely examining public characters and measures, and of free communication among the people thereon, which has ever been justly deemed, the only effectual guardian of every other right.

That this state having by its Convention, which ratified the federal Constitution, expressly declared, that among other essential rights, "the Liberty of Conscience and of the Press cannot be cancelled, abridged, restrained, or modified by any authority of the United States," and from its extreme anxiety to guard these rights from every possible attack of sophistry or ambition, having with other states, recommended an amendment for that purpose, which amendment was, in due time, annexed to the Constitution; it would mark a reproachable inconsistency, and criminal degeneracy, if an indifference were now shewn, to the most palpable violation of one of the Rights, thus declared and secured;

and to the establishment of a precedent which may be fatal to the other.

That the good people of this commonwealth, having ever felt, and continuing to feel, the most sincere affection for their brethren of the other states; the truest anxiety for establishing and perpetuating the union of all; and the most scrupulous fidelity to that constitution, which is the pledge of mutual friendship, and the instrument of mutual happiness; the General Assembly doth solemnly appeal to the like dispositions of the other states, in confidence that they will concur with this commonwealth in declaring, as it does hereby declare, that the acts aforesaid, are unconstitutional; and that the necessary and proper measures will be taken by each, for co-operating with this state, in maintaining the Authorities, Rights, and Liberties, referred to the States respectively, or to the people.

That the Governor be desired, to transmit a copy of the foregoing Resolutions to the executive authority of each of the other states, with a request that the same may be communicated to the Legislature thereof; and that a copy be furnished to each of the Senators and Representatives representing this state in the Congress of the United States.

Agreed to by the Senate, December 24, 1798.

See also: Federalist Party, p. 9; Democratic Party, 1828–60, p. 17; National Republican Party, p. 21.

More Information

- Appleby, Joyce. *Capitalism and a New Social Order: The Republican Vision of the 1790s.* New York: New York University Press, 1984.
- Banning, Lance. *The Jeffersonian Persuasion: The Evolution of Party Ideology.* Ithaca, NY: Cornell University Press, 1978.
- Ellis, Joseph J. *American Sphinx: The Character of Thomas Jefferson.* New York: Vintage, 1996.
- Graff, Henry F. (ed.) *The Presidents: A Reference History.* New York: Macmillan, 2002.

On the Web

- Virginia Resolution, The Avalon Project: http://www.yale.edu/lawweb/avalon/virres.htm.
- DNC: History of the Democratic Party. http://www.democrats.org/about/history.html.
- History of the Parties. http://www2.edgate.com/elections/inactive/the_parties.

Democratic Party, 1828–60

Flash Focus: Democratic Party

Origins

The modern Democratic Party traces its beginnings to the Democratic-Republicans of Thomas Jefferson and the Democrats of President Andrew Jackson. The name Democrats dates from Jackson's campaign for president in 1828 against John Quincy Adams, a former Democratic-Republican whose followers started using the name National Republicans. The Democrats largely represented agrarian interests of the South and also included the emerging working class in the North.

Issues

Limited government. The Democratic Party was founded on the principle that a strong central government was a threat to liberty and that the states should have more power than the federal government. This was in line with Thomas Jefferson, James Madison, and the Democratic-Republican Party. However, this vision of limited government was subtly changing under the leadership of Jackson.

The presidency. Democrats, and especially Jackson, believed that the presidency, rather than Congress, should be the focal point of the federal government. Jackson presented himself as the champion of the common man willing to do combat against monied interests in Congress.

Economic infrastructure. Democrats did not support federal funding for expanded and improved roads, canals, and other infrastructure designed to help integrate the economies of western frontier states with the populated eastern seaboard. They argued that such functions were beyond the scope of the federal government envisioned by the Constitution. Democrats also opposed tariffs (taxes on imports).

Second National Bank. The Democratic Party opposed extending the charter of the Second National Bank after its expiration on grounds that the Constitution made no provision for such a function, and that the bank wielded too much power. They accused the bank of meddling in local and national elections, constituting a danger to liberty. The Democrats favored a modified institution that would be an adjunct of the Treasury. Democrat Martin Van Buren, Jackson's successor as president, signed the Independent Treasury Act during his presidency.

Slavery. The issue of extending slavery into western territories divided the Democrats and eventually caused the party to split into northern and southern wings. Many Democrats supported slavery, which was viewed as a key economic pillar in the South, as a matter of property rights, and argued that slave owners should be able to take their "property" to any western territory without fear of losing it under antislavery laws. After acquisition of the Mexican Cession following the Mexican War of 1846-48, the question of whether slavery should be allowed in the new territories planted the seeds of the eventual split of the party.

See also: Democratic Party, 1860–76, p. 61; 1876–1900, p. 80; 1900–32, p. 111; 1932–60, p. 141; 1960–2004, p. 163.

Origins of the Democratic Party (1828–1860)

The dominance of the Democratic-Republican Party (see p. 13) in national politics from 1800 to the 1824 presidential election rendered partisanship almost obsolete in early American political history. However, the resolution of the 1824 presidential election (see Vol. 1, p. 32) signaled a drastic change in the role of political parties and their influence on elections.

The four major contestants for the presidency in 1824 all hailed from the Democratic-Republican Party. Tennessee's Andrew Jackson (see Vol. 1, p. 37), a popular figure in the nation thanks to his military exploits against the British in the Battle of New Orleans in 1815, won the popular vote by a wide margin over John Quincy Adams (see Vol. 1, p.33). However, no candidate received over 50 percent of the vote, and no candidate received the necessary number of electoral votes to win the presidency. In such cases, the Constitution instructs that the election be decided by a vote in the House of Representatives. When Henry Clay, who finished in fourth place in the presidential race (see Vol. 1, p. 41), threw his support behind Adams, Adams won the vote in the House. Adams subsequently appointed Clay secretary of state in his administration, and supporters of Jackson claimed there had been a "corrupt bargain" made between the two men. Jackson believed that the will of the people had been ignored, and he was determined to campaign for the presidency in 1828 on the conviction that in a republic, the majority should have the final say in an election, not an elite group such as the House of Representatives.

Followers of Jackson broke from the Democratic-Republicans to form their own party, the Democratic Party. The new party combined elements of grassroots efforts and a new diverse political coalition. Jackson supporters included professional politicians in New York, such as Martin Van Buren (see Vol. 1, p. 45), and Senator John Calhoun of South Carolina, Jackson's vice presidential running mate. Jackson also attracted groups of political activists who had advocated economic reform to assist indebted farmers and artisans during the Panic of 1819.

Jackson's campaign was organizationally ahead of the curve, establishing the Nashville Central Committee, which linked numerous state and local Jackson organizations to work together with political leaders in Washington. These groups fostered a more democratic style of politics that began traditions that are still seen today—rallies, parades, and personal encouragement of voters up until election day. In addition, Jackson supporters used gimmicks like political cartoons and campaign songs to strike up public enthusiasm and awareness, as well as the symbolic use of Jackson's nickname from the military, "Old Hickory." During the campaign, Democrats planted hickory trees in villages during ceremonies, built hickory poles on the corners of main city streets, and walked

FlashFocus: Andrew Jackson

Born: March 15, 1767, Waxhaw, South Carolina
Died: June 8, 1845, Nashville, Tennessee
Political Career: Representative from Tennessee 1796-97; senator from Tennessee 1797, 1824–28; Tennessee Supreme Court judge, 1797–1804; Democratic candidate for president 1824, 1828; president 1829–37.

Andrew Jackson dominated the Democratic Party as president and long afterward. He represented a new era as a "common man" in high office.

Before Jackson, presidents came from an elite group of Founding Fathers—George Washington, John Adams, Thomas Jefferson, James Madison, James Monroe—or one of their sons (John Quincy Adams). Jackson, on the other hand, was the son of Irish immigrants, grew up in rural North Carolina, and was taken prisoner by the British in the Revolutionary War at age 13 (the rest of his family died during the war).

After the war, Jackson studied law, then moved to what is now Tennessee where he was a political leader at an early age. Jackson attended the Tennessee constitutional convention (he suggested the name "Tennessee") and became the new state's first congressman, then served in the Senate for a few months before returning to serve on the Tennessee Supreme Court for seven years.

At the outset of the War of 1812, Jackson commanded the Tennessee Volunteers before he was promoted to the regular army. He gained national fame for his victory over the British in the Battle of New Orleans (1815) and led the 1818 invasion of Spanish-owned Florida, later becoming its military governor.

In 1824 Jackson returned to the Senate and ran for president as a Democratic-Republican. Although he got the most votes of all four candidates, he did not win an electoral college majority and lost the election to John Quincy Adams in the House of Representatives (see Vol. 1, p. 32). He ran again in 1828, winning handily with a coalition of Westerners, farmers, supporters of U.S. territorial expansion, and supporters of slavery.

As president, Jackson was anti-Native American and pro-expansion, although he refused to annex Texas as a new state for fear of igniting a bitter debate over expanding slavery. Jackson strengthened the power of the executive branch, for which he was criticized for overstepping his powers. He opposed renewal of the charter of the Second National Bank, which helped him win reelection in 1832.

After his second term, Jackson retired to his plantation near Nashville, Tennessee, where he exerted a strong influence on national politics and on the Democratic Party in particular. He died there in 1845.

around with hickory canes. Jackson's political opponents resorted to calling him a "jackass." Jackson picked up on the insult and turned it around on his opponents by allowing the symbol of a donkey to be put on campaign literature. Unlike today's political candidates, though, Jackson avoided active campaigning, carefully monitoring the party activity in the background.

The Democratic Party's new campaign strategy worked to perfection, and Jackson was elected as the party's first president in 1828 with the defeat of the incumbent President Adams (see Vol. 1, p. 36). This time the public left nothing to chance, and Jackson was elected with 56 percent of the popular vote and a healthy 176-83 majority in the electoral college. Jackson's inauguration ceremonies reinforced his populist appeal, when a White House reception intended for "ladies and gentlemen" was overrun by an enthusiastic crowd of well-wishers that left the new president almost crushed to death and the presidential mansion a mess. A new era of politics had dawned.

In 1832, the Democratic Party held its first national convention and nominated President Jackson for another term. He won the presidency again (see Vol. 1, p. 40), and the Democratic Party gained even more national strength and representation in Congress and across the states. In 1848, the party established the Democratic National Committee, which was charged with promoting the party between its conventions and remains today as the world's longest running political organization.

Philosophy

The Jacksonian Democrats traced their fundamental political philosophies to the party from which they came, the Democratic-Republicans of Thomas Jefferson (see Vol 1, p. 13) and James Madison (see Vol 1, p. 20). The abiding principle of the Democratic Party established by Jackson and his supporters echoed the danger of a powerful government that Jefferson and Madison identified, and an emphasis on states' rights above those of the federal government. The early Democratic Party thought that the liberty of the sovereign people was always jeopardized by excessive power, and that government was required to place a limit on its own powers. In addition, the Democratic Party promoted and emphasized public virtue—the character and spirit of the people.

These basic philosophical tenets were rooted in the agrarian society that characterized early America, but the nation's economy—with its emerging commerce, banking, and manufacturing industries—was changing rapidly when Jackson's Democrats organized, and the party was required to adapt to these new circumstances. As the leader of the party, Jackson was still devoted to the principles of the limited use of the powers of the federal government, but at the same time accepted the direction of the new economy as it related to his party's philosophies. Jackson dissatisfied some of the party's Jeffersonian purists by supporting some tariff protection and even the distribution of federal surplus back to the states. But for the most part, Jackson and the party attempted to stay close to the spirit of limited government as the essential ingredient to a free society. He attacked the formation of monopolies in business, the increasing role of banking in the United States (specifically the National Bank), and excessive government spending.

The donkey was first used as a symbol for the Democratic Party in this anonymous cartoon from 1837. Andrew Jackson rides the donkey, wielding his "veto" sword; his use of the pocket veto was blamed for the financial panic of 1837.

Under Jackson, the Democratic Party moved to make the presidency a more coequal branch of government. Opponents of Jackson, including the newly formed opposition Whig Party (see p. 27), believed that the Constitution limited the presidency to carrying out the policies and legislation enacted by Congress. While Jackson believed in limited government, he did not see the presidency as being in any way subservient to Congress. During his presidency, he expanded the veto power, basing his authority on the will of the people. He also intervened in legislative matters. As such, the Democratic Party under Jackson and its subsequent presidents greatly increased the power of the presidency, making the office the central point of American politics.

The Democratic Party was nearly as successful as the Democratic-Republican Party had been on the national scene. From its formation through 1856, Democrats won all of the presidential elections except those of 1840 and 1848. Martin Van Buren (see Vol. 1, p. 45), James Polk (see Vol. 1, p. 53), and James Buchanan (see Vol. 1, p. 65) served as Democratic presidents. The Democratic Party also enjoyed healthy representation in Congress during this period.

During this time, the main issue of contention between the parties and within the parties was the expansion of slavery into federal territories. The Whig Party dismantled over the issue, and it threatened the stability of the Democratic Party as well, as factions of Northern and Southern members of the party began to divide along the question. Senator Stephen Douglas of Illinois (see Vol. 1, p. 71), who favored the concept of popular sovereignty, which would have allowed the inhabitants of each individual territory to decide whether slavery should be permitted there, led the Northern flank. Southern Democrats believed that the institution of slavery was to be protected in the territories. This position was advanced by the likes of Senator Jefferson Davis of Mississippi. Slavery was to be the dividing line for the Union Party (see p. 56) and for the Democratic Party, which eventually placed two separate candidates on the 1860 presidential ballot (see Vol. 1, p. 68).

Democratic Party in Crisis

As was the case with the nation, the Democratic Party divided on the question of slavery. Several attempts at compromise, such as the Kansas-Nebraska Act and the Lecompton Constitution, degenerated as the squabble over whether slavery would be allowed in federal territories escalated. Democratic President James Buchanan distrusted powerful Democratic Senator Stephen Douglas of Illinois, who favored popular sovereignty to solve the slave issue. Buchanan, who was happy to admit Kansas as a slave state, and Douglas reflected the gulf that was growing between Democrats.

That split culminated in the official rupture of the party at the 1860 Democratic National Convention. Southern Democrats were determined to add a plank to the party platform that would give federal protection for territorial slavery. Aided by Buchanan, the Southern faction succeeded in delaying the selection of a presidential candidate until the platform could be debated. When the slavery protection plank was rejected, the Southern Democrats (see p. 52) walked out of the convention. They reconvened a few weeks later, nominating Buchanan's vice president, John Breckinridge (see Vol. 1, p. 72), as their candidate for president. The Northern Democrats nominated Douglas.

With two separate candidates splitting votes between themselves and a third-party candidate, Abraham Lincoln won the presidency in 1860. Several Southern states quickly seceded, and the nation moved toward civil war. The Democratic Party remained split, and many Southern Democrats found themselves in positions of leadership in the government of the Confederate States of America. Once the Civil War ended and the Union was reunited, Southern Democrats came back to the national party.

Issues

The fundamental principles of the Democratic Party were rooted in the concept of a limited central government, a philosophy advocated by Thomas Jefferson and James Madison. The Democratic Party formed by Andrew Jackson and his supporters adhered to that principle while at the same time adapting to economic changes that moved the United States away from being a strictly agrarian nation.

Democratic Platform, 1840

In the 1840 election, the Democratic Party supported the candidacy of the incumbent president, Martin Van Buren. The party's principles were outlined in the following platform.

Resolved. That the federal government is one of limited powers, derived solely from the constitution, and the grants of power shown therein, ought to be strictly construed by all the departments and agents of the government, and that it is expedient and dangerous to exercise doubtful constitutional powers.

Resolved. That the constitution does not confer authority upon the federal government the power to commence and carry on, a general system of internal improvements.

Resolved. That the Constitution does not confer authority upon the federal government, directly or indirectly, to assume the debts of the several states, contracted for local internal improvements, or other state purposes; nor would such assumption be just or expedient.

Resolved. That justice and sound policy forbid the federal government to foster one branch of industry to the detriment of another, or to cherish the interests of one portion to the injury of another portion of our common country—that every citizen and every section of the country, has a right to demand and insist upon an equality of rights and privileges, and to complete and ample protection of person and property from domestic violence, or foreign aggression.

Resolved. That it is the duty of every branch of government, to enforce and practice the most rigid economy, in conducting our public affairs, and that no more revenue ought to be raised, than is required to defray the necessary expenses of the government.

Resolved. That Congress has no power to charter a national bank; that we believe such an institution one of deadly hostility to the best interests of the country, dangerous to our republican institutions and the liberties of the people, and calculated to place the business of the country within the control of a concentrated money power, and above the laws and the will of the people.

Resolved. That Congress has no power, under the Constitution, to interfere with or control the domestic institutions of the several states, and that such states are the sole and proper judges of everything appertaining to their own affairs, not prohibited by the Constitution; that all efforts by abolitionists or others, made to induce Congress to interfere with questions of slavery, or to take incipient steps in relation thereto, are calculated to lead to the most alarming and dangerous consequences, and that all such efforts have an inevitable tendency to diminish the happiness of the people, and endanger the stability and permanency of the union, and ought not to be countenanced by any friend to our political institutions.

Resolved. That the separation of the moneys of the government from banking institutions, is indispensable for the safety of the funds of the government, and the rights of the people.

Resolved. That the liberal principles embodied by Jefferson in the Declaration of Independence, and sanctioned in the Constitution, which makes ours the land of liberty, and the asylum of the oppressed of every nation, have ever been cardinal principles in the democratic faith; and every attempt to abridge the present privilege of becoming citizens, and the owners of soil among us, ought to be resisted with the same spirit which swept the alien and sedition laws from our statute-book.

More information

- Cole, Donald B. *The Presidency of Andrew Jackson.* Lawrence: University of Kansas Press, 1993.
- McCormick, Richard. *The Second American Party System.* Chapel Hill: University of North Carolina Press, 1966.
- Remini, Robert V. *Andrew Jackson and the Course of American Freedom: 1822–1832.* New York: Harper and Row, 1981.
- Sellers, Charles. *The Market Revolution: Jacksonian America, 1815–1846.* New York: Oxford University Press, 1991.

On the Web

- Andrew Jackson's First Annual Message to Congress—1829. *http://www.geocities.com/americanpresidencynet/1829.htm.*
- Democratic National Committee: History of the Democratic Party. *http://www.democrats.org/about/history.html.*
- Great American History Fact-Finder. *http://college.hmco.com/history/readerscomp/gahff/html/ff_053000_democratpa.htm.*
- History of the Democratic Party. *http://sd.essortment.com/historydemocrat_rbur.htm.*

National Republican Party, 1828–32

FlashFocus: National Republican Party

Origins

The National Republicans emerged from the Democratic-Republicans during the presidential election of 1828, which pitted incumbent John Quincy Adams against Andrew Jackson. Both men were nominally Democratic-Republicans, but they disagreed sharply on several key issues. Adams's followers began calling themselves National Republicans, while Jackson's supporters used the term Democrats. Following Jackson's victory, his opponents held a convention under the name National Republicans in 1831 and nominated Henry Clay of Kentucky to run against Jackson the next year. The new party was reminiscent of the division between the Federalists and the Democratic-Republicans in the period before the Era of Good Feeling, with the National Republicans in some ways taking up where the Federalists left off representing the interests of manufacturers and businessmen, as well as some farmers in the West.

Issues

National Bank. The National Republicans backed renewal of the Second National Bank's charter as a means of assuring that the country had a uniform currency. Andrew Jackson vetoed the charter's renewal, and National Republicans made its renewal their signature issue in the election of 1832.

Government funding for infrastructure. National Republicans wanted the government to finance improved roads and canals linking western states with the East.

Tariffs. To help protect American business from foreign competition (as well as to raise funds for improvement projects), National Republicans backed protective tariffs on imports.

Impact

Running as a National Republican, Henry Clay captured 37.4 percent of the popular vote, against Jackson's 54.2 percent, and only 49 electoral votes. His defeat marked the end of the National Republican Party, but not the end of opposition to Jackson. The National Republican Party was a direct forerunner of the Whig Party, which campaigned for the next 20 years on the basic program of the National Republicans: a strong central government dedicated to bolstering economic development by funding public projects and running a national bank.

See also: Democratic-Republican Party, p. 13; Whig Party, p.27. Democratic Party, 1828–60, p. 17.

The emergence of the National Republicans in the election of 1828 marked the resumption of the two-party system that had been in place before the Era of Good Feeling. In 1824, all the presidential candidates—John Quincy Adams (see Vol. 1, p. 33), Andrew Jackson (see Vol. 1, p. 37), Henry Clay (see Vol. 1, p. 41), and William Crawford—were nominally Democratic-Republicans (see p. 13). When the popular election failed to give any one candidate a majority in the electoral college, Adams and Clay struck a deal that made Adams president and Clay the secretary of state. Supporters of Jackson, who won the most popular votes, were infuriated and vowed to elect Jackson in 1828. Jackson's allies built a mass political organization, the nation's first, which took control of Congress and succeeded in electing Jackson in 1828 (see Vol. 1, p. 36).

During Adams's reelection campaign in 1828, some of his supporters began calling themselves National Republicans, while Jackson's supporters dropped the term Democratic-Republicans in favor of simply Democrats. Adams, reflecting the interests of northeastern manufacturers and businessmen, supported a strong national government that would act in concert with business interests to stimulate the economy. Jackson, who was portrayed as the candidate of the common man, opposed such federal initiatives. Jackson won in a landslide with 56 percent of the popular vote and 178 electoral votes to Adams's 43.6 percent of the popular vote and 83 electoral votes.

Jackson was a divisive figure. His opponents dubbed him "King Andrew" and accused him of harboring ambitions to become a dictator. Whereas Jackson believed the presidency should be a coequal branch of government, his opponents thought the president was intended simply to carry out the wishes of Congress.

Henry Clay emerged as a leader of the anti-Jackson forces, and in December 1831, these politicians gathered in Baltimore and nominated Clay as the candidate of what they called the National Republican Party. The party's platform largely consisted of what was called the American System: a national bank to provide the nation with a uniform currency; tariffs to protect domestic manufacturers from foreign competitors; and government funding for internal improvements in roads and canals to facilitate internal trade.

Support for the National Republicans was centered in the Northeast, especially in New England. The new party had virtually no support south of Maryland, notwithstanding the fact that Clay was from Kentucky. In 1830, the National Republicans opposed Jackson's plan to forcibly remove Native Americans from their tribal lands in the Southeast to seemingly empty lands west of the Mississippi River. This position, perhaps more than any other, cost the National Republicans their support in the South.

National Republicans tended to be businessmen or manufacturers, with a smaller number of farmers. An underlying theme of the National Republicans was their aversion to Andrew Jackson. He not only opposed most elements of Clay's American System, especially the continuation of a national bank, but also seemed, in the eyes of the National Republicans, to overreach the powers of the presidency. National Republicans, like the Whigs who followed them (see p. 27), disapproved of Jackson's vetoes of bills passed by Congress—Jackson's veto of the Congressional decision to renew the charter of the Second National Bank was one outstanding example—on grounds that the executive branch should be limited to carrying out the will of Congress under all but the most exceptional circumstances.

Jackson was also viewed by the National Republicans as the popular leader of the common people. This expansion of democracy to the lower classes disturbed some National Republicans, who were more comfortable with government on the British model that limited participation to people who owned property.

End of the Party

The National Republicans ran a single presidential campaign, with Clay opposing Jackson in 1832 (see Vol. 1, p. 40). The National Republicans entered into an uneasy alliance with the Anti-Masonic Party (see p. 23), which largely represented small farmers in upstate New York, Vermont, Pennsylvania, and Ohio. But the Anti-Masonic Party was opposed to the political power of urban business interests in the Northeast, and the alliance between the two parties was a weak one at best.

Jackson's landslide victory did not mean the end of the National Republican political philosophy. Rather, the National Republican leaders—notably Clay and Adams—joined the new Whig Party, which emerged as a strong challenger to Jackson's Democrats for the next two decades.

More Information

- Lynch, William O. *Fifty Years of Party Warfare, 1789–1837.* Gloucester, MA: P. Smith, 1967.
- *National Party Conventions, 1831–2000.* Washington, D.C.: CQ Press, 2001.
- Schlesinger, Arthur M., Jr. (ed.). *History of U.S. Political Parties.* New York: Chelsea House, 1973.

On the Web

- Andrew Jackson. *http://www.presidentsusa.net/jackson.html.*
- Henry Clay. *http://coekate.murraystate.edu/kate/2004/june/clay/default.htm.*
- "National Republican Party," U-S-History.com. *http://home.u-s-history.com/pages/h1048.html.*

Anti-Masonic Party, 1827–36

FlashFocus: Anti-Masonic Party

Origins
The Anti-Masonic Party was formed in upstate New York following the kidnapping of William Morgan, a former member of the Masonic Lodge who had threatened to publish the secrets of Freemasonry, a secret fraternity with origins in Europe. Morgan's kidnapping generated a grassroots protest movement that advocated the elimination of the Masonic Order. The movement spread to New England, Pennsylvania, Ohio, and Michigan. In 1831, the Anti-Masonic Party held the first national nominating convention of any party, naming former U.S. Attorney General William Wirt of Maryland (who was, ironically, a member of the Masons) to run as president and Amos Ellmaker of Pennsylvania as vice president.

Issues
Freemasons. The alleged influence of Freemasons in politics was the single issue that gave rise to the Anti-Masonic Party. Many American leaders (including George Washington) had been members of the secret fraternal organization. The Anti-Masonic Party seized upon the kidnapping of a former Mason, who had threatened to reveal the group's secrets, to demand a ban on Masons holding political office and eradication of the perceived political influence of the Masonic organization.
Internal improvements. Anti-Masons were reluctant allies of the National Republican Party's (and later, the Whig Party's) plan for federal funds to build roads and canals.
Religious reforms. The party supported religious and moral reforms such as banning the mail and stage coaches from running on Sundays.
Egalitarianism. The Anti-Masons stood for establishment of a more egalitarian and moral political order.

Impact
William Wirt won eight percent of the popular vote and captured Vermont's seven electoral votes in the 1832 presidential election. The Anti-Masons also elected 53 U.S. representatives to the 23rd Congress (1833–35), as well as numerous representatives to state legislatures in New York, Pennsylvania, Ohio, and Michigan. After 1836, the party declined as a national force. Its main impact was limited to swinging support to either the Democratic Party or the National Republican Party, later known as the Whigs.

See also: National Republican Party, p. 21; Democratic Party, 1828–60, p. 17; Whig Party, p. 27; American (Know-Nothing) Party, p. 46.

The Anti-Masonic Party is regarded as the first alternative party in the United States. The Anti-Masons were responsible for two notable firsts: they held the first national nominating convention (in Baltimore in 1831), and they issued the first written party platform. Both concepts were shortly copied by the older, established parties, the Democrats (see p. 17) and the National Republicans (see p. 21), a party which was soon to meld into the Whig Party (see p. 27).

The Anti-Masonic Party arose in western New York state as a result of a local crime scandal: a local man, William Morgan, had been kidnapped after he resigned from the Masonic Lodge and revealed secrets of the social fraternity.

Freemasonry was, and remains, a worldwide fraternal organization representing itself as supporting moral and spiritual ideals. Over the past three centuries, some people have viewed the Masons as a dangerous cabal intent on controlling world politics. Many leaders of the American Revolution were Masons, including George Washington (see Vol. 1, p. 6), Benjamin Franklin, Patrick Henry, and Paul Revere. Masons present themselves as nothing more than a social club of middle- and upper-class men who hold no political ambition or agenda. Members give special preference to each other in their business and political lives, which causes some outsiders to conclude the Masons are an aristocratic group seeking a larger share of political influence.

The tensions between Masons and non-Masons increased with the disappearance of Morgan in 1826 from his home in Batavia, New York, near Buffalo. Morgan, a stonemason, had written a book titled *The Illustrations of Masonry* in which he exposed the group's initiation rituals, secrets, and the ways in which members dealt with one another in public business.

Before the book was printed, Morgan was arrested by police in Batavia and charged with theft. After a few days in jail he was released, but a group of local Masons kidnapped him and transported him to Fort Niagara, in Canada. He disappeared, and it was presumed that he was intentionally drowned. The investigation into Morgan's disappearance was thought to have been obstructed by sheriffs, judges, and jurors, all of whom happened to be Masons. Non-Masons became outraged, which led to the grassroots movement dedicated to banning Masons from holding positions of power and influence.

When Morgan's book was eventually published after his disappearance, the Anti-Masonic movement gained even more momentum in surrounding states. It also gained support from several newspaper publishers, notably Thurlow Weed of the *Rochester* (NY) *Editor*.

The public attention generated by Weed and others encouraged Anti-Masons to hold county nominating conventions in western New York. These conventions eventually produced candidates who won election to the state assembly in Albany. In 1828, Weed started a new publication, the *Anti-Masonic Enquirer,* to feed the growing enthusiasm for the movement and linked the New York state Anti-Masonic Party

FlashFocus: William Wirt

Born: November 8, 1772, Bladensburg, Maryland
Died: February 18, 1834, Washington, D.C.
Political Career: U.S. attorney, 1816–17; U.S. attorney general, 1817–29; Anti-Masonic candidate for president, 1832.

Both of William Wirt's parents died when he was young, and relatives and family friends helped Wirt attend elementary schools. He worked as a private tutor until age 17, when he began studying law. He practiced law in Culpeper, Virginia, and in 1799 he moved to Richmond. There he was elected clerk of the Virginia House of Delegates and later appointed chancellor of a court in Williamsburg. Wirt began his literary career around this time, publishing his first book, a commentary on Virginia society, in 1803. He continued to write and publish over the next several years.

Wirt returned to Richmond and gained national prominence for his role in prosecuting Aaron Burr, the former vice president, who was accused of treason. Wirt was elected to the Virginia House of Delegates in 1808, but resigned after one term to return to practicing law.

After Wirt argued a case before the Supreme Court in 1816, President James Madison appointed him U.S. attorney for Richmond. The next year President James Monroe appointed Wirt as attorney general, a post in which he served for 12 years. He became the first attorney general to record his opinions for use by his successors and was involved in several landmark Supreme Court cases.

Wirt resigned as attorney general when Andrew Jackson became president in 1829 and joined the anti-Jackson movement, supporting the National Republican candidate for president, Henry Clay, in 1832. When the small Anti-Masonic Party offered Wirt its presidential nomination, he accepted, hoping to create a coalition of Jackson opponents. The nomination was ironic since Wirt was a member of the Freemasons, the organization opposed by the Anti-Masons. Both the National Republicans and the Anti-Masons failed, and Jackson was elected to a second term.

Wirt died two years later in Washington, D.C.

---

to the unsuccessful reelection bid of President John Quincy Adams (see Vol. 1, p. 33), running as a National Republican.

Two years later, Weed obtained funding to start yet another newspaper, the *Albany Evening Journal,* that helped the Anti-Masonic Party spread beyond New York to areas of southeastern Pennsylvania, where a significant population of Quakers, Mennonites, and Amish began participating in the movement. Vermont also became a hotbed of Anti-Masonic fervor, and there were widespread meetings in Massachusetts to endorse candidates and form committees.

In Pennsylvania, Thaddeus Stevens rose to prominence as a spokesman for the party. The Anti-Masonic party waged a strong bid in the gubernatorial and congressional races of 1829. Also in 1829, Weed was elected to the New York Assembly, and the Anti-Masonic Party won seats in several New England state legislatures. The next year brought even more growth and legitimacy to the party, as the National Republican Party of New York simply endorsed the Anti-Masonic candidates for governor and lieutenant governor and came close to winning control of the state government. Pennsylvania elected six Anti-Masonics to the U.S. House of Representatives, and a strong Anti-Masonic coalition helped send former president John Quincy Adams back to Washington from Massachusetts as a member of the House of Representatives.

Allies with National Republicans

Weed's *Albany Evening Journal* effectively became the house organ of the Anti-Masonic Party. Weed used the paper to align the Anti-Masonic Party with the National Republicans on several issues, such as using federal funds to improve roads and canals throughout the expanding nation, which was also a primary cause of the National Republicans. On the other hand, neither Weed nor the Anti-Masonic Party was enthusiastic about another National Republican cause, the chartering of a new Bank of the United States.

For the 1832 presidential election (see Vol. 1, p. 40), the lack of a clear platform made it difficult for the Anti-Masons to unite behind a single presidential candidate and launch a sustained national campaign. The party made overtures toward John Quincy Adams as a candidate and briefly considered nominating Senator John Calhoun of South Carolina or Supreme Court Chief Justice John Marshall (see Vol. 3, p. 14). But the party could not come to a consensus.

To resolve the impasse, the Anti-Masonic Party organized the first national nominating convention, held in Baltimore in September 1831. The National Republicans and the Democrats followed suit with their own conventions shortly thereafter.

At the convention, the Anti-Masonics introduced another innovation by drafting the country's first party platform, or statement of positions. The platform focused on the abduction and apparent murder of William Morgan, the means Masons used to obstruct the investigation into his disappearance, the effect of Masonry on Christianity, and the brief history of the Anti-Masonic movement.

The convention nominated former Attorney General William Wirt of Maryland for president and Amos Ellmaker of Pennsylvania for vice president. Wirt, who was attorney general in the John Quincy Adams administration, was an odd choice for the Anti-Masonic Party. Not only was he a relatively unknown political figure, he was also a Mason.

In the 1832 election, Wirt received fewer than 40,000 votes, but managed to carry the state of Vermont and its seven electoral votes. In congressional races, the Anti-Masonics sent 53 members to the House of Representatives. After the party's disappointing results in the 1832 presidential contest, the Anti-Masonics ceased to be a factor on the presidential scene, although the party continued to function in state and local contests throughout the 1830s.

End of the Anti-Masons

After the elections of 1836, the Anti-Masonic Party declined as its members gravitated toward the new Whig Party, as did members of the National Republican Party. The Anti-Masonic movement did make a serious impact on the Masonic Order, however, which seemed to be its chief aim. The pressure exerted by Anti-Masonics and journalists like Weed forced many local Masonic lodges to break up and influenced office seekers to distance themselves from the fraternity. The movement gave men like Weed valuable political experience that was used to advance the cause of the Whig Party in later years.

The Anti-Masonic Party played on the fears of those who were suspicious of secret societies, while also alerting citizens to the potential dangers of such groups. The Anti-Masonics proved that grassroots efforts could be successful for a short period and served as a warning to politicians against ignoring the interests of minority political groups and regions.

Controversy over the Masons did not end with the demise of the Anti-Masonic Party. Into the 21st century, criticism of Masons continues to revolve around the idea that the group is engaged in secret acquisition of political power benefiting only its members. Masons, in response, made moves to make the organization more open to public view.

Platform of the Anti-Masons, 1831

Excerpts from the national platform adopted at the Anti-Masonic Party convention in Baltimore, Maryland in September 1831. The document outlines the reasons for the party's existence and specifically mentions the case of William Morgan, which spurred Anti-Masons to organize in the first place.

Resolved. That the existence of secret and affiliated societies is hostile to one of the principal defences of liberty, free discussion,— and can subserve no purpose of utility in a free government.

Resolved. That we, the American citizens, will adopt the counsel given us by the illustrious [George] Washington, "That all combinations and associations, under whatever plausible character, with the real design to direct, control, counteract, or awe the regular deliberation and action of the constituted authorities, are destructive of the fundamental principle of liberty, and of fatal tendency."

Resolved. That where evils of this nature are found existing in a free government, holding, by means of a secret combination, a majority of the civil, judicial, and military offices in the country, there are but two modes of redressing the grievance—either by revolution, or by an appeal to the ballot boxes.

Resolved. That the direct object of Freemasonry is to benefit the few, at the expense of the many, by creating a privileged class, in the midst of a community entitled to enjoy equal rights and privileges.

Resolved. That we esteem it in the plain duty of the members of that institution, as citizens of our common country, either collectively to abolish it, or individually to abandon it.

Resolved. That discussion, persuasion, and argument, in connection with the exercise of the right of suffrage, is a correct and speedy mode of diffusing information upon the subject of Freemasonry, and is the best method to ensure the entire destruction of the institution.

Resolved. That the oaths and obligations imposed upon persons when admitted into Masonic lodges and chapters, deserve the unqualified reprobation and abhorrence of every Christian, and every friend of morality and justice.

Resolved. That these oaths, being illegally administered, and designed to subserve fraudulent purposes, ought not to be regarded as binding in conscience, morality, or honor; but the higher obligations of religion and civil society require them to be explicitly renounced by every good citizen.

Resolved. That the gigantic conspiracy in New York, against the life of William Morgan, was the natural result of the oaths and obligations of masonry, understood and acted upon according to their plain and obvious meaning.

Resolved. That there is sufficient proof that the perpetrators of the abduction and murder of William Morgan, have, in several instances, been shielded from the punishment due to their crimes, by the Grand Lodge and Grand Chapter of New York, and by subordinate lodges and chapters, according to their Masonic obligations, whereby those lodges and chapters have countenanced those outrages, and become accomplices in their guilt.

Resolved. That those masons who became acquainted with and concealed the facts relative to the abduction of Capt. William Morgan, are accessory to that horrid transaction.

Resolved. That in applying the right of suffrage to effect the suppression of freemasonry, we not only exercise a right which is unalienably secured to us, but discharge a duty of the highest obligation, in thus endeavoring to abate a great political evil.

Resolved. That Anti-Masonry has for its object the destruction of Freemasonry; for its means, public opinion, manifested through the exercise of the elective franchise; that it acts upon the great principles of liberty, which made us a free people, and relies upon them to ensure the attainment of its high purpose.

Resolved. That an actual adherence, by Freemasons, to the principles contained in the obligations of the order, is inconsistent with paramount duties, which they owe to the state, and is a disqualification for offices of public trust.

Resolved. That we find, in the unexampled growth of the Anti-Masonic party, the diffusion and prevalence of its principles, the continued approbation bestowed upon them by the enlightened and wise men of the nation, abundant cause for encouragement, and perseverance with increased zeal and unabated determination, until the institution of freemasonry shall be overthrown or abandoned.

More Information

- Hesseltine, W.B. *The Rise and Fall of Third Parties.* Washington: Public Affairs Press, 1945.
- Graff, Henry F. (ed.). *The Presidents: A Reference History.* New York: Charles Scribner's Sons, 2002.
- Ratner, L. *Antimasonry.* Englewood Cliffs, NJ: Prentice-Hall, 1969.

On the Web

- Anti-Masonry Points of View. *http://www.masoninfo.com.*
- Freemasonry. *http://en.wikipedia.com/wiki/Freemasonry#History_of_Freemasonry.*
- The Proceedings of the U.S. Anti-Masonic Convention. *http://users.crocker.com/acacia/text_usmac.html.*

Whig Party, 1834–56

FlashFocus: Whig Party

Origins
The Whig Party began as a loose affiliation of diverse politicians opposed to Andrew Jackson as president. The party came to represent regional economic interests in the Northeast and West. The Whigs formally became a party in 1834, running candidates for Congress and nominated their first presidential candidate in 1836.

Issues
Role of central government. The Whigs traced their heritage to Alexander Hamilton, who had favored a strong central government with authority over the states. Whigs also worried that President Andrew Jackson took too many initiatives independently of the Congress and insisted that the president's role was limited to executing congressional policy.

Economic expansion. In a period of rapid economic growth—industrialization in the East and settlement of rural areas of the West (in states now called the Midwest)—businessmen and western farmers clamored for more and better roads, canals, and railroads to connect the populated markets in the East with the burgeoning settlements in the West. Whigs backed federal funding for such economic infrastructure.

Second National Bank. In 1832, Andrew Jackson vetoed a bill to renew the charter of the Second National Bank of the United States. The veto was the catalyst that solidified a coalition of politicians into the Whig Party. Whigs wanted the national bank to continue as an important source of loans for economic development and as a source of a uniform national currency and financial stability.

Tariffs. Whigs from the industrializing states favored higher tariffs (taxes on imports) to protect American businesses from foreign competitors, even if this meant Americans had to pay higher prices for manufactured goods.

Impact
Two Whigs were elected president: William Henry Harrison in 1840 and Zachary Taylor in 1848; both died in office. The Whigs were largely a coalition of economic interests, representing the philosophy of government as a partner of private enterprise in encouraging growth. The regional split over slavery that divided the nation eventually doomed the Whigs in the 1850s, when southern Whigs gravitated toward southern proslavery Democrats while northern Whigs joined the newly organized Republican Party or the Know-Nothing Party. General Winfield Scott was the last Whig candidate for president in 1852; he lost decisively to Democrat Franklin Pierce. The Whig Party had largely vanished by 1856.

See also: National Republican Party, p. 21; Democratic Party, 1828–60, p. 17; American (Know-Nothing) Party, p. 46; Republican Party, 1854–76, p. 55.

The Whig Party was established largely in critical response to the philosophies of President Andrew Jackson (see Vol. 1, p. 37). But just as quickly as it had formed and gained enough political influence to elect two presidents, the party split apart over the question of slavery and disbanded 30 years after its inception.

Politicians opposed to Jackson, the Democratic-Republican who narrowly lost the 1824 presidential election and who was elected president in 1828 (see Vol. 1, pp. 32, 36), thought Jackson exerted too much power, daring to take initiatives that the Whigs believed were reserved for Congress or vetoing bills passed by Congress on political, rather than legal, grounds.

Whigs also shared a second conviction: that the federal government should take an active role in promoting economic growth. In practical terms, this meant three things to the Whigs: federal funding for new roads and canals to link western farms with eastern markets; renewal of the charter of the Second National Bank; and higher tariffs to protect American businesses from foreign competition.

The Whigs echoed the support for a strong central government that had been advocated by Alexander Hamilton and the Federalists (see p. 9). These views put the Whigs squarely in opposition to Jackson's faction of the Democratic-Republican Party, which was more in line with the philosophy of Thomas Jefferson (see p. 15 and Vol. 1, p. 13) and the Democratic-Republicans (see p. 13).

Role of the President

Jackson's challengers opposed his desire to make the presidency an equal branch of government. After Jackson was elected president in 1828, his political enemies often referred to him as "King Andrew." In return, these politicians were called "Whigs," after the British political party that had challenged the authority of King James II, who ruled from 1685 to 1688 and was eventually overthrown. The Whig's idea of government was modeled after the British Parliament—a strong legislative branch that formulated national policy to be carried out by the executive branch. In the British system, a member of parliament, the prime minister, presides over professional government employees who follow the orders of the parliament.

The nucleus of the Whig Party came together in 1824, when there was still just one party, the Democratic-Republicans. Politicians who favored a more powerful central government joined to oppose Jackson's candidacy against his fellow Democratic-Republican, John Quincy Adams (see Vol. 1, p. 33). The 1824 election was eventually decided in the House of Representatives since no candidate won a majority of electoral votes in the popular election. Adams became president after a third candidate, Henry Clay of Kentucky (see Vol. 1, p. 32), threw his support in the House to Adams over Jackson.

> **FlashFocus: Cotton Whigs 1834–56**
>
> **What:** The southern faction of the Whig Party that held positions that differed significantly from northern Whigs, including strong support for states' rights and for the extension of slavery into new territories.
>
> **Who:** Hugh Lawson White of Tennessee and John Tyler of Virginia were among the best-known Cotton Whigs. White was one of three Whig presidential candidates in 1834, and Tyler was the Whig vice presidential candidate who succeeded William Harrison a month after the presidential inauguration in 1841.
>
> **When:** The Cotton Whigs coincided with the larger party, existing from 1834 to 1856.
>
> **Impact:** The Cotton Whigs were largely responsible for the successes of the Whig Party in Congress and in two presidential elections, even though they were often at odds with their more numerous northern counterparts.
>
> Prominent Cotton Whigs included Hugh Lawson White, one of three Whig candidates for president in 1836, former Democrat John Tyler, Whig vice presidential candidate in 1840 who became president after William Henry Harrison died a month after his inauguration; and John Calhoun of South Carolina, a former Democrat and advocate of the right of states to nullify (refuse to enforce) federal laws with which they disagreed.
>
> While both branches of the Whigs supported federal financing for roads and canals, Cotton Whigs like Calhoun and Tyler strongly supported states' rights and the expansion of slavery to new western territories.
>
> For over a decade, the Whigs compromised on their differences or simply ignored them to pursue their larger economic goals. But in 1848, a huge acquisition of territory from Mexico in the Mexican War (including the present states of Texas, New Mexico, Arizona, Utah, Nevada, and California, plus parts of Oklahoma, Colorado, and Wyoming) created a crisis.
>
> Most of the new territory was south of latitude 36 degrees 30 minutes, and under terms of the Compromise of 1820, it was therefore open to slavery. Many northern "Conscience Whigs" opposed expansion of slavery and supported Democratic Representative David Wilmot's proposal to bar slavery from territory acquired from Mexico; the Cotton Whigs voted against the Wilmot Proviso (see p. 43).
>
> The 1848 Whig presidential nomination of Mexican War hero General Zachary Taylor, a southern slave owner, sent some Conscience Whigs into the newly formed Free Soil Party. Although Henry Clay, a prominent Whig, temporarily papered over the crisis with the Compromise of 1850, the issue of expanding slavery proved to be fatal for the party. Many Cotton Whigs joined the Democrats, while Conscience Whigs embraced the Free Soil Party or the new Republican Party after 1854.

Jackson ran for president again in 1828 and easily defeated Adams's bid for reelection. Jackson's opponents became more tightly united, and the movement to build a national organization gained strength. The Whigs effectively became the opposition party to the Democratic-Republicans, who became known simply as Democrats.

Clay of Kentucky became a towering figure in the Whig movement, along with Adams and Senator Daniel Webster of Massachusetts (see Vol. 1, p. 46). Together their outlook was national in scope and called for an expansion of federal power. They supported federal (as opposed to state) funding for building and improving roads and canals in order to facilitate shipping goods between the rapidly developing western states and the East; the strengthening of the federal national bank as a means of establishing a national currency and economic system; and higher tariffs (taxes on imports) to protect American businesses from foreign competitors. These broad ideals and proposals appealed to the growing industrial presence in the Northeast and to agricultural interests in the West eager for improved transportation to the more heavily populated East.

A Failed Strategy

In the presidential election of 1832 (see Vol. 1, p. 40), Jackson, running for reelection as a Democrat, defeated Clay, running as the candidate of the National Republican Party (see p. 21). Four years later, elements of the Whig movement, which by then included former members of the Anti-Masonic Party (see p. 23), had gathered enough strength to mount a serious challenge to the Democrats. The Whigs became a formal political party in 1834 and made significant gains in the congressional elections that year, winning 25 seats in the Senate (three short of a majority) and 98 seats in the House of Representatives. Drawing on this momentum, the Whigs turned their attention to the contest for the White House in 1836.

But the Whigs could not agree on a single presidential candidate. Instead, they adopted a regional strategy, running three different candidates from different regions in the hope of denying the Democrat, Martin Van Buren (see Vol. 1, p. 45), a majority in the electoral college and thereby driving the election into the House of Representatives, where the Whigs were close to having a majority. The three Whig candidates were chosen on their respective sectional appeals—Daniel Webster of Massachusetts in the Northeast, William Henry Harrison (see Vol. 1, p. 49) in the Northwest, and Hugh Lawson White (see Vol. 1, p. 47) in the Southwest. The Whig strategy failed, however, and Van Buren was elected with a majority in the electoral college.

In the next election, the Whigs agreed on a single candidate, and William Henry Harrison became the first member of the party to be elected president (see Vol. 1, p. 48). Harrison died of pneumonia after only one month in office, whereupon Vice President John Tyler became president. Tyler had only recently switched to the Whig Party from long having been a Democrat, and he disagreed with Whig leaders in Congress on a variety of issues, most significantly the extent of the power of the presidency. When Tyler defied the advice of his cabinet and began vetoing bills to reestablish the Bank of the United States,

The Whig Party was founded in part as a coalition of opponents of Andrew Jackson. In this pro-Whig cartoon, Jackson's opponents surround Jackson, who is being barbequed over the fire of "public opinion."

Whigs in Congress rebelled. Clay persuaded Tyler's cabinet to resign, and Tyler was effectively expelled from the Whig Party.

Clay carried the Whig banner in the 1844 election, but lost to Democrat James Polk (see Vol. 1, p. 52). In 1848, the former Anti-Masonic Party leader Thurlow Weed managed to take control of the Whigs and arranged for General Zachary Taylor (see Vol. 1, p. 57) to become the nominee. Taylor, a military hero in the Mexican War, won the presidency, but died in office in 1850, succeeded by Vice President Millard Fillmore (see Vol. 1, p. 67). Although Fillmore managed to avoid upsetting Whig leaders in Congress during the remainder of his term, new pressures were building that doomed the Whig Party.

Slavery and the Whigs

The sectional rivalries that marked the first Whig attempt at the White House in 1836 became the main reason for the party's demise. The issue of slavery began to divide the Whigs, with many moving to new parties such as the Free Soil Party, the vehicle of abolitionists (see p. 42). In 1852, the Whig Party was crippled by the deaths of their strongest voices, Henry Clay and Daniel Webster. General Winfield Scott (see Vol. 1, p. 62) was the Whig nominee for president, but he received only 42 electoral votes. The party shattered, and many Whigs joined either the Democratic Party (which itself was dividing over the issue of slavery between northern and southern factions; see, p. 61) or the newly formed Republican Party (see p. 55). One Whig who moved to the Republican side was a former congressman named Abraham Lincoln (see Vol. 1, p. 69).

Many of the remaining Whigs from the South supported the Kansas-Nebraska Act in 1854, which established those two territories and allowed residents to decide whether or not to allow slavery. Antislavery Whigs from the North saw this as a betrayal of the Missouri Compromise of 1820 that barred slavery from either territory. Consequently, many northern Whigs left the party and joined either the Know-Nothings (see p. 46) or the new Republican Party, while southern Whigs came full circle and rejoined the Democratic Party.

The Debate over the Second National Bank

In the 1820s, debate swirled around the existence of the Second National Bank of the United States. Andrew Jackson's Democrats were opposed to the idea of a federal bank, whereas probusiness politicians—who eventually came together to form the Whig Party—supported it. The National Bank question helped meld the Whigs into a political party.

The Second National Bank was chartered by an act of Congress in 1816 (the First National Bank operated from 1791-1811, when its charter expired). It had an exclusive license to operate as a national bank (all other banks were chartered by states) and received all federal government deposits. It also was authorized to do business with the public. In particular, the Second National Bank could issue banknotes—the only form of currency at the time—which customers held as receipts for gold and silver (specie) deposited in the bank.

Opponents of the bank objected that the Constitution said nothing about allowing the federal government to charter banks and complained loudly of unwanted intrusion by the federal government into the country's economic and business affairs.

Banknotes

Like state-chartered banks, the Second National Bank was allowed to issue notes—essentially receipts for deposits of gold or silver. Anyone could exchange the notes for specie, but knowing that not everyone would try to exchange their notes at the same time, the federal bank (like state banks) could issue more notes than it could actually back up in precious metal. The National Bank was expected to maintain a conservative "margin," i.e., ratio of specie to notes, but initially the Second National Bank let this ratio bounce from as low as 12 percent to as high as 65 percent. Moreover, the Second Bank, like the First, was accustomed to suddenly demanding specie from state banks whose notes it had received, effectively regulating the specie/note ratio of state institutions. Occasionally, the public's faith in banknotes faltered, creating a "run" on banks which could not actually provide gold or silver for all their banknotes. In such cases, some depositors lost all the money they had on deposit, and economic recession followed.

Who Likes Central Banks?

Business-oriented politicians like the Whigs thought a National Bank acted as a control on state banks and thus helped prevent such "runs" or "panics." They also applauded the National Bank's role in stabilizing currency between the states.

Opponents of the National Bank, like Jackson, insisted on limiting the powers of the federal government, arguing there was no constitutional authorization for interfering in business affairs. This issue was settled in 1819, in the case of *McCulloch v. Maryland* in which the Supreme Court upheld the legality of a national bank (see Vol. 3, p. 24).

The Second National Bank symbolized the continuing argument over the role of the federal government, particularly in relation to state governments. It also put the spotlight on the economic growth of the United States at a time when the country was growing rapidly and when the Industrial Revolution was beginning to change the character of the new nation. Business interests wanted a stable economy, including a stable currency, that would facilitate trade between the states. The Whigs drew much of their political support from these interests.

Other politicians, like Andrew Jackson, mistrusted large, central institutions that had the economic power to overshadow, and even destroy, smaller state-chartered banks.

The Outcome

After Jackson vetoed the bill to renew the Second National Bank, the issue did not come up again until the Civil War, when the government enacted national banking legislation that controlled the activities of state banks and also helped the Union finance the war. Congress gained control over the production of banknotes by giving the federal government the exclusive right to engrave and print them on behalf of state banks.

Another true national bank to serve the economic functions of the First and Second National Banks did not appear until 1914, when Congress created the Federal Reserve Bank that continues to play an important role in determining the supply of money.

Whig Party Platform, 1848

In 1848, the Whigs focused their platform almost entirely on the candidacy of war hero General Zachary Taylor and avoided mention of issues that might prove controversial. For his part, Taylor expressed little interest in the Whigs or their political philosophy.

1. Resolved, That the Whigs of the United States, here assembled by their Representatives, heartily ratify the nominations of General Zachary Taylor as President and Millard Fillmore as Vice-President of the United States, and pledge themselves to their support.

2. Resolved, That the choice of General Taylor as the Whig candidate for President we are glad to discover sympathy with a great popular sentiment throughout the nation—a sentiment which, having its origin in admiration of great military success, has been strengthened by the development, in every action and every word, of sound conservative opinions, and of true fidelity to the great example of former days, and to the principles of the Constitution as administered by its founders.

3. Resolved, That General Taylor, in saying that, had he voted in 1844, he would have voted the Whig ticket, gives us the assurance—and no better is needed from a consistent and truth-speaking man—that his heart was with us at the crisis of our political destiny, when Henry Clay was our candidate and when not only Whig principles were well defined and clearly asserted, but Whig measures depended on success. The heart that was with us then is with us now, and we have a soldier's word of honor, and a life of public and private virtue, as the security.

4. Resolved, That we look on General Taylor's administration of the Government as one conducive of Peace, Prosperity, and Union. Of Peace—because no one better knows, or has greater reason to deplore, what he has seen sadly on the field of victory, the horrors of war, and especially of a foreign and aggressive war. Of Prosperity—now more than ever needed to relieve the nation from a burden of debt, and restore industry—agricultural, manufacturing and commercial—to its accustomed and peaceful functions and influences. Of Union—because we have a candidate whose very position as a Southwestern man, reared on the banks of the great stream whose tributaries, natural and artificial, embrace the whole Union, renders the protection of the interests of the whole country his first trust, and whose various duties in past life have been rendered, not on the soil or under the flag of any State or section, but over the wide frontier, and under the broad banner of the Nation.

5. Resolved, That standing, as the Whig Party does, on the broad and firm platform of the Constitution, braced up by all its inviolable and sacred guarantees and compromises, and cherished in the affections because protective of the interests of the people, we are proud to have, as the exponent of our opinions, one who is pledged to construe it by the wise and generous rules which Washington applied to it, and who has said, (and no Whig desires any other assurance) that he will make Washington's Administration the model of his own.

6. Resolved, That as Whigs and Americans, we are proud to acknowledge our gratitude for the great military services which, beginning at Palo Alto, and ending at Buena Vista, first awakened the American people to a just estimate of him who is now our Whig Candidate. In the discharge of a painful duty—for his march into the enemy's country was a reluctant one; in the command of regulars at one time and volunteers at another, and of both combined; in the decisive though punctual discipline of his camp, where all respected and beloved him; in the negotiations of terms for a dejected and desperate enemy; in the exigency of actual conflict, when the balance was perilously doubtful—we have found him the same—brave, distinguished and considerate, no heartless spectator of bloodshed, no trifler with human life or human happiness, and we do not know which to admire most, his heroism in withstanding the assaults of the enemy in the most hopeless fields of Buena Vista—mourning in generous sorrow over the graves of Ringgold, of Clay, or of Hardin—or in giving in the heat of battle, terms of merciful capitulation to a vanquished foe at Monterey, and not being ashamed to avow that he did it to spare women and children, helpless infancy, and more helpless age, against whom no American soldier ever wars. Such a military man, whose triumphs are neither remote nor doubtful, whose virtues these trials have tested, we are proud to make our Candidate.

7. Resolved, That in support of this nomination we ask our Whig friends throughout the nation to unite, to co-operate zealously, resolutely, with earnestness in behalf of our candidate, whom calumny cannot reach, and with respectful demeanor to our adversaries, whose Candidates have yet to prove their claims on the gratitude of the nation.

More Information

- Brown, Thomas. *Politics and Statesmanship: Essays on the American Whig Party.* New York: Columbia University Press, 1985.
- Ershkowitz, Herbert, *The Origin of the Whig and Democratic Parties.* Lanham, MD: University Press of America, 1983.
- Holt, Michael F. *The Rise and Fall of the American Whig Party: Jacksonian Politics and the Onset of the Civil War.* New York: Oxford University Press, 1999.
- Howe, Daniel Walker. *The American Whigs: An Anthology.* New York: Wiley, 1973.

Periodicals

- Atkin, Jonathan. "The Whig Party vs. the 'Spoilsmen' of Tennessee," *The Historian,* Winter 1994, p. 329.

On the Web

- Whig Party. *http://www.1upinfo.com/encyclopedia/W/Whigpart.html.*
- Whig Platform of 1856. The American Presidency Project. University of California at Santa Barbara. *http://www.presidency.ucsb.edu/ocs/platforms/other/W1856.htm.*

Locofocos, 1835–48

FlashFocus: Locofocos

Origins

The Locofocos were organized in New York City by reform-minded activists of the Democratic Party. The name derived from an incident in which entrenched Democratic Party members, meeting in New York City's Tammany Hall, attempted to disrupt the proceedings and prevent an official tabulation of a vote for party leaders that was not going their way. When they realized that their candidates were losing to the reform faction, they cut off the gas lights in the hall. The dissenting members responded by lighting candles with new self-igniting matches called Locofocos, and the voting went on.

Issues

National bank. Locofocos opposed state-owned banks, business monopolies, and the paper money system, partly on grounds that the Constitution did not explicitly authorize the federal government to own a bank or issue currency. (At the time, private banks chartered by states issued their own currency, which entitled holders to exchange it for gold or silver).

Rights of workers. Locofocos supported legal protection for labor unions and opposed policies they perceived as too favorable to privileged interests. When the Locofocos broke away from the Tammany Democrats, the Industrial Revolution was gaining momentum, and the first labor unions were taking shape to protect the rights of industrial workers. Protection for unions was a leading concern of the new party, comprised mainly of laborers.

Impact

No member of the Locofocos ever served in national office, but the party's principal aim was achieved in 1840 when President Martin Van Buren signed the Independent Treasury Act separating government from the banking industry. After the act was signed, the influence of Locofoco members was confined to New York. By the late 1840s, the Locofocos had aligned themselves with northern Democrats who eventually split from the Democratic Party on the issue of slavery.

See also: Democratic Party, 1828–60, p. 17.

Radical subgroups of organized political parties have often focused their attention on one particular issue or cause they believe their party should advocate above all others. Sometimes those radical elements split from the larger party in protest and try to achieve their particular narrow aims on their own. Such was the case with the Locofocos, formally known as the Equal Rights Party.

Organized in New York City in 1835, the Locofocos faction counted among its members working people and politically minded reformers who opposed any government policies that seemed to be antidemocratic or susceptible to abuse by special interest groups. The main goal of the Locofocos was not to build a base from which they could reach and sustain political power, but rather to persuade fellow Democrats to adopt their economic platform.

The Locofocos rose in opposition to the political group in New York City known as the Tammany Democrats, the local chapter of the Democratic Party. The Locofocos broke away from the Tammany Democrats, whom they viewed as being under the control of wealthier individuals (the word Tammany came from the name of a Delaware chief called Tamanend; after the Revolutionary War, Tammany Societies formed in the larger cities of the nation, including New York, to serve local political interests).

In the early to mid-1830s, some Tammany Democrats began supporting the policies of President Andrew Jackson (see Vol. 1, p. 37) and his opposition to renewing the charter of the Second National Bank. These individuals, who later formed the Locofocos faction, believed that the fight against government-owned banks should extend to state-owned banks as well. Their opposition to government banks extended to paper money, tariffs, and business monopolies, putting the Locofocos at the opposite end of the spectrum from the Whig Party, which was emerging at about the same time (see p. 27).

Like Jacksonian Democrats, these New Yorkers believed that government involvement in financial affairs was a drastic overreach of the powers of the central government. One of the more outspoken members of this faction was the editor of the *New York Evening Post,* William Leggett, who made his position clear in editorials and public demonstrations. This created tension within the Tammany organization, and in September 1835, Tammany leaders voted to expel Leggett from the party, spurring like-minded radicals into action.

On October 29, 1835, at a Tammany Democrats meeting to nominate and elect party officers, the dissenters voted down the chairman selected by the party hierarchy. But before the vote could be officially recognized, Tammany loyalists turned off the gas-powered lights inside the meeting hall. Undaunted, the protestors lit candles using the new self-igniting friction matches known as locofocos and continued the meeting until they nominated their own slate of candidates. Thereafter, the group became known in both derision and praise as the Locofocos.

Following their candlelight revolt, the group of Tammany radicals officially formed the Friends of Equal Rights, often called the Equal Rights Party, in January 1836, but the early nickname stuck, and the Equal Rights Party forever remained "Locofocos." The party quickly made its presence felt in local political contests. In April 1836, the Locofocos defeated Tammany Democrats for city office by enlisting Whig candidates to align with them, even though the two parties often held radically different positions (the Whigs, for example, supported a national bank). Two Locofocos were elected that year to the state assembly in Albany.

The party's greatest triumph came when President Martin Van Buren (see Vol. 1, p. 45), a New Yorker, successfully persuaded Congress to pass the Independent Treasury Act, which required the federal government to completely separate itself from the banking industry by establishing federal repositories for public funds instead of keeping the money in national or state banks. Van Buren was pressured to propose the legislation in the wake of the economic panic of 1837, in which much public money was lost when state banks failed when they could not convert paper money into gold and silver during a "panic." This led in turn to the fall of real estate prices, a halt to bank-financed internal improvements, and widespread unemployment.

Van Buren signed the legislation on July 4, 1840. Tammany Democrats—recognizing a winning issue when they saw one—adopted a large portion of the Locofocos platform with an emphasis on the financial planks. Their mission successfully completed, most members of the Locofocos were reabsorbed into the Democratic Party.

End of the Locofocos

President Van Buren's signing of the Independent Treasury Act in 1840 marked the peak of the Locofocos. Their goal of persuading the government not to interfere with the banking industry had reached the federal level, and their job was complete. Following this victory, the party's political influence reverted to local skirmishes in New York, and by the end of the 1840s, most of the radicals who had begun their journey by the light of the candle had been welcomed back to the mainstream of the Democratic Party. However, many of those who had battled the Tammany Democrats would once again become disillusioned with the party over the question of slavery in the years to come.

Platform of the Locofocos, 1835

The following resolutions were adopted by candlelight at the Tammany Hall meeting on October 29, 1835, during which the Locofocos took form.

Resolved—That in a free state all distinctions but those of merit are odious and oppressive, and ought to be discouraged by a people jealous of their liberties.

Resolved—That all laws which directly or indirectly infringe the free exercise and enjoyment of equal rights and privileges by the great body of the people, are odious, unjust, and unconstitutional in their nature and effect, and ought to be abolished.

Resolved—For all amounts of money, gold and silver are the only legitimate, substantial, and proper, circulating medium of our country.

Resolved—That perpetuities and monopolies are offensive to freedom, contrary to the genius and spirit of a free state and the principles of commerce, and ought not to be allowed.

Resolved—That we are in favor of a strict construction of the Constitution of the United States, and we are therefore opposed to the United States Bank, as being unconstitutional and opposed to the genius and spirit of our democratic institutions, and subversive of the great and fundamental principles of equal rights and privileges, asserted in the charter of our liberties.

Resolved—That we are opposed to all bank charters granted by individual states, because we believe them founded on, and as giving an impulse to, principles of speculation and gambling, at war with good morals and just and equal government, and calculated to build up and strengthen in our country the odious distribution of wealth and power against merit and equal rights; and every good citizen is bound to war against them as he values the blessings of free government.

More Information

- Allen, Oliver E. *The Tiger: The Rise and Fall of Tammany Hall.* Reading, MA: Addison-Wesley, 1993.
- Mushkat, Jerome. *Tammany: The Evolution of a Political Machine.* Syracuse, NY: Syracuse University Press, 1971.

On the Web

- Locofocos. http://tomcourses.tripod.com/locofoc1.htm.
- Locofocos on Encyclopedia.com. http://www.encyclopedia.com/html/L/locofocos.asp.

Liberty Party, 1840–48

Flash Focus: Liberty Party

Origins
The Liberty Party was organized by abolitionists as a means of ending slavery through political action. The Liberty Party first met in Warsaw, New York, on April 1, 1840, and nominated James Birney as its presidential candidate.

Issues
Abolition of slavery. The Liberty Party's single focus was abolishing the institution of slavery in the United States. Party members accepted that there were intermediate measures that might advance the cause of abolition short of freeing all slaves immediately.
Extension of slavery. The Liberty Party fought the establishment of slavery in newly admitted states and territories, notably territory gained from Mexico in the course of the Mexican War of 1846–48. The party specifically advocated passage of the Wilmot Proviso, which would have banned slavery from states formed from territory won in the Mexican War. The proviso was repeatedly passed by the House of Representatives but was defeated in the Senate.
Three-fifths clause. The Liberty Party advocated amending the Constitution to remove the three-fifths clause, which counted slaves as three-fifths of a person in calculating the number of representatives of southern states in Congress.
Abolition in Washington, D.C. The party campaigned to abolish slavery in the federal capital.

Impact
The Liberty Party nominated James Birney for president in 1840 and again in 1844. In the first of these races, Birney received 7,000 votes; in the second, he received 62,000 votes. His 1844 campaign likely denied the Whig candidate, Henry Clay of Kentucky, the electoral votes of New York and consequently the presidency. In 1848, the party nominated John Hale for president, but he abruptly withdrew from the race. Consequently, the Liberty Party dissolved, with many of its members joining the Free Soil Party. Some prominent abolitionists of the era, notably William Lloyd Garrison, viewed political maneuvers—which might include compromises or settling on half-way measures—as ineffective and even immoral and futile when applied to the issue of abolishing slavery. Despite its lack of success on the national level, the Liberty Party exerted strong political pressure on various state legislatures to combat slavery.

See also: Republican Party, 1854–76, p. 55; Free Soil Party, p. 42; Abolitionism, Vol. 4, p. 21; American Anti-Slavery Society, Vol. 4, p. 25; The Emancipation Proclamation, Vol. 4, p. 42.

A concerted campaign to abolish slavery in the United States gained momentum in the 1830s, largely as a moral crusade against the cruelty and injustice of slavery, which abolitionists termed the "peculiar institution." Within the ranks of abolitionists there were two schools of thought. One side, represented by William Lloyd Garrison (see Vol. 4, p. 24), the fiery newspaperman and abolitionist leader from Boston, demanded an immediate end to slavery without compromise. The other side believed in using political means to end slavery, even if this meant accepting intermediate steps short of complete abolition.

Garrison, who was leader of the American Anti-Slavery Society (AASS, see Vol. 4, p. 25), argued that direct political action was sinful as well as futile. Garrison and his followers in the organization wanted antislavery groups to exist as forums in which all views were presented and no official political positions were taken or advertised.

Other members of the AASS disagreed with Garrison's strategy and thought that the previous efforts to influence the government had been ineffective. The leaders of the political faction of AASS, Henry Stanton (husband of Elizabeth Cady Stanton, see Vol. 4, p. 156) and James Birney (see p. 36), tried to force the society to choose between resistant and nonresistant action in 1839. The AASS decided to back Garrison and his followers, and those who advocated political action were encouraged to form their own political party.

On April 1, 1840, abolitionists from six states met at Albany, New York, to discuss the formation of a new political party and to nominate a presidential and vice presidential ticket. The group, calling themselves the National Convention of Friends of Immediate Emancipation, agreed that they wanted a protest party focused on the single issue of abolition. Consequently, their brief party platform simply advocated abolishing slavery within the Union. The group then nominated Birney, a lawyer and legislator from Kentucky, for president and Thomas Earle of Ohio for vice president. The convention adopted the name Liberty Party, and members were often called Libertymen.

The 1840 Election

The new Liberty Party was neither highly organized nor well prepared for the 1840 presidential campaign (see Vol. 1, p. 48). Libertymen tried unsuccessfully to persuade Garrison and his followers to join their campaign—especially since Birney was not very well known outside of abolitionist circles. The party also failed to persuade Whig (see p. 27) voters to abandon their presidential candidate, William Harrison, the eventual winner (see Vol. 1, p. 48). Birney managed to collect only about 7,000 votes, a little over two percent of the popular vote total.

This cartoon shows a marriage ceremony between Martin Van Buren and a black slave woman. The Liberty and Free Soil parties both opposed the expansion of slavery, but for different reasons.

Undaunted, the Liberty Party spurned suggestions that it try to appeal to a wider range of voters by expanding its political platform to address the other issues of the day, such as tariffs, internal improvements to roads and canals, and a national bank—issues that the Whigs had successfully exploited. The party declined this advice, believing that incorporating other issues into its platform might compromise its mission to end slavery.

Despite holding firm on its one-issue agenda, the party had an impact on state and local elections. In 1842, for example, the Democratic candidate for governor in Ohio beat his Whig opponent by less than 4,000 votes, while the Liberty Party candidate, Leicester King, got 5,405 votes; it was thought that the Liberty votes might otherwise have gone to the Whig.

In 1844 (see Vol. 1, p. 52), the Liberty Party again nominated Birney for president and expanded its platform to include support for public education and Irish independence from England, an issue designed to attract support from recent immigrants. The incremental success of the party at the local level helped Birney gain more votes in that election and prompted worried operatives for the Whig Party to publish a forged letter under Birney's name in which he allegedly promised not to campaign against slavery. Birney and the Libertymen drew 62,103 votes in the general election (about 2.3 percent of the total), again failing to win any votes in the electoral college. But in New York, Birney won enough votes to prevent the Whig candidate, Henry Clay (see Vol. 1, p. 41), from winning the state; if Clay had taken New York, he would have won the presidency. Instead, James Polk (see Vol. 1, p. 53), a Democrat, won in 1844 (see Vol. 1, p. 52).

End of the Liberty Party

Gearing up for the 1848 presidential election (see Vol. 1, p. 56), some Libertymen wanted to expand the party platform still further and establish a coalition with factions of other parties. After the failed effort to adopt the Wilmot Proviso (a law that would have banned slavery in any lands acquired by the United States from Mexico after the Mexican War in 1848; see p. 43), many members of the Liberty Party wanted to join forces with northern Democrats who introduced the legislation. Some northern Democrats joined in the effort, and the Liberty Party nominated Senator John Hale of New Hampshire to be its 1848 presidential nominee. But Hale soon abandoned his candidacy to join the new Free Soil Party (see p. 42) along with other former Whigs and other Liberty Party members. The Liberty Party then nominated Gerritt Smith of New York for president, but he also withdrew his candidacy.

The defection of Liberty Party supporters to the Free Soil Party was, in some ways, a fulfillment of Garrison's original

FlashFocus: James Gillespie Birney

Born: February 4, 1792, Danville, Kentucky
Died: November 25, 1857, Eagleswood, New Jersey
Political Career: Kentucky State Legislature, 1816–18; Alabama General Assembly, 1819–23; Liberty candidate for president, 1840, 1844.

James Birney was educated at Transylvania University in Lexington, Kentucky, and graduated from the College of New Jersey (now Princeton University) in 1810. After studying law in Philadelphia and passing the bar in 1814, he returned to Danville to practice law. He was elected to the lower house of the Kentucky State Legislature in 1816. After serving his term, he moved to Alabama and was elected to the Alabama General Assembly in 1819, serving one term. He moved to Huntsville, Kentucky, to resume his private law practice.

During this time, Birney's attitudes toward slavery evolved. Initially, he was not an abolitionist but rather advocated gradual emancipation and the return of slaves to Africa. After visits to the North, he became increasingly convinced of the need to abolish slavery completely through political means.

In 1832, Birney received a commission as an agent for the American Colonization Society (see Vol. 4, p. 11). However, he resigned as vice president of the Kentucky Colonization Society as his views became more strongly abolitionist. In 1835, he helped form the Kentucky Antislavery Society. He planned to publish a weekly antislavery newsletter, but strong opposition to the project and threats to Birney himself led him to move to Ohio, where he helped found the Ohio Antislavery Society and published the antislavery newsletter *Philanthropist* from 1836–37. He then moved to New York in 1837 to become executive secretary of the American Antislavery Society.

In 1840, an antislavery convention representing six states nominated Birney as their candidate for president. The convention, which would become the Liberty Party, had no platform, but nevertheless won 7,069 votes from the states represented at the convention. After the election, Birney moved to England to serve as vice president of the World Antislavery Convention. In 1842, he returned to the United States, settling in Michigan. In 1844, a more firmly established Liberty Party again nominated Birney for president. Representing twelve states, and campaigning on a long platform focused on abolition, Birney collected 62,300 votes.

The following year, Birney fell from a horse and was partially paralyzed. His political career over, he moved to Eagleswood, New Jersey, in 1853, where he died in 1857.

objections to using elective politics to achieve abolition. The Free Soilers did not favor abolition of slavery; their approach was to ban the expansion of slavery into new territories. Their primary motivation was to reserve this territory for free white labor, rather than allow southern slave owners to use black slaves to work new lands.

By limiting itself to its original sole objective—the complete abolition of slavery within the United States—without a detailed plan to achieve this goal, the Liberty Party had trouble competing on the national level for votes. Many Libertymen tried to argue that the Constitution itself was an antislavery document and that simple congressional resolutions and legislation could end slavery constitutionally.

The 1848 election marked the end of the Liberty Party. When Republican President Abraham Lincoln (see Vol. 1, p. 69) signed the Emancipation Proclamation in January 1863 (see Vol. 4, p. 42), freeing slaves still living in Confederate territory, he did so as a military maneuver, hoping to inspire slaves to revolt and complicate the causes of the Confederacy against the Union. Emancipation of the slaves did not occur until the Thirteenth Amendment was ratified on December 6, 1865 (see Vol. 4, p. 47).

Platforms of the Liberty Party, 1840 and 1844

The Liberty Party platforms of 1840 and 1844 demonstrated the growth of the party in just four years. While the 1840 platform was simple and direct, the 1844 platform was broad and outlined the goals of a more organized and formidable political entity.

1840 Platform

Resolved, That, in our judgment, every consideration of duty and expediency which ought to control the action of Christian freemen requires of the Abolitionists of the United States to organize a distinct and independent political party, embracing all the necessary means for nominating candidates for office and sustaining them by public suffrage.

1844 Platform

1. Resolved, That human brotherhood is a cardinal principle of true democracy, as well as of pure Christianity, which spurns all inconsistent limitations; and neither the political party which repudiates it, nor the political system which is not based upon it, can be truly democratic or permanent.

2. Resolved, That the Liberty party, placing itself upon this broad principle, will demand the absolute and unqualified divorce of the general government from slavery, and also the restoration of equality of rights among men in every state where the party exists or may exist.

3. Resolved, That the Liberty party has not been organized for any temporary purpose by interested politicians, but has arisen from among the people in consequence of a conviction, hourly gaining ground, that no other party in the country represents the true principles of American liberty, or the true spirit of the Constitution of the United States.

4. Resolved, That the Liberty party has not been organized merely for the overthrow of slavery: its first decided effort must, indeed, be directed against slaveholding as the grossest and most revolting manifestation of despotism, but it will also carry out the principle of equal rights into all its practical consequences and applications, and support every just measure conducive to individual and social freedom.

5. Resolved, That the Liberty party is not a sectional party, but a national party; was not originated in a desire to accomplish a single object, but in a comprehensive regard to the great interests of the whole country; is not a new party, nor a third party, but is the party of 1776, reviving the principles of that memorable era, and striving to carry them into practical application.

6. Resolved, That it was understood in the times of the Declaration and the Constitution that the existence of slavery in some of the states was in derogation of the principles of American liberty, and a deep stain upon the character of the country; and the implied faith of the states and the nation was pledged that slavery should never be extended beyond its then existing limits, but should be gradually, and yet at no distant day wholly, abolished by state authority.

7. Resolved, That the faith of the states and the nation thus pledged was most nobly redeemed by the voluntary abolition of slavery in several of the states, and by the adoption of the ordinance of 1787 for the government of the territory northwest of the river Ohio, then the only territory in the United States, and consequently the only territory subject in this respect to the control of Congress, by which ordinance slavery was forever excluded from the vast regions which now compose the States of Ohio, Indiana, Illinois, Michigan, and the Territory of Wisconsin, and an incapacity to bear up any other than free men was impressed on the soil itself.

8. Resolved, That the faith of the states and the nation, thus pledged, has been shamefully violated by the omission, on the part of many of the states, to take any measures whatever for the abolition of slavery within their respective limits; by the continuance of slavery in the District of Columbia and in the Territories of Louisiana and Florida; by the legislation of Congress; by the protection afforded by national legislation and negotiation of slaveholding in American vessels, on the high seas, employed in the coastwise slave traffic; and by the extension of slavery far beyond its original limits by acts of Congress admitting new slave states into the Union.

9. Resolved, That the fundamental truths of the Declaration of Independence, that all men are endowed by their Creator with certain inalienable rights, among which are life, liberty, and the pursuit of happiness, were made the fundamental laws of our national government by that amendment of the Constitution which declares that no person shall be deprived of life, liberty, or property without due process of law.

10. Resolved, That we recognize as sound the doctrine maintained by slaveholding jurists, that slavery is against natural rights, and strictly local, and that its existence and continuance rests on no other support than state legislation, and not on any authority of Congress.

More Information

- Greene, Jack P. (ed.). *Encyclopedia of American Political History.* New York: Scribners, 1984.
- Graff, Henry F. (ed.). *The Presidents: A Reference History.* New York: Macmillan, 2003.

On the Web

- Liberty Party Platform. *http://www.geocities.com/CollegePark/Quad/6460/doct/839lib.htm.*
- The Liberty Party. *http://www.geocities.com/CollegePark/Quad/6460/dir/839lib.html.*

Law and Order Party of Rhode Island, 1841–51

FlashFocus: Law and Order Party of Rhode Island

Origins
The government of Rhode Island, founded by a charter (constitution) granted in 1663, was challenged by a statewide popular vote in 1841 over the issue of who had the right to vote. Since colonial times, only property owners had been allowed to vote in Rhode Island. By 1841, fewer than half the white males in the state were qualified to vote. The state legislature refused to eliminate property ownership as a condition of voting rights, which led to Dorr's Rebellion, a mostly (but not entirely) peaceful attempt to replace the established state government with one popularly chosen by an expanded electorate. The Law and Order Party rose as a coalition of Whigs and rural Democrats opposed to Thomas Dorr's "People's Constitution."

Issues
Male Suffrage. Rhode Island, like most states, experienced a steady influx of immigrants in the 1830s, many of whom were poor and could not vote because they did not own property. The state legislature refused repeated pleas to expand male suffrage. These refusals caused lawyer Thomas Dorr to organize an unofficial convention in 1841 to write a new state constitution that included the right to vote for all white males.
Right to rebellion. The organizers of the constitutional convention organized a popular referendum, in which all white males could vote, that approved the new constitution by a wide margin. But the established state government refused to recognize either the new constitution or the government headed by Dorr as governor. The established government eventually used the state militia to drive Dorr out of the state, raising the issue of whether the majority of the population had the right to change forms of government without the permission of the established government.

Impact
The Law and Order Party defeated the Rhode Island suffragists by force of arms and by arresting Dorr. Realizing that popular sentiment was against them, the party organized its own constitutional convention and allowed all male citizens—including African Americans—who had lived in Rhode Island for at least three years to vote for delegates. The constitution adopted by the official convention greatly expanded the right to vote, just as Dorr's party had insisted, while maintaining the principle that only an established government could organize a new constitution. The Law and Order Party thus became responsible for giving African American Rhode Islanders, as well as most other males, the right to vote.

In 1842, Rhode Island's government was still operating under a royal charter granted to Rhode Island and Plymouth Plantations in 1663. The American Revolution notwithstanding, the charter had not changed in 180 years. It allowed only freeholders (land owners) to vote and gave each town equal representation in the state legislature, ignoring the enormous growth of Providence over such colonial era towns as Newport and Warwick.

Starting in the 1830s, a large number of immigrants had settled in Rhode Island, working in textile mills and other factories (the first water-powered mill for spinning thread in America was established in Pawtucket, Rhode Island, in 1793, marking the unofficial start of the American Industrial Revolution). The newcomers did not own property and could not vote. Efforts had been made since 1817 to drop property ownership as a condition for voting and holding office, but the state legislature, where representatives of smaller towns clung to their colonial era political influence, refused to agree. In this way, Rhode Island was an exception to the rule in an era when property ownership was dropped as a condition of the right to vote.

In 1840, only about a third of the white males in Rhode Island had the right to vote, prompting advocates of expanded white male suffrage to form the Rhode Island Suffrage Association in March. The following autumn, the association convened a statewide meeting with delegates chosen without regard to property ownership. Calling themselves the People's Convention, the delegates drafted a new state constitution that extended the right to vote to all white males without a property qualification and reorganized the state legislature on a more equitable geographical basis. The convention considered, but rejected, efforts by the Rhode Island Anti-Slavery Society to remove the word "white" from the new constitution.

In January 1841, the Suffrage Association arranged a statewide popular vote on its new constitution and proclaimed that it was accepted by a wide margin. Four months later, in April, an election was conducted under the Suffrage Constitution, and Thomas Dorr (see p. 39), a prominent lawyer and a Democrat, was elected governor.

In the meantime, the established government refused to accept the People's Constitution and instead proposed its own document, called the Legal Constitution (sometimes called the Freemen's Constitution). A coalition of Whigs (see p. 27) and rural Democrats formed the Law and Order Party to back the established government and the new proposed constitution. In an election in March 1842, the Legal Constitution failed to win popular acceptance by 676 votes. Nevertheless, the established government insisted that it was the legitimate authority under the original colonial charter.

The result was a short period in which there were two competing governments in Rhode Island, one headed by Dorr and the other by Samuel King of the Law and Order Party, who had been chosen in a separate, competing election. On May 18, 1842, Dorr tried to seize the government's Providence Arsenal, but the state militia controlled by King repelled the attack. Dorr fled to New Hampshire to avoid arrest, only to return in June with about 1,000 armed supporters intent on convening the People's Constitution legislature in Chepachet, Rhode Island.

The Law and Order Party rallied about 2,500 men to oppose Dorr. The conflict resulted in only a few minor armed confrontations, and Dorr again went to New Hampshire. African American citizens strongly supported King's government and may have been decisive in the outcome. The reason: King's Law and Order Party had proposed yet another constitutional convention to be held in September 1842, with delegates to be elected in August. The Law and Order Party dropped the word "white" from the description of which males were allowed to vote for delegates, an issue of great interest to African Americans, who remembered that Dorr's party had resisted black suffrage.

The new constitution was not wholly free of property qualifications for voters. Naturalized citizens, which largely meant Irish Roman Catholics at the time, were required to own property worth $134 (worth about $2,200 in 2002), a restriction aimed squarely at depriving poor immigrants of the right to vote. (The restriction was lifted in 1888.) The Legal Constitution also retained for rural towns disproportionate representation in the state senate (one senator from each town regardless of population).

Despite these shortcomings, the new constitution was accepted by a vote of 7,024 to 51 (out of 23,000 eligible voters). In the wake of the events in the summer, many opponents abstained from voting. The new constitution took effect the following May 2. In the summer of 1843, Dorr was found guilty of treason and sentenced to life in prison in solitary confinement at hard labor. His sentence was commuted in 1845, and he was released from prison. His political rights were restored in 1851 by the state assembly, then controlled by Democrats, and his conviction for treason was reversed in 1854. Nevertheless, Dorr never again exerted political influence.

In 1845, Charles Jackson of the Liberation Party was elected governor of Rhode Island, followed in 1846 by Byron Diman of the Law and Order Party who was in turn succeeded by Elisah Harris of the Law and Order Party in 1847. The last Law and Order candidate was Henry Anthony, elected to a two-year term as governor in 1849 as the joint candidate of the Law and Order Party and the Whig Party. Thereafter, the Law and Order Party disappeared.

The irony of the Law and Order Party was that it started as the stronghold of freeholders who resisted an expansion of the franchise and ended as the champion of universal male suffrage, including the right of African Americans to vote.

FlashFocus: Thomas Dorr

Born: November 5, 1805, Providence, Rhode Island
Died: December 27, 1854, Providence, Rhode Island
Political Career: Thomas Dorr attended the Latin Grammar School in Providence, Rhode Island, and Phillips Exeter Academy in Exeter, New Hampshire, before entering Harvard University at age 14. After graduating from Harvard in 1823, he went to New York to study law, passing the bar in 1827. Dorr returned to Providence to practice law, concentrating on commercial and maritime cases. He became an abolitionist and advocate of political and religious liberty.

In 1834, Dorr was elected to the Rhode Island state general assembly where he worked for reforms in the state constitution and in banking, as well as for expanded education and rights for nonlandowners (a minority in Rhode Island at the time). The reform movement evolved into the Constitutional Party, founded in 1834 with Dorr as the party's secretary. In 1837, he was the Constitutional Party candidate in an unsuccessful bid for governor. The Constitutional Party dissolved after the election, and Dorr joined the Democratic Party, becoming its state chairman in 1838.

Two competing constitutional conventions were held in Rhode Island in 1841—the People's Convention and the Landowners' Convention—and Dorr was selected as a delegate to both. He supported the expansion of voting rights to all white and black males, but the People's Convention voted to extend suffrage only to whites. When voters overwhelmingly approved the constitution put forward at the People's Convention, Dorr encouraged the general assembly to accept the new constitution, but the assembly, dominated by landowners, refused. In response, the People's Party set up its own state government and elected Dorr governor. When the official government declared martial law, Dorr left Rhode Island to seek help from other states, but was unsuccessful. He and his followers returned to Rhode Island and attacked the arsenal in Providence; again, Dorr was unsuccessful and fled the state.

When the general assembly revised the state constitution and expanded voting rights in 1842, Dorr returned to Rhode Island but was promptly arrested and convicted of treason. He was sentenced to life in prison in 1844 but was released in 1845 when the Law and Order Party lost control of the government to the Democrats. Dorr remained in Providence until his death in 1854.

The Suffrage Party in Rhode Island
By Orestes A. Brownson
October 1844

Orestes Brownson was a writer and political philosopher who published *Brownson's Quarterly Review*, a journal of political opinion, in the midnineteenth century. In October 1844, he published an essay defending the Rhode Island Law and Order Party and arguing against Dorr's Rebellion. Excerpts:

We, in common with the great body of the American people, wished to see the elective franchise extended to the great mass of those who could not be electors under the old established freehold qualification. Though ...very far from believing the acquisition of universal suffrage equivalent to the acquisition of liberty, or that universal suffrage affords any considerable guaranty, in a country where inequality of property obtains, of wise or just government, we have yet believed it essential to the perfection of the political system adopted in this country, and have therefore always advocated its general adoption. Accordingly, we were among those who encouraged the formation of the [Rhode Island] suffrage association, believing, as we did, that its only design was to act on public opinion, and by the force of opinion, to compel the [royal] charter government to take measures for the formation and adoption of a more liberal constitution....

[W]hen the new government under the people's constitution was preparing to organize itself [we] regarded the whole proceedings under that constitution as illegal and revolutionary; but we were not disposed to condemn them with much severity, because we could not perceive how any amendment could be legally introduced, or the evils complained of legally redressed. We supposed the restriction on suffrage was a provision of the charter, and, if so, it could not be altered by any legal authority in the state, as the charter did not provide for its own amendment.

Taking this view of the question, we argued, that, let the measures for the extension of suffrage, or the formation of a new constitution emanate from what source they might, from the suffrage association or from the general assembly, since not authorized by the charter from which existing authorities derive their existence and power, they must needs be, in fact, illegal and revolutionary. The people's constitution is, we said, confessedly illegal in its origin; but so also must be a constitution framed by a convention called by the general assembly, for the general assembly has no authority from the charter to call a convention. Since, then, the suffrage association have called a convention, since that convention has framed a constitution, and since a majority of the people of Rhode Island, as it is alleged, have voted for it, it is decidedly best to let it go peaceably into operation. It ... contains several very objectionable features; but as it provides for its own amendment, it may hereafter be amended; and, bad as it is, it is better than the old charter. Presuming, from the information we received, that an immense majority of the people were satisfied with it, we concluded that nothing was wanted but a little firmness on the part of Mr. Dorr and his friends in its defense, to induce the charter party to yield, and suffer the new government to go quietly into operation....

But, after Mr. Dorr's failure, it came out that the limitation of suffrage to a freehold qualification was not a provision of the charter, but an act of the legislature. This changed the whole aspect of the case; for now it could no longer be pretended that there was no legal authority in the state competent to extend the elective franchise to all to whom it could be advisable to extend it. We

When the Rhode Island state government, dominated by landowners, refused to implement reforms voted upon by the people, Thomas Dorr set up a new, parallel government. In this poster, followers of Thomas Dorr are accused of being "traitors."

saw that we had reasoned from false premises, and had therefore come to false conclusions....

On one point, however, the controversy growing out of the Rhode Island suffrage movement has led us to reflect more than we had previously done, and on which our views, if not changed, have at least become clearer and more definite. We refer to what is called the sacred right of revolution. We believe the political sovereignty ... resides in the body of the nation.... The term nation conveys always the idea of a corporation, an organic body; while the word people may mean only a numerical collection of individuals. A nation never exists without a legal constitution of some sort, written or unwritten, and some legal forms or modes for collecting the national sense. Now, since the nation has a corporate existence by virtue of the fact that it is a nation, it possesses in itself the supreme political power, which commissions all the officers of government, and to which they are responsible. When these officers, or what is called the government, betray their trust, break the fundamental laws of the nation, whether those laws are written on parchment, or in the customs of the people existing from time immemorial, the nation, acting in accordance with these laws and customs, may unmake the administrators of the government, commission new ones, and institute new guaranties against abuses, and even by force of arms, if necessary. So far as this is a right of revolution, we are advocates of that right, but no further. But so long as the legitimate administrators of the government observe the national laws, and administer the government in accordance with them, honestly, and with a single eye to the maintenance of justice, we hold all resistance to the civil authority to be criminal. A revolution, for the mere purpose of changing the form of government, of substituting one form of government for another, as monarchy for aristocracy, or democracy for monarchy, or vice versa, we hold to be never justifiable. The authorities must themselves transgress the national laws, and put themselves thus out of the protection of the law, before the citizen or subject can have the right to resist them. We may resist tyrants and usurpers, but never the lawful magistrate in the lawful discharge of his official functions.

The principles here laid down will justify the colonists in their separation from Great Britain, but not Mr. Dorr in his attempted revolution in Rhode Island. Our fathers took up arms to resist an aggression on their constitutional and chartered rights. They contended, not that the British government had invaded or failed to secure certain assumed abstract rights of man, but their rights as recognized by the British constitution and the colonial charters. It is against George III as a tyrant, as violating the national laws, that they profess to take up arms; not against the king in the legal exercise of his constitutional prerogative.

But the suffrage party planted themselves on no national law of Rhode Island, written or unwritten, they alleged, and could allege, no transgression, on the part of the charter government, of any public law, no usurpation, no act of tyranny. They simply alleged that the charter government did not correspond to their notions of the best possible form of government, did not secure what they regarded as the abstract rights of man; and they took up arms, not to expel a tyrant or usurper, but to establish a new form of government, more conformable to their notions of abstract truth and justice.

Here is a broad difference between the suffrage men and the patriots of the revolution, which the author of the work before us has failed to recognize, and which would have prevented her, had she recognized it, from placing the heroes of Federal Hill [in Providence, Rhode Island] and Chepachet [Rhode Island] on the same line with the heroes of Saratoga and Yorktown [revolutionary war sites]. The former were, view them in what light you will, rebels against legitimate authority; but the latter were resisting aggression, and vindicating the violated majesty of the laws. The suffrage men may have meant well… [but] they were politically rebels, and could be treated only as such by a government that respected itself, and resolved to discharge its legal functions.

We regard this question as one of vital importance in our country. The laws have, with us, their chief support in public opinion. Let that opinion become unsound or corrupt, and the laws lose their force, and we are without protection. If the doctrine once obtain among us, that legal authority may be set aside for the purpose of making the government conform to our abstract theories of human rights, there is no foreseeing the lawlessness and anarchy which will ensue. The symptoms are already threatening; and recent riots and mobs, and, worse of all, the delay and hesitancy of authority in using force for their suppression, and the very extensive doubts which obtain as to the rightfulness of resorting to force at all, are to us really not a little alarming….

[We] feel more and more the necessity of rebuking the mobocratic spirit [rule of the mob], in whatever form it may manifest itself, and more and more the necessity of inculcating a reverence for law, and strict obedience to the lawful magistrate in the discharge of his lawful duties. We cannot afford, in this country, to insist on 'the sacred right of insurrection,' for we shall, if we do, have bands of insurgents in every town, village, and hamlet in the land. Whatever we may think of Mr. Dorr and his friends personally, we cannot approve their measures, or defend their doctrines, without a terrible hazard to the country, to all security of peace, life, property, and conscience.

More Information

- Ness, Immanuel and James Ciment. *The Encyclopedia of Third Parties in America.* Armonk, NY: Sharpe Reference, 2000.
- Kruschke, Earl R. *Encyclopedia of Third Parties in the United States.* Santa Barbara, CA: ABC-CLIO, 1991.

On the Web

- Arnold, Noah J. "The History of Suffrage in Rhode Island." *Narragansett Historical Register*, July 1890. http://www.rootsweb.com/~rigenweb/article229.html.
- Orestes Brownson Society. http://orestesbrownson.com/.

Free Soil Party, 1848–54

FlashFocus: Free Soil Party

Origins
The Free Soil Party reflected the debate over whether slavery should be permitted in new states formed from territory acquired after the Mexican War of 1846–48. The party was initially organized by a faction of Democrats from New York called Barnburners who opposed expansion of slavery into new states while refusing to advocate abolition of slavery everywhere. The party also attracted Conscience Whigs who opposed Whig presidential candidate Zachary Taylor, a slave owner, in the election of 1848, and some members of the abolitionist Liberty Party.

Issues
Expansion of slavery. The Free Soil Party's signature issue was its objection to the expansion of slavery into new states formed from territory gained from the Mexican War of 1846–48. This position was first put forward in the proposed Wilmot Proviso in 1846 and was rooted in a desire to keep western territories open for free white labor rather than enslaved black labor. Although some abolitionists supported the Free Soil Party, many others did not.
Homesteads. Hoping to attract working-class Democrats, the party proposed giving western settlers free land to establish farms as a way of attracting more settlers to the West. This plank was consistent with preserving western territory for free whites rather than enslaved blacks.
Public improvements. Reflecting the influence of Whigs over the new party, the Free Soil platform endorsed public funding for "river and harbor improvements" in the West.
Smaller government. Other planks of the Free Soil platform pledged to reduce the size of the federal government and to lower postage rates.

Impact
The Free Soil Party ran presidential candidates in 1848 and again in 1852; both fared poorly. In 1848, former President Martin Van Buren and his running mate, Charles Francis Adams of Massachusetts, polled just over 10 percent of the popular vote and won no electoral votes. The party elected two senators and 14 representatives. In 1852, the Free Soil ticket of John Hale and George Julian won just 155,210 votes, or 4.9 percent of the total. By then, most of the Democratic Barnburners had returned to the Democratic Party, leaving Free Soil with support from some Whigs and some abolitionists from the Liberty Party.

See also: Whig Party, p. 27; Republican Party, 1854–76, p. 55; American (Know Nothing) Party, p. 46; Liberty Party, p. 34.

The Free Soil Party lasted only six years (1848–54), but it served as an important catalyst in shaping the growing debate over slavery, as well as the balance of power between North and South over control of the federal government.

The origins of the party lay in the long-simmering dispute over expansion of slavery beyond the South at a time when settlers were streaming west. In 1845, Democratic President James Polk (see Vol. 1, p. 53) had annexed Texas, which recognized slavery, over the vehement objections of the Whig Party (see p. 27). Northern Democrats recognized that their constituents also opposed the expansion of slavery into new territories. One of them, Representative David Wilmot of Pennsylvania, proposed an amendment to a war spending bill (the Wilmot Proviso; see p. 43) that would have banned slavery from any future state formed by territory that might be acquired from Mexico.

The opposition to expansion of slavery expressed by the Wilmot Proviso was not rooted in the abolitionist opposition to the institution of slavery. Rather, it reflected the attitudes of the white working class represented by the Northern Democrats, who wanted new western territories reserved for free whites and feared that the introduction of slavery would eliminate the prospect of whites working in agriculture. The Wilmot Proviso passed the House of Representatives in 1846, but the Senate never voted on it. Wilmot reintroduced the measure in 1847, when the House again passed it but the Senate did not. The Wilmot Proviso subsequently became an issue leading up to the 1848 presidential election (see Vol. 1, p. 56).

Splitting from the Democrats

The New York State Convention of the Democratic Party held in Syracuse, New York, in September 1847 was sharply divided between two factions, the Barnburners, who demanded widespread economic reforms and supported the Wilmot Proviso, and the more conservative Hunkers. Defeated by the Hunker faction, the Barnburners stormed out of the state convention and met separately in Utica, New York, the next February, while the Hunkers also held a separate convention in Albany. Both factions sent delegations to the National Democratic Convention in Baltimore in May 1848. There, the dispute over which New York delegation should be seated resulted in the Barnburners walking out and demanding another convention, to be held in Utica, New York, the following month. Democrats from Wisconsin, Ohio, Massachusetts, Illinois, and Connecticut joined the Barnburners and nominated former president (and Barnburner) Martin Van Buren (see Vol. 1, p. 45) to run for president. The Barnburner Convention also called for yet another national convention to be held in Buffalo, New York, in August of 1848 to unite the party on the basis of free soil, meaning a ban on the expansion of slavery into new territories.

In the meantime, the Whigs nominated Mexican War hero Zachary Taylor (see Vol. 1, p. 57), a slave owner, as their candidate, alienating the Conscience Whigs who also opposed the expansion of slavery. Some dissident Whigs arrived in Buffalo for a boisterous meeting that resulted in formation of the Free Soil Party. Democrats nominated Lewis Cass of Michigan (see Vol. 1, p. 58), who supported popular sovereignty—the position that residents of western territories should vote on whether to recognize slavery in new states.

Platform: Something for Everyone

Stopping the extension of slavery to any more territories was at the center of the platform adopted by the new Free Soil Party. Some abolitionists, such as Frederick Douglass (see Vol. 4, p. 33), recognized that the Free Soil Party position was far short of abolishing slavery, but reasoned that it was at least a step in the right direction. Other abolitionists continued to support a separate party, the Liberty Party (see p. 34), which was dedicated to outright abolition of slavery.

The Free Soil position on the Wilmot Proviso was not the only element in a party platform that also called for a federal homestead act to grant free land to settlers heading west, a platform plank consistent with the party's desire to preserve new territories for free white labor rather than black slaves. Indeed, the Wilmot Proviso was sometimes called the "white man's proviso." The Free Soil platform in 1848 insisted that new territories "be kept free for the hardy pioneers of our own land and the oppressed and banished of other lands," which was taken to mean that black people, free or slave, were not considered welcome.

The Free Soil platform also contained clauses designed to appeal variously to disaffected Whigs and northern workers who had been loyal to the Democrats. It endorsed federal funding for transportation improvements, tariffs on imports to raise federal revenues, cheaper postage, and a reduction in federal appointments.

The convention nominated Martin Van Buren as president and Charles Francis Adams of Massachusetts, son of former president and Whig leader John Quincy Adams (see Vol. 1, p. 33), as vice president. The Free Soil ticket polled just 291,501 popular votes, or 10.1 percent, and did not carry a single state. (The Whig candidate, Zachary Taylor, was elected with 1.3 million votes, or 47.3% of the total and 163 electoral votes.) Even in New York, where the Barnburners were strong, the party polled only 26 percent of the popular vote, drawing support from both the Democrats and Whigs. The party did manage to elect two senators and 14 congressmen.

The weak showing caused many Barnburners to return to the Democratic Party, and in 1850 Congress adopted the Compromise of 1850, a set of laws proposed by the Whig leader Henry Clay (see Vol. 1, p. 41) to try to resolve the slavery issue. Under the compromise, Texas, a slave state, gave up claims to western territories in exchange for $10 million from the federal government (which was used to pay debts to Mexico). Territory that would eventually become New Mexico,

FlashFocus: The Wilmot Proviso

What: A proposal to ban slavery from any territory acquired from Mexico during the Mexican War of 1846-48. The Wilmot Proviso was twice passed by the House of Representatives, but not by the Senate.
Who: David Wilmot, a Democratic representative from Pennsylvania, sponsored the proposal that bore his name.
When: The Wilmot Proviso was first proposed in 1846 and was put forward again in 1847.
Impact: The Wilmot Proviso was a catalyst for dividing the Democratic Party between proslavery southerners and antislavery northerners. It was the focus of the newly organized Free Soil Party in 1848.

The issue of expanding slavery in formerly Mexican territory first arose in 1836, when American settlers in the Mexican state of Texas declared independence. Their request in 1837 to join the United States was rejected by the administration of President Martin Van Buren, partly to avoid war with Mexico and partly to prevent expansion of slave territory. Van Buren's action cost him the support of Southern Democrats in 1840. In 1843, President John Tyler became concerned that Britain had designs on Texas, not as part of the British empire but as a means of blocking westward expansion of U.S. territory. To block the British, Tyler proposed annexing Texas. The Senate rejected Tyler's proposal, which became an issue in the 1844 election. The Democratic candidate James Polk favored annexation, and after he was elected president, he proceeded to annex Texas to the United States in 1845.

War with Mexico

On April 25, 1846, Mexican troops fired on a U.S. garrison stationed along the southern border of Texas, sparking the two-year war that ended with a U.S. victory and annexation of the northern part of Mexico, including present-day California and other territory of the Southwest.

In August 1846, Representative David Wilmot of Pennsylvania, a Democrat, proposed an amendment to a bill financing the war. The amendment, known as the Wilmot Proviso, would have made it a condition of the war that slavery would not be permitted in any state formed from territory acquired from Mexico. The Wilmot Proviso was adopted by the House, but the Senate did not include it in its version of the war funding. Wilmot made the same proposal in another war-funding bill in 1847; again the House accepted it, but the Senate did not.

In 1848, the Wilmot Proviso became a rallying cry for a faction of New York Democrats, called the Barnburners, who opposed expansion of slavery to new territories.

See also: Election of 1844, Vol. 1, p. 52; Election of 1848, Vol. 1, p. 56.

Arizona, and Nevada would be organized without mentioning slavery; their residents would be allowed to decide the issue later. The slave trade was abolished in the national capital, and California would be admitted as a free state. To pacify

In this cartoon, Free Soil leader Martin Van Buren tries to bridge the gap between the Democrats and the Whigs. The Free Soil platform attempted to attract new members from both the Democratic and Whig parties.

Southern supporters of slavery who were unhappy that California would tip the balance of slave and free states, the Fugitive Slave Act required that runaway slaves captured in free states be returned to their owners.

Demise of the Free Soil Party

The Compromise of 1850 took a good deal of wind out of the sails of the Free Soilers, and many Democratic Barnburners returned to their original party, leaving the Free Soil Party as a collection of Conscience (antislavery) Whigs and remnants of the Liberty Party (see p. 34). In 1852 the Free Soil Party nominated John Hale, the 1848 Liberty Party presidential candidate, for president. In their second try for national office, the Free Soilers collected only about half as many votes as they had four years earlier—a total of 155,210 or 4.19 per cent—and carried no states (see Vol. 1, p. 60).

In 1854, the Kansas-Nebraska Act undid the Compromise of 1850 by establishing two new territories west of Missouri, Kansas and Nebraska, and providing that residents would decide whether to allow slavery when the territories became states. At first, Free Soilers saw the law, sponsored by Democratic Senator Stephen Douglas of Illinois (see Vol. 1, p. 71) as a means of reuniting a badly divided Democratic Party, as an opportunity to revive the Free Soil Party. Instead, the passions evoked by the Kansas-Nebraska Act led to formation of the new Republican Party in 1856 (see p. 55) which swept aside the Free Soil Party along with the last remnants of the Whigs and the emerging anti-immigrant Know-Nothings (see p. 46). The Free Soil Party ceased to function after 1854.

Platform of the Free Soil Party, 1848

Excerpts from the platform of the Free Soil Party in 1848:

We have assembled in convention as a union of free men, for the sake of freedom, forgetting all past political differences, in a common resolve to maintain the rights of free labor against the aggression of the slave power, and to secure free soil to a free people; and

Whereas, The political conventions recently assembled at Baltimore and Philadelphia—the one stifling the voice of a great constituency entitled to be heard in its deliberations, and the other abandoning its distinctive principles for mere availability—have dissolved the national party organization heretofore existing, by nominating for the chief magistracy of the United States, under the slaveholding dictation, candidates neither of whom can be supported by the opponents of slavery extension without a sacrifice of consistency, duty and self-respect; and

Whereas, These nominations so made furnish the occasion and demonstrate the necessity of the union of the people under the banner of free democracy, in a solely and formal declaration of their independence of the slave power, and of their fixed determination to rescue the federal government from its control,—

1. Resolved, Therefore, that we, the people here assembled, remembering the example of our fathers in the days of the first Declaration of Independence, putting our trust in God for the triumph of our cause, and invoking his guidance in our endeavors to advance it, do now plant ourselves upon the national platform of freedom, in opposition to the sectional platform of slavery.

2. Resolved, That slavery in the several states of this Union which recognize its existence depends upon the state law alone, which cannot be repealed or modified by the federal government, and for which laws that government is not responsible. We therefore propose no interference by Congress with slavery within the limits of any state.

3. Resolved, That the proviso of Jefferson, to prohibit the existence of slavery after 1800 in all the territories of the United States, southern and northern; the votes of six states and sixteen delegates in the Congresses of 1784 for the proviso, to three states and seven delegates against it; the actual exclusion of slavery from the Northwestern Territory, by the Ordinance of 1787, unanimously adopted by the states in Congress, and the entire history of that period,—clearly show that it was the settled policy of the nation not to extend, nationalize, or encourage, but to limit, localize, and discourage slavery; and to this policy, which should never have been departed from, the government ought to return.

4. Resolved, That our fathers ordained the Constitution of the United States in order, among other great national objects, to establish justice, promote the general welfare, secure the blessings of liberty; but expressly denied to the federal government, which they created, a constitutional power to deprive any person of life, liberty, or property, without due legal process.

…

6. Resolved, That it is the duty of the federal government to relieve itself from all responsibility for the existence or continuance of slavery wherever the government possesses constitutional power to legislate on that subject, and is thus responsible for its existence.

7. Resolved, That the true and, in the judgment of this convention, the only safe means of preventing the extension of slavery into territory now free is to prohibit its extension in all such territory by an act of Congress.

8. Resolved, That we accept the issue which the slave power has forced upon us; and to their demand for more slave states and more slave territory, our calm but final answer is: No more slave states and no more slave territory. Let the soil of our extensive domain be kept free for the hardy pioneers of our own land and the oppressed and banished of other lands seeking homes of comfort and fields of enterprise in the new world.

…

12. Resolved, That we demand cheap postage for the people; a retrenchment of the expenses and patronage of the federal government; the abolition of all unnecessary offices and salaries; and the election by the people of all civil officers in the service of the government so far as the same may be practicable.

13. Resolved, That river and harbor improvements, when demanded by the safety and convenience of commerce with foreign nations, or among the several states, are objects of national concern, and that it is the duty of Congress, in the exercise of its constitutional power, to provide therefore.

14. Resolved, That the free grant to actual settlers, in consideration of the expenses they incur in making settlements in the wilderness, which are usually fully equal to their actual cost, and of the public benefits resulting therefrom, of reasonable portions of the public lands under suitable limitations, Is a wise and just measure of public policy, which will promote, in various ways, the interest of all the states of this Union; and we therefore recommend it to the favorable consideration of the American people.

15. Resolved, That the obligations of honor and patriotism require the earliest practical payment of the national debt, and we are therefore in favor of such a tariff of duties as will raise revenue adequate to defray the expenses of the federal government, and to pay annual installments of our debt, and the interest thereon.

16. Resolved, That we inscribe on our banner, " Free Soil, Free Speech, Free Labor, and Free Men," and under it we will fight on, and fight forever, until a triumphant victory shall reward our exertions.

More Information

- Bilotta, James D. *Race and the Rise of the Republican Party, 1848–1865.* New York: P. Lang, 1992.
- Johnson, Donald Bruce (ed.). *National Party Platforms: Volume I, 1840–1846.* Champaign-Urbana, IL: University of Illinois Press, 1978.
- *Political Parties in America.* Washington: Congressional Quarterly Press, 2001.
- Smith, Theodore Clarke. *The Liberty and Free Soil Parties in the Northwest.* New York, Russell & Russell, 1967.

On the Web

- Free Soil Party. African American Journey. *http://www2.worldbook.com/wc/popup?path=features/aajourney _new&page=html/aa_2_freesoil.shtml&direct=yes.*
- Free Soil Party. Encyclopedia Americana. *http://ap.grolier.com/article?assetid=0165940- 00&templatename=/article/article.html.*
- Free Soil Party. Reader's Companion to American History. *http://college.hmco.com/history/readerscomp/rcah/html/ ah_033800_freesoilpart.htm.*
- 1848 Platform, Free Soil Party. *http://www.geocities.com/ CollegePark/Quad/6460/doct/848frsl.html.*
- Great American History Fact-Finder. *http://college.hmco.com/history/readerscomp/gahff/html/ ff_044000_constitutio3.htm.*

American (Know-Nothing) Party, 1849–57

> ### Flash Focus: American (Know-Nothing) Party
>
> **Origins**
>
> Large-scale immigration from Germany and Ireland in the 1840s caused American-born Protestants to feel threatened, both politically and economically. In New York City, a group opposed to the rising tide of immigration formed the secret Order of the Star-Spangled Banner. Local chapters soon formed in other cities. Members were instructed to reply, "I know nothing," when asked about the group, which gave it nickname of the Know-Nothing Party. As its membership and influence began to grow, the group began to shed its secrecy and adopted an official name, the American Party, in 1855.
>
> **Issues**
>
> **Immigration restrictions.** Know-Nothings advocated laws to limit immigration, which they blamed for driving down wages and for increases in crime and urban slums.
>
> **Eligibility for citizenship.** The party advocated a 21-year residence requirement for immigrants to become citizens or to hold political office. They insisted that no one should hold office who recognized an allegiance to a foreign power or who refused to recognize the federal and state constitutions as supreme law.
>
> **Separation of church and state.** Know-Nothings were suspicious that Roman Catholic priests exerted undue influence over Catholic immigrants. They worried about Catholics' allegiance to the Vatican, and the party demanded a strict separation of church and state.
>
> **Impact**
>
> The party was formed in 1849 and held its last meeting in 1857. The Know-Nothing Party grew rapidly, and in 1852 it scored impressive victories in state and local elections in the Northeast, especially in Massachusetts. The party appealed to many conservative voters who were unhappy siding with either proslavery Democrats or antislavery Whigs or Republicans. The party's electoral peak came in 1854, when 43 Know-Nothings were elected to the House of Representatives, and Henry J. Gardner was elected governor of Massachusetts. As with the Whig Party, slavery proved the Know-Nothing Party's undoing. A wild debate ensued after a proslavery resolution was read at the party's 1855 convention; it ended with a broad defection of members. Personal animus between party leaders in New York also contributed to the party's dissolution. The party's last gasp came in 1856 when it nominated former President Millard Fillmore to run for president; he ran a distant third. The last national meeting of the Know-Nothings took place in 1857.
>
> *See also:* Free Soil Party, p. 42; Republican Party, 1854–76, p. 55.

In the 1840s, the United States absorbed over three million German and Irish immigrants. It was the first time since American independence that such a large number of non-British immigrants had come to the United States in such a short period.

The immigration surge occurred at a time when new industrial enterprises were growing rapidly, especially in cities of the Northeast. Factory jobs were attracting many of the immigrants, as well as drawing people from rural areas into cities and towns. The immigration of the 1840s also coincided with the Great Awakening, a period of intense religious fervor in the United States. Unlike earlier immigrants, who were predominantly Protestants, many of the newcomers from Ireland and Germany were Roman Catholics. Underscoring their religious differences, immigrants from Ireland also brought with them ancient antipathies toward the English.

The immigrants gave rise to anti-immigrant sentiment among native-born American Protestants who feared the recent arrivals would threaten their political and economic well-being.

Party Origins

The Know-Nothings originated from the Order of the Star-Spangled Banner in New York City, one of many anti-immigrant secret societies that sprang up throughout the Northeast. The Order of the Star-Spangled Banner was led by Charles Allen, one of the most prominent leaders of the nativist movement.

The nativist groups blamed immigrants for a host of social problems emerging in the rapidly growing industrial cities—increased crime, overcrowded tenements, and severe competition for jobs that kept wages low.

On top of hostilities rooted in the growth of industrialization, native Protestants had long been suspicious of the intentions of the Catholic Church, which in many European countries was the official religion and exercised significant influence over the government. Protestants feared that a large increase in the number of Catholic voters could lead to a papal plot to control the United States. Native Protestants also accused Catholic immigrants of undermining public schools by sending their children to church schools.

Role of Secret Societies

The secret societies that formed in the wake of increased immigration believed they could help establish a new political party dedicated to applying pressure on existing political parties—notably the Democrats and Whigs—to nominate only native American Protestants for political office. The leaders of these secret groups instructed their members to say, "I know

Members of the Know-Nothing Party were particularly suspicious of the Catholic Church and its influence in politics. Here, a boatful of Catholic bishops threaten the American way of life.

nothing," when asked about the secret groups, giving rise to the "Know-Nothing" nickname of the American Party. In 1854, the order secretly promoted its members or other candidates with anti-immigrant positions for office and managed to elect candidates whom the opposition did not even realize were in the race as "Know-Nothings." As its membership and influence grew, the party abandoned its secretive approach and officially became known as the American Party in 1855. It was the fastest-growing political party in the United States, with membership estimated at between 800,000 and 1.5 million.

The party came to light just as the issue of slavery was splitting both the two major parties, the Whigs (see p. 27) and the Democrats (see p. 17). Disenchanted Whigs and Democrats both found a home with the Know-Nothings, who amplified their themes of American interests and the stability of the Union. Some newcomers to the American Party may have hoped that a campaign aimed against immigrants could ease tensions over slavery. Some opportunistic politicians took advantage of the beginning of the demise of the Whig Party to form a new base of support with the Know-Nothings. The new party also promoted itself as a party of the people, devoid of professional politicians and not aligned with a particular political machine.

A Changing Economy

The economic landscape of the United States was quickly changing in the 1840s and '50s. The increase in industrialization led to economic slumps and unemployment. Rapidly expanding railroads happily hired immigrants, who were often willing to work for extremely low wages. This aroused resentment and animosity toward new immigrants among more established workers, and this disgruntlement created fertile ground for recruitment of new Know-Nothings.

The party's effort to bring together different sectional and political factions meant that its membership and leadership varied widely across the country. In New York, the American

Party attracted former Whigs who opposed the antislavery elements of their former party, whereas in New England, Know-Nothing leaders tended to favor the antislavery part of the Whig platform. One such New England Know-Nothing, Henry Gardner, was elected governor of Massachusetts in 1854. Southerners, who did not experience the influx of foreign immigrants comparable to the North, viewed new immigrants in the North as troublesome simply based on the assumption that they would oppose slavery. Know-Nothings had limited impact in the South, and even less in states like Illinois, Indiana, and Ohio.

The high-water mark for the Know-Nothings came in 1854. In addition to Gardner's victory in Massachusetts, 43 Know-Nothings took the oath of office when the House of Representatives convened in 1855.

But election to state legislatures did not result in successful implementation of nativist laws. Because of legislative inexperience, the Know-Nothing representatives in Massachusetts, for example, failed to pass an amendment to the state constitution restricting voting rights of immigrants. They succeeded only in passing a literacy test for voting and in appointing an investigation board looking into the Catholic schools. Nationally, Know-Nothing congressmen failed to get immigration bills out of committees. This failure to produce results disenchanted many supporters of the new movement.

End of the Know-Nothings

Nationally, the Know-Nothings became caught up in the divisions over slavery. To present themselves as a national party, northern Know-Nothing leaders stressed that it was unwise to criticize southern Know-Nothings despite serious misgivings about slavery.

At the 1855 party convention in Philadelphia, a large number of Know-Nothings left the convention—and the party—after a proslavery resolution was introduced. Massachusetts nativists led a walkout by several state delegations.

The party tried to regroup in 1856, when southerners and a minority of northern Know-Nothings nominated former President Millard Fillmore for president (see Vol. 1, p. 64). But Fillmore had joined a nativist association as a political maneuver and was never a dedicated Know-Nothing loyalist. Many northern Know-Nothings voted instead for the Republican candidate, John C. Frémont (see Vol. 1, p. 66). Fillmore won only 22 percent of the popular vote and eight electoral votes (all from Maryland).

After the election of 1856, party membership dwindled. The party held its last national conference in 1857, during which it adopted a resolution calling on each state Know-Nothing council to draft rules for its organization that would best suit that particular state.

The Know-Nothings began to disappear gradually following the final national conference. In the North, the party struggled as a small minority party, but most of its members joined the Republican Party. In the South, many former Know-Nothings ended up backing the presidential candidacy of John Bell of the Constitutional Union Party in 1860 (see p. 50 and Vol. 1, p. 68).

1856 Platform of the Know-Nothing Party

The Know-Nothing Party was dedicated to restricting immigration and was unabashedly anti-Catholic. The party tried to avoid the divisive issue of slavery by attracting diverse elements from other parties on the basis of a common enemy—immigrants. The party platform from 1856 outlined their general aim. Excerpts:

Americans must rule America; and to this end, native-born citizens should be selected for all state, federal, or municipal offices of government employment, in preference to naturalized citizens.

No person should be selected for political station who recognizes any alliance or obligation of any description to any foreign prince, potentate or power, who refuses to recognize the federal and state constitutions as paramount to all other laws, as rules of particular action.

The unequalled recognition and maintenance of the reserved rights of the several states, and the cultivation of harmony and fraternal good-will between the citizens of the several states, and to this end, non-interference by Congress with questions appertaining solely to the individual states, and non-intervention by each state with the affairs of any other state.

The recognition of the right of the native-born and naturalized citizens of the United States, permanently residing in any territory thereof, to frame the constitution and laws, and to regulate their domestic and social affairs in their own mode, subject only to the provisions of the federal Constitution, with the right of admission into the Union whenever they have the requisite population for one representative in Congress. Provided, always, that none but those who are citizens of the United States, under the Constitution and laws thereof, and who have a fixed residence in any such territory, are to participate in the formation of the constitution, or in the enactment of laws for said territory or state.

An enforcement of the principles that no state or territory can admit other than native-born citizens to the right of suffrage, or of holding political office unless such persons shall have been naturalized according to the laws of the United States.

A change in the laws of naturalization, making a continued residence of twenty-one years, of all not heretofore provided for, an indispensable requisite for citizenship hereafter, and excluding all paupers or persons convicted of crime from landing upon our shores; but no interference with the vested rights of foreigners.

Opposition to any union between Church and State; no interference with religious faith or worship, and no test oaths for office…

Opposition to the reckless and unwise policy of the present administration in the general management of our national affairs, and more especially as shown in removing "Americans" (by designation) and conservatives in principle, from office, and placing foreigners and ultraists in their places, as shown in a truckling [fawning] subserviency to the stronger, and an insolent and cowardly bravado toward the weaker powers; as shown in opening sectional agitation, by the repeal of the Missouri Compromise; as shown in granting to unnaturalized foreigners the right of suffrage in Kansas and Nebraska, as shown in vacillating course on the Kansas and Nebraska question…

A free and open discussion of all political principles embraced in our platform.

More Information

- Greene, Jack P. (ed.) *Encyclopedia of American Political History.* New York: Scribners, 1984.
- Mulken, John R. *The Know-Nothing Party in Massachusetts: The Rise and Fall of the People's Movement.* Boston: Northeastern University Press, 1990.
- Schlesinger, Arthur M., Jr. (ed.). *History of U.S. Political Parties: Vol. 1, 1789–1860.* New York: Chelsea House, 1973.
- *Political Parties in America.* Washington, D.C.: Congressional Quarterly Press, 2001.

On the Web

- Know-Nothing Movement, Encyclopedia Americana. *http://ap.grolier.com/article?assetid=0233110-00&templatename=/article/article.html.*
- Knownothingism, The Catholic Encyclopedia. *http://www.newadvent.org/cathen/08677a.htm.*
- Know-Nothing Movement, U-S-History.Com. *http://www.u-s-history.com/pages/h140.html.*

Constitutional Union Party, 1860

FlashFocus: Constitutional Union Party

Origins
The Constitutional Union Party was formed by conservative members of the former Know-Nothing and Whig Parties in an effort to head off the Civil War. Members urged national conciliation and support for the Constitution without regard for sectional disputes.

Issues
Preservation of the Union. The party identified the very real danger that some states would decide to secede from the Union over the issue of slavery and urged that this be prevented.

The Constitution. Constitutional Unionists argued that adherence to the principles of the Constitution would guide the nation back to conciliation. The party platform argued that political divisions within other parties were the result of partisan bickering and disregard for the founding principles of the nation.

Impact
The party nominated John Bell for president in 1860. He won 39 electoral votes (in Kentucky, Tennessee, and Virginia) and finished last in the four-way race. Bell's presence siphoned votes from the Democrats, who were already split between two presidential candidates representing Northern and Southern wings, and helped give victory to Republican Abraham Lincoln.

The 1860 election dashed the party's hopes of avoiding secession by states in the South. The start of the Civil War in 1861 rendered the party's single goal irrelevant, and the party dissolved.

See also: Election of 1860, Vol. 1, p. 68; John Bell, Vol. 1, p. 73; Republican Party, 1854-76, p. 55; Democratic Party, 1860–76, p. 61.

The question of slavery, and whether or not the federal government should allow it to exist in new states and territories, caused rising dissension among politicians, officeholders, and political parties in all parts of the United States in the 1850s. The Constitutional Union Party was a one-issue party dedicated to preserving the Union; after a single season in the political sun, the party left virtually no legacy.

The Constitutional Union Party served as a temporary home for former Democrats (see p. 61) and Whigs (see p. 27) who could no longer abide the sectional bickering over slavery and the potential rupture of the Union. But the party failed to present any practicable solutions to the issue of slavery, and after entering a candidate in the 1860 presidential election (see Vol. 1, p. 68), the party dissolved, ending as a historical footnote to the period just before the Civil War.

Origin and Philosophy

The Constitutional Union Party was formed after some Democrats became dissatisfied with the divisions in their party that arose over the Lecompton Constitution, a document drafted at Lecompton, Kansas, which was designed to bring Kansas into the Union as a proslavery state. The collapse of the Whig Party had left many southerners without a viable political home, and perceived shortcomings of the American Party ("Know-Nothing" Party, see p. 46) provided fertile ground for the formation of a new political party.

Senator John Crittenden of Kentucky gathered 50 conservative congressmen in Baltimore, Maryland, on May 9, 1860, to attend the first and only convention of the Constitutional Union Party.

Intentionally avoiding a discussion of slavery, the most controversial subject of the day, the convention drafted and adopted a brief platform that urged support for a Constitution and a Union unchanged. The platform was specifically aimed at border states such as Kentucky and Tennessee that were sometimes viewed as neutral on the slavery issue. The newly organized party nominated Senator John Bell of Tennessee (see Vol. 1, p. 73), a former Speaker of the House of Representatives, for president and Edward Everett, the president of Harvard University, for vice president.

Bell and Everett ran a somewhat dull campaign and managed to win about 12.5 percent of the popular vote. The party collected 39 electoral votes from Virginia, Kentucky, and Tennessee, out of a possible 303. Coupled with the split in the Democratic Party, the Constitutional Unionists effectively ensured the election of the Republican candidate, Abraham Lincoln (see Vol. 1, p. 69), who captured the necessary majority of electoral votes to become president in the election of 1860 (see Vol. 1, p. 68).

End of the Constitutional Unionists

Despite Lincoln's victory in 1860, the Constitutional Union Party initially tried to press on, campaigning against the threat of secession. Despite these efforts, seven Southern states voted to secede from the Union, followed by four more at the beginning of hostilities in the Civil War, and formed the Confederate States of America. The Constitutional Union Party then disappeared, many of its members supporting the Confederacy during the Civil War.

Platform of the Constitutional Union Party

The Constitutional Union Party ran its one and only candidate for the presidency in 1860 on a platform with one issue: the preservation of the Union. Its platform was simple and direct:

Whereas, Experience has demonstrated that Platforms adopted by the partisan Conventions of the country have had the effect to mislead and deceive the people, and at the same time to widen the political divisions of the country, by the creation and encouragement of geographical and sectional parties; therefore

Resolved, that it is both the part of patriotism and of duty to recognize no political principle other than THE CONSTITUTION OF THE COUNTRY, THE UNION OF THE STATES, AND THE ENFORCEMENT OF THE LAWS, and that, as representatives of the Constitutional Union men of the country, in National Convention assembled, we hereby pledge ourselves to maintain, protect, and defend, separately and united, these great principles of public liberty and national safety, against all enemies, at home and abroad; believing that thereby peace may once more be restored to the country; the rights of the People and of the States re-established, and the Government again placed in that condition of justice, fraternity and equality, which, under the example and Constitution of our fathers, has solemnly bound every citizen of the United States to maintain a more perfect union, establish justice, insure domestic tranquility, provide for the common defense, promote the general welfare, and secure the blessings of liberty to ourselves and our posterity.

More Information

- Johnson, Donald Bruce (ed.). *National Party Platforms: Volume I, 1840–1846.* Champaign-Urbana: University of Illinois Press, 1978.
- *Political Parties in America.* Washington: Congressional Quarterly Press, 2001.

On the Web

- Constitutional Union Party. Readers' Companion to American History. *http://college.hmco.com/history/readerscomp/rcah/html/ah_019900_constitutio2.htm.*
- Constitutional Union Party. The American Presidency, Encyclopedia Americana. *http://ap.grolier.com/article?assetid=0106240-00&templatename=/article/article.html.*
- Constitutional Union Party. The Handbook of Texas Online. *http://www.tsha.utexas.edu/handbook/online/articles/view/CC/wac1.html.*

Southern Democratic Party, 1860

FlashFocus: Southern Democratic Party

Origins
At the Democratic Party's 1860 national convention in Charleston, South Carolina, a faction of delegates representing the southern slave states demanded a plank in the platform establishing a federal slave code that would permit slavery to be extended to territories in the West. The measure was defeated, and the members of the group walked out of the convention. They regrouped and held their own convention, nominating the incumbent vice president, John Breckinridge, for president. The split in the Democratic Party foreshadowed the withdrawal of southern states from the Union, starting with South Carolina on December 20, 1860, a move that led directly to Civil War in 1861.

Issues
Slave codes. Southern Democrats supported a federal law that would protect slaveholders bringing their "property" into western territories. In effect, Southern Democrats demanded that the government recognize the legitimacy of slavery in territories not yet states, viewing the issue as one of protecting private property.
Fugitive Slave Law. The Fugitive Slave Law had been passed in 1850, requiring that states where slavery was not recognized nevertheless must hand over fleeing slaves. Southern Democrats strongly supported the legislation and insisted that it be applied to western territories as well.

Impact
Breckinridge finished third in the four-way race for president in 1860, winning the popular votes in 11 of the 15 states that recognized slavery. While Breckinridge and Democrat Stephen Douglas together received more votes than Republican Abraham Lincoln, Lincoln won an absolute majority in northern states which gave him a victory in the electoral college. During the Civil War from 1861 to 1865, Southern Democrats were the main leaders of the Confederate States of America, including its president, Jefferson Davis. When the Civil War ended with defeat of the Confederacy and abolition of slavery by constitutional amendment, the issues that brought together the Southern Democrats as a separate party vanished. The faction did not attempt to sustain a separate party, but instead returned to the national Democratic Party.

See also: Election of 1860, Vol. 1, p. 68; Democratic Party, 1828–60, p. 17; Republican Party, 1854–76, p. 55; Constitutional Union Party, p. 50; Democratic Party, 1860–76, p. 61.

Never before had a major American political party split so dramatically as did the Democratic Party leading up to the 1860 presidential election. Throughout the middle of the nineteenth century, the Democrats had presented a united front by endorsing legislation that sought a middle ground on the issue of slavery—protecting slavery in southern states and leaving the issue up to a popular vote in the western territories. As the decade wore on, Democrats from the South grew increasingly frustrated with compromise.

At the 1860 Democratic National Convention, held in Charleston, South Carolina, Senator Jefferson Davis of Mississippi led a contingent of Southern Democrats that called for a plank in the party platform explicitly protecting slavery in U.S. territories. The resolution was defeated, and most of the southern delegates to the convention simply left. The northerners who were left decided to regroup six weeks later in Baltimore, Maryland, where they nominated Senator Stephen Douglas of Illinois (see Vol. 1, p. 71) for president.

The Southern Democrats, plus some delegates from California and Oregon, also met again and nominated incumbent Vice President John Breckinridge (see Vol. 1, p. 72) as their candidate for president. Breckinridge accepted the nomination, and two separate Democratic national committees opened offices in the nation's capital to manage the separate campaigns of Douglas and Breckinridge.

The two halves of the Democratic Party shared some positions. Both Northern and Southern Democrats supported enforcement of the Fugitive Slave Law, which punished runaway slaves and those who harbored them. However, the Southern Democrats went a step further in arguing for the enactment of a federal slave code to govern U.S. territories as well as the states. In addition, Southern Democrats supported slaveholders who wished to take their slaves into western territories, even if slavery was not recognized in those areas.

Douglas and the Northern Democrats believed such decisions should be decided by the Supreme Court. The Republican Party, headed by presidential candidate Abraham Lincoln (see Vol. 1, p. 68), opposed any sort of federal slave code. Breckinridge stated that he was not necessarily anti-Union, but believed that slavery could be banned in a territory only after it was admitted as a state. He saw himself as the Democratic candidate—indeed the only candidate—who could prevent secession of the slave states of the South.

Breckinridge finished third in the popular vote for the presidency in 1860, behind Lincoln and Douglas. Breckinridge won the popular vote—and thus the electoral votes—in 11 of the 15 slave states and finished second in the electoral college with 72 votes. Lincoln benefited from the split of the Democratic Party and from the candidacy of John Bell (see Vol. 1, p. 73) of the Constitutional Union Party (see p. 50). After the election, Breckinridge (who was still vice president of the United States) worked with other Democrats to achieve a compromise that might prevent war between the states. Lincoln was adamant that slavery should not be allowed in

In a reference to Abraham Lincoln's log-splitting days as a youth, this cartoon shows Lincoln as the force behind the split between North and South. It was this split that inspired the formation of the Southern Democratic Party.

federal territories, and a reconciliation could not be reached. Between Lincoln's election in November 1860 and his inauguration in March 1861, 11 Southern states seceded from the Union, forming the Confederate States of America. Breckinridge went on to serve as a major general in the Confederate Army and later as the secretary of war in the Confederate government.

End of the Southern Democrats

With the onset of the Civil War and the formation of the Confederate States of America, Southern Democrats focused on Richmond, Virginia, the capital of the Confederacy. Many Southern Democratic officeholders who had once served in Washington remained to serve the new government, and many fought in the Confederate Army. Once the war ended in defeat for the Confederacy, and with slavery no longer legal anywhere in the United States, the issues and positions that gave rise to the Southern Democratic Party in 1860 had vanished. The Southern Democrats made no effort to function separately from the rest of the Democratic Party and rejoined the national organization.

Platform, Southern Democratic Party, 1860

After the Southern Democrats walked out of the Democratic Party National Convention in 1860, they reconvened and held a convention of their own. Vice President John Breckinridge was nominated as the presidential candidate of the Southern Democrats, and a platform was debated and adopted.

Resolved, That the platform adopted by the Democratic party at Cincinnati be affirmed, with the following explanatory resolutions:

1. That the Government of a Territory organized by an act of Congress is provisional and temporary, and during its existence all citizens of the United States have an equal right to settle with their property in the Territory, without their rights, either of person or property, being destroyed or impaired by Congressional or Territorial legislation.

2. That it is the duty of the Federal Government, in all its departments, to protect, when necessary, the rights of persons and property in the Territories, and wherever else its constitutional authority extends.

3. That when the settlers in a Territory, having an adequate population, form a State Constitution, the right of sovereignty commences, and being consummated by admission into the Union, they stand on an equal footing with the people of other States, and the State thus organized ought to be admitted into the Federal Union, whether its constitution prohibits or recognizes the institution of slavery.

Resolved, That the Democratic party are in favor of the acquisition of the Island of Cuba, on such terms as shall be honorable to ourselves and just to Spain, at the earliest practicable moment.

Resolved, That the enactments of State Legislatures to defeat the faithful execution of the Fugitive Slave Law are hostile in character, subversive of the Constitution, and revolutionary in their effect.

Resolved, That the Democracy of the United States recognize it as the imperative duty of this Government to protect the naturalized citizen in all his rights, whether at home or in foreign lands, to the same extent as its native-born citizens.

WHEREAS, One of the greatest necessities of the age, in a political, commercial, postal and military point of view, is speedy communication between the Atlantic and Pacific coasts. Therefore be it

Resolved, that the National Democratic party do hereby pledge themselves to use every means in their power to secure the passage of some bill, to the extent of the constitutional authority of Congress, for the construction of a Pacific Railroad from the Mississippi River to the Pacific Ocean, at the earliest practicable moment.

More Information

- Auchampaugh, Phillip. *James Buchanan and His Cabinet on the Eve of Secession.* Boston: J. S. Canner, 1965 (© 1926).
- Crenshaw, Ollinger. *The Slave States in the Presidential Election of 1860.* Baltimore: Johns Hopkins Press, 1945.
- Donald, David Herbert. *Lincoln.* New York: Simon and Schuster, 1995.
- Graff, Henry F. (ed.). *The Presidents: A Reference History.* New York: Macmillan, 2002.
- *Political Parties in America.* Washington: Congressional Quarterly Press, 2001.

On the Web:

- 1860 Democratic Convention Number 1—Charleston, South Carolina. *http://usgovinfo.about.com/library/weekly/aa080400b.htm.*
- 1860 Platform of the Southern Democrats. *http://www2.vscc.cc.tn.us/socialscience/FinalDocs/coming/sernDem1860.htm.*

Republican Party, 1854–76

FlashFocus: Republican Party, 1854–76

Origins
The Republican Party originated in 1854 as the party of free soil, opposed to expanding slavery into western territories. The new party attracted many northern Whigs (whose southern colleagues had joined Democrats in supporting the right to take slaves to western territories) as well as northern free soil Democrats. After coming to power with the election of Abraham Lincoln in 1860, Republicans oversaw Union participation in the Civil War (1861–65) and a period of Reconstruction in the South. In 1876, the Republican presidential candidate lost the popular vote to the Democratic candidate, ending two decades of virtual monopoly on power in the federal government.

Issues
Free Soil. The principle issue around which the Republican Party was organized was stopping the expansion of slavery into western territories—not to benefit slaves, but to preserve the West for independent white farmers.
Union and Reconstruction. During the Civil War, the Republican Party led the North in preserving the union of the states. After the war, radical Republicans in Congress took the lead in overseeing the vanquished Confederacy and enforcing civil rights for emancipated slaves, including the right to vote.
Emancipation of slaves. In the midst of the Civil War, President Lincoln signed the Emancipation Proclamation, freeing slaves living in areas under Confederate control as of January 1, 1863. This marked an evolution of the Republican position on free soil and reflected the position of radical Republicans intent on reconstructing Southern society after the war.
Homesteading. Despite the distraction of the Civil War, the Republicans passed a homesteading law in 1862 providing white settlers in the West with 160 acres of free land to start family farms.

Impact
Republicans captured the White House in 1860, six years after the party was founded, guided the country through four years of Civil War, and remained in power for another 12 years largely without effective challenge from the Democrats. Republicans held uninterrupted majorities in both houses of Congress from 1861 to 1877. But the Republicans remained almost exclusively a party of the North and West during the Civil War and Reconstruction eras and long after.

See also: Whig Party, p. 27; Free Soil Party, p. 42; American (Know Nothing) Party, p. 46; Republican Party, 1876–1900, p. 75; Republican Party, 1900–32, p. 105; Republican Party, 1932–68, p. 135; Republican Party, 1968–2004, p. 169; Democratic Party, 1860–76, p. 61.

On the surface, the story of the Republican Party was one of unparalleled success. Founded in 1854, the party captured the White House just six years later and held onto it for 44 of the next 52 years (or, in terms of elections, Republicans won the White House 11 times in the next 13 presidential elections). The Republicans effectively replaced the Whigs (see p. 27) as the party of business interests in a two-party system.

Of course, below the surface lies a more complex and more interesting story of politics and policies in an era when positions were sometimes defended in fistfights and knife fights, even among members of Congress. The Republican Party was initially founded in 1854 around one basic principle: free soil, or the idea that slavery should not be allowed in newly settled Western territories. After an extended struggle with other major contenders, including the badly divided Democrats (see p. 17) and the anti-immigrant Know-Nothings (see p. 46), the Republicans emerged victorious in the election of 1860 (see Vol. 1, p. 68), electing their presidential candidate, Abraham Lincoln (see Vol. 1, p. 69), in a four-way race in which Lincoln failed to receive a majority of votes. Following the Civil War (1861–65), the Republicans continued to dominate the national government for another 12 years of Reconstruction in the South. After 1876, the party faced a much tougher fight to maintain control of the White House and constantly traded control of Congress with the Democrats.

The Debate over Free Soil

The Republican Party was formally organized in July 1854 in Jackson, Michigan, as an alliance of Free Soilers (see p. 42), Democrats, and Whigs (see p. 27) who came together to oppose the Kansas-Nebraska Act of 1854. Sponsored by Illinois Democratic Senator Stephen Douglas (see Vol. 1, p. 71), the Kansas-Nebraska Act had repealed a key provision of the Missouri Compromise of 1820 in order to allow settlers in the territory of present day Kansas and Nebraska to decide whether slavery would be legal there when the territories became states. (The Missouri Compromise of 1820 had barred slavery in territory north of latitude 36 degrees 30 minutes, roughly the southern border of Missouri.) The Republican free soil position—that slavery should be barred in newly settled western territories—was quite distinct from abolitionism, which advocated the end of slavery everywhere. Free soilers were less interested in the fate of African American slaves than in the future of white settlers who wanted to set up farms on homesteads in the West and who feared competition from large southern-style plantations worked by slaves. In this fight, the Republicans attracted Whigs, such as Abraham Lincoln of Illinois. The Whigs had been irreparably split over the free soil issue, with southern Whigs joining Democrats in supporting the Kansas-Nebraska Act and northern Whigs

> ### FlashFocus: Union Party, 1864
>
> **What:** The Union Party was the name adopted by Republicans during the 1864 presidential election to attract Democrats who supported the Civil War effort in the North. To further promote an alliance with prowar Democrats, the Union Party chose Andrew Johnson of Tennessee, a Democrat, as President Abraham Lincoln's vice presidential running mate.
>
> **Who:** Abraham Lincoln, the Republican president, was the Union Party presidential candidate in 1864. Andrew Johnson of Tennessee, a Democrat, was Lincoln's vice presidential running mate.
>
> **When:** The Union Party was purely a vehicle to demonstrate national unity in the North in the midst of the Civil War. The Union victory in early 1865 eliminated any need, or justification, for continuation of the party.
>
> **Impact:** Lincoln and his supporters in the Republican Party took political advantage of the split between northern Democrats who favored continuation of the war and those who favored a peace settlement (called Peace Democrats, or Copperheads). The Democratic Party nominated former Union army general George McClellan—fired by Lincoln for not pursuing Confederate armies with enough vigor—but on a platform advocating negotiation with the South and a cessation of armed conflict.
>
> To make themselves more appealing to Democrats, Republicans adopted the name Union Party and welcomed Democrats who supported the war effort and Lincoln's demand that slavery be abolished throughout the United States. They also nominated a Democrat, Andrew Johnson of Tennessee, a flamboyant supporter of the war, as vice president.
>
> Lincoln was reelected with 55 percent of the vote, overwhelming Democrat George McClellan. By the following April, the Confederacy had surrendered to the Union and the Civil War was over, and with it the Union Party. Democrats who had supported the war effort realigned themselves with their original party.

looking for a new political home. Also joining the new Republican Party were a significant number of northern Democrats, known as Barnburners, who also opposed expansion of slavery.

In the first presidential election after its founding, in 1856 (see Vol. 1, p. 64), the Republicans nominated California Senator John Frémont (see Vol. 1, p. 66) for president. Frémont, a well-known explorer and veteran of the 1848 war with Mexico, ran second to Democrat James Buchanan (who carried every slave state in the South, plus Illinois, Indiana, Pennsylvania and New Jersey; see Vol. 1, p. 65) and ahead of American (Know-Nothing) Party candidate Millard Fillmore (see Vol. 1, p. 67). The Kansas-Nebraska Act stayed in place, touching off fierce battles over the future of Kansas in particular, including John Brown's famous raid (see Vol. 4, p. 31).

It was a period when political passions were strongly felt. Republican Representative (and for two years Speaker of the House) Galusha Grow of Pennsylvania, for example, had a fistfight with Democrat Laurence Keitt of South Carolina, while Republican John Potter of Wisconsin, challenged to a duel by Democrat Roger Pryor of Virginia, chose Bowie knives as the weapon.

By 1860, with the Democrats divided between fervent slavery supporters in the South and more moderate party members in the North, the Republicans were themselves divided into three wings: the radicals, who refused any compromise on the issue of extending slavery to the West; moderates, including Lincoln, who were willing to seek a compromise over the issue of free soil; and conservatives, who were less committed to the principle of free soil and more interested in simply defeating Democrats. Lincoln won the 1860 Republican presidential nomination and went on to win the presidency over three other candidates.

During the Civil War, Lincoln assembled a coalition of Republicans and northern Democrats to conduct the Civil War with a united front, although some Democrats known as Copperheads (see p. 62) advocated negotiating peace with the Confederacy. The bedrock Republican principle of free soil evolved into ending slavery altogether, partly as a tactic to win the war by inspiring a slave revolt (which never occurred). In September 1862, in an effort to persuade wavering Confederates to come over to the Union side, Lincoln threatened to free all slaves living in Confederate territory as of January 1863. He followed through on the threat by issuing the Emancipation Proclamation (see Vol. 4, p. 42) on January 1, 1863, freeing slaves living in areas of breakaway states not under Union control. In the summer of 1864, with the outcome of the war still in doubt, Lincoln nominated a Democrat (and slave owner), Andrew Johnson of Tennessee (see Vol. 1, p. 75), as his vice presidential running mate in his reelection campaign. Lincoln's victory was then virtually guaranteed by a string of Union military victories in the weeks just before the election.

Lincoln was assassinated in April 1865, just days after the surrender of the Confederate Army, paving the way for radical Republicans in Congress to force through a program of "reconstruction" of the South against the instincts of Johnson, who became president. Reconstruction included not only emancipating all slaves (see Thirteenth Amendment, Vol. 4, p. 47), but also guaranteeing full civil rights to freed slaves (see Fourteenth Amendment, Vol. 4, p. 51) and full voting rights (see Fifteenth Amendment, Vol. 4, p. 55, and Civil Rights Act of 1866, Vol. 4, p. 49).

Reconstruction of the South under the direction of the radical Republicans was carried out in the South by the Army, which continued to occupy portions of the South until 1877. General Ulysses Grant (see Vol. 1, p. 79), who had played the critical role in defeating the South, was elected president as a Republican in 1868 and again in 1872. Grant was largely sympathetic with the radicals' program of reconstruction, although he resisted more extreme measures during his second term. The Reconstruction era in the South was marked by con-

Thomas Nast was the first to use the elephant to symbolize the Republican Party. Here, the dominant Republican elephant destroys everything in its path. The Democratic Party is represented by the small fox hiding under a bush.

tinuing efforts by whites to reassert local control of state government and to discourage former slaves from taking advantage of their civil rights.

Republicans after Reconstruction

From 1865 to 1877, the dozen years immediately following the Civil War, Republicans maintained control of the White House and both houses of Congress by campaigning successfully on three major issues: reconstruction of the South (including military occupation, which limited the political power of white Democrats), the "bloody shirt" of Civil War veterans, and Democratic disloyalty in both the South and in the North. Republicans were fond of reminding voters of the sacrifices made in the Civil War (a tactic referred to as "waving the bloody shirt") and also of the role in the war of Northern Democrats, some of whom had advocated a compromise and peace treaty with the Confederacy during the early years of conflict. But at the same time the radical Republicans were reliving the Civil War, other priorities began to clamor for attention; westward expansion, rapid industrial growth, and increasing European immigration all began changing the face of America. Southern whites, more committed than ever to the Democratic Party, regained control of state governments, even though it sometimes meant resorting to terrorism (see Ku Klux Klan, Vol. 4, p. 53) to discourage freed slaves from exercising their newfound political rights. Democrats reappeared to challenge Republican control of Congress, rising from just 11 senators in 1865 to 28 in 1875, and from 38 representatives to 103 in the same period.

Republicans, on the other hand, were forced to deal with the political fallout of government scandals uncovered during Grant's second term, as well as with the rising strength of Democrats in the Middle Atlantic states, parts of the Midwest, and the newly settled territories of the West. New England remained the most reliable bastion of Republican strength, just as it had been the bastion of the Federalists (see p. 9) and the Whigs before.

The Republican Party was split in 1872 when a group of newspaper editors objected to the policies of the Grant administration, including growing rumors of serious corruption. The editors helped encourage foundation of the Liberal Republican Party (see p. 69), which nominated Horace Greeley (see Vol. 1, p. 83) as president. Democrats also nominated Greeley in hopes that a combination of Democrats and disaffected Republicans could unseat the long Republican domination of the federal government. Greeley proved to be an inept candidate, and Grant was easily reelected. Nevertheless, the long Republican domination of national politics was nearing an end. Although Republicans managed to control both houses of Congress from 1873 to 1877, their domination based on the linked issues that drove the nation to the Civil War—free soil and slavery—was beginning to fade, replaced by rapid westward expansion, explosive growth of industry, and a flood of refugees from eastern and southern Europe.

In 1876, the Democrats mounted the most serious challenge for the White House in 20 years (see Vol. 1, p. 86), and the election proved to be a major turning point for the Republicans. The Democratic presidential candidate, Samuel Tilden of New York (see Vol. 1, p. 88), won 51 percent of the popular vote to 48 percent for Republican Rutherford Hayes of Ohio (see Vol. 1, p. 87). Republicans challenged the outcome of voting in four states—Louisiana, South Carolina, Florida, and Oregon. A spe-

FlashFocus: Charles Sumner

Born: January 6, 1811, Boston, Massachusetts
Died: March 11, 1874, Washington, D.C.
Political Career: Cofounder, Free Soil Party, 1848; U.S. Senator from Massachusetts, 1851 (as a Free Soil candidate); reelected as a Republican, 1856, 1862, 1868.

The story of Charles Sumner in some ways parallels the early years of the Republican Party. The Boston native, Harvard graduate, and prominent lawyer entered politics as a Whig but declined that party's nomination for Congress in 1846. Two years later, Sumner helped found the Free Soil Party, opposing expansion of slavery into western federal territories, an issue brought to the forefront by the U.S. acquisition of territory after war with Mexico (1846-48). Proslavery southerners insisted they had the right to carry their "property"—including African American slaves—into new U.S. territory; free soilers like Sumner insisted new territories be reserved for free white farmers.

Sumner ran for Congress on the Free Soil Party ticket in 1848 but lost. Two years later, he was elected to the Senate as the Free Soil candidate. He was reelected three times as a Republican, in 1856, 1862, and 1868. Sumner was assaulted in the Senate chamber by Representative Preston Brooks of South Carolina on May 22, 1856, in a violent objection to Sumner's attacks on slavery. Sumner's injuries kept him out of the Senate until December 1859.

During the Civil War and the period of Reconstruction that followed, Sumner was a leader of the radical Republicans intent on reconstructing southern society on the basis of equal rights for all. During the Civil War, Sumner had advocated use of African American troops to aid the Union Army and acted diplomatically to prevent European countries from intervening to support the South, an important source of cotton for European textile mills. Taking a lead in designing the postwar program called Reconstruction, Sumner opposed the conciliatory policies of President Andrew Johnson and led the effort to impeach him. Sumner backed extensive economic aid and education for freed slaves, including redistribution of white-owned plantations to former slaves, as well as legislation to give African Americans equal civil rights.

In 1872, Sumner accused Republican President Ulysses Grant of not doing enough to advance black political power. Sumner instead backed the Liberal Republican candidate that year, Horace Greeley, who lost. Sumner died of a heart attack two years later, on March 11, 1874, in Washington.

cial commission comprised of senators, representatives, and Supreme Court justices examined the disputed votes and voted along party lines to award the electoral votes of all four states—and with them, the presidency—to Republican Hayes. In an apparent backroom deal, never officially confirmed, Democrats agreed to let the commission's findings go through Congress in exchange for an agreement to withdraw the Army from its remaining occupation duties in the South. The impact was to deliver political control of the South to Democrats for the next 90 years, to effectively disenfranchise freed slaves, and to end Reconstruction. After 1876, the United States had returned to a two-party democracy similar to the situation that had existed from 1828 to 1860. Democrats used their southern base to exert strong influence, or even control, over Congress and to begin challenging Republicans for the White House.

The Republicans, having abandoned thoughts of competing in the South on the strength of African American voters, turned their attention to the rapid growth of industrialization (and an accompanying expansion of population) in the North, succeeding the Whigs as the party representing business interests. The Democrats in turn sought to expand beyond their southern base by building support among the rapidly growing group of low-paid industrial workers, many of whom were immigrants from eastern and southern Europe, and among small farmers in western states and territories.

Republican Philosophy, 1854-1876

The Republicans, somewhat like the Whigs before them, became a major party by creating an alliance of diverse interests. In the period from the party's founding in 1854 until 1876, the principal areas of political interest for Republicans were:

Free soil, or the idea that the institution of slavery should not be permitted outside the states where it was already allowed. The Republican position was rooted in a genuine hatred of slavery, even if many Republicans expressed the view that African Americans were not necessarily the equals of white men.

Emancipation. At first, the party did not endorse freeing all slaves everywhere. It was only during the Civil War that the party moved gradually toward the view that slavery should be ended—in part as a tactic to arouse a rebellion among slaves in the Confederacy in order to shorten the Civil War. In addition to issuing the Emancipation Proclamation, Lincoln helped push the Thirteenth Amendment through Congress, ending slavery everywhere.

Reconstruction. A set of policies pushed through by radical Republicans in the Senate was designed to "reconstruct" southern society and make sure that emancipated slaves were able to exercise political rights—or even control—in the states where slavery had existed before the war. Reconstruction was the era of military occupation of the South by the army of the North. Changes forced onto the South by the Republicans were strongly resisted by whites; and after northern whites grew tired of the effort (or as radical Republicans died or retired), Reconstruction was effectively allowed to lapse after the army occupation ended in 1877.

Homesteading. Even in the midst of the Civil War, the Republicans passed a homestead bill in 1862 to give settlers 160 acres of land in western territories at no charge. The act proved critical in the westward migration that followed the Civil War.

Tariffs. Even while the disintegration of the Union threatened in 1860, the Republicans endorsed higher tariffs to protect domestic manufacturers from foreign competition. Like the Whigs before them, the Republicans endorsed other measures designed to aid business, such as improvements to harbors to aid commerce and a national railroad to link the western and eastern halves of the country.

Republican Platform, 1860

Meeting in Chicago in 1860, Republicans nominated Abraham Lincoln of Illinois for president and adopted a platform that called for a ban on extending slavery beyond the states of the South where it already existed. Excerpts:

Resolved, That we, the delegated representatives of the Republican electors of the United States, in Convention assembled … unite in the following declarations:

1. That the history of the nation, during the last four years, has fully established the propriety and necessity of the organization and perpetuation of the Republican party, and that the causes which called it into existence are permanent in their nature, and now, more than ever before, demand its peaceful and constitutional triumph.

2. That the maintenance of the principles promulgated in the Declaration of Independence and embodied in the Federal Constitution, "That all men are created equal; that they are endowed by their Creator with certain inalienable rights; that among these are life, liberty, and the pursuit of happiness; that to secure these rights, governments are instituted among men, deriving their just powers from the consent of the governed," is essential to the preservation of our Republican institutions; and that the Federal Constitution, the rights of the States, and the Union of the States, must and shall be preserved.

3. That to the Union of the States this nation owes its unprecedented increase in population, its surprising development of material resources, its rapid augmentation of wealth, its happiness at home and its honor abroad; and we hold in abhorrence all schemes for Disunion, come from whatever source they may: And we congratulate the country that no Republican member of Congress has uttered or countenanced the threats of Disunion so often made by Democratic members without rebuke and with applause from their political associates; and we denounce those threats of Disunion, in case of a popular overthrow of their ascendancy, as denying the vital principles of a free government, and as an avowal of contemplated treason, which it is the imperative duty of an indignant People sternly to rebuke and forever silence.

4. That the maintenance inviolate of the rights of the States, and especially the right of each State to order and control its own domestic institutions according to its own judgment exclusively, is essential to that balance of powers on which the perfection and endurance of our political fabric depends; and we denounce the lawless invasion by armed force of the soil of any State or Territory, no matter under what pretext, as among the gravest of crimes.…

7. That the new dogma, that the Constitution, of its own force, carries Slavery into any or all of the Territories of the United States, is a dangerous political heresy, at variance with the explicit provisions of that instrument itself, with contemporaneous exposition, and with legislative and judicial precedent; is revolutionary in its tendency, and subversive of the peace and harmony of the country.

8. That the normal condition of all the territory of the United States is that of freedom; That as our Republican fathers, when they had abolished Slavery in all our national territory, ordained that "no person should be deprived of life, liberty, or property, without due process of law," it becomes our duty, by legislation, whenever such legislation is necessary, to maintain this provision of the Constitution against all attempts to violate it; and we deny the authority of Congress, of a territorial legislature, or of any individuals, to give legal existence to Slavery in any Territory of the United States.

9. That we brand the recent reopening of the African slave-trade, under the cover of our national flag, aided by perversions of judicial power, as a crime against humanity and a burning shame to our country and age; and we call upon Congress to take prompt and efficient measures for the total and final suppression of that execrable traffic.

10. That in the recent vetoes, by their Federal governors, of the acts of the legislatures of Kansas and Nebraska, prohibiting slavery in those territories, we find a practical illustration of the boasted Democratic principle of Non-Intervention and Popular Sovereignty, embodied in the Kansas-Nebraska bill, and a demonstration of the deception and fraud involved therein.…

12. That, while providing revenue for the support of the General Government by duties upon imports, sound policy requires such an adjustment of these imposts as to encourage the development of the industrial interest of the whole country; and we commend that policy of national exchanges which secures to the working men liberal wages, to agriculture remunerative prices, to mechanics and manufacturers an adequate reward for their skill, labor, and enterprise, and to the nation commercial prosperity and independence.…

14. That the Republican party is opposed to any change in our Naturalization Laws or any State legislation by which the rights of citizenship hitherto accorded to immigrants from foreign lands shall be abridged or impaired; and in favor of giving a full and efficient protection to the rights of all classes of citizens, whether native or naturalized, both at home and abroad.

15. That appropriations by Congress for River and Harbor improvements of a National character, required for the accommodation and security of an existing commerce, are authorized by the Constitution, and justified by the obligations of Government to protect the lives and property of its citizens.

16. That a Railroad to the Pacific Ocean is imperatively demanded by the interest of the whole country; that the Federal government ought to render immediate and efficient aid in its construction; and that, as preliminary thereto, a daily Overland Mail should be promptly established....

More Information

- Benedict, Michael Les. *A Compromise of Principle: Congressional Republicans and Reconstruction, 1863–1869.* New York: Norton, 1974.
- Bennett, Lenore. *Forced Into Glory: Abraham Lincoln's White Dream.* Chicago: University of Chicago Press, 2000.
- Crandall, Andrew W. *The Early History of the Republican Party, 1854–1856.* Gloucester, MA: P. Smith, 1960.
- Donald, David Herbert. *Lincoln.* New York: Simon and Schuster, 1995.
- Gienapp, William E. *The Origins of the Republican Party, 1852–1856.* New York: Oxford University Press, 1987.
- Graff, Henry F. *The Presidents: A Reference History.* New York: Macmillan, 2002.
- Hesseltine, William B. *Ulysses S. Grant: Politician.* New York: Dodd, Mead & Company, 1935.
- Montgomery, David. *Beyond Equality: Labor and the Radical Republicans, 1862–1872.* New York: Knopf, 1967.
- Paludan, Philip Shaw. *The Presidency of Abraham Lincoln.* Lawrence: University of Kansas Press, 1994.
- Polakoff, Keith Ian. *The Politics of Inertia: The Election of 1876 and the End of Reconstruction.* Baton Rouge: Louisiana State University Press, 1979.
- Smith, Jean Edward. *Grant.* New York: Simon and Schuster, 2001.

On the Web

- Formation of the Republican Party (plus links to related topics). U-S-History.com. *http://www.u-s-history.com/pages/h141.html.*
- National Union Party. *http://www.unionparty.rantweb.com/.*
- Origins of the Republican Party. *http://www.ushistory.org/gop/hist/origins.htm.*
- Republican Party Platform, 1864. *http://www.sewanee.edu/faculty/Willis/Civil_War/documents/republican.html*
- Republican Party, Republican History. h*ttp://www.gop.com/About/GOPHistory/Default.aspx.*
- Union Party. *http://college.hmco.com/history/readerscomp/gahff/html/ff_183200_unionparty.htm.*
- United States Republican Party. History World Search.com (hyperlinks to related subjects). *http://history.worldsearch.com/united_states_republican_party/.*

Democratic Party, 1860–76

FlashFocus: Democratic Party, 1860–76

Origins
Democrats split in 1860 over the issue of slavery. Southern Democrats led the withdrawal of states from the Union in 1861 and remained a distinct branch of the party for over a century. Northern Democrats divided between those urging reconciliation with the South (Copperheads) and those supporting the Union. After the Civil War, the Democrats were largely out of power for a decade until they began to benefit from the support of the rapidly growing industrial working class and hard-pressed western farmers.

Issues
Civil War. The South was the key base of Democratic support since Andrew Jackson's era. When the South withdrew from the Union in 1861, Democratic power over the federal government disappeared. In the North, Democrats split over the war. One branch, the Copperheads, urged a negotiated settlement; other Democrats joined with Republicans in supporting the Union. After the Civil War, Democrats in both the North and South were often labeled as traitors.

Civil Liberties. Democrats objected to the suspension of civil liberties in the North during the Civil War. Many Democratic critics of the war were arrested for publishing articles or making speeches against the war; some of them were promptly voted into office as a form of voter protest on the issue of civil rights.

Reconstruction. Postwar Union occupation of the South, called Reconstruction, became the basis of the party's solid support by southern whites. The party opposed most Reconstruction policies, including Republican efforts to transfer political power to freed African Americans.

Leadership. No strong statesmen emerged to lead the Democrats in the 1860s and '70s. The party largely remained bogged down on issues of the Civil War and Reconstruction, and did not develop its strategy of linking to the rapidly emerging working class in the industrial North until the 1880s.

Government reform. Corruption during the Republican administration of President Ulysses Grant gave Democrats a claim on government reform to end abuses of the system of political patronage (government jobs for political supporters). It was this issue that helped the Democrats regain a voice in the national government.

Impact
Democrats exercised relatively little influence over national affairs from 1860 to 1876. No Democrat was elected president throughout the period, and Republicans retained control of the Senate. The Democrats could not claim a majority in the House until the 44th Congress, elected in 1874.

See also: Democratic Party, 1828–1860, p. 17; Democratic Party, 1876–1900, p. 80. Republican Party, 1854–76, p. 55.

The election of 1860 (see Vol. 1, p. 68) was a disaster for the Democrats. Unable to agree on the issue of slavery and its expansion into western territories, the party split between southern Democrats who insisted slavery was a matter of property rights, and northern and western Democrats who agreed not to threaten slavery in states where it existed but wanted to control its expansion into the West. The division of the party resulted in a Republican victory, secession by the southern states, and the Civil War, effectively ending Democratic influence over the federal government for the next 16 years.

Stephen Douglas (see Vol. 1, p. 71) came into the 1860 Democratic convention held in Charleston, South Carolina, as the most likely presidential candidate. On the critical issue of whether slavery should be permitted in western territories soon to become states, Douglas believed the decision should be left to residents of the territories. Die-hard southern supporters of slavery viewed slavery as a question of protecting private property—slaves—wherever they might be taken by their owners. The debate was vociferous, and often far from polite, with delegates using terms like "nigger-stealing thiefs" (sic) and "black hearted scoundrels" to describe their opponents within the same party. Supporters of slavery lost their bid for the convention to approve a platform plank in support of slavery in the territories. Instead, the convention voted for a minority plank endorsing Douglas's view of popular sovereignty, whereupon the delegations from Alabama, Mississippi, Texas, and Florida walked out of the convention along with a majority of delegates from Virginia, South Carolina, Georgia, and Arkansas. The actions of the delegates presaged the withdrawal of those states from the Union a few months later.

After 57 ballots, the remaining delegates failed to reach the party's traditional two-thirds consensus for Douglas as the 1860 presidential candidate and decided to adjourn until June 18, planning to reconvene in Baltimore, Maryland. In the meantime, delegates who had left the Charleston meeting planned another meeting in Richmond, Virginia, for June 11. At Baltimore, Douglas won the Democratic nomination, but without the support of southern delegates, who again withdrew from the convention and instead voted to nominate John Breckinridge (see Vol. 1, p. 72) in a separate caucus. The southern Democrats based their platform on three main principles: "1. That the government of a territory organized by an act of Congress is provisional and temporary, and during its existence all citizens of the United States have an equal right to settle with their property in the Territory, without their rights, either of person or property, being destroyed or impaired by Congressional or Territorial legislation; 2. That it is the duty of the federal government, in all its departments, to protect, when necessary, the rights of persons and property in the ter-

FlashFocus: The Copperheads (Peace Democrats)

What: The Copperheads, also known as the Peace Democrats, were a faction of the Democratic Party in the North that favored negotiating a peace with the Confederacy. Copperhead was a derogatory term referring to the snake that strikes without warning. The term was first used in conjunction with the political party by the *New York Tribune* in 1861.

Who: Clement Vallandigham, a congressman from southern Ohio, was the leader of the Copperheads.

When: The Copperheads emerged shortly after war broke out in 1861 and continued as a faction of the Democratic Party until the war's end in 1865.

Impact: Copperheads drew strength mainly from the Midwest (Illinois, Indiana, and Ohio), where many families had southern roots and relatives still living in the region. Midwestern farmers also had been hurt economically by the Civil War as a result of having to ship their crops by rail, which was more expensive than shipping via the Mississippi River that ran through the Confederacy. Some Midwestern farmers were beginning to oppose policies of a Republican Party that they saw as too friendly to industrialists. Copperheads also found support from Irish immigrants in the Northeast, whose jobs were threatened when shipment of manufactured goods to the Confederacy was cut off, and who feared that freed slaves would journey north and take their jobs. Another subgroup of Copperheads simply objected to Lincoln's suspension of certain civil rights during the Civil War.

The Copperheads gained influence in the 1862 congressional races and in state and local contests. They blocked prowar legislation in Indiana, and they briefly controlled the Illinois House of Representatives. A prominent Eastern Copperhead, Horatio Seymour, was elected New York's governor in 1862.

The Copperheads arrived at the Democratic National Convention in 1864 ready to wield their newfound influence. They managed to gain control of the platform and added a plank that denounced the war, calling it a failure and demanding a negotiated settlement with the Confederacy. But then the Democrats nominated former Union General George McClellan for president. He did not want to associate with the Copperheads and disavowed the peace plank, as did northern Democrats who went over to the Union Party. When the war ended in 1865, so did the Copperhead faction.

---

ritories, and wherever else its constitutional authority extends; 3. That when the settlers in a territory, having an adequate population, form a state constitution, the right of sovereignty commences, and being consummated by admission into the Union, they stand on an equal footing with the people of other States, and the State thus organized ought to be admitted into the Federal Union, whether its constitution prohibits or recognizes the institution of slavery."

In early summer 1860, the political party that with a few exceptions had dominated national politics since Thomas Jefferson's election in 1800 (see Vol. 1, p. 12) was left sharply divided in the face of the candidate of a unified Republican Party, Abraham Lincoln (see Vol. 1, p. 69). The fourth presidential candidate in 1860, John Bell of the Constitutional Union Party (see Vol. 1, p. 73), largely competed with Democrats for votes, further enhancing Lincoln's chance for election.

Lincoln's election victory in November was soon followed by the secession of South Carolina, followed by other traditional Democratic strongholds in the South and formation of the Confederate States of America. By April 1861, the country was at war, North against South.

Democrats during the Civil War

During the Civil War (1861–65), while Democrats continued to exercise power in the Confederate states, Northern Democrats were divided. One faction, the Copperheads, advocated a negotiated peace with the South, effectively agreeing to the South's secession. Many other Democrats lined up to back the North's war effort. But despite the support of many Democrats for the war effort, the combination of Democratic control of the South, plus the position of the Copperheads, enabled the Republicans to label Northern Democrats the party of rebellion. While military setbacks for the North in the early years of the Civil War helped the Democrats reduce the Republican majority in the House of Representatives, elections two years later only complicated the picture for Democrats. The Democratic 1864 convention accepted the war platform proposed by the Copperheads, calling for a negotiated settlement of the conflict, but also nominated General George McClellan for president (see Vol. 1, p. 76). McClellan rejected the party's "peace plank" and did not hesitate to say so during the campaign. Many Democrats joined the newly dubbed Union Party—actually, the Republican Party plus prowar Democrats—which nominated a Democrat, Senator Andrew Johnson of Tennessee (see Vol. 1, p. 75), as vice president. The outcome, in which Lincoln won an unprecedented 55 percent of the popular vote, simply reinforced what a disaster the Civil War had been for the Democratic Party.

Often overlooked in the win-loss numbers during the Civil War were political trends that would eventually prove to be the salvation of the Democratic Party. For example, many Irish workers living in New York, New Jersey, and Pennsylvania had been economically hurt when their employers who depended on southern markets were no longer able to sell goods in the Confederate states. Western farmers also suffered an economic downturn during the Civil War and agitated for a quick end to the conflict. These two groups in particular later proved critical to Democratic successes in the last quarter of the century.

Postwar Democrats

After the Civil War ended in 1865, the country entered into a period of rocky reunion called Reconstruction. Northern

William "Boss" Tweed was a favorite target of the political cartoonist Thomas Nast. In this cartoon, Nast presented Tweed in a striped suit resembling a prison uniform, pointing proudly to the corrupt principles that guided his political career in New York.

Republicans insisted on remaking ("reconstructing") southern society, which had been based on slave labor on large plantations. Their program included eliminating slavery and providing help for newly freed African Americans to lead lives as free men. Whites in the South strongly resisted Reconstruction, often resorting to terrorizing freed African Americans to discourage them from taking advantage of their new freedom and civil rights. The occupying U.S. Army tried, with varying success, to protect African Americans and to enforce Reconstruction laws. In this struggle, northern Democrats were torn between wanting to reconstitute their alliance with southern Democrats in order to gain control of the federal government, and not wanting to be too closely associated with the former "rebels." Republicans happily insisted on pinning the rebel label on Democrats in both regions, which helped prevent Democrats from electing a president until 1884.

In their efforts to reconstruct their North-South alliance, Democrats effectively helped the Republicans promote the rebel image by opposing passage and ratification of the Fifteenth Amendment (see Vol. 4, p. 55) that guaranteed the right to vote for all free men including African Americans, and by trying to thwart other Reconstruction policies of President Ulysses Grant (see Vol. 1, p. 79) from 1869 to 1877. These efforts were aimed at Republican programs designed to guarantee

FlashFocus: William ("Boss") Tweed

Born: April 3, 1823, New York City
Died: April 12, 1878, New York City
Political Career: William Tweed was the prototype of corrupt political party "bosses" in the midnineteenth century. As chairman of the New York City Democratic committee, called Tammany Hall, Tweed oversaw a scheme of corruption in which bribes were paid to obtain government contracts or goods and services, which the party then resold at inflated prices. Largely through the political cartoons of Thomas Nast and an exposé by the *New York Times*, Tweed came to symbolize political party leaders (the term "bosses" made them seem more ominous) who controlled parties' choices of candidates, manipulated election results, and influenced government operations.

Tweed was born into modest circumstances, the son of a chairmaker. He began his political career as a volunteer fireman in New York City. Tweed won his first elective office, to the New York City board of aldermen, as a Democrat by persuading a friend to run as an "independent Whig," thereby splitting the Whig vote and giving Tweed the victory.

Tweed held a string of city and state elective offices and was elected to the U.S. House of Representatives for one term, from 1853 to 1855. But it was in his role as chairman of the Democratic Party in New York City that he managed his network of corruption, collecting bribes from businessmen who wanted city government contracts or other favors. Typical of Tweed's schemes was his purchase of a marble quarry in Massachusetts, and his arrangement to sell his marble at inflated prices for an enormous new courthouse. Tweed used his official positions to steer government contracts to other companies he owned, or that were owned by friends and colleagues, while using his position as chairman of the Democratic Party in the nation's largest city to dictate who would be nominated for city office.

Tweed's influence peaked in the 1860s, but not before spreading to include state government as well. In 1871, a slate of reform Democrats led by Samuel Tilden defeated most of Tweed's candidates, and Tweed was arrested for bribery. He served a year in jail and was then arrested again on other similar charges. Tweed fled to Cuba, then to Spain, where he was recognized on the basis of a Nast cartoon and extradited to the United States. He died in prison two years later.

equal rights to newly freed African Americans—a position that found few objectors among the Democrats' white working-class constituency in the North.

Nevertheless, Democratic intransigence in the South gave the radical Republicans the ammunition they needed to delay reentry of Southern Democrats into national political life. Republicans won an overwhelming majority in the House in the elections of 1866, enabling them to impose strict conditions on the return of Southern Democrats to the national legislature.

A division of a different sort, over monetary policy, also prevented the Democrats from gaining power. Western farmers, who had been a mainstay of Jacksonian Democratic support, had been harmed by the war. They resented Republican tariffs that increased the cost of manufactured goods. They also favored "greenbacks," or currency not supported by gold, which made money more plentiful. But the eastern wing of the Democratic Party, led by Samuel Tilden of New York (see Vol. 1, p. 88) among others, supported the gold standard. Thus developed an East-West split in the Democratic party, between "soft money" advocates of the West and "hard money" advocates in the East, which further weakened the party's challenge to the dominant Republicans in the elections of 1868.

By 1872, the Democratic Party felt desperate. Hoping to take advantage of a split in Republican ranks, which saw the emergence of the Liberal Republican Party (see p. 69), the Democrats chose to nominate the Liberal Republican presidential nominee, Horace Greeley, as their own (see Vol. 1, p. 82). Greeley proved to be an inept campaigner, often delivering speeches to northern audiences that could be expected to appeal to southerners and vice versa. The incumbent Republican president, Ulysses Grant, won the popular vote by a wide margin (55.6% to 43.8%). In some respects, 1872 was a nadir for the Democratic Party.

Democratic Platform 1864

The Democratic Party platform adopted in 1864 underscored the underlying weakness of the party from the period 1860 to 1876. The most notable plank in the platform was a call for a negotiated peace with the Confederate States of America. To many Northerners, the platform seemed disloyal to the Union cause; to Southerners, who might have embraced the platform, it made no difference, since they were not voting in the Union election. Although the party's presidential candidate rejected the platform, it made little difference; he lost to incumbent Abraham Lincoln by an overwhelming margin of 55 percent to 45 percent.

Resolved, That in the future, as in the past, we will adhere with unswerving fidelity to the Union under the Constitution as the only solid foundation of our strength, security, and happiness as a people, and as a framework of government equally conducive to the welfare and prosperity of all the states, both Northern and Southern.

Resolved, That this convention does explicitly declare, as the sense of the American people, that after four years of failure to restore the Union by the experiment of war, during which, under the pretense of a military necessity of war-power higher than the Constitution, the Constitution itself has been disregarded in every part, and public liberty and private right alike trodden down, and the material prosperity of the country essentially impaired, justice, humanity, liberty, and the public welfare demand that immediate efforts be made for a cessation of hostilities, with a view of an ultimate convention of the States, or other peaceable means, to the end that, at the earliest practicable moment, peace may be restored on the basis of the Federal Union of the States.

Resolved, That the direct interference of the military authorities of the United States in the recent elections held in Kentucky, Maryland, Missouri, and Delaware was a shameful violation of the Constitution, and a repetition of such acts in the approaching election will be held as revolutionary, and resisted with all the means and power under our control.

Resolved, That the aim and object of the Democratic Party is to preserve the Federal Union and the rights of the States unimpaired, and they hereby declare that they consider that the administrative usurpation of extraordinary and dangerous powers not granted by the Constitution; the subversion of the civil by military law in States not in insurrection; the arbitrary military arrest, imprisonment, trial, and sentence of American citizens in States where civil law exists in full force; the suppression of freedom of speech and of the press; the denial of the right of asylum; the open and avowed disregard of State rights; the employment of unusual test-oaths; and the interference with and denial of the right of the people to bear arms in their defense is calculated to prevent a restoration of the Union and the perpetuation of a Government deriving its just powers from the consent of the governed.

Resolved, That the shameful disregard of the Administration to its duty in respect to our fellow-citizens who now are and long have been prisoners of war and in a suffering condition, deserves the severest reprobation on the score alike of public policy and common humanity.

Resolved, That the sympathy of the Democratic Party is heartily and earnestly extended to the soldiery of our army and sailors of our navy, who are and have been in the field and on the sea under the flag of our country, and, in the events of its attaining power, they will receive all the care, protection, and regard that the brave soldiers and sailors of the republic have so nobly earned.

More Information

- Abrahamson, James L. *The Men of Secession and Civil War, 1859–1861*. Wilmington, DE: SR Books, 2000.
- Brock, William R. *An American Crisis: Congress and Reconstruction, 1865–1867*. New York: St. Martin's Press, 1963.
- Cox, James H. *Politics, Principle, and Prejudice, 1865–1866*. New York: Atheneum, 1963.
- Johnson, Donald Bruce (ed.). *National Party Platforms: Volume 1, 1840–1856*. Champaign-Urbana: University of Illinois Press, 1978.
- Mitchell, Stewart. *Horatio Seymour of New York*. Cambridge: Harvard University Press, 1938.
- Morin, Isobel. *Politics, American Style: Political Parties in American History*. Brookfield, CT: Millbrook Press, 1999.
- *Political Parties in America*. Washington, D.C.: Congressional Quarterly Press, 2001.
- Porterfield, Jason. *Problems and Progress in American Politics: The Growth of the Democratic Party in the Late 1800s*. New York: Rosen Pub. Group, 2004.
- Ridgway, James M. *Little Mac: Demise of an American Hero*. Princeton, NJ: Princeton University Press, 2000.
- Trefousse, Hans L. *Andrew Johnson: A Biography*. New York: Norton, 1989.

On the Web

- CNN-Time Magazine, Democratic Convention History, A Historical Overview from 1831–1992. *http://www.cnn.com/ALLPOLITICS/1996/conventions/chicago/facts/convention/index.shtml.*
- Democratic Party Platforms, 1860–1900. American Presidency Project, University of California at Santa Barbara. *http://www.presidency.ucsb.edu/site/docs/platforms.php.*
- Jensen, Richard. American Political History On-Line (collection of links to primary documents and related historical materials). *http://tigger.uic.edu/~rjensen/pol-gl.htm.*

Prohibition Party, 1869–

FlashFocus: Prohibition Party

Origins
The Prohibition Party emerged from a web of influences including industrialization, immigration, and populism to become the longest-lived third party in the United States. It ran presidential candidates in every election from 1872 to 2000. The party's platform consistently went beyond its signature issue, banning alcoholic beverages, to include a broad range of subjects designed to appeal to the middle and working classes.

Issues
Prohibition of alcohol. Whatever issues came and went from the party platform, banning alcoholic beverages has always been foremost. The party blames alcohol for a broad range of social problems afflicting people who drink and their families.
Women's rights. Long before mainstream parties supported the right of women to vote and to be paid wages equal to men, the Prohibition Party endorsed both concepts.
Easy currency. In 1892, the year the party turned in its strongest performance in a presidential election, the party endorsed basing currency on both gold and silver, and producing enough currency to meet full employment of labor, positions designed to compete with populist parties of that era.
Tax reduction. The party's 2004 platform, published in 2003, endorsed a balanced budget amendment, a limit on the taxing powers of Congress, and sale of government-owned businesses.
Abortion. The 2004 party platform endorsed an antiabortion Constitutional amendment.

Impact
The strongest showing of the Prohibition Party was in 1892, when presidential candidate John Bidwell polled 270,770 votes (2.2 percent). But no Prohibitionist ever carried a state or collected a single electoral vote. While some might credit the party with passage of the Eighteenth Amendment, which banned alcohol sales, the Women's Christian Temperance Union (WCTU) and the Anti-Saloon League, working with the mainstream political parties, were much more influential in adoption of Prohibition. Rather than acting the role of a broad-based mainstream party, tacking on a broad range of objectives to their namesake goal of prohibiting alcohol, the Prohibitionists found it difficult to influence mainstream politicians. It would be hard to identify even a single case in which the Prohibition Party influenced a state legislature.

See also: 1892, Vol. 1, p. 102.

The Prohibition Party likes to claim the title of longest-lived "third party" in the United States, having run a presidential candidate in every election from 1872 to 2000. But longevity does not necessarily connote success. Unlike minor parties formed to pursue one specific goal (abolition of slavery, for example), the Prohibition Party has consistently tried to broaden its appeal by adopting complex platforms endorsing a multitude of planks while still centering on the party's main goal—eliminating the manufacture and sale of alcoholic beverages. The party has never collected a single electoral vote for its presidential nominee, nor can it claim to have affected the outcome of any presidential or congressional election.

Opposition to alcoholic beverages predates formation of the Prohibition Party by many decades. As early as 1785, Benjamin Rush, a signer of the Declaration of Independence, wrote an essay on the deleterious effects of alcohol on "the human mind and body." By 1829, temperance societies claimed over 100,000 members in the United States, and by 1856, eleven states had passed temperance laws following the lead of Maine in 1851. (The other states were Connecticut, Delaware, Indiana, Iowa, Michigan, Minnesota, Nebraska, New Hampshire, New York, Rhode Island, and Vermont.). For much of the nineteenth century, temperance, alongside abolition of slavery, was an entré into politics for women who were not allowed to vote. From 1870, temperance and women's suffrage were the dual pillars of the Women's Christian Temperance Union (WCTU, see Vol. 4, p. 166) which gained substantial influence over traditional politicians.

The Prohibition Party was formally organized at a convention held in Chicago in September 1869. Originally named the Temperance Party, the name was changed to Prohibition Party in 1873. About 500 delegates, most of them women, attended the original convention, pledging to run a candidate in every presidential election starting in 1872.

The party's first presidential nominee, James Black, received only 5,608 votes out of nearly 6.5 million cast. The party took its biggest leap in 1884, when it polled 147,482 votes (1.5 percent of the total). It reached its all-time height in 1892, when its presidential candidate, John Bidwell (see p. 67), polled 270,770 votes, or 2.2 percent of the total. The party's next highest total came in 1904, when it received 258,539 votes (1.9 percent).

Passage of the Eighteenth Amendment, Prohibition, was followed by a sharp drop-off in Prohibition Party support; its votes fell from 188,391 (when the amendment had passed but not been implemented) to 54,833 in 1924. For the last two-thirds of the twentieth century, the party's support steadily fell until it polled fewer than 2,000 votes in both 1992 and 1996. In 2000, the Prohibition candidate received just 208 votes, all from one state, Colorado.

The party had slightly better luck in some state elections. Prohibition candidate Sidney Catts was elected governor of Florida in 1916; U.S. representatives elected on the party's ticket include Kittel Halvorson of Minnesota in 1890 and Charles

Randall of California in 1914 and 1916. No Prohibitionist candidate was ever elected to the Senate.

A Lesson for Third Parties

Launching a political party to achieve a specific goal, such as banning alcohol, is but one way of achieving success. The other principal approach is to campaign outside the structure of political parties to influence politicians from major parties to adopt particular goals. This was the overall approach of both the Women's Christian Temperance Union (WCTU) and the Anti-Saloon League, and is the reason these two organizations are largely credited with passage of the Eighteenth Amendment.

The WCTU and Anti-Saloon League also adopted a slightly different approach: they relied on inducing guilt for the harm done to families by excessive drinking on the part of the male wage-earner, rather than promoting prohibition as a positive goal in and of itself. There was a subtle difference between protecting families by controlling, or shutting down, excessive drinking by banning the sale of alcohol, and persuading politicians to adopt a moral position that all drinking was evil all the time. In any case, even on the eve of adopting the Eighteenth Amendment, the Prohibition Party received only 188,391 votes in 1920, compared to over 16 million for the victorious Republican, Warren Harding (see Vol. 1, p. 128).

The structure of American electoral politics has never favored special-interest parties. By awarding all the electoral votes of a state to the winner, the system makes it almost impossible for minority parties such as Prohibition to achieve even one electoral vote. Voters, recognizing this problem, are often loath to cast a vote that is unlikely to affect the outcome of a state's election, i.e., for a party besides one of the two largest parties. This pattern has occasionally been broken—the Progressive ("Bull Moose") Party (see p. 121), comprised of breakaway Republicans following Theodore Roosevelt (see Vol. 1, p. 114) carried a few states in 1912, for example—but the exceptions have tended to prove the rule.

For its first half century, the Prohibition Party also suffered another inherent disadvantage: the bulk of its supporters could not vote at all because they were women.

Platform of the Prohibition Party 1892

The Prohibition Party, in national Convention assembled, acknowledging Almighty God as the source of all true government, and His law as the standard to which human enactments must conform to secure the blessings of peace and prosperity, presents the following declaration of principles:

> *The liquor traffic is a foe to civilization, the arch enemy of popular government, and a public nuisance. It is the citadel of the forces that corrupt politics, promote poverty and crime, degrade the nation's home life, thwart the will of the people, and deliver our country into the hands of rapacious class interests. All laws that under the guise of regulation legalize and protect this traffic or make the government share its ill-gotten gains, are 'vicious in*

FlashFocus: John Bidwell

Born: August 5, 1819, Chautauqua County, New York
Died: April 4, 1900, Rancho Chico, California
Political Career: California State Senate, 1849; vice president, Democratic state convention; representative, U.S. House of Representatives, 1864.

As Bidwell was growing up, his family spent time in California, Pennsylvania, and Ohio. In 1836 he entered Kingsville Academy, and when he graduated in 1838, he returned to Ohio to teach. He wanted to go out West, and in 1841 he moved to Missouri, where he continued to teach until 1841, when he traveled to California as part of a wagon train.

In California, Bidwell worked at Fort Sutter with John Sutter himself. He was naturalized and received a land grant in 1844. When California declared its independence from Mexico in 1846, Bidwell was a member of the committee that wrote the declaration. He served in the California army for some years and was one of the first discoverers of gold. In 1849, Bidwell bought the 22,000-acre Rancho Chico and remained devoted to agriculture for the rest of his life.

Bidwell traveled to the Democratic National Convention in 1860 as a supporter of Stephen Douglas. When the Civil War broke out in 1861, Bidwell joined the Union Party. He was made brigadier-general of the militia in 1863 due in part to his strong unionist ideals. Toward the end of the war, however, Bidwell moved to the Republican Party. He attended the Republican National Convention in 1864 and was elected to Congress from California.

Bidwell ran several times for governor of California, without success. In 1867, he ran as a Republican. In the following years he became increasingly interested in third parties. In 1875, he ran for governor as an Anti-Monopolist, and in 1890 he ran as a Prohibitionist. He remained affiliated with the Prohibition Party and was the Prohibition candidate for president in 1892. He received 264,133 votes, the most votes won by any Prohibition presidential candidate.

After the election, Bidwell retired from politics and concentrated on his ranch. He died there in 1900.

> *principle and powerless as a remedy.' We declare anew for the entire suppression of the manufacture, sale, importation, exportation and transportation of alcoholic liquors as a beverage by federal and state legislation, and the full powers of government should be exerted to secure this result....*
>
> *No citizen should be denied the right to vote on account of sex, and equal labor should receive equal wages, without regard to sex.*
>
> *The money of the country should consist of gold, silver, and paper, and be issued by the general government only, and in sufficient quantity to meet the demands of business and give full opportunity for the employment of labor. To this end an increase in the volume of money is demanded....*

The lobby of liquor companies and saloons is depicted in this political cartoon as an octopus trying to strangle the world with tentacles depicting the negative effects of alcoholic beverages, such as debauchery, poverty, crime, and disease.

Tariff should be levied only as a defense against foreign governments which levy tariff on or bar out our products from their markets....

Railroad, telegraph, and other public corporations should be controlled by the government in the interest of the people....

Foreign immigration has become a burden upon industry...; therefore our immigration laws should be revised and strictly enforced....

Non-resident aliens should not be allowed to acquire land in this country....

All men should be protected by law in their right to one day's rest in seven....

We stand unequivocally for the American Public School, and opposed to any appropriation of any public moneys for sectarian schools....

Recognizing and declaring that prohibition of the liquor traffic has become the dominant issue in national politics, we invite to full party fellowship all those who on this one dominant issue are with us agreed, in the full belief that this party can and will remove sectional differences, promote national unity, and insure the best welfare of our entire land....

More information

▶ Blocker, Jack S., Jr. *American Temperance Movements: Cycles of Reform.* Boston: Twayne Publishers, 1989.
▶ Hamm, Richard F. *Shaping the Eighteenth Amendment: Temperance Reform, Legal Culture, and the Polity, 1880–1920.* Chapel Hill: University of North Carolina Press, 1995.
▶ Johnson, Donald Bruce (ed.). *National Party Platforms.* Urbana: University of Illinois Press, 1978.

On the Web

▶ The Prohibition Party's Web site. *http://www.prohibitionists.org*
▶ Bidwell's Letter Formally Accepting His Nomination. California Prohibitionist, August 25, 1892. Library of Congress. *http://memory.loc.gov/cgi-bin/query/r?ammem/calbk:@field(DOCID+@lit(calbk046div31))*.

Liberal Republican Party, 1872

FlashFocus: Liberal Republican Party

Origins
The Liberal Republican Party was an offshoot of the regular Republican Party for a single election, in 1872. The party was a collection of a variety of politicians, many of whom believed they were being loyal to the principles laid down by the founders of the party two decades earlier. Formation of the Liberal Republicans was the work of an alliance of four newspaper publishers, joined by former members of Abraham Lincoln's cabinet. The party was viewed by some Democrats as a vehicle through which they could possibly regain the White House, and the Liberal Republicans and Democrats nominated the same person, Horace Greeley, for president in 1872.

Issues
Reconstruction. The Liberal Republicans advocated easing the stringent Reconstruction programs of the post-Civil War administration of President Ulysses Grant and urged an amnesty for officials of the defeated Confederate government.

Civil service reform. The Grant administration had been marked by corruption of government officials, and the Liberal Republicans campaigned on a program of reform, even though their presidential candidate, Horace Greeley, was not strongly in favor of such changes.

End to government aid to companies. Liberal Republicans disagreed with the active probusiness stance of the regular Republican Party which included, for example, extensive land grants to railroads in exchange for expanding in the West. They advocated instead a smaller federal government less involved with helping business expand economically.

Impact
The Liberal Republicans had a dismal showing in the presidential election, garnering only 43.8 percent of the vote to 55.6 percent for President Grant. Their candidate, Greeley, ran an unorganized campaign in which he delivered speeches meant to appeal to northerners in the South, and vice versa. The party did slightly better in Congressional elections, sending five of its candidates to the U.S. Senate and 14 to the House of Representatives. After losing the popular vote, Greeley collapsed and died before the electoral college vote was tabulated. After 1872, many Liberal Republicans returned to the mainstream Republican Party.

See also: Eelection of 1872, Vol. 1, p. 82; Republican Party, 1854–76, p. 55; Democratic Party, 1860–76, p. 61.

The Liberal Republicans came and went in a single year, 1872, and posed no serious challenge either to the regular Republicans or to the Democrats. However, this absence of electoral success may understate the longer-term impact of the Liberal Republicans. The administration of President Ulysses Grant (see Vol. 1, p. 79), who was reelected in 1872, introduced significant changes in response to Liberal Republican accusations. These reforms undercut the campaign of the Liberal Republicans, but effectively introduced some of the party's positions as government policy.

The driving force behind formation of the Liberal Republican Party in 1872 was opposition to President Ulysses Grant, the Civil War general who had been elected president in 1868 (see Vol. 1, p. 78). Grant had followed the program of radical Reconstruction advocated by some Republicans in the North, a program opposed by both Democrats (many of whose supporters lived in the former Confederacy) and some Republicans. In Congressional elections of 1870, Republicans lost seats to Democrats in the House of Representatives and the Senate. In Missouri, particularly, the election of Republican dissidents B. Gratz Brown as governor and Carl Schurz as Senator gave hope to other Republicans who disagreed with Grant's policies.

A group of former abolitionists and founders of the Republican Party gathered in April 1872 in New York City under the leadership of four newspaper editors: Samuel Bowles of the *Springfield* (Massachusetts) *Republican,* Mural Halstead of the *Cincinnati Commercial,* Horace White of the *Chicago Tribune,* and Colonel Henry Watterson of the *Louisville* (Kentucky) *Courier-Journal.* Other prominent Republican newspaper publishers, such as Whitelaw Reid of the *New York Tribune,* also supported the Republican dissidents.

The next month, May 1872, the newly organized Liberal Republicans nominated yet another newspaperman, Horace Greeley (see Vol. 1, p. 83) of the *New York Tribune* for president after six ballots. Other contenders included Charles Francis Adams, son of John Quincy Adams (see Vol. 1, p. 33) and grandson of John Adams (see Vol. 1, p. 10), Brown of Missouri, Senator Lyman Trumbull of Illinois, and Supreme Court Justice David Davis (see Vol. 3, p. 39).

The choice of Greeley was both controversial and tactical. Because Greeley had an uneven and controversial record of supporting the North during the Civil War (he had, for example, recently offered bail to imprisoned Confederate President Jefferson Davis), the Liberal Republicans hoped he would appeal to Democrats. But the same record that seemed appealing to Democrats also repelled some Republicans who might otherwise have been attracted to a reform movement in their own party.

On other issues, as well, the Liberal Republicans did not present a united front. Some Liberal Republicans advocated civil service reform—the movement to fill government jobs on the basis of competence rather than as political favors—but others were lukewarm on the subject. Most Liberal Republicans rejected protective tariffs—taxes on imports designed to protect

A cartoonist's depiction of Horace Greeley, the Liberal Republican candidate for president.

domestic manufacturers from foreign competition—but the party did not present a strong position on this topic either.

The largest unifying force for the Liberal Republicans was their dislike of Grant. In this, they were joined by the Democrats who had been out of office for 12 years. At the Democratic convention in Baltimore on July 9 and 10, Greeley became the Democratic nominee as well in the hope that the combination of Democrats and dissident Republicans could carry the day in the election. The strategy was largely theoretical, however, and in the end many Democrats ended up not voting for either candidate.

Because the Liberal Republicans had no prior history (and no history after the election), much of the party's reputation lay on Greeley's positions, which were in some ways contradictory. He condemned slavery, but declined to condemn the southern culture built around the "peculiar institution." The Liberal Republicans advocated widespread amnesty for southerners after the Civil War, which conflicted with feelings by many northerners that southern politicians active in the Confederacy should not hold office.

Weak Campaign

Greeley's campaign, rather than minimizing some of the party's contradictory positions, seemed intent on emphasizing them. In the North, Greeley gave speeches advocating universal amnesty for officers of the Confederate government and the withdrawal of the Union Army from the South—positions that appealed to southerners but not to northerners. While in the South, Greeley tended to advocate equal rights for African Americans, a position that did not generate enthusiasm among white Democrats.

Because the party had been hastily formed just months before the campaign, the Liberal Republicans lacked an extensive network of local supporters. By contrast, the Republicans and Democrats could rely on help from many government officials at both the state and federal levels who owed their jobs to party-directed appointments. The principle motivating factor for the Liberal Republicans—corruption in the Grant administration—failed to ignite support for Greeley's candidacy.

Moreover, as 1872 wore on, President Grant took moves that effectively canceled the Liberal Republicans' positions. Grant arranged for protective tariffs (which raised prices on products for consumers, even as wealthy business owners benefited) to be lowered, for the national debt to be reduced, and for the Civil War-era federal income tax to be repealed. Grant oversaw enactment of civil service reforms, and many Confederate officials were offered amnesty.

The U.S. economy was generally strong in the early 1870s, which led to an atmosphere of contentment—and support for the status quo.

The combined forces of the Liberal Republicans and Democrats collected 2.8 million votes, or 43.8 percent of the total, compared to 3.6 million (55.6 percent) for Grant and the regular Republicans. The death of Greeley shortly after the election but before the electoral college vote further complicated the situation. His electoral votes were divided between Thomas Hendricks of Indiana (who had run for president as an independent Democrat) and Brown of Missouri (the official Liberal Republican vice presidential nominee). The presidential electors from Georgia cast three votes for the deceased Greeley, but the House of Representatives voted to disregard them.

The failure of the Liberal Republicans to make a serious dent in the success of the regular Republicans marked the party's end after a single election. However, the outcome of the election did result in changes in the Republicans. Noting that Grant received a bare majority (50.1 percent) of votes in the South, the Republicans soon eased their policy of Reconstruction and adopted policies more conciliatory with whites in the region.

Liberal Republican Platform, 1872

The Administration now in power has rendered itself guilty of wanton disregard of the laws of the land and of powers not granted by the Constitution. It has acted as if the laws had binding force only for those who are governed, and not for those who govern. It has thus struck a blow at the fundamental principles of constitutional government, and the liberties of the citizen. The President of the United States has openly used the powers and opportunities of his high office for the promotion of personal ends. He has kept notoriously corrupt and unworthy men in places of power and responsibility to the detriment of the public interest. He has used the public service of the Government as a machinery of partisan and personal influence, and interfered with tyrannical arrogance in the political affairs of States and municipalities. He has rewarded with influential and lucrative offices men who had acquired his favor, by valuable presents, thus stimulating demoralization of our political life by his conspicuous example. He has shown himself deplorably unequal to the tasks imposed upon him by the necessities of the country, and culpably careless of the responsibilities of his high office....

We, the Liberal Republicans of the United States in National Convention assembled at Cincinnati, proclaim the following principles as essential to just government.

First: We recognize the equality of all men before the law, and hold that it is the duty of Government in its dealings with the people to mete out equal and exact justice to all of whatever nativity, race, color, or persuasion, religious or political.

Second: We pledge ourselves to maintain the union of these States, emancipation, and enfranchisement, and to oppose any re-opening of the questions settled by the Thirteenth, Fourteenth, and Fifteenth Amendments to the Constitution.

Third: We demand the immediate and absolute removal of all disabilities imposed on account of the Rebellion, which was finally subdued seven years ago, believing that universal amnesty will result in complete pacification in all sections of the country.

Fourth: Local self-government, with impartial suffrage, will guard the rights of all citizens more securely than any centralized power. The public welfare requires the supremacy of the civil over the military authority, and freedom of person under the protection of the habeas corpus. We demand for the individual the largest liberty consistent with public order: for the State, self-government, and for the nation a return to the methods of peace and constitutional limitations of power.

Fifth: The Civil Service of the Government has become a mere instrument of partisan tyranny and personal ambition and an object of selfish greed. It is a scandal and reproach upon free institutions and breeds a demoralization dangerous to the perpetuity of republican government. We therefore regard such thorough reforms of the Civil Service as one of the most pressing necessities of the hour; that honesty, capacity, and fidelity constitute the valid claim to public employment; that the offices of the Government cease be a matter of arbitrary favoritism and patronage, and that public station become again a post of honor. To this end it is imperatively required the President shall be a candidate for re-election.

Sixth: We demand a system of Federal taxation which shall not unnecessarily interfere with the industry of the people, and which shall provide the means necessary to pay the expenses of the Government economically administered, the pensions, the interest on the public debt, and a moderate reduction annually of the principal thereof; and, recognizing that there are in our midst honest but irreconcilable differences of opinion with regard to respective systems of Protection and Free Trade, we remit the discussion of the subject to the people in their Congress Districts, and to the decision of Congress thereon, wholly free of Executive interference or dictation.

Seventh: The public credit must be sacredly maintained, and we denounce repudiation in every form and guise.

Eighth: A speedy return to specie payment is demanded alike by the highest considerations of commercial morality and honest government.

Ninth: We remember with gratitude the heroism and sacrifices of the soldiers and sailors of the Republic, and no act of ours shall ever detract from their justly-earned fame or the full reward of their patriotism.

Tenth: We are opposed to all further grants of lands to railroads or other corporations. The public domain should be held sacred to actual settlers.

Eleventh: We hold that it is the duty of the Government, in its intercourse with foreign nations to cultivate the friendship of peace, by treating with all on fair and equal terms, regarding it alike dishonorable either to demand what is not right, or to submit to what is wrong.

Twelfth: For the promotion and success of these vital principles and the support of the candidates nominated by this Convention, we invite and cordially welcome the co-operation of all patriotic citizens, without regard to previous affiliations.

More Information

- Haynes, Fred E. *Third Party Movements Since the Civil War, with Special Reference to Iowa: A Study in Social Politics.* New York: Russell & Russell, 1966.
- Nash, Howard P., Jr. *Third Parties in American Politics.* Washington, D.C.: Public Affairs Press, 1959.
- Simpson, Brooks D. *The Reconstruction Presidents.* Lawrence: University Press of Kansas, 1998.

On the Web

- Liberal Republicans. http://www.u-s-history.com/pages/h216.html.
- "Republican Party." Encyclopedia Americana. http://ap.grolier.com/article?assetid=0331130-00&templatename=/article/article.html.

Equal Rights Party, 1872–88

FlashFocus: Equal Rights Party

Origins

The Equal Rights Party was largely the vehicle for one woman, Victoria Woodhull, who sought an equal role for women in public life about a century before the women's movement took root in the twentieth century. Woodhull's party had no significant impact on government in its day and was not even successful in attracting widespread support among those advocating women's right to vote. Nevertheless, the Equal Rights Party platform was remarkably foresighted in the demands it made.

Issues

Women's right to vote. The women's suffrage movement was already well established by the time Woodhull formed her party and ran for president in 1872. Her approach—a new political party to press for women's equal rights—attracted only limited support among suffragists, most of whom preferred to try to work within the established Republican and Democratic parties.

Equal rights for women. The right to vote was just one of several rights issues pursued by the Equal Rights Party. Woodhull's candidacy represented a much broader challenge to male domination of social institutions and was a precursor of the women's movement of the late twentieth century.

Improved civil rights. Symbolic of Woodhull's advocacy of civil rights was her nomination of black leader Frederick Douglass as vice president on her party's ticket, an offer he declined. Woodhull's party went beyond abolition of slavery and pushed for equal civil rights for African Americans throughout society.

Impact

Woodhull was in jail when the election of 1872 took place, accused of libel for charges published in her newspaper accusing a prominent New York City clergyman of having an affair with a married woman (she was eventually found not guilty). The fact that Woodhull had not reached age 35, the minimum age for a president, kept her off the ballot in most areas. Even ardent suffragettes such as Susan Anthony declined to go along with Woodhull's platform, which they found too extreme for their tastes. Woodhull soon gave up on running for political office as a vehicle to change society. Her party supported the Greenback and Greenback-Labor Parties in 1876 and 1880. In 1884, Belva Ann Lockwood ran as the party's candidate for president. She attracted even fewer votes than Woodhull. Nevertheless, Lockwood ran a second time in 1888, although there are no official records of her receiving any votes. Shortly afterwards the party dissolved.

See also: Equal Rights Party, Vol. 4, p. 163

Victoria Woodhull was a remarkable pioneer in the long campaign to achieve equal rights for women. Of the many better remembered women's leaders in the nineteenth century, including such characters as Susan B. Anthony (see Vol. 4, p. 159) and Elizabeth Cady Stanton (see Vol. 4, p. 156), Woodhull stood out for the modernity of her approach. Many positions she advocated in the late nineteenth century would became issues again a century later.

In many respects, the Equal Rights Party was established as an extension of Woodhull's larger campaign for an equal role for women. With her sister, she had already established a successful Wall Street stock brokerage, the first invasion by women of what had been a man's exclusive preserve, and founding the Equal Rights Party was in many ways an extension of her campaign into another all-male area of American life.

Woodhull's political opponents, who included many women as well as men, often focused on her unconventional lifestyle and personal history in an effort to attack her larger political and social philosophy. Having been married as a teenager to a man who turned out to be an abusive husband, Woodhull was a divorcée who lived an unconventional life in New York City.

Despite her personal habits—or perhaps because of them—Woodhull attracted widespread publicity. In January 1871, she appeared before Congress to testify in favor of women's right to vote, arguing that the Fourteenth and Fifteenth Amendments (see Vol. 4, pp. 51 and 55) had already enfranchised women—a view shared by other feminists, but not upheld by the U.S. Supreme Court.

A year after her Washington appearance, Woodhull organized the first convention of the Equal Rights Party in New York City as part of a planned joint meeting with the National Woman Suffrage Association (NWSA; see Vol. 4, p. 158) and the International Workingmen's Association. Woodhull was nominated for president on a platform that covered both equal rights for women and new rights for workers in an era of rapidly expanding corporate enterprises.

Woodhull's effort to expand the campaign for women's rights by founding a new party was not universally supported. Susan B. Anthony, for example, rejected Woodhull's approach in favor of trying to persuade established political parties to support the feminist platform. Anthony's colleague, Elizabeth Cady Stanton, disagreed with her on this and supported Woodhull. Feminists affiliated with the more conservative American Woman Suffrage Association (AWSA; see Vol. 4, p. 161) actively opposed Woodhull's candidacy. They denounced her for being too adventuresome and too liberal. Horace Greeley (see Vol. 1, p. 83), also a candidate for president in 1872, used his *New York Tribune* to attack Woodhull's stance on sexual liberation as dangerous. Shortly after the new party's convention, one of Woodhull's allies, the International Workingmen's Association, also turned against her.

A week before the 1872 election, Woodhull used her own newspaper to expose a sexual affair between a prominent New York City clergyman, Henry Ward Beecher (who was president of the AWSA), and a married woman. She was arrested under an antiobscenity law but found not guilty eight months later.

Woodhull's 1872 campaign was a nonstarter from the beginning since she was below the constitutional age for president (35).

Twelve passed before the Equal Rights Party ran another candidate of its own, Belva Ann Lockwood, who was one of the few female trial attorneys practicing in the United States. Lockwood, a leader of the NWSA, ran with another feminist, Marietta L. B. Stow, on a platform that called for female suffrage, "equal and exact justice to every class of our citizens, without distinction of color, sex, or nationality," a policy on controlling alcoholic beverages, and changes in local laws governing marriage and divorce. As in 1872, many feminist leaders, including Anthony, rejected the Equal Rights Party and backed the Republican nominee, James Blaine (see Vol. 1, p. 96).

As was the case with her predecessor Woodhull, Lockwood's campaign was condemned by many men and women as inappropriate for a woman. The ticket registered just over 4,000 votes; reportedly, in some cases, ballots with their names checked off were simply thrown out as false votes.

Lockwood ran again in 1888 with even less enthusiasm and gathered even fewer votes. Indeed, there is no established record that she received any votes in the last campaign, after which the Equal Rights Party dissolved as women's rights became planks in the platforms of other parties.

Platform of the Eqal Rights Party, 1872

The May 25, 1872, edition of *Woodhull and Claflin's Weekly*, published by Victoria Woodhull and her sister, contained what was titled the "Official Report of the Equal Rights Convention" which was held in New York City from May 9 to 11, 1872, including the party's platform. Extracts:

> We, women citizens of the United States, in national convention assembled at New York, proclaim the following principles as essential to just government:
>
> 1. We recognize the equality of all before the law, and hold that it is the duty of government in its dealings with the people to mete out equal and exact justice to all, of whatever nativity, race, color, sex or persuasion, religious or political.
>
> 2. We pledge ourselves to maintain the union of the States, and to oppose any reopening of the questions settled by the Thirteenth, Fourteenth and Fifteenth amendments of the Constitution, which have emancipated and enfranchised the slaves and the women of the nation.
>
> 3. We demand the immediate and absolute removal of all disabilities now imposed on rebels and women, believing that universal suffrage and universal amnesty will result in complete purification in the family, and in all sections of the country.
>
> 4. We demand for the individual the largest liberty consistent with the public order, for the state self-government and for the national administration the methods of peace, and the constitutional limitations of power.
>
> 5. We demand a thorough civil service reform as one of the pressing necessities of the hour.... The first step in this reform is the one term principle, and the election of President, Vice President and United States Senators by the whole people.
>
> 6. We affirm that no form of taxation is just or wise which puts burdens upon the people by means of duties intended to increase the price of domestic products and which are unnecessary for purposes of revenue....
>
> 7. The highest consideration of commercial morality and honest government requires a thorough reform of the present financial system. The interests of the people demand a cheap, sound, uniform, abundant, and elastic currency....
>
> 8. We remember with gratitude the heroism and sacrifices of the wives, sisters and mothers throughout this republic in the late war; the grand sanitary work they did in the hospital, on the battlefield, and in gathering in the harvest at home, have justly earned for the women of the country the generous recognition of all their political rights by every true American statesman.
>
> 9. We are opposed to all grants of lands to railroads or other corporations. The public domain should be held sacred to actual settlers, an inviolable homestead secured to every man and woman.
>
> 10. We believe in the principles of the referendum, minority representation, and a just system of graduation taxation.
>
> 11. It is the duty of government to regard children and criminals as wards of the State; to secure to the one the best advantages of education, and for the other more humane legislation and better methods of reform.
>
> 12. We hold it is the duty of the government in its intercourse with foreign countries to cultivate the friendships of peace, by treating with all on just and equal terms, and by insisting on the settlement of all differences by a congress of nations.
>
> 13. For the promotion of these vital principles and the establishment of a party based on them, we invite the cooperation of all "citizens," without distinction of race, color, sex, nationality or previous political affiliations.

More Information

▶ Boynick, David K. *Women Who Led the Way; Eight Pioneers for Equal Rights.* New York: Crowell, 1972 (© 1959).

▶ Gabriel, Mary. *Notorious Victoria: The Life of Victoria Woodhull, Uncensored.* Chapel Hill, NC: Algonquin Books of Chapel Hill, 1998.

▶ Goldsmith, Barbara. *Other Powers: The Age of Suffrage, Spiritualism, and the Scandalous Victoria Woodhull.* New York: Knopf, 1998.

On the Web

▶ Victoria Woodhull. National Women's History Project. http://www.nwhp.org/tlp/biographies/woodhull/woodhull_bio.html.

- Puz, Susan. "The First Woman to Run for President." http://www.class.csupomona.edu/his/skpuz/hst202/Woodhull/WQart.html.

- Victoria Woodhull, the Spirit to Run the White House. http://www.victoria-woodhull.com/.

Republican Party, 1876–1900

FlashFocus: Republican Party, 1876–1900

Origins

The last quarter of the nineteenth century presented the Republicans with an entirely different set of circumstances than those from 1854 to 1876, when the party won national dominance. The nation was ready to put the Civil War and Reconstruction eras behind it and focus on a period of rapid industrial growth, large-scale immigration from southern and eastern Europe, and continuing westward expansion. Industrialization was the hallmark of the era, with massive fortunes built up in industries such as steel and petroleum. The Republicans, as natural heirs of the Whigs, took on the role of political defender of business interests.

Issues

Hard currency. Republicans consistently defended basing currency on government stores of gold bullion, while Democrats and third parties often campaigned for the unlimited coinage of silver. Retaining gold as the sole basis for currency was generally favored by those who already owned substantial wealth.

Business. The Republicans succeeded the Whig Party in adopting aggressive probusiness positions, particularly tariffs designed to protect American companies from foreign competitors even at the expense of raising prices for ordinary workers and farmers. Republicans also resisted calls for regulations to protect the interests of workers.

Foreign expansion. In 1898, the United States went to war with Spain, seizing control of Spanish colonies in Cuba and the Philippines. The war established the United States as a global military power at a time when European powers ruled much of Africa and parts of Asia as colonial masters.

Impact

Republicans captured the White House four times in the period—in 1876, 1880, 1888, and 1896—losing to Democrats only twice (1884 and 1892). The Republicans were less successful in congressional elections, holding onto majorities in both houses in just four Congresses—1889 to 1891 and 1895 to 1901. The party remained largely a party of the North and West, while Democrats completely dominated the South after 1876.

See also: Republican Party, 1854–76, p. 55; Republican Party, 1900–32, p. 105; Republican Party, 1932–68, p. 135; Republican Party, 1968–2004, p. 169; Democratic Party, 1876–1900, p. 80.

After its rise to dominance during the Civil War (1861–65) and Reconstruction, the Republican Party effectively replaced the Whigs (see p. 27) and Federalists (see p. 9) as the party of business interests during the last 24 years of the nineteenth century, a period marked by the rapid expansion of unfettered capitalism.

Republicans after Reconstruction

The election of 1876 (see Vol. 1, p. 86) proved to be a major turning point for the Republicans. The Democratic candidate, Samuel Tilden of New York, (see Vol. 1, p. 88) won 51 percent of the popular vote to 48 percent for Republican Rutherford Hayes of Ohio (see Vol. 1, p. 87). Republicans challenged the outcome of voting in four states—Louisiana, South Carolina, Florida, and Oregon. A special commission comprised of senators, representatives, and Supreme Court justices examined the disputed votes and voted along party lines to award the electoral votes of all four states—and with them, the presidency—to Hayes. In an apparent backroom deal, never officially confirmed, Republicans arranged with some Democrats to let the commission's findings go through Congress in exchange for an agreement to withdraw the Union Army from its remaining occupation duties in the South. The impact was to deliver political control of the South to Democrats for the next 90 years, effectively disenfranchising freed slaves, and to end Reconstruction. Democrats used their southern base to exert strong influence over Congress and again began challenging Republicans for control of the White House.

The Republicans, having abandoned any ideas of competing in the South on the strength of African American support, turned their attention to the rapid growth of industrialization and an accompanying expansion of population in the North, succeeding the Whigs as the party representing business interests. The Democrats in turn sought to expand beyond their southern base by building support among the rapidly growing group of low-paid industrial workers, many of whom were immigrants from eastern and southern Europe, and among small farmers in the West.

Republican Philosophy

Even while the aftermath of the Civil War attracted the attention of politicians from 1865 to 1876, the United States was undergoing a radical social and economic transformation brought about by a combination of new technology (such as the replacement of coal with petroleum and, later, electricity to drive both large machines and smaller engines), completion of transcontinental railroad and telegraph links, and a growing wave of immigration from southern and eastern Europe. The period between 1880 and 1900 is sometimes called the Gilded Age, suggesting a time when enormous fortunes were made by such industrialists as Andrew Carnegie (steel), John D. Rockefeller (petroleum), and J. P. Morgan (finance). In the Republican view, the role of government was to support policies that would help American industry grow—on terms acceptable to corporate owners. This largely meant two principles: protective tariffs to shield American manufacturers from foreign competitors (especially British competitors), and

FlashFocus: Mark Hanna

Born: September 24, 1837, Lisbon, Ohio
Died: February 15, 1904, Washington, D.C.
Political Career: Industrialist Mark Hanna was the first national political "boss" who introduced large sums of corporate money into the presidential election process.

Hanna (born as Marcus Alonzo Hanna) started his career working for his father's wholesale grocery business. After serving in the Civil War, Hanna became a successful shipper and broker of iron ore in Cleveland, a major link between Great Lakes iron ore deposits and Ohio steel mills. Hanna expanded into banking, transportation, and publishing, becoming a millionaire.

Intrigued by the relationship between politics and business, Hanna became active in the Republican Party, working to elect candidates he thought would help business. Hanna became closely associated with Ohio Representative William McKinley. McKinley was elected governor of Ohio in 1892 with Hanna's financial aid and advice, and four years later Hanna managed McKinley's successful 1896 campaign for the Republican presidential nomination.

For his work with McKinley, Hanna was appointed Republican Party chairman, becoming the first national political boss. Democratic newspapers portrayed Hanna as a puppet master who directed McKinley's every decision and policy position. Hanna had planned to let other Republican strategists run the general election campaign, but changed his mind after Democrats nominated William Jennings Bryan of Nebraska for president. Bryan strongly backed unlimited coinage of silver, a policy popular with small farmers and workers, but unpopular with large business interests.

In the campaign, Hanna exploited the fear Bryan generated among the heads of large corporations. Hanna raised $3.5 million for McKinley's campaign, the largest amount so far raised for a political campaign. Hanna hired 1,400 people to distribute campaign leaflets—the equivalent of modern television advertising—which were credited with McKinley's victory in 1896. Hanna had launched the modern era in politics in which campaign contributions from wealthy interests played an increasingly important role.

Hanna, who himself became a senator, came into conflict with another Republican, then Navy Secretary Theodore Roosevelt. When Roosevelt became McKinley's vice presidential running mate in 1900, Hanna told McKinley that his job for the next four years was to stay alive in order to prevent "that damned cowboy" from becoming president. McKinley was assassinated on September 14, 1901. As Roosevelt's opposite within the Republican Party, Hanna was viewed as Roosevelt's leading challenger for the 1904 presidential nomination. Before he could mount a challenge, Hanna died of typhoid fever on February 15, 1904.

The figure of Senator Mark Hanna overwhelms the small figure of President William McKinley in this cartoon, pointing out the influence Hanna wielded over McKinley and the Republican Party.

"hard money," currency backed by deposits of gold owned by the government. It also meant, in the Republican view, resisting calls for government control or regulation of business.

Ranged against the Republicans in the last quarter of the century were Democrats, who formed an alliance among southern politicians, industrial workers in the North and Midwest, small farmers in the West, and a bevy of much smaller third parties built around principles either of socialism or noneconomic issues such as the prohibition of alcohol.

In five presidential elections between 1880 and 1896, Republicans won three (1880, 1888, 1896), and Democrats won two (1884 and 1892). In Congress during the last two decades of the nineteenth century, Republicans controlled both the House and Senate just over half the time—from 1880 to 1883, 1889 to 1891, and from 1895 to 1900 (see Vol. 1, pp. 90-112).

Politics in the era also took on religious overtones, with many Catholic immigrants supporting the Democrats and native Protestants supporting Republicans. The seemingly religious divisions along political lines largely reflected the fact that many Catholics had immigrated recently from southern and eastern Europe and worked at low-paying factory jobs, which made them prime candidates for Democratic recruiters. Resentment or fear that immigrants were changing the social character of the country caused native Protestants to turn to Republicans.

In 1880, Republican James Garfield (see Vol. 1, p. 91) barely won the poplar vote by fewer than 2,000 votes out of nearly 8.9 million cast, but managed to carry the electoral college by 214 to 155 (see Vol. 1, p. 90). Four years later, New York Governor Grover Cleveland (see Vol. 1, p. 95), a Democrat, broke a long

FlashFocus: Silver Republicans

What: A minority faction within the Republican Party active between 1891 and 1900 that supported recognition of silver, alongside gold, as legal tender. The group considered running its own candidate for president but ended up supporting the Democratic candidate.

Who: Senator Henry Teller of Colorado was the most prominent leader of the Silver Republicans, who reflected the interests of western farmers and miners who had invested in silver mines.

Impact: The Silver Republicans managed to elect six senators in 1894 (Henry Teller of Colorado, Richard Pettigrew of South Dakota, Lee Mantle of Montana, Frank Cannon of Utah, and William Stewart and John Jones of Nevada), but never succeeded in their principal aim of persuading their party to abandon the gold standard.

On one level, the Silver Republicans were participating in a long debate over the basis of money. In the nineteenth century, paper currency usually represented government holdings of precious metals, generally gold but also silver, at different times and in different countries. A $100 bill could be traded for a set amount of gold (or, in some cases, an amount of silver). This meant governments could not simply print more money at will without first acquiring precious metals to back it up. Supporters of the "gold standard" believed that unless paper currency could be exchanged for a fixed amount of gold, currencies would become worthless, prices would soar, and the value of wealth would decline. Bankers were especially fearful that inflation would result in debts being paid off in currency that would buy less, in terms of hard goods, than it would have bought when the loans were made. Something like this had already occurred during the Civil War (1861–65) when the federal government abandoned the gold standard and simply printed money, called "greenbacks." After the war, the United States reverted to a policy of bimetallism, recognizing both gold and silver as a legitimate basis for issuing currency. In 1873, however, silver was demonetized, meaning that gold was the sole recognized basis for legal tender (money that could be used to pay debts and taxes, for example).

The gold standard had the effect of sharply limiting the increase of currency in circulation, even as the population increased rapidly thanks to immigration. People who already owned gold were happy with the situation; others, particularly western farmers, felt squeezed, especially when greatly increased production caused crop prices to fall, thereby making it much harder to pay off loans taken out to buy land or plant crops. The question of whether to use silver as currency, which would have greatly increased the money supply at a time of high silver production, was a burning issue during the 1880s. In addition to a party centered around the issue, factions within both the Republican and Democratic Party argued for recognition of silver as money.

The question of the gold standard versus bimetallism went beyond pure monetary policy. It also reflected a power struggle between eastern industrialists and western farmers and miners, many of whom were deeply invested in silver mines at a time when silver production was robust. In 1894, a group of western Republicans was elected to the Senate on a platform of bimetallism, threatening the Republican majority. The westerners fought for inclusion of a bimetallism plank in the 1896 presidential platform and walked out of the Republican convention when they lost.

The Silver Republicans then debated whether to join the National Silver Party or whether to join the Democratic Party and try to nominate their leader, Senator Henry Teller of Colorado, as president. The Silver Republicans decided to wait until after the Democratic convention to decide what to do.

Surprisingly, the Democrats nominated William Jennings Bryan, who had given a rousing prosilver speech at their convention, effectively coming out of nowhere to win the nomination. The Silver Republicans rallied behind Bryan, but he lost to Republican William McKinley, a supporter of the gold standard.

In 1897, the Silver Republicans, led by Teller, tried to gain control of the Senate by arranging a new coalition around the issue of bimetallism. The coalition would have linked Silver Republicans, the People's Party (also known as Populists), and sympathetic Democrats. But the prospective allies were divided on many other issues, and the effort soon collapsed.

On issues besides silver, most Silver Republicans were members of the progressive wing of the Republican Party. They backed a graduated income tax, government control of monopolies, government ownership of public utilities (such as electricity), and direct election of senators (rather than appointment by state legislatures). In international affairs they supported a canal across Panama, limited immigration, and regulated foreign ownership of U.S. companies.

Despite widespread support in the West, the Silver Republicans had little influence over the Republican Party, which dominated both the White House and Congress. By 1904, the movement had all but disappeared.

---

string of Republican presidential victories by defeating James Blaine (see Vol. 1, p. 96). Republicans won the White House back in 1888 (in the electoral college; Blaine lost the popular vote to Cleveland), only to lose again to Cleveland in 1892 in both the popular vote and the electoral college (see Vol. 1, p. 102).

A year after Cleveland's second victory, a severe economic depression struck. Cleveland's administration was further complicated by a wave of strikes in the railroad and coal industries that reflected growing tensions between business owners and their employees in an era of low wages and severe working conditions. The combination of economic downturn and tensions brought on by labor strife returned the Republicans to control of Congress in 1894.

The economic crisis also brought the issue of currency to the forefront of national politics. Republicans generally favored basing American currency exclusively on the gold bullion, whereas Democrats were increasingly attracted to supporting unlimited coinage of silver. Basing money on silver as well as gold resulted in increasing the amount of available money to repay debts, but it also had the effect of diminishing the value of wealth represented by limited stores of gold. The presidential campaign of 1896 pitted Republican William McKinley (see Vol. 1, p. 106) against Democrat William Jennings Bryan of Nebraska (see Vol. 1, p. 107), a vehement supporter of using silver to back currency. Bryan's powerful rhetoric helped his opponent McKinley raise significant campaign contributions from business owners who felt threatened by Bryan, thereby ushering in an era in which Republicans reinforced their friendliness toward business interests.

Republican Platform, 1876

The Republican Party platform of 1876 was a relatively simple document as far as major party platforms are concerned. This document succinctly demonstrates the party's stance on various issues such as equal rights, tariffs, and support for the public school system (a disguised form of anti-immigrant sentiment, since many Catholic immigrants sent their children to church-based schools). Excerpts:

When, in the economy of Providence, this land was to be purged of human slavery, and when the strength of government of the people by the people and for the people was to be demonstrated, the Republican party came into power. Its deeds have passed into history, and we look back to them with pride. Incited by their memories, and with high aims for the good of our country and mankind, and looking to the future with unfaltering courage, hope, and purpose, we, the representatives of the party, in national convention assembled, make the following declaration of principles:—

1. The United States of America is a nation, not a league. By the combined workings of the national and state governments, under their respective constitutions, the rights of every citizen are secured at home and abroad, and the common welfare promoted.

2. The Republican party has preserved these governments to the hundredth anniversary of the nation's birth, and they are now embodiments of the great truth spoken at its cradle, that all men are created equal; that they are endowed by their Creator with certain inalienable rights, among which are life, liberty, and the pursuit of happiness; that for the attainment of these ends governments have been instituted among men, deriving their just powers from the consent of the governed. Until these truths are cheerfully obeyed, and if need be, vigorously enforced, the work of the Republican party is unfinished.

3. The permanent pacification of the Southern section of the Union and the complete protection of all its citizens in the free enjoyment of all their rights, are duties to which the Republican party is sacredly pledged. The power to provide for the enforcement of the principles embodied in the recent constitutional amendments [Thirteenth, Fourteenth and Fifteenth] is vested by those amendments in the Congress of the United States; and we declare it to be the solemn obligation of the legislative and executive departments of the government to put into immediate and vigorous exercise all their constitutional powers for removing any just causes of discontent on the part of any class, and securing to every American citizen complete liberty and exact equality in the exercise of all civil, political, and public rights....

5. ... The invariable rule for appointments [to government office] should have reference to the honesty, fidelity, and capacity of the appointees, giving to the party in power those places where harmony and vigor of administration require its policy to be represented, but permitting all others to be filled by persons selected with sole reference to the efficiency of the public service and the right of citizens to share in the honor of rendering faithful service to their country.

6. We rejoice in the quickened conscience of the people concerning political affairs. We will hold all public officers to a rigid responsibility, and engage that the prosecution and punishment of all who betray official trusts shall be speedy, thorough, and unsparing.

7. The public school system of the several states is the bulwark of the American republic; and, with a view to its security and permanence, we recommend an amendment to the constitution of the United States, forbidding the application of any public funds or property for the benefit of any school or institution under sectarian control.

8. The revenue necessary for current expenditures and the obligations of the public debt must be largely derived from duties upon importations, which, so far as possible, should be so adjusted as to promote the interests of American labor and advance the prosperity of the whole country.

9. We reaffirm our opposition to further grants of the public lands to corporations and monopolies, and demand that the national domain be devoted to free homes for the people....

11. It is the immediate duty of congress fully to investigate the effects of the immigration and importation of Mongolians on the moral and material interests of the country.

12. The Republican party recognizes with approval the substantial advances recently made toward the establishment of equal rights for women, by the many important amendments effected by Republican legislatures in the laws which concern the personal and property relations of wives, mothers, and widows, and by the appointment and election of women to the superintendence of education, charities, and other public trusts. The honest demands of this class of citizens for additional rights, privileges, and immunities should be treated with respectful consideration....

15. We sincerely deprecate all sectional feeling and tendencies. We therefore note with deep solicitude that the Democratic party counts, as its chief hope of success, upon the electoral vote of a united South, secured through the efforts of those who were recently arrayed against the nation and we invoke the earnest attention of the country to the grave truth, that a success thus achieved would reopen sectional strife and imperil national honor and human rights.

16. We charge the Democratic party with being the same in character and spirit as when it sympathized with treason; with making its control of the House of Representatives the triumph and opportunity of the nation's recent foes; with reasserting and applauding in the national capitol the sentiments of unrepentant rebellion; with sending Union soldiers to the rear, and promoting Confederate soldiers to the front; with deliberately proposing to repudiate the plighted faith of the government; with being equally false and imbecile upon the over-shadowing financial question; with thwarting the ends of justice, by its partisan mismanagements and obstruction of investigation; with proving itself, through the period of its ascendancy in the lower house of congress, utterly incompetent to administer the government; and we warn the country against trusting a party thus alike unworthy, recreant, and incapable....

18. We present as our candidates for President and Vice-President of the United States two distinguished statesmen, of eminent ability and character, and conspicuously fitted for those high offices, and we confidently appeal to the American people to entrust the administration of their public affairs to Rutherford B. Hayes and William A. Wheeler.

More Information

- Felt, Thomas. *The Rise of Mark Hanna.* East Lansing: Michigan State University Press, 1960.
- Garraty, John A. *The New Commonwealth, 1877–1890.* New York: Harper & Row, 1968.
- Polakoff, Keith Ian. *The Politics of Inertia: The Election of 1876 and the End of Reconstruction.* Baton Rouge: Louisiana State University Press, 1973.
- Russell, Francis. *The President Makers.* New York: Little, Brown & Company, 1976.
- Seip, Terry L. *The South Returns to Congress: Men, Economic Measures, and Intersectional Relationships.* Baton Rouge: Louisiana State University Press, 1983.
- Trask, David F. *The War with Spain in 1898.* New York: MacMillan, 1981.
- Trefousse, Hans L. *Rutherford B. Hayes.* New York: Times Books, 2002.
- White, Leonard D. *The Republican Era: A Study in Administrative History, 1869–1901.* New York: Free Press, 1965 (© 1958).

On the Web:

- The Republican Party, GOP History. *http://www.gop.com/About/GOPHistory/Default.aspx.*
- Republican Party Platforms. The American Presidency Project. *http://www.presidency.ucsb.edu/site/docs/platforms.php.*
- United States Republican Party. History World Search.com (hyperlinks to related subjects). *http://history.worldsearch.com/united_states_republican_party/.*

Democratic Party, 1876–1900

FlashFocus: Democratic Party

Origins

The Democratic Party split in 1860 over the issue of slavery. Southern Democrats supported the withdrawal of states from the Union to form the Confederacy and remained a distinct branch of the Democratic Party for over a century after the end of the Civil War in 1865. Northern Democrats were divided between those wanting reconciliation with the South and those supporting the Union. After the Civil War, the Democrats were largely out of power for 20 years until they began to benefit from support by the rapidly growing working class in industrialized cities and hard-pressed farmers in the West during the last 16 years of the nineteenth century.

Issues

Reconstruction. The Civil War, and especially Reconstruction, resulted in the Democrats gaining a long-term hold on white voters throughout the South. The Democratic Party opposed many aspects of post-Civil War Reconstruction, including the Fifteenth Amendment, giving voting rights to black men in the South. Supporters of the Democrats often tried to intimidate African Americans to keep them from exercising their rights.

Free silver. Democrats were long split over whether the government should issue currency ("greenbacks") not backed by gold bullion and whether to allow unlimited coinage of silver ("free silver"). Western farmers favored both moves; northeastern industrialists did not.

Tariffs. Democrats opposed high tariffs designed to protect American companies from foreign competition on grounds that such taxes on imports made goods more expensive for the benefit of business owners. Some industrialists agreed with this position since tariffs raised the cost of raw materials for their factories.

Government reform. Corruption during the Republican administration of President Ulysses Grant gave Democrats a claim on government reform to end abuses of the system of political patronage (government jobs for political supporters).

Impact

Democrats controlled the White House for just eight years between 1861 and 1913, during the two nonconsecutive terms of Grover Cleveland (1885–89 and 1893–97). Democrats controlled both houses of Congress for just four years (1879–81 and 1893–95). Only in the last two decades of the century did Democrats begin to achieve success as an alliance of immigrant industrial workers in the North, farmers in the West, and whites in the South, but their impact on the federal government from 1860 to 1900 was slight.

See also: Democratic Party, 1828–60, p. 17; Democratic Party, 1860–76, p. 61; Democratic Party, 1876-1900, p. 80; Democratic Party, 1900–32, p. 111; Democratic Party, 1932–68, p. 141; Democratic Party, 1968–2004, p. 163; Republican Party, 1876–1900, p. 75.

Not until 1876 did the Democratic Party begin to regain the influence over national affairs it had held before the Civil War. Between 1877 and 1901, Democrats held a majority in the House of Representatives in seven of the 12 Congresses that met during that time. The Senate remained out of reach, however, and only one Democrat, Grover Cleveland, won the White House—twice, in 1884 and 1892 (see Vol. 1, p. 94 and p. 102).

The Election of 1876

The first sign of renewed Democratic strength came in 1874, when Democrats won a majority in the House of Representatives, aided by the economic downturn that followed the Panic of 1873. Despite continued Republican efforts to "wave the bloody shirt" of the Civil War, American society was changing. New industries were being built in the North, the first members of a significant flood of European immigrants were filling new factory jobs in cities like New York and Chicago, and westward expansion was proceeding rapidly.

In 1876, the Democrats nominated New York Governor Samuel Tilden (see Vol. 1, p. 88) for president, a corporate lawyer who made his reputation effectively fighting government corruption in New York City. Tilden narrowly won the popular vote against Republican Rutherford Hayes (see Vol. 1, p. 86), but in four states (Louisiana, Florida, South Carolina, and Oregon) the outcome was contested. A special commission comprised of judges and legislators, voting along party lines, awarded the electoral votes of the states to Hayes. The commission's vote required ratification by the House of Representatives (where the Democrats had won a majority two years earlier). In the House, Southern Democrats made a bargain: they would not object to the commission's findings if Hayes would commit himself to removing Army troops from the South. The deal was struck: Hayes became president and soon after taking office withdrew the troops, effectively marking the end of Reconstruction. Southern Democrats could claim credit for ending military occupation, reinforcing their claim to represent the interests of the white majority. Democrats dominated the "solid South" for nearly a century, during which African Americans continued to be denied full civil rights.

Although Tilden did not become president, his strong showing was further evidence that the Democratic Party was again a major player in national politics. The decade of the 1880s was one marked by extremely close contests between the two parties and without sharp distinctions in their policies. One historian described the election of 1880, for example, as one marked by "purchased votes, forgery, calumny, and vindictive politics." Political energies were largely directed to fights inside both the Democratic and Republican Parties during the decade, rather than against each other.

The 1880s

The decade of the 1880s marked a period of rapid change and development in the United States, characterized by rapid growth of industrialization, a heavy influx of European immigrants who flooded into industrial cities such as New York, Cleveland, and Chicago, and continuing westward expansion. These three threads were woven together inside the Democratic Party, which became an alliance of noncompeting interests. In the South, the white establishment was firmly entrenched as the Republicans retreated from enforcing the policies of Reconstruction. In the North and Midwest, Democrats represented the interests of industrial workers, while in the West, Democrats came to represent the interests of small farmers.

This alliance was built around an array of issues, including:

Civil rights. The rights guaranteed to freed slaves by the Fourteenth Amendment (see Vol. 4, p. 51) were largely ignored by the Republicans after 1876 and had always been resisted by whites who were almost unanimously Democratic.

Tariffs. Many industrialists favored high tariffs (taxes on imports) as a means of protecting their companies from foreign competition, especially from Britain. Democrats favored lowering tariffs, a position also taken by some industrialists who resented paying higher prices for imported raw materials.

Silver. The term "silver" in the context of the late nineteenth century refers to efforts by western Democrats to adopt "free" (that is, unlimited) use of silver as currency. Western farmers believed more money in circulation would help them pay their debts; as long as gold was the only basis for currency, debts were hard to pay off. More money in circulation, they reasoned, would make it easier to pay their debts, even if it simultaneously drove up prices for everything else.

The 1880s were a transitional decade for the Democratic Party on several of these issues. The successful Democratic nominee for president in 1884, Governor Grover Cleveland of New York, was sometimes called the "Businessman's President." He supported "sensible" tariffs—lower than what some Republicans wanted but not as low as what some Democrats insisted upon—and opposed use of silver as money.

Cleveland was a strong proponent of civil service reform, however, which helped him win election in 1884. At the time, out of 126,000 federal jobs, only 16,000 were filled on the basis of competency demonstrated by testing; the other 110,000 were filled by appointment, judged by many voters to be a prime source of corruption.

Cleveland won the popular election in 1888 by about 90,600 votes, but lost in the electoral college to Republican Benjamin Harrison, 233-168. (see Vol. 1, p. 98). Four years later, Cleveland defeated Harrison (see Vol. 1, p. 102). But although he had been reelected, in some respects Cleveland was already losing touch with his own party. The western leg of the Democratic alliance in particular was losing support to the Populists (see p. 98), for whom the issue of "free silver" (unlimited use of silver, which was plentiful, for coinage to supplement gold at a fixed ratio) was a leading issue.

FlashFocus: Adlai Stevenson

Born: October 23, 1835, Christian County, Kentucky
Died: June 14, 1914, Chicago, Illinois
Political Career: U.S. House of Representatives, 1874–76, 1878–80; vice president, 1892–96; Democratic candidate for vice president, 1900; Democratic candidate for governor of Illinois, 1908.

Adlai Stevenson, Sr. (not to be confused with his grandson, Adlai Stevenson III, see Vol. 1, p. 160), was born in Kentucky, the son of a slave-owning planter who could afford to provide Stevenson with an above-average education. Stevenson taught school before entering Illinois Wesleyan University and then Centre College in Danville, Kentucky. Stevenson left college upon the death of his father and never graduated. Instead, he studied law, passed the bar, and opened a law practice in Metamora, Illinois. He won election as a state attorney before moving to Bloomington, Illinois, in 1868 to join the law office of James Ewing.

Along the way, Stevenson deepened his interest in politics and his involvement in the Democratic Party. He campaigned actively for Illinois Democrats seeking statewide offices, and he himself was elected to Congress in 1874. He lost his reelection bid in 1876, but ran again in 1878 and regained his seat for a second term.

When President Grover Cleveland took office in 1885, he appointed Stevenson as first assistant postmaster-general, with the delicate task of dismissing several postmasters who had been Republican political appointees in order to make room for Cleveland's own Democratic appointees. For this, Stevenson drew harsh criticism; and when Cleveland appointed Stevenson to the supreme court of the District of Columbia, Republicans in the Senate blocked the appointment.

Stevenson attended the Democratic National Convention in 1892 as a Cleveland supporter and was chosen by the convention to be the vice presidential candidate. Incoming president William McKinley named Stevenson to a monetary commission to Europe.

Upon his return to the United States, Stevenson remained an important figure in the Democratic Party. He ran for vice president as William Jennings Bryan's running mate in 1900, but the ticket lost. Stevenson ran for governor of Illinois in 1908, but again was unsuccessful. He retreated from politics to focus on writing. He died in Chicago in 1914.

Free Silver and the Democrats

This trend in the Democratic party came thundering out of Nebraska in 1896 with the nomination of William Jennings Bryan (see Vol. 1, p. 107) for president. Bryan was spokesman for hard-pressed western farmers who found prices for their crops falling while costs for raw materials and shipping were rapidly climbing. For Bryan, the answer was "free silver."

Bryan had supported the Peoples' Party candidate, James Weaver, for president in 1892 (see p. 98 and Vol. 1, p. 102), and after Cleveland's retirement at the end of his second term, Bryan brought many of the populist issues into the Democratic Party platform, foremost among them the free coinage of silver. At the 1896 Democratic convention in Chicago, silver forces led by Bryan fought northeastern Democrats who favored the gold standard. Bryan delivered one of the most famous orations of the age, his "Cross of Gold" speech, at the convention, carrying the cause for free silver, but at a price: the support of gold standard Democrats. Outgoing President Cleveland himself preferred the Republican candidate, William McKinley (see Vol. 1, p. 106), who supported the gold standard.

Bryan's vigorous campaigning helped Republicans persuade businessmen to make large contributions to the Republican Party, leading to a victory by McKinley. But Bryan, populism, and the gold standard would remain campaign issues well into the twentieth century.

Democratic Platform, 1876

The Democratic Party tried to take advantage of scandals within the administration of Republican Ulysses Grant to argue that a change in party was needed in the White House. The Democrats offered a variety of reform measures, and their candidate, New York corporate lawyer Samuel Tilden, had already earned a reputation for combating government corruption in New York City. In 1876, the Democrats were just beginning to recover from their reputation as the party of the Confederacy in the Civil War a decade earlier, but had not yet become strongly identified with the emerging industrial working class. Excerpts from the party's 1876 platform:

We, the delegates of the Democratic party of the United States, in National Convention assembled, do hereby declare the administration of the Federal Government to be in great need of immediate reform; do hereby enjoin upon the nominees of this Convention, and of the Democratic Party in each State, a zealous effort and co-operation to this end, and do here appeal to our fellow citizens of every former political connection to undertake with us this first and most pressing patriotic duty for the Democracy of the whole country.

We do here reaffirm our faith in the permanence of the Federal Union, our devotion to the Constitution of the United States, with its amendments universally accepted as a final settlement of the controversies that engendered civil war, and do here record our steadfast confidence in the perpetuity of republican self-government; in absolute acquiescence in the will of the majority, the vital principle of republics; in the supremacy of the civil over the military; in the two-fold separation of church and state, for the sake alike of civil and religious freedom; in the equality of all citizens before just laws of their own enactment; in the liberty of individual conduct unvexed by sumptuary laws; in the faithful education of the rising generation, that they may preserve, enjoy and transmit these best conditions of human happiness and hope....

Reform is necessary to rebuild and establish in the hearts of the whole people the Union eleven years ago happily rescued from the danger of the secession of states, but now to be saved from a corrupt centralism which, after inflicting upon ten states [of the South] the rapacity of carpetbag tyrannies, has honeycombed the offices of the federal government itself with incapacity, waste and fraud; infected states and municipalities with the contagion of misrule, and locked fast the prosperity of an industrious people in the paralysis of hard times. Reform is necessary to establish a sound currency, restore the public credit and maintain the national honor....

We denounce the present tariff levied upon nearly four thousand articles as a masterpiece of injustice, inequality and false pretense, which yields a dwindling and not a yearly rising revenue, has impoverished many industries to subsidize a few....

Reform is necessary in the scale of public expense, federal, state, and municipal. Our federal taxation has swollen ... from less than five dollars per head to more than eighteen dollars per head....

Reform is necessary to correct the omissions of a Republican Congress and the errors of our treaties and our diplomacy which has ... exposed our brethren of the Pacific coast to the incursions of a race [the Chinese] not sprung from the same great parent stock....

Reform is necessary in the civil service. Experience proves that efficient economical conduct of the government is not possible if its civil service be subject to change at every election, be a prize fought for at the ballot box....

All these abuses, wrongs, and crimes, the product of sixteen years' ascendancy of the Republican party, create a necessity for reform, confessed by Republicans themselves; but their reformers are voted down in convention and displaced from the cabinet. The party's mass of honest voters is powerless to resist the eighty thousand office-holders, its leaders and guides. Reform can only be had by a peaceful civic revolution. We demand a change of system, a change of administration, a change of parties, that we may have a change of measures and of men....

Bryan's "Cross of Gold" speech, July 9, 1896

William Jennings Bryan, the eventual Democratic presidential nominee in 1896 (and in 1900 and 1908), delivered a fiery defense of freely coining silver to the Democratic convention on July 9, 1896. Bryan's passionate oratory on the subject, which was dear to economically hard-pressed western farmers, helped propel him to the Democratic nomination. Not all Democrats agreed with Bryan; his speech was part of an intense debate over whether the party should endorse the gold standard (backing all currency with government stores of gold bullion).

Mr. Chairman and Gentlemen of the Convention:

I would be presumptuous, indeed, to present myself against the distinguished gentlemen to whom you have listened [in favor of a gold standard] if this was a mere measuring of abilities; but this is not a contest between persons. The humblest citizen in all the land, when clad in the armor of a righteous cause, is stronger than all the hosts of error. I come to speak to you in defense of a cause as holy as the cause of liberty—the cause of humanity.

When this debate is concluded, a motion will be made to lay upon the table the resolution offered in commendation of the administration and also the resolution offered in condemnation of the administration. We object to bringing this question down to the level of persons. The individual is but an atom; he is born, he acts, he dies; but principles are eternal; and this has been a contest over a principle.

Never before in the history of this country has there been witnessed such a contest as that through which we have just passed. Never before in the history of American politics has a great issue been fought out, as this issue [of free silver] has been, by the voters of a great party. On the fourth of March, 1895, a few Democrats, most of them members of Congress, issued an address to the Democrats of the nation, asserting that the money question was the paramount issue of the hour; declaring that a majority of the Democratic party had the right to control the action of the party on this paramount issue; and concluding with the request that the believers in the free coinage of silver in the Democratic party should organize, take charge of, and control the policy of the Democratic party. Three months later, at Memphis, an organization was perfected, and the silver Democrats went forth openly and courageously proclaiming their belief, and declaring that, if successful, they would crystallize into a platform the declaration which they had made. Then began the conflict. With a zeal approaching the zeal which inspired the crusaders who followed Peter the Hermit, our silver Democrats went forth from victory unto victory until they are now assembled, not to discuss, not to debate, but to enter up the judgment already rendered by the plain people of this country. In this contest brother has been arrayed against brother, father against son. The warmest ties of love, acquaintance and association have been disregarded; old leaders have been cast aside when they have refused to give expression to the sentiments of those whom they would lead, and new leaders have sprung up to give direction to this cause of truth. Thus has the contest been waged, and we have assembled here under as binding and solemn instructions as were ever imposed upon representatives of the people....

We say to you that you have made the definition of a businessman too limited in its application. The man who is employed for wages is as much a businessman as his employer; the attorney in a country town is as much a businessman as the corporation counsel in a great metropolis; the merchant at the cross-roads store is as much a businessman as the merchant of New York; the farmer who goes forth in the morning and toils all day—who begins in the spring and toils all summer—and who by the application of brain and muscle to the natural resources of the country creates wealth, is as much a businessman as the man who goes upon the board of trade and bets upon the price of grain; the miners who go down a thousand feet into the earth, or climb two thousand feet upon the cliffs, and bring forth from their hiding places the precious metals to be poured into the channels of trade are as much businessmen as the few financial magnates who, in a

The issue of whether to use silver as money was of tremendous importance in the last quarter of the nineteenth century and caused rifts in both the Democratic and Republican parties. Here, the Democratic Party, symbolized by the donkey, suffers under the burden of the currency debate within the party.

back room, corner the money of the world. We come to speak for this broader class of businessmen.

Ah, my friends, we say not one word against those who live upon the Atlantic coast, but the hardy pioneers who have braved all the dangers of the wilderness, who have made the desert to blossom as the rose—the pioneers away out there [pointing to the West], who rear their children near to Nature's heart, where they can mingle their voices with the voices of the birds—out there where they have erected school houses for the education of their young, churches where they praise their Creator, and cemeteries where rest the ashes of their dead—these people, we say, are as deserving of the consideration of our party as any people in this country. It is for these that we speak. We do not come as aggressors. Our war is not a war of conquest; we are fighting in the defense of our homes, our families, and posterity. We have petitioned, and our petitions have been scorned; we have entreated, and our entreaties have been disregarded; we have begged, and they have mocked when our calamity came. We beg no longer; we entreat no more; we petition no more. We defy them....

We say in our platform that we believe that the right to coin and issue money is a function of government. We believe it. We believe that it is a part of sovereignty, and can no more with safety be delegated to private individuals than we could afford to delegate to private individuals the power to make penal statutes or *levy taxes.... Those who are opposed to this proposition tell us that the issue of paper money is function of the bank, and that the government ought to go out of the banking business. I stand with [Thomas] Jefferson ... and tell them, as he did, that the issue of money is a function of government, and that the banks ought to go out of the governing business....*

And now, my friends, let me come to the paramount issue. If they ask us why it is that we say more on the money question than we say upon the tariff question, I reply that, if protection has slain its thousands, the gold standard has slain its tens of thousands. If they ask us why we do not embody in our platform all the things that we believe in, we reply that when we have restored the money of the constitution all other necessary reforms will be possible; but that until this is done there is no other reform that can be accomplished....

You come to us and tell us that the great cities are in favor of the gold standard; we reply that the great cities rest upon our broad and fertile prairies. Burn down your cities and leave our farms and your cities will spring up again as if by magic; but destroy our farms and the grass will grow in the streets of every city in the country....

Having behind us the producing masses of this nation and the world, supported by the commercial interests, the laboring interests, and the toilers everywhere, we will answer their demand for a gold standard by saying to them: 'You shall not press down upon the brow of labor this crown of thorns; you shall not crucify mankind upon a cross of gold!'

More Information

- Ashby, LeRoy. *William Jennings Bryan: Champion of Democracy.* Boston: Twayne Publishers, 1987.
- Cherny, Robert W. *A Righteous Cause: The Life of William Jennings Bryan.* Boston: Little, Brown, 1985.
- Flick, Alexander. *Samuel Jones Tilden; A Study in Political Sagacity.* New York: Dodd, Mead & Company, 1939.
- Garraty, John A. *The New Commonwealth, 1877–1890.* New York: Harper & Row, 1968.
- Graff, Henry F. *Grover Cleveland.* New York: Times Books, 2002.
- Josephson, Matthew. *The Politicos: 1865–1896.* New York: Harcourt, Brace, and World, 1963.
- Morris, Roy. *Fraud of the Century: Rutherford B. Hayes, Samuel J. Tilden and the Stolen Election of 1876.* New York: Simon & Schuster, 2003.
- Polakoff, Keith Ian. *The Politics of Inertia: The Election of 1876 and the End of Reconstruction.* Baton Rouge: Louisiana State University Press, 1973.

On the Web

- Bryan, William Jennings, biography and Web links. http://www.fact_index.com/w/wi/william_jennings_bryan.html.
- Cleveland, Grover. Inaugural addresses. 1885: http://www.bartleby.com/124/pres37.html; 1893: http://www.bartleby.com/124/pres39.html.
- CNN-Time Magazine, Democratic Convention History, A Historical Overview from 1831–1992. http://www.cnn.com/ALLPOLITICS/1996/conventions/chicago/facts/convention/index.shtml.
- Democratic Party Platforms, 1860–1900. American Presidency Project. http://www.presidency.ucsb.edu/site/docs/platforms.php.
- Jensen, Richard. American Political History On-Line (collection of links to primary documents and related historical materials). http://tigger.uic.edu/~rjensen/pol-gl.htm.
- Tilden, Samuel. Speech to the Manhattan Club Conceding the Election of 1876. *New York Herald,* June 13, 1877. http://www.rbhayes.org/tilden_concession.htm.

Workingmen's Party of California, 1877–80

FlashFocus: Workingmen's Party of California

Origins
Jobless whites in San Francisco, who blamed their unemployment on immigrant Chinese workers, formed a political party to denounce railroad companies that hired immigrants. The Workingmen's Party of California aimed to represent the interests of white California laborers.

Issues
Immigration. The party became incensed at the increasing trend of railroad companies to hire skilled Chinese immigrants to build new tracks. Unemployed workers blamed the immigrants for driving down wages. They demanded that immigrants be dismissed from their jobs, and they wanted companies to be barred from hiring immigrants.
Eight hour workday. This plank of the party platform was a universal demand of American workers during the late nineteenth century.
New tax system. Enraged at the level of profits earned by railroad company owners and stockholders, the party proposed a new tax system to prevent monopolies and the accumulation of what it regarded as outsized wealth.

Impact
The party won nearly one-third of the seats in the 1878 election for representatives to the California state constitutional convention. In 1879 the party won every elective office in San Francisco except one. When the California courts overturned anti-Chinese legislation in 1880, factories rehired Chinese immigrants, and the Workingmen's Party collapsed by the end of the year.

See also: Chinese Immigration, Vol. 4, p. 186; Chinese Exclusion Act of 1882, Vol. 4, p. 188.

Periodic economic slowdowns in the nineteenth century coincided with a rapid rise in immigration from both Europe and Asia. In California, Chinese laborers often were the target of European-Americans who resented being out of work. The Workingmen's Party of California combined populism—a call for popular control of the economy—with intense anti-Chinese sentiments in the late 1870s, when economic depression gripped much of the nation.

Origin and Philosophy

The Workingmen's Party of California was organized by an Irish immigrant, Denis Kearney, in reaction to low farm prices, high unemployment, and a standstill in manufacturing. The first iteration of the Workingman's Party was established in New York City in 1829, but proved largely ineffective; Kearney's party was a revival of the New York party with a distinctly Californian flavor.

The railroad industry in particular was in turmoil as companies waged price wars in an attempt to hold onto their passengers and to attract new ones. To compensate for reduced revenues, railroad companies also cut wages. In July 1877, violent strikes by railroad workers sprang up spontaneously in Baltimore, West Virginia, and along the West Coast. Workers in San Francisco, already upset over a growing trend by railroads to drive down wages by hiring skilled Chinese immigrants, were in a rebellious mood.

The newly formed Workingmen's Party called a mass meeting on July 23, 1877, in San Francisco. Police were on alert for violence, but nevertheless an anti-Chinese mob stormed away from the rally after no mention was made of Chinese workers by the official speakers. By the next day, 20 Chinese laundry businesses had been looted, and the Chinese Methodist Mission had been destroyed.

Kearney's political ambition led him to deliver a series of speeches in San Francisco advocating violence against the Chinese. He popularized the party slogan "The Chinese Must Go," which appeared in campaign literature and drawings. In one speech, Kearney demanded that the Central Pacific Railroad, a major employer in California, dismiss all of its employees of Chinese descent. Otherwise, Kearney threatened to stage a violent takeover of the city government. As a result of this speech—and on the basis of others he and various party operatives had made—Kearney and several members of the party were arrested. Kearney was sentenced to six months in jail, but the California State Supreme Court soon ordered him released on a legal technicality.

In late January 1878, the Workingmen's Party held its first statewide convention in San Francisco. The party declared that the United States government had ignored the rights of its citizens and urged that "coolie" (Chinese) labor (see Vol. 4, p. 187) be abolished. The party advocated an eight-hour workday and a new tax system that would prevent massive wealth accumulation and monopolies.

Workingmen's Party members won a third of the seats at a scheduled California constitutional convention that convened in 1878, and it was highly influential in the document that resulted. The new constitution, replacing one adopted in 1849, was approved by California voters in a referendum held on May 7, 1879.

Among other provisions, the new state constitution included clauses to regulate railroads and other companies and to change the state's tax structure to benefit farmers. The new

An artist's depiction of an anti-Chinese demonstration in California. The Workingmen's Party opposed Chinese immigration because they feared immigrants, willing to work for lower wages, would take jobs away from Americans.

constitution was particularly noteworthy for its attacks on Chinese immigrants. It included an absolute ban on government employment of Chinese at any level, and it instructed the state legislature to "delegate all necessary power to the incorporated cities and towns of this state for the removal of Chinese without the limits of such cities and towns, or for their location within prescribed portions of those limits." The new constitution went on to declare that Chinese immigrants ineligible to become American citizens were "dangerous to the well-being of the state," and ordered the legislature to discourage future Chinese immigration.

In 1879, the Workingmen's Party of California won nearly every elective office in San Francisco, including the office of mayor. The new mayor, Isaac Kalloch, was a clergyman who ironically ran a large Chinese Sunday school at his church. Kalloch nevertheless supported the anti-Chinese stance of the party, despite having been wounded during the campaign by a gunshot fired by the editor of the San Francisco Chronicle after Kalloch had stormed the newspaper's offices. Kalloch survived and won the election in a landslide.

Kearney tried to carry his anti-Chinese message elsewhere in the country. In August 1878, for example, he delivered a speech in Lowell, Massachusetts, where he spoke against employment of Chinese immigrants in textile factories.

End of the Party

By 1880, unemployed workers were gathering daily to march through the streets of San Francisco demanding the mass firings of Chinese workers from factories. Many business owners capitulated for fear of violent reprisals, but in the spring, state courts overturned the anti-Chinese laws and regulations passed by the legislature at the party's insistence. Following the repudiation of these laws, many factories rehired Chinese workers.

The Workingmen's Party collapsed by the end of 1880. At that time, the economy began to improve, resulting in more jobs, and the party's legislation was declared invalid. Nevertheless, some party members strongly supported labor and labor-friendly politicians for years to come.

Ideology

Kearney, in his role as president of the Workingmen's Party of California, in February 1878 sent the following letter to the *Indianapolis* (Indiana) *Times* laying out his party's platform and seeking support from other areas.

> Our moneyed men have ruled us for the past thirty years. Under the flag of the slaveholder they hoped to destroy our liberty. Failing in that, they have rallied under the banner of the millionaire, the banker and the land monopolist, the railroad king and the false politician, to effect their purpose.
>
> We have permitted them to become immensely rich against all sound republican policy, and they have turned upon us to sting us to death. They have seized upon the government by bribery and corruption. They have made speculation and public robbery a science. The have loaded the nation, the state, the county, and the city

with debt. They have stolen the public lands. They have grasped all to themselves, and by their unprincipled greed brought a crisis of unparalleled distress on forty millions of people, who have natural resources to feed, clothe and shelter the whole human race....

We, here in California, feel it as well as you. We feel that the day and hour has come for the Workingmen of America to depose capital and put Labor in the Presidential chair, in the Senate and Congress, in the State House, and on the Judicial Bench....

To add to our misery and despair, a bloated aristocracy has sent to China—the greatest and oldest despotism in the world—for a cheap working slave. It rakes the slums of Asia to find the meanest slave on earth—the Chinese coolie—and imports him here to meet the free American in the Labor market, and still further widen the breach between the rich and the poor, still further to degrade white Labor.

These cheap slaves fill every place. Their dress is scant and cheap. Their food is rice from China. They hedge twenty in a room, ten by ten. They are whipped curs, abject in docility, mean, contemptible and obedient in all things. They have no wives, children or dependents.

They are imported by companies, controlled as serfs, worked like slaves, and at last go back to China with all their earnings. They are in every place, they seem to have no sex. Boys work, girls work; it is all alike to them.

The father of a family is met by them at every turn. Would he get work for himself? Ah! A stout Chinaman does it cheaper. Will he get a place for his oldest boy? He can not. His girl? Why, the Chinaman is in her place too! Every door is closed. He can only go to crime or suicide, his wife and daughter to prostitution, and his boys to hoodlumism and the penitentiary.

Do not believe those who call us savages, rioters, incendiaries, and outlaws. We seek our ends calmly, rationally, at the ballot box. So far good order has marked all our proceedings. But, we know how false, how inhuman, our adversaries are. We know that if gold, if fraud, if force can defeat us, they will all be used. And we have resolved that they shall not defeat us. We shall arm. We shall meet fraud and falsehood with defiance, and force with force, if need be.

We are men, and propose to live like men in this free land, without the contamination of slave labor, or die like men, if need be, in asserting the rights of our race, our country, and our families.

California must be all American or all Chinese. We are resolved that it shall be American, and are prepared to make it so. May we not rely upon your sympathy and assistance?

More Information

▶ Bruce, Robert V. *1877: Year of Violence*. Indianapolis: Bobbs-Merrill, 1959.

▶ Graff, Henry F., ed. *The Presidents: A Reference History*. New York: Macmillan, 2000.

▶ Shumsky, Neil. *The Evolution of Political Protest and the Workingmen's Party of California*. Columbus: Ohio State University Press, 1991.

FlashFocus: Denis Kearney

Born: February 1, 1847, County Cork, Ireland
Died: April 24, 1907, Alameda, California
Political Career: Denis Kearney, a native of County Cork, Ireland, went to sea as a boy and settled in San Francisco in 1877 at age 30. There, he went into the local hauling business and achieved success. In the city, it was customary to hold public outdoor meetings on Sundays, which is where Kearney made the transition from small business owner to politician.

Kearney initially made his mark denouncing a public rifle range, declaring that marksmen there were practicing to shoot striking workers. Kearney was a persuasive orator, and his speeches were printed by two newspapers, the *Call* and the *Chronicle*, which were engaged in a war to gain circulation. Consequently Kearney became well known throughout the city.

Kearney quickly focused on a single theme—the city's large Chinese immigrant community. Kearney claimed Chinese workers were taking jobs from European Americans at a time of general economic slowdown. He regularly ended his speeches by demanding, "The Chinese must go!" He combined his anti-Chinese invective with a stream of abuse against the rich, speaking in his distinctive Irish accent of lynching millionaires, burning rich men's "palaces," and swimming in "rivers of blood."

Kearney invigorated the Workingmen's Party by taking advantage of his popularity as an orator. Under Kearney's leadership, the party was influential in drafting a new state constitution that was adopted by popular vote in 1879. The new constitution contained many provisions introduced by Kearney and his party, notably an insistence on expelling any Chinese not in the country legally. The rabid anti-Chinese feelings in California that Kearney helped build were later reflected in the federal Chinese Exclusion Act of 1882, which was repeatedly renewed, effectively stopping Chinese immigration to the United States for nearly a century—but which also robbed Kearney of his main political issue.

Toward the end of 1880, the national economy began improving, and Kearney's appeals faded. His efforts to expand the Workingman's Party to other states largely fell on deaf ears. Kearney died in 1907.

On the Web

▶ Kearneyism, the Chinese, and Labor Unrest in California. The Virtual Museum of the City of San Francisco. *http://www.sfmuseum.org/hist6/kearneyism.html*.

▶ Workingman's Party. *http://www.californiahistory.net/7_pages/chinese_party.htm*.

▶ Workingmen's Party. *http://www.shapingsf.org/ezine/labor/workingmens/main.html*.

Greenback Party, 1874–1940

FlashFocus: Greenback Party

Origins
The Greenback Party (also known as the National Independent or Greenback-Labor Party) was formed in November 1874 at a meeting in Indianapolis, Indiana. The party was an outgrowth of the Panic of 1873, an economic depression that hurt both farmers and industrial workers. The Greenback Party initially represented farmers who advocated the creation of paper money not backed by gold, in order to make it easier for farmers to pay their debts. Two years later, groups representing factory workers joined the Greenback Party to form the Greenback-Labor Party, bringing together the interests of rural workers and urban industrial workers.

Issues
Currency. The Greenbacks opposed a return to the gold standard (paper money backed by government-owned gold bullion) in favor of retaining paper money (popularly called greenbacks). The party believed that issuing more paper money would aid farmers and industrial workers who had been hurt during the Panic of 1873. The party also argued vehemently against the passage of the Specie Resumption Act, which would have required paper money to be backed by gold or silver, a policy the Greenbacks insisted would favor wealthy business owners and bankers over general workers.
Women's suffrage. The Greenback Party called for a constitutional amendment to give women the right to vote.
Labor reform. After their initial national campaign in 1876, the Greenbacks added government regulation of factories and mines and abolition of child labor to thier platform. The growth of industrialization had also given rise to squalid working conditions in factories, a development that several political parties began to address.
Graduated income tax. The party argued for a proportional tax on property and income.

Impact
The Greenback Party first ran a candidate for president in 1876. In the Congressional elections of 1878, the party combined support from urban workers and farmers and won 14 seats in the House of Representatives. Its 1880 presidential nominee, Representative James Weaver of Iowa, received 305,997 votes (3.3 percent of the total popular vote). Although Weaver's showing disappointed many party members, it was the party's high point. In 1884, Greenback presidential nominee Benjamin F. Butler managed only 175,096 votes. Rising national prosperity further weakened the Greenback Party, which achieved no more electoral successes.

See also: National Silver Party, p. 92; People's Party (Populists), p. 98; Republican Party, 1876–1900, p. 75; Democratic Party, 1876–1900, p. 80; Election of 1880, Vol. 1, p. 90; Election of 1892, Vol. 1, p. 102; Election of 1896, Vol. 1, p. 105.

The Greenback Party, also known as the National Independent Party or the Greenback-Labor Party, was founded in November 1874 in Indianapolis, Indiana, in response to growing economic pressures on farmers brought about by an economic downturn known as the Panic of 1873.

Origins of the Greenbacks

During the Civil War, the federal government had been in desperate need of money to finance the Union Army. Until the war, paper currency issued by the U.S. Treasury had been backed by specie, or deposits of gold, which limited the amount of currency that could be issued. In 1862, the federal government began issuing paper money not backed by precious metal. This currency, called "greenbacks," pumped money into the economy and helped the government pay the cost of the Civil War. But many bankers opposed printing money not supported by deposits of gold since doing so enabled the government to print money whenever it seemed convenient. Such money tended to drive inflation (higher prices) and diminish the value of debts, since obligations could be paid off with paper money that did not represent something, like gold, of lasting value. On the other hand, some economists argued that maintaining a flexible supply of paper money served the interests of farmers and industrial workers, as opposed to a gold and silver-based treasury, which benefitted wealthier individuals.

In 1873, an economic downturn that had plagued Europe reached the United States. The nation's most powerful banking firm, Jay Cooke and Company (which backed many of the nation's railroad projects), failed. Unable to collect money it had loaned, it could not pay gold to its depositors. The bank's demise began a chain of events that led to the closing of the New York Stock Exchange for 10 days, the evaporation of credit, the subsequent failure of other banks across the country, and a rash of foreclosures (banks seizing property that was used as collateral for loans). These conditions hurt farmers who depended on loans to get through the sowing and growing seasons and factory employees thrown out of work by business failures.

The Greenback Party favored retaining the paper money used during the Civil War as a means of ending the economic crisis. Farm groups such as the National Grange and labor organizations such as the Knights of Labor were instrumental in the formation of the new party.

The party tried but failed to prevent the passage of the Specie Resumption Act of 1875 that returned the nation to hard money (currency backed by gold and silver). In 1876, the Greenback Party based its national campaign on the repeal of the Specie Resumption Act. Peter Cooper, a New York philanthropist, was nominated as the Greenback Party's presidential candidate at the national convention in Indianapolis. He ran on a platform that focused only on the issue of currency.

This cartoon illustrates several of the monetary issues taken up by the Greenback Party.

Because the economic panic was a disaster for farmers, Cooper collected many rural votes, but only managed 75,973 votes (0.9 percent of the total) overall. Republican Rutherford Hayes won the presidency (see Vol. 1, p. 86).

The Greenback Party regrouped at its national convention in 1878. Bolstered by the continuing economic slump, the party welcomed labor reform groups to its ranks and wrote a platform that added labor concerns to the currency plank. The addition of labor gave the party new momentum, as did a general willingness among many voters to blame bankers and business leaders for hard times. The Greenback Party won more than a million votes in the 1878 congressional elections, sending 14 men to the U.S. House of Representatives.

The party failed to achieve its goal of repealing the Specie Resumption Act, but this did not prevent the nation's economy from resuming growth in the 1880s. The Greenback Party continued to argue for unlimited coinage of silver (a precious metal much more plentiful than gold), the abolition of child labor, an end to prison labor for hire (which the party argued denied jobs to law-abiding workers), a graduated income tax, and granting the right to vote to all Americans, including women. Beginning the 1880 campaign with high hopes, the party won eight seats in the House of Representatives. Its presidential candidate, James Weaver, received a disappointing 3.3 percent of the vote (see Vol. 1, p. 90).

End of the Greenbacks

After the 1880 campaign, the Greenbacks were further hampered by an economic rebound that caused their core issue to decline in importance. The 1884 presidential campaign was the last for the party. The Greenbacks attacked both the Republican and Democratic parties, accusing them of being instruments of large corporations that needed to be regulated. Former Massachusetts governor Benjamin Butler was the Greenback nominee; he received 175,096 votes, or 1.7 percent (see Vol. 1, p. 94). Although the Greenbacks had expanded their appeal and adopted a wider range of issues, such as the income tax and female suffrage, many party members moved into the agrarian reform movement that became the People's Party (Populist; see p. 98).

What remained of the Greenback Party merged with the Union Labor Party in the presidential elections of 1888 (see Vol. 1, p. 98), but voters virtually ignored it (see Vol. 1, p. 98). The Greenbacks then aligned themselves with the People's Party (Populists) in the election of 1892 (see Vol. 1, p. 102), which again proved meaningless in terms of increased influence and electoral success.

The Greenback Party continued to function, however, and reemerged in 1918 when a reformer from Indiana, John Zahnd, became its candidate for the election of 1920. Zahnd ran on the party ticket in every successive presidential election until 1940. By the 1950s, the party had grown so weak that it

FlashFocus: James Baird Weaver

Born: June 12, 1833, Dayton, Ohio
Died: February 6, 1912, Des Moines, Iowa
Political Career: District attorney, 1866–67; federal assessor, 1867–73; representative from Iowa, 1878–82, 1884–88; Greenback candidate for president, 1880; Populist candidate for president, 1892; mayor of Colfax, Iowa, 1896–1912.

Weaver attended country schools in Iowa while working as a mail carrier. He graduated from Cincinnati Law School in 1855 and opened a private law practice in Bloomfield, Iowa.

Initially a Democrat, Weaver became interested in the Free Soil movement (a movement to ban slavery from new states entering the Union), then was active in Republican Party politics from 1857 until the Civil War. Weaver rose from lieutenant to colonel in the Union Army.

Weaver ran unsuccessfully for lieutenant governor of Iowa in 1865 and was elected district attorney in 1866. He then served as a federal tax collector from 1867 to 1873.

Weaver began to diverge from the Republican Party on the key issue of whether paper currency must be backed by government stores of gold bullion (as the Republicans believed) or whether the government should issue money without such backing. Weaver was popular with voters, and only political maneuvering within the Republican Party denied him the Republican nomination for Congress in 1874 and for governor in 1875.

Weaver turned to the Greenback Party, which shared his view on currency. He was elected to Congress as the Greenback candidate in 1878 and became the unsuccessful Greenback candidate for president in 1880. Weaver lost his seat in Congress in 1882, but won it back in 1884 and 1886.

When the Farmers' Alliance succeeded the Greenback Party as the party of "soft money," Weaver helped build the Alliance into the populist People's Party. He ran for the White House a second time in 1892, as the People's Party candidate, and won over a million popular votes and 22 electoral college votes. Four years later, Weaver encouraged a fusion between Populists and Democrats, and arranged for the People's Party to support Democrat William Jennings Bryan for president. Bryan lost to Republican William McKinley, and the People's Party disappeared, along with the political careers of its leaders.

His national political career over, Weaver had already returned to Iowa where he was elected mayor of Colfax in 1895 for two years. He died in Des Moines in 1912.

did not appear on the ballots in many states and eventually faded from the scene.

Greenback Party Platform, 1884

The Greenback Party was initially formed around the single issue of supporting paper currency. Later, its platform expanded to include other issues, such as women's right to vote, federal regulation of interstate commerce, and a federal tax on incomes. The party's broader outlook is outlined in the 1884 platform.

1. That we hold the late decision of the Supreme Court on the legal-tender question to be a full vindication of the theory which our party has always advocated on the right and authority of Congress over the issue of legal-tender notes, and we hereby pledge ourselves to uphold said decision, and to defend the Constitution.... We demand the issue of such money in sufficient quantities to supply the actual demands of trade and commerce, in accordance with the increase of population and the development of our industries. We demand the substitution of greenbacks for national-bank notes, and the prompt payment of the public debt. We want that money which saved our country in time of war and which has given it prosperity and happiness in peace. We condemn the retirement of the fractional currency and the small denomination of greenbacks, and demand their restoration. We demand the issue of the hoards of money now locked up in the United States Treasury, by applying them to the payment of the public debt now due.

2. We denounce as dangerous to our republican institutions, those methods and policies of the Democratic and Republican parties which have sanctioned or permitted the establishment of land, railroad, money, and other gigantic monopolies; and we demand such governmental action as may be necessary to take from such monopolies the power they have so corruptly and unjustly usurped, and restore them to the people, to whom they belong.

3. The public lands being the natural inheritance of the people, we denounce that policy which has granted to corporations vast tracts of land, and we demand that immediate and vigorous measures be taken to reclaim from such corporations, for the people's use and benefit, all such land-grants as have been forfeited by reason of non-fulfilment of contract, or that may have been wrongfully acquired by corrupt legislation, and that such reclaimed lands and other public domain be henceforth held as a sacred trust, to be granted only to actual settlers in limited quantities; and we also demand that the alien ownership of land, individual or corporate, shall be prohibited.

4. We demand Congressional regulations of interstate commerce, we denounce " pooling," stock-watering, and discrimination in rates and charges, and demand that Congress shall correct these abuses, even, if necessary, by the construction of national railroads. We also demand the establishment of a government postal-telegraph system.

5. All private property, all forms of money and obligations to pay money, should bear their just proportion of the taxes. We demand a graduated income-tax.

6. We demand the amelioration of the condition of labor by enforcing the sanitary laws in industrial establishments, by the abolition of the convict labor system, by a rigid inspection of mines and factories, by a reduction of the hours of labor in Industrial establishments, by fostering educational institutions, and by abolishing child labor.

7. We condemn all importations of contract labor, made with a view of reducing to starvation wages the workingmen of this country, and demand laws for its prevention.

8. We insist upon a constitutional amendment reducing the terms of United States Senators.

9. We demand such rules for the government of Congress as shall place all representatives of the people upon an equal footing, and take away from committees a veto-power greater than that of the President.

10. The question as to the amount of duties to be levied upon various articles of import has been agitated and quarreled over, and has divided communities for nearly a hundred years. It is not now and never will be settled unless by the abolition of indirect taxation. It is a convenient issue—always raised when the people are excited over abuses in their midst. We favor a wise revision of the tariff laws, with a view to raising a revenue from the luxuries rather than necessaries; we insist that as an economic question its importance is insignificant as compared with financial issues; for, whereas we have suffered our worst panics under low and also under high tariff, we have never suffered from a panic or seen our factories or workshops closed while the volume of money in circulation was adequate to the needs of commerce. Give our farmers and manufacturers money as cheap as you now give it to our bankers, and they can pay high wages to labor and compete with all the world.

More Information

- Keller, Morton. *Affairs of State: Public Life in Late-Nineteenth Century America.* Cambridge: Harvard University Press, 1977.
- Mitchell, Wesley. *Gold, Prices, and Wages under the Greenback Standard.* New York: A.M. Kelley, 1966.
- Nugent, Walter T. K. *Money and American Society, 1865–1880.* New York: Free Press, 1968.

On the Web

- Greenback Party Platform. *http://www.geocities.com/CollegePark/Quad/6460/doct/884grbk.html.*
- Greenbacks. *http://www.bartleby.com/65/gr/Greenbac.html.*
- Morris, Charles (ed.) "Financial Panic of 1873." excerpt from *The Great Republic by the Master Historians, Vol. III.* New York: Belcher, 1902. *http://www.publicbookshelf.com/public_html/The_Great_Republic_By_the_Master_Historians_Vol_III/panicof1_hd.html.*
- Panic of 1873. *http://www.u-s-history.com/pages/h213.html.*

National Silver Party, 1880–1904

FlashFocus: National Silver Party

Origins

The National Silver Party was an alliance of politicians, mostly from western states, determined to reestablish silver's role as money (in the form of coins) alongside gold during the last two decades of the nineteenth century. The party began as a state organization in Nevada; when it expanded its reach to other western states (including those with significant silver deposits, such as Colorado, Idaho, and Utah), it was in the form of backing Democratic William Jennings Bryan in the 1896 presidential election (which Bryan lost). As a single-issue party, National Silver faded quickly from national politics, although it remained active in Nevada.

Issue

Bimetallism. The National Silver Party had a single issue: restoration of silver as recognized legal money, in the form of coins. Silver had lost this status in 1873, leaving gold as the sole basis for U.S. currency. The National Silver Party rose in Nevada, the source of new silver discoveries in the 1880s; it also gained support from other western states where farmers advocated an increase in the money supply (which silver would have facilitated) in order to make it easier to pay debts. Against the silver interests were eastern industrialists, dominant in the Republican Party, who insisted that all currency should be based on gold.

Impact

The National Silver Party in the end had minimal impact, either on monetary policy or on any other topic. Following Bryan's loss of the 1896 presidential election to Republican William McKinley, an economic recovery starting in 1898 resulted in easier times for hard-pressed western farmers, who soon lost interest in the cause of free silver (unlimited coinage of silver) and reverted to supporting either the Democrats or Republicans.

See also: Silver Republicans, p. 77; People's Party, p. 98; Greenback Party, p. 88; Election of 1896, Vol. 1, p. 105.

The National Silver Party never ran a candidate for president or even began to challenge the dominant Republicans and Democrats for control of Congress. Rather, the party illustrated the inherent weakness of parties that have a single issue—in this case, the unlimited use of silver as money in the form of coins (free silver)—appealing to a limited constituency.

In a larger sense, however, the free silver issue symbolized a larger political struggle occurring in the last two decades of the nineteenth century, pitting entrenched interests of eastern bankers and industrialists against western farmers and miners. Two decades after the Civil War, the East-West competition for influence had largely supplanted the older North-South rivalry for power and influence on the federal level. As in the earlier contest, the interests of the Northeast were victorious.

Genesis of the National Silver Party

The Civil War created a financing crisis for the government. President Abraham Lincoln (see Vol. 1, p. 69) pushed through statehood for Nevada in 1863 in order to acquire gold and silver output from the Comstock Lode, a major discovery of gold and especially silver ore near what is now Virginia City, Nevada, but even this was insufficient to meet the government's military expenses. Consequently, the government began printing paper money not backed by metal (meaning, paper currency could not be exchanged for gold or silver). The downside of such currency (called "greenbacks" because one side was printed in green ink) was that the supply of money grew without regard to growth in real economic output (goods and services), leading to inflation (higher prices). After the Civil War (1861–65), the federal government stopped printing greenbacks and gradually returned to a bimetallic standard (currency backed by either gold or silver). In 1873, there was an imbalance of gold and silver supplies, and under pressure from bankers, both in the United States and abroad, the United States passed the Coinage Act. The act listed all the coins to be minted by the government—and made no mention of the silver dollar. In this way, silver was eliminated as a source of currency, leaving only gold to be used as coins or to back paper currency (which in effect were certificates that a bank had a certain amount of gold on deposit). The Coinage Act was followed by the Panic of 1873, ushering in a prolonged economic recession that was followed by two decades of deflation (falling prices). Falling prices hit western farmers particularly hard. While their crops brought in fewer dollars, payments on their debts remained steady. Desperate for economic relief, farmers turned to free silver as a solution—the unlimited coinage of silver, with the expectation that more money in circulation would send prices upward. In the 1880s and 1890s, monetary policy became a focus of attention, especially in the West, and lay behind the rise of the Greenback Party (see p. 88) and the Silver Republicans (see p. 77), as well as the National Silver Party. To eastern bankers and industrialists, who generally owned significant amounts of gold (or currency that could be converted into gold), the prospect of adding to the money supply was unacceptable. They feared that a sudden bulge in the supply of currency without a corresponding increase in economic activity would lead to inflation (higher prices) and would also have the effect of reducing the value of debts (since each dollar repaid would be worth less in terms of goods). Many industrial workers also feared inflation, reckoning their cost of rent and food might go up faster than wages.

Thus, a seemingly abstract debate over the monetary policy (whether all currency should be backed by gold versus allow-

The principal issue advocated by the National Silver Party was the use of both gold and silver as currency. This prosilver cartoon shows American workers and farmers being weighed down by the burden of the gold standard, forced upon them by a wealthy businessman.

ing currency to be backed by both gold and silver) translated into a struggle for both political and economic power between eastern banking and manufacturing interests. In Nevada, especially, government purchases of silver slowed after 1873, which had an adverse effect on the state's economy.

National Silver Party

In 1892, a local Silver Party in Nevada swept state elections, including the governor's office. Support for the Silver Party came from disaffected Republicans as well as some Democrats. In the 1892 presidential election, the electoral votes of Nevada, Colorado, and Idaho all went to the People's Party (also called Populists, see p. 98), which endorsed free coinage of silver.

In 1896, a national Silver Party held its convention in St. Louis, its first (and last) national meeting for the purpose of nominating a president. The Republicans that year nominated William McKinley of Ohio (see Vol. 1, p. 106), who supported the gold standard. The Democrats, carried along by a dramatic prosilver speech delivered by William Jennings Bryan (see Vol. 1, p. 107), nominated the little known Nebraska politician as president and also adopted a free silver plank in their platform.

With a free silver candidate running as a Democrat, the nascent National Silver Party debated what to do. Should they proceed with their own presidential ticket, back Bryan for president but nominate their own vice president, or simply back the Democratic ticket of Bryan and Arthur Sewall of Maine? (The People's Party, or Populists, also nominated Bryan, but named their own vice presidential candidate, Thomas Watson of Georgia.) The Silver Party decided that the best way to guarantee success for their platform issue was to join in supporting Bryan and the Democratic ticket, but at the same time to adopt their own platform.

Defeat and Demise

Bryan lost the election to William McKinley (see Vol. 1, p. 106), the Republican, marking the end of the Silver Party's involvement as a national party. Under the name Silver-Democrat Party, prosilver advocates elected local candidates in Nevada for several years, but the era of the silver parties ended in 1896. An economic recovery in 1898, followed by passage of the Gold Standard Act in 1900, effectively ended the campaign for free silver, although Silver Republicans continued their quest with a convention in Kansas City in 1900.

Platform of the National Silver Party, 1896

The fact that the National Silver Party had a single issue—the reintroduction of silver as part of the American monetary system—is reflected in the party's sole national platform, adopted at its 1896 convention in St. Louis, when the party endorsed the Democratic presidential candidate, William Jennings Bryan:

The National Silver Party in convention assembled hereby adopts the following declaration of principles:

First—The paramount issue at this time in the United States is indisputably the money question. It is between the gold standard, gold bonds and bank currency on the one side, and the bimetallic standard, no bonds and Government currency on the other side.

On this issue we declare ourselves to be in favor of a distinctively American financial system. We are unalterably opposed to the single gold standard and demand the immediate restoration to the constitutional standard of gold and silver by the restoration by this government, independent of any foreign power, of the unrestricted coinage of gold and silver as the standard money at the ratio of 16 to 1 and upon terms of exact equality as they existed prior to 1873; the silver coin to be a full legal tender, equally with gold, for all debts and use, public and private; and we favor such legislation as will prevent for the future the demonetization of any kind of legal tender money by private contract.

We hold that the power to hold and regulate a paper currency is inseparable from the power to coin money, and hence that all currency intended to circulate as money should be issued and its volume controlled by the general Government only, and should be legal tender.

We are unalterably opposed to the issue by the United States of interest-bearing bonds in time of peace, and we denounce as a blunder worse than a crime the present Treasury policy, incurred by a Republican House [of Representatives], of plunging into debt by hundreds of millions in the vain attempt to maintain the gold standard by borrowing gold; and we demand the payment of all coin obligations of the United States, as provided by existing laws, in either gold or silver coin, at the option of the Government and not at the option of the creditor.

Second—That over and above all other questions of policy, we are in favor of restoring to the people of the United States the time-honored money of the Constitution—gold and silver; not one but both—the money of Washington and Hamilton, and Jefferson and Monroe, and Jackson and Lincoln, to the end that the American people may receive honest pay for an honest product; that the American debtor may pay his just obligations in an honest standard and not in a standard that has appreciated 100 percent above all the great staples of our country; and to the end, further, that silver standard countries may be deprived of the unjust advantage they now enjoy in the difference in exchange between gold and silver—an advantage which tariff legislation cannot overcome.

We therefore confidently appeal to the people of the United States to leave in abeyance for the moment all other questions, however important and even momentous they may appear, to sunder if need be all former ties and affiliations and unite in one supreme effort to free themselves and their children from the domination of the money power—a power more destructive than any which has ever been fastened upon the civilized men of any race or in any age. And upon the consummation of our desires and efforts, we invoke the gracious favor of divine Providence.

More Information

▶ *Congressional Quarterly's Guide to U.S. Elections.* Washington, D.C.: Congressional Quarterly, 1994.
▶ Dewey, Davis Rich. *National Problems, 1885–1897.* New York: Greenwood Press, 1968.
▶ Morgan, H. Wayne. *From Hayes to McKinley; National Party Politics, 1877–1896.* Syracuse, NY: Syracuse University Press, 1969.
▶ Ness, Immanuel (ed.). *The Encyclopedia of Third Parties in America.* Armonk, NY: M. E. Sharpe Reference, 1998.

On the Web

▶ McMaster, John Bach. *A Brief History of the United States,* Chapter 33, A Quarter Century of Struggle over Industrial Questions, 1872 to 1897. Electronic text from Project Gutenburg. *http://www.nalanda.nitc.ac.in/resources/english/etext-project/history/briefusa/chapter35.html.*
▶ Political History of Nevada, Nevada State Library and Archives. *http://dmla.clan.lib.nv.us/docs/nsla/archives/political/politic.htm.*
▶ The Silver Party. 1896: The Presidential Campaign. Vassar University. *http://projects.vassar.edu/1896/silverparty.html.*

Socialist Labor Party, 1874–1976

FlashFocus: Socialist Labor Party

Origins

Formed in 1874 in New York, the Socialist Labor Party was the first national party advocating socialism. Initially calling themselves the Social Democratic Workingmen's Party, the group changed its name three years later to the Socialist Labor Party. The party favored democratic control of economic institutions, such as corporations, as well as political institutions. It advocated workers' rights and an equitable distribution of wealth.

Issues

Socialist revolution. The party advocated the seizure of the "means of production"—factories and farms—by organized workers from private owners. Socialists believed that capitalism fostered the concentration of wealth among an elite few and reduced the individual worker to being nothing more than a dehumanized, replaceable part. The party blamed social ills, like widespread poverty and crime, on the capitalist system.

Government. The Socialist Labor Party envisioned a government made up of democratically elected representatives from industrial and agricultural workers. The party called for the abolition of the executive branch of the federal government and the Senate. In the place of the presidency would be an executive board elected by the public. The House of Representatives would then be the sole legislative body.

Legal code. The party called for a uniform criminal and civil law to be applicable throughout United States and to be administered at no cost to citizens. The party also opposed capital punishment.

Impact

The Socialist Labor party ran presidential candidates in every election from 1892 through 1976. The high point of the party's success came in 1896, when Simon Wing won 36,356 votes (three-tenths of one percent). The party was one of several socialist political organizations active in the United States. When Socialist Labor leader Daniel DeLeon lost the support of party moderates due to his overbearing and rigid positions, the Socialist Party of Eugene Debs welcomed them, reducing the Socialist Laborites to a much smaller membership.

See also: Social Democratic Party, p. 102; Socialist Party, p. 116; Communist Party, p. 128.

During the nineteenth century, the Industrial Revolution dramatically changed the character of the American economy and the conditions of its workforce. As new factories sprang up, laborers were often subject to hazardous working conditions and low wages. The attractions of socialism—public ownership and control of "the means of production," meaning factories—resonated with many workers, and socialist political organizations gained strength in the United States.

The Socialist Labor Party was formed in 1874 by members of the European-based Socialist International in New York, officially adopting the name Socialist Labor Party in 1877 after first being known as the Socialist Democratic Workingman's Party. The party was the first national party in the United States that endorsed Marxism (the theory enunciated by writer Karl Marx stating that control of society by the working class is inevitable and should be speeded along by revolution). At first, the party worked in conjunction with other small parties on the left wing of the political spectrum, including the Greenback Party (see p. 88).

In 1886, the Socialist Labor Party gained notoriety for its indirect involvement with the Haymarket Square bombings in Chicago during a widespread strike. In one case, a bomb was thrown into a group of police officers battling strikers. Although no evidence was ever produced proving responsibility, several former members of the Socialist Labor Party were convicted of a conspiracy to murder the policemen and sentenced to death.

One of the most prominent members of the Socialist Labor Party in its heyday was Daniel DeLeon, a former law professor at New York's Columbia University. DeLeon was influenced by the writings of socialist theorist Edward Bellamy, and in 1890 DeLeon joined the Socialist Labor Party. Within a year he was editing the party's newspaper, *The People,* and he won about 13,000 votes in the New York gubernatorial race of 1891. DeLeon also wrote two books—*Socialist Reconstruction of Society* and *As to Politics*—in which he argued for the integration of Marxism into the American political system.

For DeLeon, integrating Marxism meant the violent overthrow of capitalist society. He argued that American workers, abused by the forces of capitalism, were ready for a revolution. DeLeon hoped the party would benefit from the depression and unemployment that characterized the American economy for much of the 1890s. His vision was that workers, in their new role as factory owners, could control the economy and administer it in the best interests of the society at large. Under DeLeon's militant leadership, the Socialist Labor Party made its best electoral showings in local New York races in 1898.

The party ran its first presidential candidate in 1892. Simon Wing of Massachusetts was the party's candidate, running on a platform that argued that the inalienable rights outlined by Thomas Jefferson (see Vol. 1, p. 13) in the Declaration of Independence (life, liberty, and the pursuit of happiness) were impossible to fulfill under the American economic system. Instead, these ideals could only be achieved if the people owned and controlled government and the means of industrial production. Wing collected only 21,173 votes in the presidential election.

FlashFocus: Daniel DeLeon

Born: December 14, 1852, Curacao, Venezuela
Died: May 11, 1914, New York, New York
Political Career: Socialist Labor candidate for governor of New York, 1891, 1902; Socialist Labor candidate for several New York state assembly seats and for representative from New York.

DeLeon was home schooled until the death of his father, after which he studied in Germany and in Amsterdam. He came to New York in 1874 and first worked as editor of a Spanish paper that supported Cuban revolutionaries. He also worked as a schoolteacher. During this time DeLeon took law and political science classes at Columbia University, graduating in 1878. He opened a private law practice in Texas, and after practicing for a few years, he returned to New York in 1883. He won a lectureship at Columbia, which he held until 1889.

While lecturing at Columbia, DeLeon developed an interest in social issues. He joined the Knights of Labor in 1888, the Nationalist movement in 1889, and the Socialist Labor Party in 1890. He was made the party lecturer in 1891 and was the Socialist Labor candidate for governor of New York that same year. In 1892, he became editor of the party's newspaper, *The People*. He was again candidate for governor of New York in 1902 and ran several other unsuccessful campaigns for seats in the state assembly and Congress.

DeLeon became a clear leader in the party soon after joining and maintained this leadership for many years. Then, because of an ideological split in the party over issues of organized labor, a faction broke away from the Socialist Labor Party to form the Socialist Party of America. DeLeon helped found the International Workers of the World, but again ideological differences with other leaders of the group led DeLeon and his followers to break away and form their own rival group, the Workers' International Industrial Union. As before, DeLeon's smaller and weaker group ultimately could not compete with its larger rival. He continued to work for the socialist cause and wrote many pamphlets that were later admired by Vladimir Lenin, leader of the Russian Revolution in 1917. DeLeon died at a New York hospital in 1914.

The Socialist Labor Party made modest gains in the 1896 presidential election when they presented Charles Matchett, also of Massachusetts, as their candidate. Running on a platform that advocated a progressive income tax, demanded mandatory education for children 14 and under, and called for universal suffrage, the party won 36,356 votes. Another Massachusetts nominee, Joseph Malloney, garnered around 41,000 votes in the 1900 presidential election.

Thinning of the Ranks

While DeLeon's program appealed to many industrial workers, his autocratic style and opposition to the organized labor movement, which aimed to improve workers' lives through labor unions rather than revolution, drove many party members away and stirred internal rebellions. The Jewish Socialists in New York were eliminated from membership in 1897. Many disaffected former members of the Socialist Labor Party found a new home in the ranks of the Socialist Party (see p. 116) led by Eugene Debs (see Vol. 1, p. 110), organized in 1901.

Throughout the early to midtwentieth century, the Socialist Labor Party platforms were generally consistent in their main themes. The party urged workers to organize with the common goal of destroying capitalism, eventually calling for a "Socialist industrial republic" to be administered by workers.

Because of the much stronger Socialist Party organization, as well as the New Deal policies of President Franklin Roosevelt (see Vol. 1, p. 141) in the 1930s, the Socialist Labor Party found itself on the margins of the political scene. Its warnings of social upheaval in the wake of the Depression went unheard, and in 1936 the party's presidential candidate managed to win only 12,790 votes.

The Socialist Labor Party continued to run presidential candidates without much impact. The party blamed the American economic system for ills ranging from economic recessions to mental illness and alcoholism. The party's last presidential candidate was Jules Levin of New Jersey, who ran in 1976, although the party continued to exist and to advocate seizure of the means of production. In the early twenty-first century, the party continued publishing *The People* six times a year.

Platform of the Socialist Labor Party, 1892

The Socialist Labor Party's first presidential candidate was Charles Wing of Massachusetts, who ran in 1892. The party platform that year gave the party a fundamental base and theme for subsequent election campaigns. Excerpts from the 1892 platform:

The Socialist Labor Party of the United States, in convention assembled, reasserts the inalienable right of all men to life, liberty, and the pursuit of happiness.

With the founders of the American republic, we hold that the purpose of government is to secure every citizen in the enjoyment of this right; but in the light of our social conditions we hold, furthermore, that no such right can be exercised under a system of economic inequality, essentially destructive of life, of liberty, and of happiness.

With the founders of this republic we hold that the true theory of politics is that the machinery of government must be owned and controlled by the whole people; but in the light of our industrial development we hold, furthermore, that the true theory of economics is that the machinery of production must likewise belong to the people in common.

To the obvious fact that our despotic system of economics is the direct opposite of our democratic system of politics, can plain-

ly be traced the existence of a privileged class, the corruption of government by that class, the alienation of public property, public franchises and public functions to that class, and the abject dependence of the mightiest of nations upon that class. Again, through the perversion of democracy to the ends of plutocracy, labor is robbed of the wealth which it alone produces, is denied the means of self-employment, and, by compulsory idleness in wage-slavery, is even deprived of the necessaries of human life. Human power and natural forces are thus wasted, that the plutocracy may rule. Ignorance and misery, with all their concomitant evils, are perpetuated, that the people may be kept in bondage. Science and invention are diverted from their humane purpose to the enslavement of women and children.

Against such a system the Socialist Labor Party once more enters its protest. Once more it reiterates its fundamental declaration, that private property in the natural sources of production and in the instruments of labor is the obvious cause of all economic servitude and political dependence; and

WHEREAS, the time is fast coming when, in the natural course of social evolution, this system, through the destructive action of its failures and crises, on the one hand, and the constructive tendencies of its trusts and other capitalistic combinations, on the other hand, shall have worked out its own downfall; therefore, be it

RESOLVED, That we call upon the people to organize with a view to the substitution of the co-operative commonwealth for the present state of planless production, industrial war, and social disorder – a commonwealth in which every worker shall have the free exercise and full benefit of his faculties, multiplied by all the modern factors of civilization. We call upon them to unite with us in a mighty effort to gain by all practicable means the political power.

In the meantime, and with a view to immediate improvement in the coalition of labor, we present the following "Demands":

Social Demands

1. Reduction of the hours of labor in proportion to the progress of production.

2. The United States shall obtain, possession of the railroads, canals, telegraphs, telephones, and all other means of public transportation and communication.

3. The municipalities to obtain possession of the local rail roads, ferries, water-works, gas-works, electric plants, and all industries requiring municipal franchise.

4. The public lands to be declared inalienable. Revocation of all land grants to corporations or individuals, the conditions of which have not been complied with.

5. Legal incorporation by the States of local Trade Unions which have no national organization.

6. The United States to have the exclusive right to issue money.

7. Congressional legislation providing for the scientific management of forests and waterways, and prohibiting the waste of the natural resources of the country.

8. Inventions to be free to all; the inventors to be remunerated by the nation.

9. Progressive income tax and tax on inheritances; the smaller incomes to be exempt.

Political Demands

1. The people have the right to propose laws and to vote upon all measures of importance, according to the Referendum principle.

2. Abolition of the Presidency, Vice-Presidency, and Senate of the United States. An Executive Board to be established, whose members are to be elected, and may at any time be re-called by the House of Representatives as the only legislative body.

More Information

▶ Kraditor, Aileen S. *The Radical Persuasion, 1890–1917*. Baton Rouge: Louisiana State University Press, 1981.

▶ Sassoon, Donald. *One Hundred Years of Socialism*. New York: New Press, 1996.

On the Web

▶ Socialist Labor Party. *http://reference.allrefer.com/encyclopedia/S/SocLab.html*.

▶ Socialist Labor Party of America. *http://www.slp.org/*.

People's Party (Populists), 1891–1908

Flash Focus: People's Party (Populists)

Origins

Disaffected farmers struggling with poor economic conditions gathered in Cincinnati, Ohio, in May 1891 to form a political party. The membership of the party came mainly from a group called the Farmers' Alliance. The party nominated James Weaver of Iowa for president in the 1892 election; he carried four states. In 1896, the party nominated William Jennings Bryan, who was simultaneously the nominee of the Democratic Party. Bryan lost to Republican William McKinley.

Issues

Silver. The party demanded that the government coin silver and gold at a ratio of 16:1 without the consent of foreign governments. (Under the monetary system in effect at the time, the value of the U.S. dollar depended on international acceptance of how much money the U.S. government put into circulation.) The party expected that if the amount of currency in circulation rose, it would result in higher commodity prices and make it easier for farmers to pay off their loans.

Railroads. Reflecting the feeling of many farmers that they were victimized by railroad charges to haul their crops to market, the Populists advocated government ownership and operation of the railroads. The party believed that the government would be best suited to maintain the rights of citizens.

Civil rights. James Weaver, the party's 1892 presidential candidate, campaigned for full and equal civil rights for black Americans and a free and fair ballot in the South, where African Americans were often denied the right to vote.

Graduated income tax. Populists of all stripes generally agreed on the principle that those with a greater amount of wealth should bear a greater amount of the tax burden.

Direct democracy. The party advocated the direct election of the president and U.S. senators. Many states elected senators by a vote of the state legislature during this period.

Impact

Using silver as legal coins alongside gold was a key goal of the People's Party. Its failure to push through this policy caused the party to lose support. Aligning with the Democratic Party in 1896 created an identity crisis for the People's Party as an institution separate from the Democrats, and the party declined thereafter. Despite its lack of electoral success, many Populist causes, such as direct election of senators, a graduated income tax, and civil rights for African Americans, eventually came to pass.

See also: Greenback Party, p. 88; Social Democratic Party, p. 102; Progressive ("Bull Moose") Party, p. 121.

After the Civil War (1861–65) and for the rest of the nineteenth century, economic conditions in the United States did not favor farmers. Commodity prices fell, the cost of shipping crops to market by railroad rose, and many farmers found themselves with mortgage debts that were unmanageable. As a group, farmers became frustrated, and many came to believe they were victims of the nation's new industrial economy, even though the reasons for their economic plight had more to do with fluctuations in international markets for crops such as corn and wheat.

Origins of the People's Party

The fundamental problem with the agricultural economy beginning in the 1870s was the steady drop in commodity prices. After the Civil War, more land came under cultivation, and the market for agricultural goods became saturated. Crops from newly cultivated land in the West were brought to eastern markets by newly constructed railroads. The result was a new abundance of crops, and prices were driven down by the law of supply and demand. Pressed by the low prices their crops brought, American farmers focused on the rates charged by railroads to haul farm products to eastern markets, rates that did not fall in line with agricultural prices. As commodity prices declined, debts of the individual American farmer began to increase. To compensate for low prices, farmers produced ever more crops to bring in consistent income and thereby exacerbated the problem of excess supply.

The People's Party focused much attention on railroads, which in the last half of the nineteenth century were politically active in many states and often enjoyed special government favors. Some state governments invested in railroads; in other cases, federal land grants (later sold to prospective farmers) helped finance the expansion of railroads westward. Thus, an industry that was intimately linked to the financial viability of western farming became a prime target of farmers during hard times.

The first group that tried to give farmers a significant political voice was the Patrons of Husbandry, known as the Grange. It was headed by a clerk in the federal Agriculture Department, Oliver Hudson Kelley. The Grange advocated a cooperative movement among farmers to build strength—a form of trade union among independent farmers—but this strategy was largely unsuccessful. Many Grangers looked to the National Farmers' Alliance, a group that viewed any and all agricultural difficulties as economic in nature. The Farmers' Alliance also stressed cooperative marketing to end farmers' reliance on banks, which made loans in exchange for liens on crops (a lien is a legal claim which enabled a banks to claim the crops if farmers failed to repay their loans). Most of the leaders of the Farmers' Alliance came from the Greenback Party (see p. 88) and from southern and Midwestern farm cooperative associations.

A People's Party was formed in Kansas in 1890 based on a platform that was later adopted by the national party—government ownership of railroads (to control freight rates), unlimited coinage of silver (to put more money in circulation and drive down the value of mortgage debts), and a system called a "sub treasury" in which farmers could hand over ownership of a crop to a government warehouse and receive a loan for 80 percent of the crop's value at two percent annual interest, effectively making the government, instead of banks, the preferred lender to farmers.

When the Kansas People's Party expanded to become a national party in 1891 at a convention in Cincinnati, Ohio, the People's Party (also known as the Populist Party) sought an alliance with industrial workers in the belief that the "public good" should take precedence over private interests. To that end, the party supported eight-hour workdays in factories and restrictions on immigration (effectively limiting the flow of new industrial workers competing for available jobs). The party also tried to bring black farmers into the party, but this caused the movement to stall in the South, where race relations overshadowed economic reform. In the end, the Populist Party received the support of white land-owning cotton farmers in the South and wheat farmers in the West.

The Populists nominated James Weaver (see p. 90) of Iowa as their 1892 presidential candidate. Weaver, who had lost in the 1880 presidential election (see Vol. 1, p. 90) as the Greenback candidate, campaigned mainly in the West before enthusiastic crowds. Weaver carried five states and won 1,024,280 votes (8.5 percent). The party elected six senators and seven representatives to Congress.

While the People's Party candidates who won election in state government positions struggled—the party did not win enough legislative seats to effect much change—the dour economic climate throughout the country gave rise to populist fervor. President Grover Cleveland (see Vol. 1, p. 95) alienated supporters of free silver (unlimited use of silver as money) through his support of the gold standard that required paper currency to be backed by gold deposits. Workers were also put off by Cleveland's use of the army to defeat a strike conducted by railroad workers. Although the People's Party did not do as well as it had hoped in the 1894 congressional elections, the stage was set for a serious run at the presidency in 1896, when the party decided to focus on the silver issue as its main appeal to the electorate.

Populists were faced with a political dilemma, however, when the Republican Party nominated William McKinley (see Vol. 1, p. 106), who favored the gold standard, and the Democratic Party nominated William Jennings Bryan (see Vol. 1, p. 107), who was for free silver. The Populists had to decide whether to nominate their own candidate, thereby risking a split in the free silver vote, or join in the endorsement of Democrat Bryan. The party decided to endorse Bryan as its own candidate,

FlashFocus: Charles William Macune

Born: May 20, 1851, Kenosha, Wisconsin
Died: November 3, 1940, Fort Worth, Texas
Political Career: President of Farmers' Alliance, 1886–90.

After his father's death, Charles Macune moved with his mother to Freeport, Illinois, where he attended school until going to work on a farm at age 10 to help support his family. After the Civil War, Macune moved to California and worked as a rancher, then moved to Kansas where he joined the circus and later worked as a cattle driver. He traveled to Burnett, Texas, in 1874, and then to San Saba, Texas, where he worked as a house painter while studying medicine and law. He passed his medical exam and for the next few years practiced medicine.

Macune joined the Farmers' Alliance, a trade group by which farmers tried to join forces to get better prices and pursue their financial interests. In 1886, Macune became chairman of its executive committee. Macune worked to expand the Farmers' Alliance and to join together with other state chapters. The Texas Farmers' Alliance soon merged with several other similar alliances in the South, forming a new group called the Farmers' Alliance and Industrial Union, of which Macune was president.

Macune was wary of the notion of taking the Farmers' Alliance to the status of a political third party; but when the People's Party emerged in 1892, nominating a candidate for president, Macune gave it his enthusiastic support. There were, however, accusations that Macune was paid to tell Farmers' Alliance supporters to support Grover Cleveland for president, rather than the People's Party candidate, and this cost him the trust of members of the larger populist movement. At the 1892 Farmers' Alliance convention, he was defeated by a Populist for the presidential nomination. He left the movement in 1893 and returned to Texas. He briefly published a newspaper in Cameron, Texas, then moved to Beaumont to practice law. He also served as a preacher in small rural towns and did volunteer medical work. He died in Fort Worth, Texas, in 1940.

although it nominated a separate candidate for vice president.

Despite efforts by Democrats and Populists to combine forces in individual states, Bryan was beaten by the well-organized and handsomely financed Republican Party.

End of the People's Party

The People's Party lost a great deal of its identity as a separate party in 1896. New discoveries of gold in South Africa and the Yukon also robbed the issue of free silver of some of its appeal, even as prices for agricultural goods began to recover. The People's Party made several attempts at revival—in 1904, a Populist convention nominated a presidential ticket that won over 114,000 votes—but it could not sustain a strong effort. No members of the Populist Party sat in Congress after 1903.

People's Party Platform 1892 "The Omaha Platform"

Excerpts from the 1892 national platform of the People's Party, adopted in Omaha, Nebraska, on July 4, 1892:

We declare…

First.—That the union of the labor forces of the United States this day consummated shall be permanent and perpetual; may its spirit enter into all hearts for the salvation of the republic and the uplifting of mankind.

Second.—Wealth belongs to him who creates it, and every dollar taken from industry without an equivalent is robbery. "If any will not work, neither shall he eat." The interests of rural and civil labor are the same; their enemies are identical.

Third.—We believe that the time has come when the railroad corporations will either own the people or the people must own the railroads; and should the government enter upon the work of owning and managing all railroads, we should favor an amendment to the constitution by which all persons engaged in the government service shall be placed under a civil-service regulation of the most rigid character, so as to prevent the increase of the power of the national administration by the use of such additional government employees.

FINANCE.—We demand a national currency, safe, sound, and flexible issued by the general government only, a full legal tender for all debts, public and private, and that without the use of banking corporations; a just, equitable, and efficient means of distribution direct to the people, at a tax not to exceed 2 per cent, per annum, to be provided as set forth in the sub-treasury plan of the Farmers' Alliance, or a better system; also by payments in discharge of its obligations for public improvements.

We demand free and unlimited coinage of silver and gold at the present legal ratio of 16 to 1.

We demand that the amount of circulating medium be speedily increased to not less than $50 per capita.

We demand a graduated income tax.

We believe that the money of the country should be kept as much as possible in the hands of the people, and hence we demand that all State and national revenues shall be limited to the necessary expenses of the government, economically and honestly administered. We demand that postal savings banks be established by the government for the safe deposit of the earnings of the people and to facilitate exchange.

TRANSPORTATION.—Transportation being a means of exchange and a public necessity, the government should own and operate the railroads in the interest of the people. The telegraph and telephone, like the post-office system, being a necessity for the transmission of news, should be owned and operated by the government in the interest of the people.

LAND.—The land, including all the natural sources of wealth, is the heritage of the people, and should not be monopolized for speculative purposes, and alien ownership of land should be prohibited. All land now held by railroads and other corporations in excess of their actual needs, and all lands now owned by

KILLING THE GOOSE THAT LAID THE GOLDEN EGG

A Populist beheads "the goose that laid the golden egg," representing the Democratic Party, in this cartoon.

aliens should be reclaimed by the government and held for actual settlers only.

Expressions of Sentiments

Your Committee on Platform and Resolutions beg leave unanimously to report the following: Whereas, Other questions have been presented for our consideration, we hereby submit the following, not as a part of the Platform of the People's Party, but as resolutions expressive of the sentiment of this Convention.

RESOLVED, That we demand a free ballot and a fair count in all elections and pledge ourselves to secure it to every legal voter without federal intervention, through the adoption by the states of the unperverted Australian or secret ballot system.

RESOLVED, That the revenue derived from a graduated income tax should be applied to the reduction of the burden of taxation now levied upon the domestic industries of this country….

RESOLVED, That we condemn the fallacy of protecting American labor under the present system, which opens our ports to the pauper and criminal classes of the world and crowds out our wage-earners; and we denounce the present ineffective laws against contract labor, and demand the further restriction of undesirable emigration.

RESOLVED, That we cordially sympathize with the efforts of organized workingmen to shorten the hours of labor, and demand a rigid enforcement of the existing eight-hour law on Government work, and ask that a penalty clause be added to the said law....

RESOLVED, That we commend to the favorable consideration of the people and the reform press the legislative system known as the initiative and referendum.

RESOLVED, That we favor a constitutional provision limiting the office of President and Vice-President to one term, and providing for the election of Senators of the United States by a direct vote of the people....

(Reported in the Omaha, Nebraska, *Morning World-Herald*, July 5, 1892.)

More Information

- Hollingsworth, J. Rogers. *The Whirligig of Politics: The Democracy of Cleveland and Bryan.* Chicago: University of Chicago Press, 1963.
- Keller, Morton. *Affairs of State: Public Life in Late-Nineteenth Century America.* Cambridge: Harvard University Press, 1977.
- McSeveney, Samuel T. *The Politics of Depression: Political Behavior in the Northeast, 1893–1896.* New York: Oxford University Press, 1972.
- Tindall, George B. "The People's Party," in *History of U.S. Political Parties,* Arthur M. Schlesinger, Jr., ed. New York: R. R. Bowker Company, 1973.
- Watson, Thomas. *The People's Party Campaign Book, 1892.* New York: Arno Press, 1975.

On the Web

- People's Party Platform, 1896. *http://projects.vassar.edu/1896/peoplesplatform.html.*
- People's Party Platform. *http://usinfo.state.gov/usa/infousa/facts/democrac/29.htm.*
- Political Crisis of the 1890s: Populism. Digital History. *http://www.digitalhistory.uh.edu/database/article_display.cfm?HHID=157.*
- Rural Life in the Late 19th Century, Library of Congress. *http://memory.loc.gov/learn/features/timeline/riseind/rural/rural.html.*

Social Democratic Party, 1897

> ### Flash Focus: Social Democratic Party
>
> **Origins**
>
> The Social Democratic Party was formed in 1897 by politically active members of trade unions and left-wing journalists to advance the causes of socialism. It was one of numerous third parties to raise the socialism banner in the United States. Leading figures in the Social Democratic party were Eugene V. Debs, Victor Berger and Ella Reeve Bloor.
>
> **Issues**
>
> **Capitalism as a barrier to freedom.** The Social Democratic Party argued that as the working class became more and more dependent on corporations owned by a wealthy elite, freedom of the individual would suffer. Socialists saw capitalists (businessmen) as people willing to sacrifice the lives of their employees for higher profits. Social Democrats wanted to establish a new order in which the workers controlled their own destiny.
>
> **Public ownership of factories.** The Social Democratic Party called for public ownership of "all industries," as well as natural resources such as gold, silver, coal, and oil.
>
> **Rights of workers.** The party advocated a reduction of hours in the workday, federally funded insurance for workers, and government public works projects for the unemployed.
>
> **Voting.** Social Democrats favored the introduction of the referendum in national elections as opposed to devices such as the electoral college. The party supported the right to recall elected officials.
>
> **Impact**
>
> Two Social Democratic party members were elected to the state legislature in Massachusetts in 1898. Eugene Debs was the party's presidential nominee in 1900, gathering 96,978 votes. Many party members, including Debs, united with other small socialist parties in 1901, forming the Socialist Party of America.

See also: Socialist Party, p. 116; People's Party (Populists), p. 98; Eugene Debs, Vol. 1, p. 110.

Like many other smaller factions of what would eventually merge into the larger Socialist Party, the Social Democratic Party was founded on the underlying principle of socialism—democratic government control of industry. During the Industrial Revolution in the United States, corporations that mass-produced goods became more and more prevalent, and individual skilled workmen declined in relative importance. Workers were often exposed to dangerous working conditions and low wages. Socialists deplored the private ownership of what they referred to as "the means of production"—by which socialists meant factories, mines, and land—and advocated a takeover of private interests by an organized class of workers.

Like most socialists, the Social Democrats believed that capitalists—owners of businesses—controlled government actions as well as the economy. Their objective was to put the working class, with its far greater numbers, in charge of both government and economic institutions such as large companies.

Origins of the Social Democratic Party

The public face of the Social Democratic Party was Eugene V. Debs of Indiana, a former state legislator with a long history of political activism on behalf of labor. He had organized and led the American Railway Union and was serving as its president when the Social Democratic Party (originally named the Social Democracy of America) was organized. The railway union's participation in the 1894 strike of Pullman car workers landed Debs in jail for violating a federal court order to end the strike. In prison, Debs began studying socialist theory and was won over.

In the presidential election of 1900 (see Vol. 1, p. 109), Debs ran for president on the Social Democratic ticket, receiving 96,978 votes. He did not win any electoral votes.

The party later merged with the larger Socialist movement in the United States. Debs and the leaders of the Social Democrats jumped at the opportunity to advance the movement, and Debs was eventually nominated for president numerous times as the candidate of the Socialist Party, the surviving entity after the merger with the Socialist Labor Party (see p. 95) led by Morris Hillquit.

Debs also became the editor of the Socialist Party's weekly publication *Appeal to Reason* and built up a national following as a popular lecturer. In 1918, Debs was sentenced to prison for 10 years after being convicted of sedition for his opposition to American involvement in World War I. Campaigning from his jail cell, Debs polled nearly a million votes in the presidential election of 1920 (see Vol. 1, p. 128).

Platform of the Social Democrats, 1900

Eugene Debs first ran for the presidency under the banner of the Social Democratic Party in 1900. At the party convention in Rochester, New York, the delegates adopted a platform of principles.

The Social Democratic party, of the United States, in convention assembled, reaffirms its allegiance to the revolutionary principles of international socialism and declares the supreme political issue in America today to be the contest between the working class and the capitalist class for the possession of the powers of government. The party affirms its steadfast purpose to use those powers, once achieved, to destroy wage slavery, to abol-

ish the institution of private property in the means of production, and establish the co-operative commonwealth.

In the United States, as in all other civilized countries, the natural order of economic development has separated society into two antagonistic classes—the capitalists, a comparatively small class, the possessors of all the modern means of production and distribution (land, mines, machinery, and means of transportation and communication), and the large and ever-increasing class of wage-workers, possessing no means of production.

This economic supremacy has secured to the dominant class the full control of the government, the pulpit, the schools, and the public press; it has thus made the capitalist class the arbiter of the fate of the workers, whom it is reducing to a condition of dependence, economically exploited and oppressed, intellectually and physically crippled and degraded, and their political equality rendered a bitter mockery.

The contest between these two classes grows ever sharper. Hand in hand with the growth of monopolies goes the annihilation of small industries and of the middle class depending upon them; ever larger grows the multitude of destitute wage-workers and of the unemployed, and ever fiercer the struggle between the class of the exploiter and the exploited, the capitalists and the wage-workers....

The introduction of a new and higher order of society is the historic mission of the working class. All other classes, despite their apparent or actual conflicts, are interested in upholding the system of private ownership in the means of production. The Democratic, Republican, and all other parties which do not stand for the complete overthrow of the capitalist system of production, are alike the tools of the capitalist class. Their policies are injurious to the interest of the working class, which can be served only by the abolition of the profit system.

The workers can most effectively act as a class in their struggle against the collective power of the capitalist class only by constituting themselves into a political party, distinct and opposed to all parties formed by the propertied classes.

We, therefore, call upon the wage-workers of the United States, without distinction of color, sex, race, or creed, and upon all citizens in sympathy with the historic mission of the working class, to organize under the banner of the Social Democratic party, as a party truly representing the interests of the toiling masses and uncompromisingly waging war upon the exploiting class, until the system of wage slavery shall be abolished and the co-operative commonwealth shall be set up. Pending the accomplishment of this, our ultimate purpose, we pledge every effort of the Social Democratic party for the immediate improvement of the condition of labor and for the securing of its progressive demands.

More Information

▶ Buhle, Mari Jo, Paul Buhle, and Dan Georgakas (eds.) *Encyclopedia of the American Left*. New York: Oxford University Press, 1998.
▶ Kraditor, Aileen S. *The Radical Persuasion, 1890–1917*. Baton Rouge: Louisiana State University Press, 1981.

FlashFocus: Victor Louis Berger

Born: February 28, 1860, Nieder-Rehbach, Austria-Hungary
Died: July 16, 1929, Milwaukee, Wisconsin
Political Career: U.S. Representative from Wisconsin, 1910–12, 1923–28.

Victor Berger was educated at universities in Vienna, Austria, and Budapest, Hungary. At age 18 he immigrated to the United States, living first in Bridgeport, Connecticut, and then moving to Milwaukee, where he worked as a schoolteacher and was active in politics. He also founded a German-language newspaper, *Vorwarts*.

He was a member of the Socialist Labor Party, then joined a faction that broke away to form Social Democracy of America in 1897. When disagreements arose among the leaders, Berger and others broke away yet again to found the Social Democratic Party in 1898.

Berger was a clear leader in the Social Democratic Party; and when it merged with the Socialist Labor Party to form the Socialist Party of America, Berger was named to the national executive board. The Milwaukee branch of the party was well organized under Berger's leadership. Berger made a particular effort to establish a strong presence in the city, and the party organized numerous events in the community, regularly distributing pamphlets on various issues in order to maintain its visibility.

Berger was elected a city alderman-at-large in 1910 and was elected to Congress later the same year. He was the first Socialist to serve in the House of Representatives. After one term, he lost bids for reelection in 1912 and 1914.

Berger, like many other Socialists, opposed American involvement in World War I. In 1918, Berger was sentenced to 20 years in prison for opposing the war. While he was appealing the case, he was reelected to Congress, but the House of Representatives voted to deny him his seat because of his views on the war. A special election was then held to find a replacement, but Berger won the special election by an even greater margin. The House again refused to seat him. The Supreme Court heard his appeal and overturned his conviction in 1921, and Berger was reseated in the House in 1923. He continued to serve in the House until 1928. He died in 1929 after being injured in a streetcar accident.

▶ Ray, Ginger. *The Bending Cross: A Biography of Eugene Victor Debs*. Kirksville, MO: Thomas Jefferson University Press, 1992.
▶ Weinstein, James. *The Long Detour: The History and Future of the American Left*. Boulder, CO: Westview Press, 2003.

On the Web

▶ The American Movement. *http://www.marxists.org/archive/debs/*.
▶ Eugene V. Debs. h*ttp://www.iww.org/culture/biography/EugeneDebs1.shtml*.

- Guide to the Social-Democratic Party of America Records 1900–1905. Tamiment Library/Robert F. Wagner Labor Archives, New York University. *http://dlib.nyu.edu:8083/tamwagead/servlet/SaxonServlet?source=/sdp.xml&style=/saxon01t2002.xsl&part=body.*

Republican Party, 1900–32

> **FlashFocus: Republican Party, 1900–1932**
>
> **Origins**
>
> The Republican Party was well-positioned to govern at the beginning of the twentieth century, having elected William McKinley president and enjoying a majority in both houses of Congress. But changes in American society originating during the last three decades of the nineteenth century gave the Republicans a much rougher ride in the first half of the twentieth century. The party split between conservative and progressive wings in 1912, giving Democrats two consecutive presidential victories. After a period of prosperity in the 1920s, the Great Depression of the 1930s and World War II resulted in five consecutive Democratic victories between 1932 and 1948.
>
> **Issues**
>
> **Government regulation.** Theodore Roosevelt vigorously prosecuted businesses that established monopolies and championed federal regulations to insure fair and safe working conditions. Taft pulled back on Roosevelt's program, preferring to bring about change through the courts. Republicans were generally friendly to business as the economy boomed in the 1920s, and Calvin Coolidge lowered taxes and federal expenditures. Coolidge did, however, propose constitutional amendments to restrict child labor and to establish a minimum wage for women.
>
> **Cuts in military.** The horrors of World War I and the false assumption that the peace would last led to cuts in the military, as well as outlawing of the use of poisonous gas, which was widely employed in the war.
>
> **Depression.** The Republican Party suffered enormously due to being the administration in power at the onset of the Great Depression. Herbert Hoover made modest attempts at reviving the economy, but his policies were blamed for the lack of recovery.
>
> **Impact**
>
> Republicans dominated the first three decades of the twentieth century, electing Presidents William McKinley (1900), Theodore Roosevelt (1904), William Howard Taft (1908), Warren Harding (1920), Calvin Coolidge (1924), and Herbert Hoover (1928). The party controlled both houses of Congress from 1901 to 1911 and again from 1921 to 1933.

See also: Republican Party 1876–1900, p. 75; Republican Party 1932–68, p. 135; Democratic Party 1900–32, p. 111.

The Republican Party entered the twentieth century seemingly in a dominant position. Democrats had succeeded in electing a president only twice since the Civil War (1861–65) and would succeed only twice again between 1900 and 1932. But the outward appearances of Republican influence masked deep divisions within the party: between staunch probusiness conservatives and reform-minded progressives, and between the eastern, urban middle-class and rural farmers. In the period from 1900 to 1932, the divisions within the Republican Party were not just along economic lines but also along cultural and ethnic lines. Similar divisions tore at the Democratic Party. The twentieth century's first third was a time of rapid social change as well as economic change, all taking place in an unstable world.

Origins of the Republican Era

The Republican Party entered the twentieth century having dominated national politics since the end of the Civil War in 1865. Democrats could count on both congressional and electoral college votes from the states of the former Confederacy, but these were not enough to elect a president or control Congress. In the period from 1865 to 1933, covering 17 administrations, Republicans were in the White House for all but four. In the same period, Republicans had a majority in the House of Representatives for 20 of the 34 Congresses and a Senate majority for 28.

This long stretch of Republican domination covered a period of enormous change in the United States. Industrialization changed the face of the nation, replacing agriculture as the primary economic engine. With industrialization came a large mass of immigrants, including many from southern and eastern Europe, who did not share the northern European ethnic and religious background of earlier Americans. African Americans were liberated from slavery and gained the vote, as did women, after a long struggle. Through all these changes, the Republican Party generally managed to dominate, aided in part by sharp divisions among the Democrats.

As a general rule, Republicans represented middle- and upper-middle-class voters, including small businessmen, the growing class of white-collar workers, and professionals, as well as the corporate elite who counted on Republicans to represent their interests. Republicans were largely perceived as the party of native-born "old stock" Protestants, while newer immigrants from southern and eastern Europe, more likely to be working-class Catholics, were captured by the Democrats. Initially, Republicans also claimed the loyalty of African Americans, following the party's role in emancipation, although this loyalty was waning by 1932. As the twentieth century advanced, Republicans also made inroads among conservative white farmers in the Midwest and West against the Democrats on social issues, such as prohibition, which many urban Democrats openly opposed and flouted.

Although economics played an important role in elections—especially in 1896 (see Vol. 1, p. 105), when the nation was still trying to recover from a severe economic depression—there were other considerations at work in politics, particularly a strong sense of morality in government. Moral issues, for example, led Republicans to support measures like mandatory school attendance, limits on use of child labor, enforcement of blue laws (required business closure on Sundays), and laws banning birth control. Moral impulses often led rank-and-file Republicans to support legislation that was opposed by large corporations. It also fed the progressive wing of the party, especially in the first dozen years of the twentieth century, even while the more conservative, entrenched congressional Republican leaders could be counted on by corporate owners to back protective tariffs and the gold standard (all money to be based on gold deposits).

This progressive-conservative division in the Republican Party was captured by an editorial in the *New York Sun*, a probusiness newspaper, in 1904, after the presidential election victory of Theodore Roosevelt (see Vol. 1, p. 114), a progressive Republican: "We prefer the impulsive candidate of the party of conservatism," the paper said, "to the conservative candidate of the party which the business interests regard as permanently and dangerously impulsive."

The ethnic composition of Republicans also tended to coincide with geography. The party was dominant in New England states and across a swath of states from the Midwest to California, populated by people whose ancestors had moved west from New England. The ethnic backgrounds of these areas, and of the Republican Party generally, tended to be English, Scottish, Scotch-Irish, or Scandinavian, with a portion of the Protestant-German population.

Party Dominance

In 1900, the Republicans nominated incumbent President William McKinley (see Vol. 1, p. 106) to run against Democrat William Jennings Bryan (see Vol. 1, p. 107). At the Republican convention, McKinley yielded to the popular choice of the delegates and agreed to accept as his running mate former New York Governor Theodore Roosevelt. Roosevelt was, moreover, an energetic, young campaigner who carried the ball for the Republicans in a campaign largely masterminded by Senator Mark Hanna (see p. 76). The contest was a virtual rerun of the 1896 election, especially after Bryan insisted on running on the identical platform that emphasized the free coinage of silver alongside gold. After McKinley had defeated Bryan for a second time, Hanna (who once called Roosevelt a "madman") wrote to McKinley: "Your duty to the country is to live for four years from next March"—lest Roosevelt become president.

In fact, however, McKinley was assassinated in September 1901, just six months into his second term, leading Hanna to cry, "Now that damned cowboy is president!" The progressive wing of the party, represented by Roosevelt, had replaced the more conservative, business-friendly stream, represented by McKinley. The new president's first dramatic move came in 1902 when he ordered his attorney general to file suit to break up the Northern Securities Company, a trust that owned three previously competitive railroads (see Vol. 3, p. 80). Roosevelt was easily elected in his own right in 1904 (see Vol. 1, p. 113) against Democrat Alton Parker (see Vol. 1, p. 115), a conservative judge from New York running on a campaign of states' rights and the gold standard.

In his second term, Roosevelt pushed a program he called the "Square Deal": ending special privileges for the wealthy, regulation of large corporations, affirming the right of workers to organize in unions, and creating a professional federal civil service based on merit. It was a program designed to appeal to the middle- and lower-middle-class voters of the Republican progressive wing. Roosevelt promoted the Hepburn Act to institute federal meat inspection (a popular cause after publication of *The Jungle* by Upton Sinclair in 1907) and the Pure Food and Drug Act. By 1907, conservative Republicans, who remained in control of Congress, were in open rebellion against Roosevelt. Their ability to thwart popular opinion, especially in the Senate, reflected two facts of political life: state legislatures appointed most senators, and most state legislatures were dominated by conservative rural interests as a result of legislative districting that reflected a preindustrial era. This malapportionment of state legislatures also enabled conservatives to gerrymander House districts to give an advantage to conservatives that did not necessarily reflect popular opinion.

For his running mate in 1904, Roosevelt had chosen another Ohio politician, William Howard Taft (see Vol. 1, p. 118), whose real ambition in life was to become a judge (he became chief justice of the Supreme Court in 1921; see Vol. 3, p. 95). With Roosevelt's blessing, Taft became the Republican nominee in 1908, to run against Democrat William Bryan in the Nebraskan's third and final campaign for the White House (see Vol. 1, p. 117). Taft garnered 51.6 percent of the vote to Bryan's 43.1 percent, and Republicans retained control of both houses of Congress. As president, the legal-minded Taft was far more cautious than Roosevelt, believing there was no constitutional justification for some of Roosevelt's progressive reforms. Taft pulled back the reins on presidential power as it had been exercised by Roosevelt, preferring instead to use legal action in the courts to reform business practices. Roosevelt, who at first removed himself from the scene by going on an African safari, became increasingly frustrated with Taft's failure to follow through on his reforms, as did rank-and-file Republicans in the progressive wing of the party.

These progressives begged Roosevelt to challenge Taft for the 1912 nomination, which the former president reluctantly agreed to do. In presidential primaries that year, Roosevelt outpolled Taft by nearly two-to-one, but at the Republican convention, Roosevelt was thwarted by convention chairman Elihu Root, representing the more conservative, corporate-friendly branch of the party. Taft became the nominee, after which Roosevelt bolted from the party and ran as the candidate of the Progressive

("Bull Moose") Party (see p. 121). The contradictions between the probusiness conservatives and reform-minded progressives had broken out into the open and could no longer be contained within a single party. The result of the election in 1912 was that Taft, the third-place finisher after Roosevelt and Democrat Woodrow Wilson (see Vol. 1, p. 122), skimmed off enough conservative Republican votes to deny Roosevelt reelection (see Vol. 1, p. 121). Wilson, who had been elected governor of New Jersey on a progressive platform in 1910, gave Democrats control over the White House, while the party kept its majority in the House of Representatives and won control of the Senate.

End of the Progressive Era

After the Democratic victory of 1912, conservative Republicans in Congress waged steady warfare on most of Wilson's progressive program of social and economic reform, including creation of the Federal Reserve to regulate the supply of money (in lieu of the gold standard), enacted in 1913. In 1916, Roosevelt declined to run on the Progressive ticket. Progressives held their convention simultaneously with the Republicans in the same city (Chicago), waiting to see whom the Republicans would nominate. The Republicans turned to Supreme Court Justice Charles Hughes (see Vol. 3, p. 104 and Vol. 1, p. 126), a former governor of New York who had won progressive credentials with an investigation of the insurance industry in 1905. The Progressives also endorsed Hughes, effectively going out of business, ending what is sometimes called the Progressive Era.

But by 1916, the Great War in Europe between Britain and France on one side and Germany, the Austrian Empire, and the Ottoman Empire on the other, had largely displaced progressivism as the chief focus of the Republicans. New strains appeared in the Party over foreign policy. Republicans were now divided among isolationists, determined to keep the United States out of the European war; moderate internationalists; and ultranationalists, who thought the United States had a mission in the world and wanted to achieve national greatness. These divisions were not entirely new. The Spanish American War of 1898, which had established Roosevelt as a war hero and given the United States control of the Philippines, was an earlier expression of the ultranationalist wing of the party. On the other hand, Republican Senator Robert La Follette of Wisconsin (later founder of the Progressive Party of 1924; see p. 132), was a strict isolationist during Wilson's first term, urging that the United States not be drawn into the European conflict.

President Wilson was reluctant to enter the war, but by 1917 he was given little choice, as American shipping on the Atlantic came under attack by the German Navy. In April 1917, Wilson sent American soldiers to Europe on the side of Britain and France "to make the world safe for democracy."

Although entering the war had been controversial, it was Wilson's proposal for a League of Nations that generated the political heat after the war ended in November 1918. Republican ultranationalists, led by Senator Henry Cabot Lodge of Massachusetts (see p. 108), strongly opposed the League and made it a major campaign theme in 1920. Wilson, who made the League his major theme in the election, suffered a debilitating stroke, however, and American membership in the League was defeated in the Senate, which the Republicans had recaptured in 1919 and held until 1931.

The Roaring Twenties

The next 12 years largely belonged to the Republicans. They won three consecutive presidential elections: in 1920 with Warren Harding (see Vol. 1, p. 129); in 1924 with Harding's vice president, Calvin Coolidge (see Vol. 1, p. 133); and in 1928 with Herbert Hoover, a former commerce secretary and coordinator of U.S. food aid to Europe after World War I (see Vol. 1, p. 137).

In the decade known as the Roaring Twenties, social issues, rather than economic concerns or foreign policy, came to the forefront in Republican politics. To be sure, economic issues did not disappear, and Republicans generally came down on the side of corporations in the form of tariff protection against foreign competition, in favor of tax cuts, and in favor of injunctions against labor union strikes. In general, Republicans endorsed the spirit of *laissez faire*, preferring to avoid government involvement in economic affairs.

Instead, Republicans focused on three principle social issues: nativism, prohibition of alcohol, and anti-Catholicism.

Nativism refers to opposition to immigration. Starting in the 1880s, a large number of southern and eastern European immigrants had begun to change the ethnic character of the United States, from a nation of people whose ancestors predominantly came from the British Isles or northwestern Europe, to a much more diversified country. (An influx of Asian immigrants, which might have brought further changes to the ethnic mix, had largely been stopped by legislation in the 1880s; see Vol. 4, p. 188.) In the South and Midwest, particularly, a revived version of the Ku Klux Klan (see Vol. 4, p. 53) had attracted many members, including many conservative, rural Republicans, during the 1920s. In Indiana and Colorado, the Klan largely took over the Republican Party, promoting a campaign against civil rights for African Americans and against the Catholic Church. The Klan's program sometimes resulted in violence, particularly the lynching of African Americans, and was more often based on intimidation, with robed, hooded Klansmen burning crosses in nighttime rallies.

By no means did the Republican Party endorse the Ku Klux Klan or act in concert with it (with the exceptions of the party in Indiana and Colorado). But the party did support positions in line with the anti-immigrant sentiments, pushing through the Immigration Act of 1924 (see Vol. 4, p. 199) that effectively halted the flow of immigrants. Republicans also supported the Volstead Act, to enforce the Eighteenth Amendment, banning the sale of alcoholic beverages. The act was popular in the Republican "heartland" but largely opposed or ignored in big cities, where "speakeasies" represented a set of values and lifestyles that were abhorred in the countryside.

As a sign of the importance of such issues, in 1928 Hoover captured the electoral votes of Virginia, North Carolina, Tennessee, and Texas—the first defections of Confederate states to the Republicans since the era of Reconstruction (see Vol. 1, p. 136). Republicans also began to see the first signs that support by African Americans, originally secured during the Civil War, was beginning to slip.

Crash!

The economy came roaring back as the driving issue in politics in September 1929, when a sharp decline in stock prices on the New York Stock Exchange led to economic contraction. Unprecedented speculation in stock prices was a hallmark of the Roaring Twenties, when small investors got caught up in enthusiasm for quick riches through rising stock prices. That era, and the era of Republican domination, began unraveling in September 1929, when prices began falling. Between September 9 and November 13, 1929, stocks lost 47.9 percent of their value, making that crash the fourth worst in stock market history. Although the crash of 1929 marked the beginning of a prolonged economic depression, and is often thought of as "the crash," a worse decline occurred the next spring, from April 17 to July 8, 1930, when stocks lost 86 percent of their value.

The crash wiped out the equity of many investors. Business could not raise capital for expansion, and with so many savings gone (including the savings of small individual investors), the stock market decline ushered in the worst single economic depression of American history. Up to a quarter of the workforce suddenly became unemployed. Although President Hoover attempted countermeasures, such as persuading corporate leaders to avoid precipitous layoffs of workers, accelerating federal work projects, and calling on states to do the same, his efforts fell far short of countering the developing economic crisis. Even though Hoover had overseen government food aid to a Europe devastated by World War I, he declined to expand government involvement to social welfare during his administration.

Well into the 1930s, encampments of destitute workers, or farmers driven off their land by a devastating drought that accompanied the collapse of the industrial economy in the 1930s, were known as Hoovervilles.

Hoover was nominated to run for a second term in 1932, but he stood little chance against the Democratic candidate, Franklin Roosevelt (see Vol. 1, p. 141). Roosevelt won 57.4 percent of the vote to Hoover's 39.6 percent, and Democrats gained control of both houses of Congress for the first time since 1917 (see Vol. 1, p. 140).

Republican Philosophy, 1928

Herbert Hoover served the nation as secretary of commerce, U.S. Food Administrator, and as a relief administrator in Europe. Hoover had the misfortune of being elected president shortly before the great stock market crash of 1929. Below are excerpts from his first and only inaugural address in March 1929.

FlashFocus: Henry Cabot Lodge

Born: May 12, 1850, Boston, Massachusetts
Died: November 29, 1924, Boston, Massachusetts
Political Career: Massachusetts house of representatives, 1879–81; U.S. Representative from Massachusetts, 1886–93; U.S. Senator from Massachusetts, 1893–1924.

Henry Cabot Lodge was born into a prominent family in Boston. He attended Harvard University, graduating in 1871. He went on to attend Harvard Law School, graduating in 1874, and received the first Ph.D. ever granted by Harvard in political science in 1876. He then wrote several works of history before becoming involved in politics.

Lodge began his career in the Massachusetts house of representatives in 1879, serving until 1881. His work for and loyalty to the Massachusetts Republican Party earned him the party's nomination for U.S. House of Representatives in 1886. He narrowly won that election, but was reelected in 1888 and 1890 by larger margins. He won election to the U.S. Senate in 1892, where he served for over 30 years.

During his time in the Senate, Lodge supported imperialist policies. He was in favor of the Spanish-American War, the annexation of Hawaii and the Philippines, the construction of the Panama Canal, and the involvement of the United States in World War I. However, he also represented the ultranationalist wing of the Republican Party, supporting protective tariffs, restrictions on immigration, and increased defense spending, and opposing the Treaty of Versailles and U.S. participation in the League of Nations. While he believed that "commerce follows the flag" and that the U.S. should expand its economic influence, he also believed that the United States should avoid alliances that might restrict its political and diplomatic power and sovereignty. When Democratic President Woodrow Wilson presented the Treaty of Versailles and the League of Nations proposal to the Republican-controlled Senate, Lodge led the opposition movement to both, and neither was ever ratified by the Senate. Lodge also was against American participation in the World Court, proposed in 1922.

Throughout his career in the Senate, Lodge remained an important leader in the Republican Party. He served as the Republican National Convention chairman in 1900, 1908, and 1920. Although he opposed woman suffrage, he supported the right of black men to vote, perhaps in order to encourage blacks to vote Republican and thus maintain Republican dominance in the South. Lodge died in Boston in 1924.

If we survey the situation of our Nation both at home and abroad, we find many satisfactions; we find some causes for concern. We have emerged from the losses of the Great War and the reconstruction following it with increased virility and strength. From this strength we have contributed to the recovery and progress of the world. What America has done has given renewed hope and courage to all who have faith in government by the people. In the large view, we have reached a higher degree of comfort and security than ever existed before in the history of the world. Through liberation from widespread poverty we have reached a higher degree of individual freedom than ever before. The devotion to and concern for our institutions are deep and sincere. We are steadily building a new race—a new civilization great in its own attainments. The influence and high purposes of our Nation are respected among the peoples of the world. We aspire to distinction in the world, but to a distinction based upon confidence in our sense of justice as well as our accomplishments within our own borders and in our own lives. For wise guidance in this great period of recovery the Nation is deeply indebted to Calvin Coolidge.

But all this majestic advance should not obscure the constant dangers from which self-government must be safeguarded. The strong man must at all times be alert to the attack of insidious disease.

Of the undoubted abuses which have grown up under the eighteenth amendment, part are due to the causes I have just mentioned; but part are due to the failure of some States to accept their share of responsibility for concurrent enforcement and to the failure of many State and local officials to accept the obligation under their oath of office zealously to enforce the laws. With the failures from these many causes has come a dangerous expansion in the criminal elements who have found enlarged opportunities in dealing in illegal liquor.

But a large responsibility rests directly upon our citizens. There would be little traffic in illegal liquor if only criminals patronized it. We must awake to the fact that this patronage from large numbers of law-abiding citizens is supplying the rewards and stimulating crime.

I have been selected by you to execute and enforce the laws of the country. I propose to do so to the extent of my own abilities, but the measure of success that the Government shall attain will depend upon the moral support which you, as citizens, extend. The duty of citizens to support the laws of the land is coequal with the duty of their Government to enforce the laws which exist. No greater national service can be given by men and women of good will—who, I know, are not unmindful of the responsibilities of citizenship—than that they should, by their example, assist in stamping out crime and outlawry by refusing participation in and condemning all transactions with illegal liquor. Our whole system of self-government will crumble either if officials elect what laws they will enforce or citizens elect what laws they will support. The worst evil of disregard for some law is that it destroys respect for all law. For our citizens to patronize the violation of a particular law on the ground that they are opposed to it is destructive of the very basis of all that protection of life, of homes and property which they rightly claim under other laws. If citizens do not like a law, their duty as honest men and women is to discourage its violation; their right is openly to work for its repeal.

To those of criminal mind there can be no appeal but vigorous enforcement of the law. Fortunately they are but a small percentage of our people. Their activities must be stopped.

The larger purpose of our economic thought should be to establish more firmly stability and security of business and employment and thereby remove poverty still further from our borders. Our people have in recent years developed a new-found capacity for cooperation among themselves to effect high purposes in public welfare. It is an advance toward the highest conception of self-government. Self-government does not and should not imply the use of political agencies alone. Progress is born of cooperation in the community—not from governmental restraints. The Government should assist and encourage these movements of collective self-help by itself cooperating with them. Business has by cooperation made great progress in the advancement of service, in stability, in regularity of employment and in the correction of its own abuses. Such progress, however, can continue only so long as business manifests its respect for law.

There is an equally important field of cooperation by the Federal Government with the multitude of agencies, State, municipal and private, in the systematic development of those processes which directly affect public health, recreation, education, and the home. We have need further to perfect the means by which Government can be adapted to human service.

In our form of democracy the expression of the popular will can be effected only through the instrumentality of political parties. We maintain party government not to promote intolerant partisanship but because opportunity must be given for expression of the popular will, and organization provided for the execution of its mandates and for accountability of government to the people. It follows that the government both in the executive and the legislative branches must carry out in good faith the platforms upon which the party was entrusted with power. But the government is that of the whole people; the party is the instrument through which policies are determined and men chosen to bring them into being. The animosities of elections should have no place in our Government, for government must concern itself alone with the common weal.

More Information

- Cutright, Paul B. *Theodore Roosevelt: The Making of a Conservationist.* Champaign-Urbana: University of Illinois Press, 1985.
- Gould, Lewis L. *The Presidency of Theodore Roosevelt.* Lawrence: University Press of Kansas, 1991.
- Manners, William. *TR and Will: A Friendship That Split the Republican Party.* New York: Harcourt, Brace & World, 1969.
- Morris, Edmund. *Theodore Rex.* New York, Random House, 2001.
- Murray, Robert K. *The Politics of Normalcy: Governmental Theory and Practice in the Harding-Coolidge Era.* New York: Norton, 1973.
- Romasco, Albert U. *The Poverty of Abundance: Hoover, the Nation, the Depression.* New York: Oxford University Press, 1965.
- Schlesinger, Arthur M. Jr. *The Imperial Presidency.* Boston: Houghton Mifflin, 1973.

- Smith, Richard Norton. *An Uncommon Man: The Triumph of Herbert Hoover.* New York: Simon and Schuster, 1984.
- Sobel, Robert. *Coolidge: An American Enigma.* Washington, D.C.: Regnery Pub, 1998.

On the Web:
- Bailey, Charles W. "The Odd Couple: Uncle Mark and Teddy." *http://www.cosmos-club.org/journals/1997/bailey.html.*
- From War to Normalcy. The Library of Congress (includes links to audio files). *http://memory.loc.gov/ammem/nfhtml/nfexhome.html.*
- Inaugural Addresses of the President of the United States. *http://www.bartleby.com/124/.*
- John Calvin Coolidge. AmericanPresident.org. *http://www.americanpresident.org/history/calvincoolidge/.*
- McKinley Webfinder. McKinley Memorial Library and Museum (links to resources on the Web). *http://www.mckinley.lib.oh.us/McKWeb/home.htm.*
- Political Party Platforms. The American Presidency Project. *http://www.presidency.ucsb.edu/site/docs/platforms.php.*
- Theodore Roosevelt Association. *http://www.theodoreroosevelt.org/.*
- Warren Gamaliel Harding. AmericanPresident.org. *http://www.americanpresident.org/history/warrenharding/.*
- William Howard Taft. Ohio State University. Biography and links to related topics. *http://1912.history.ohio-state.edu/taft.htm.*

Democratic Party, 1900–32

> ### *FlashFocus: Democratic Party, 1900–32*
> #### Origins
> For most of the first three decades of the twentieth century, Democrats were divided between the rural interests of the South and West and the urban interests of the East. Progressive farm interests, championed by William Jennings Bryan, dominated the party from 1900 to 1912. Democrats were in power under President Woodrow Wilson from 1913 to 1921, then suffered a period of lackluster conservative leadership that echoed many Republican positions. Late in the 1920s, progressive urban and labor interests, symbolized by Governor Al Smith of New York, rose to dominate.
>
> #### Issues
> **Farm vs. labor.** Democrats began the century largely representing the interests of farmers; by 1930, the party largely represented urban workers, including many immigrants. Failure to create a consistent, strong alliance between the two groups kept the party out of power for all but eight years of the first 32 years in the twentieth century.
> **Monetary policy.** Initially, Democrats backed free coinage of silver, a position mistrusted by many urban workers and business interests. Democrats later accepted the gold standard, then backed creation of the Federal Reserve system to regulate the nation's currency.
> **Religion.** Rural Protestants distrusted the influence of the Catholic Church over urban Democratic voters, an issue central to the 1928 presidential campaign, in which Democratic nominee Al Smith was a proud Catholic.
> **World War I.** In 1916, the Democratic platform praised incumbent President Woodrow Wilson for having kept the country out of Europe's Great War. After his reelection, Wilson led the country into the war to "make the world safe for democracy." The war was an election issue in 1920, when Wilson's support for the League of Nations and the Treaty of Versailles cost Democrats votes.
> **Prohibition.** The Eighteenth Amendment (1919) banned the sale of alcoholic beverages. Some urban Democrats, notably New York Governor Al Smith, opposed Prohibition, which nevertheless remained popular in the West and South.
>
> #### Impact
> Democrats elected just one president, Woodrow Wilson (in 1912 to 1916), in the first 32 years of the twentieth century. Wilson's election was largely due to a split in the Republican Party. Democrats controlled the House of Representatives from 1911 to 1919 and the Senate from 1913 to 1919. It took a devastating economic depression after the stock market crash of 1929 for the Democrats to regain power in 1932.
>
> *See also:* Democratic Party, 1876–1900, p. 80; Democratic Party, 1932–68, p. 141; Democratic Party, 1968–2004, p. 163; Progressive Party, 1924, p. 132; Republican Party, 1900–32, p. 105.

Political success for political parties inevitably hinges on a party's ability to fashion a coalition of diverse interests. In the first three decades of the twentieth century, the Democratic Party generally failed at doing so. At first, following William Jennings Bryan of Nebraska, the Democratic candidate for president in 1896, 1900, and 1908 (see Vol. 1, p. 107), the party promoted the interests of western and southern farmers, sometimes at the expense of urban industrial workers in the East. After an eight-year interval when Democrat Woodrow Wilson (see Vol. 1, p. 122) was president—largely because of a split in the Republican Party in 1912 (see p. 105) between progressives led by Theodore Roosevelt (see Vol. 1, p. 114) and the more conservative William Taft (see Vol. 1, p. 118)—Democrats still failed to fashion a program that would attract both farm interests and labor interests. Consequently, the period from 1900 to 1932 was primarily one of Republican domination. Even within these major blocs of voters, Democrats experienced continuing splits between reformers and party "machines" in large cities, such as Tammany Hall in New York or the Pendergasts in Kansas City, Missouri.

These three decades also represented a period of rapid change in the United States. The wave of immigration that had begun in the middle of the nineteenth century with Irish and German immigrants became a flood after 1880. The newest immigrants, from southern and eastern Europe, were largely Roman Catholics or Jews, rather than Protestants, who had long constituted the American religious majority. The newcomers settled in cities and worked at industrial jobs, in stark contrast to the Protestant farmers of the West and South. These two groups—immigrants and farmers—disagreed on many economic issues, such as free coinage of silver (a popular cause among farmers for two decades, beginning in the late 1880s) and the role of labor unions (popular among industrial workers). By the 1920s, these two groups were also separated by cultural issues, ranging from prohibition of alcoholic beverages (supported in the conservative West and South, largely ignored in cities and in the Northeast) to Roman Catholicism (feared by many western and southern Protestants). It was a time when the Ku Klux Klan (see Vol. 4, p. 53) succeeded in becoming an important political voice in the South and Midwest, opposing civil rights for African Americans and the influence of Catholicism.

New Century, Old Issues

Democrats entered the twentieth century firmly rooted in the nineteenth. For president in 1900 they again nominated William Jennings Bryan of Nebraska, their losing candidate in 1896, who insisted on retaining the same party platform he had run on previously. The principal plank in the platform was the free coinage of silver—a position opposed by Bryan's chief rival

FlashFocus: James Curley

Born: November 20, 1874, Boston, Massachusetts
Died: November 12, 1958, Boston, Massachusetts
Political Career: Mayor of Boston, 1914–18, 1922–26, 1930–34, 1947–51. Governor of Massachusetts, 1935–37; U.S. House of Representatives, 1943–47.

The son of Irish immigrants, James Curley grew up in Boston's Roxbury neighborhood, leaving high school before graduating to work as a delivery boy for a grocery store. He gravitated toward politics and earned the attention of politicians for his steady work for the party.

Urged to run for office, Curley entered the race for Boston's Common Council, a good starting point for ambitious politicians. Curley's initially solid campaign was undermined by dirty tricks by Democratic opponents who even had Curley fired from his grocery job after he lost the election. Taking a sales job, Curley developed his speaking skills while campaigning for the next Common Council election, which he won. Rather than punishing his political enemies, Curley won them over by retaining many in their patronage jobs and advocating fair working hours.

Curley moved up the Democratic Party ladder with his election to the Massachusetts state legislature in 1902. He returned to local Boston politics to run for alderman in 1904, but ran into trouble for taking a civil service exam on behalf of a supporter who was afraid he would not pass on his own. He spent two months in jail, but continued to campaign from his cell and won the election, as many voters determined Curley was only trying to help a friend.

Curley continued to attract support from Irish immigrants, advocating increases in government services for the poor and standing up to wealthy Boston leaders. Curley won election as mayor of Boston in 1914 and served two additional mayoral terms (1922–26 and 1930–34). He was elected governor of Massachusetts in 1935 and served until 1937 before moving on to serve two terms in Congress from 1943–47, where he supported the New Deal policies of President Roosevelt.

Curley was again elected mayor of Boston in 1947 and took office once his congressional term was finished. During this latest term as mayor, Curley lent his name to a business venture that turned out to be fraudulent, and the misuse of the U.S. Postal Service by the business landed Curley in federal prison for mail fraud. Curley managed to run the city from his prison cell before being pardoned by President Truman. Curley ran for reelection in 1951 and 1955 but failed both times. He died in Boston on November 12, 1958.

---

in the Republican Party, former President Grover Cleveland (see Vol. 1, p. 95). Bryan insisted that both silver and gold should form the basis of U.S. currency; Republicans, and many eastern Democrats, were fearful that free silver would translate into higher prices, especially for food. Bryan's platform remained unchanged, but after 1896, an influx of gold from Alaska contributed to a rise in economic prosperity, undercutting his arguments.

Another new political issue in 1900 was the Spanish-American War of 1898 and its aftermath. The war had resulted in the Philippines becoming a United States possession, which Democrats criticized as being imperialistic and contrary to the historic origins of the United States. Bryan opposed imperialism without making it his central theme. Had he chosen to emphasize it, he might have gained the White House.

Bryan lost to Republican William McKinley (see Vol. 1, p. 106) in 1900, 51.7 percent to 45.5 percent (see Vol. 1, p. 109), a slightly worse margin than his showing in 1896 (see Vol. 1, p. 105). Republicans also maintained a firm hold over both houses of Congress. Democrats carried the South—a continuing legacy of the Civil War—plus the relatively lightly populated silver states of Colorado, Nevada, Idaho, and Montana. Bryan did not even carry his home state of Nebraska.

In the 1904 presidential election (see Vol. 1, p. 113), Bryan agreed not to run a third time, although he continued to battle for a free silver platform. Instead, eastern Democrats nominated a New York state court judge, Alton Parker (see Vol. 1, p. 115), who was thought to be more attuned to eastern industrial interests than Bryan. After he was nominated, Parker unexpectedly insisted that the Democrats endorse the gold standard, a studied insult to Bryan and his loyal silver supporters. Moreover, Parker proved to be a dismal campaigner running against the vigorous Republican incumbent President Theodore Roosevelt (see Vol. 1, p. 114). Parker won a mere 37.6 percent of the vote to Roosevelt's 56.4 percent. Republicans picked up 42 seats in the House of Representatives and maintained their control of the Senate.

Ironically, Roosevelt's victory paved the way for Bryan to recapture the Democratic party nomination in 1908. During his presidency, Roosevelt had adopted a series of progressive positions, such as regulating corporations in areas like inspection of meat, that seemed to echo many planks that were in Bryan's 1896 Democratic platform. Moreover, Roosevelt was not running for reelection in 1908, enabling Bryan to run as the natural successor to the popular Roosevelt against the conservative Republican William Howard Taft of Ohio. The outcome in 1908, however, echoed Bryan's campaign in 1900: 51.6 percent for Taft to 43.1 percent for Bryan (see Vol. 1, p. 117).

In 1912, the Republicans gave Democrats a golden opportunity when Roosevelt challenged incumbent President Taft for the party's nomination. Roosevelt lost the Republican nomination largely because of support for Taft by Republican Party insiders. He then bolted from his party to form the Progressive ("Bull Moose") Party (see p. 121) and proceeded to split the Republican vote.

The main contender for the Democratic nomination in 1912 was Governor Woodrow Wilson of New Jersey. Wilson was a native of Virginia who attracted support in the South while campaigning as a moderate progressive in the North. He was challenged by Speaker of the House Champ Clark of Missouri, heir to Bryan's western populist tradition. Wilson won the nomination on the 46th ballot, then managed to avoid alienating either western progressives or big city machines while campaigning under the slogan "New Freedom." With Republicans split between Roosevelt and Taft, Wilson became the first Democrat since Grover Cleveland in 1892 (see Vol. 1, p. 102) to win the presidency, albeit with just 41.8 percent of the popular vote (see Vol. 1, p. 121).

War in Europe broke out in 1914, and the United States was determined to remain neutral. Nevertheless, Wilson began strengthening the armed forces, and as the war dragged on, he led the United States into the conflict on the side of Britain and France against Germany, Austria, and the Ottoman Empire. Wilson was reelected in 1916 largely by forging an alliance between progressives and labor. He endorsed federal legislation to set an eight-hour workday, for example, and campaigned on a promise to continue to keep the country out of war. He was reelected with 49.2 percent of the vote to 46.1 percent for Republican Charles Hughes, a former chief justice of the Supreme Court (see Vol. 1, p. 126 and Vol. 3, p. 104). Despite Wilson's peace promises, the United States entered World War I in 1917 and fought alongside Britain and France until the armistice in 1918. At the war's conclusion, Wilson played a key role in the peace negotiations. Since the war was long over by the time the elections of 1920 rolled around, it was Wilson's postwar policies that generated the most controversy. Wilson, debilitated by a stroke in 1919, nevertheless insisted on supporting the new League of Nations and certain clauses in the Treaty of Versailles that burdened Germany with stiff reparations (financial punishments for starting the war). These positions, plus the suspension of civil liberties under Wilson in 1918 and 1919 during a red scare (fear of undue communist influence that resulted in deporting hundreds of leftist immigrants), made the Republican call for a "return to normalcy" in 1920 all the more appealing.

The Roaring Twenties

In 1920, the Democrats again lost power to Republicans and remained the minority party for the next 12 years. The Democrats lost three consecutive presidential elections (1920, 1924, and 1928) and after 1919 did not have a majority in either the House or the Senate until 1931 (see Vol. 1, pp. 128-39).

There were two large themes that helped keep the Democrats in political exile during the 1920s:

Western farm support went to the Republicans. Although independent western farmers were a declining percentage of the population, loss of their support hurt Democrats in the 1920s. Farm prices were falling, even while the Esch-Cummins Act of 1920 allowed railroad freight rates to rise. Wilson, in his last year as president, did little to help farmers.

"Values." Rural dwellers were concerned about the spread of urban influences in areas like music and art during

FlashFocus: Thomas Pendergast

Born: July 22, 1872, St. Joseph, Missouri
Died: January 26, 1945, Kansas City, Missouri
Political Career: Thomas Pendergast was born in St. Joseph, Missouri, in 1872 and arrived in Kansas City in the 1890s to work in a saloon owned by his older brother, Jim, who had risen to the top of the Democratic Party. Tom learned the intricacies of politics from his brother as he deepened his own involvement in the party, and when Jim died in 1911, the leadership of the party was handed to Tom.

Under Pendergast, the party maintained control of elected offices through various criminal methods, such as counting the votes of the dead and paying citizens to vote multiple times on election day. Pendergast rewarded associates who delivered victories by keeping alcohol and gambling legal in Kansas City and by awarding lucrative government building contracts to companies favored by the machine.

One of the political entities that the Pendergast machine controlled was the three-man Jackson County Court, which included an elected "presiding judge." Because of a family connection, Tom Pendergast chose to put forward a little-known owner of a haberdashery, Harry Truman, to run for the office. In return for Pendergast's support, Truman awarded patronage jobs to Pendergast supporters when he could. In 1934, Pendergast backed Truman for senator. Truman won, launching the national career that would lead him to the White House.

As Pendergast grew more powerful, however, local reformers in Kansas City grew more vocal in protesting his grip on the political process. Critics urged the ouster of Pendergast-backed officeholders through the use of a recall election in 1932. Reform efforts began to bear fruit in the 1934 elections, as several opposition candidates won seats on the City Council.

The Pendergast machine began to break apart as law enforcement officials began investigating Tom Pendergast's finances, and the reform movement gathered more strength. Pendergast was convicted of income tax evasion in 1939 and sentenced to serve time at the federal prison in Leavenworth, Kansas. He was paroled after a year in jail on the promise that he refrain from any political activity. Pendergast died on January 26, 1945.

the 1920s. This was combined with fears of Roman Catholic influence over urban voters. These concerns were reflected by the growth of the Ku Klux Klan, not just in the South but also in the Midwest. The Klan was overtly opposed to civil rights for African Americans, to Jews, and to Catholics. This alienation came to a head in 1928 when the Democrats nominated Al Smith, governor of New York and a Catholic, for the presidency (see Vol. 1, p. 138). The urban-rural division was further accentuated by differences over the prohibition of alcohol (favored by many rural interests, opposed by urban politicians).

Democrats in the 1920s also failed to nominate candidates who would capture the national imagination. In 1920, their presidential candidate was publisher James Cox (see Vol., 1, p. 130) of Ohio, a lackluster campaigner who chose to make the League of Nations his principal issue—an issue that fell flat among most voters. Four years later, the party was sharply split between Al Smith of New York and William McAdoo, a native of Georgia who practiced law in New York City but nevertheless became heir apparent to William Bryan's support among culturally conservative farmers. McAdoo supported Prohibition and denounced the influences of big cities. Deadlocked in their convention over 102 ballots, the party compromised on John Davis (see Vol., 1, p. 134), a lawyer born in West Virginia who previously was U.S. ambassador to Britain, as the candidate for president and William Bryan's brother Charles Bryan, governor of Nebraska, as the candidate for vice president. Davis was a shy man and an entirely ineffective campaigner; he later complained that he could never succeed in uniting the Democratic faction that supported McAdoo and the faction that supported Smith. Davis managed to collect just 28.8 percent of the popular vote against his taciturn Republican opponent, Calvin Coolidge (running as an incumbent, see Vol. 1, p. 133) and Progressive Party (see p. 132) candidate Robert La Follette (see p. 133), who won 16.6 percent, largely at the expense of the Democrats.

In 1928, Smith of New York won the nomination he had fought for in 1924. Again, cultural differences began to intrude. The fact that Smith was a proud Roman Catholic—an autographed portrait of the Pope hung in his office in Albany, New York—and former mayor of New York City helped the Republicans attract the more conservative voters living on farms and in small towns of the South and West. The cultural hoopla associated with the Roaring Twenties—including bootleg violations of Prohibition—did not play well down on the farm. Smith exacerbated these concerns by endorsing repeal of Prohibition and by naming a millionaire Catholic businessman (and antiprohibitionist), John Raskob, as party chairman. Rather than downplaying aspects of his background and politics that might alienate western and southern voters, Smith seemed to play them up. The result was a drubbing of the Democratic ticket, with a decisive loss of the presidential race to the Republicans, 50.2 percent to 40.8 percent (see Vol. 1, p. 136). Republicans gained 30 seats in the House of Representatives and seven in the Senate. But the Republican joy was cut short in September 1929 when stock prices crashed, ushering in the worst economic depression in the country's history. President Herbert Hoover (see Vol. 1, p. 137), persuaded that he lacked constitutional power to relieve the economic crisis or the suffering of unemployed workers, turned out to be the last Republican president for the next 24 years.

Democratic Party Platform, 1912

Excerpts from the platform of the Democratic Party in 1912:

We declare it to be a fundamental principle of the Democratic party that the Federal government, under the Constitution, has no right or power to impose or collect tariff duties, except for the purpose of revenue, and we demand that the collection of such taxes shall be limited to the necessities of government honestly and economically administered.

The high Republican tariff is the principal cause of the unequal distribution of wealth; it is a system of taxation which makes the rich richer and the poor poorer; under its operations the American farmer and laboring man are the chief sufferers; it raises the cost of the necessaries of life to them, but does not protect their product or wage.... We favor the immediate downward revision of the existing high and in many cases prohibitive tariff duties....

A private monopoly is indefensible and intolerable. We therefore favor the vigorous enforcement of the criminal as well as the civil law against trusts and trust officials, and demand the enactment of such additional legislation as may be necessary to make it impossible for a private monopoly to exist in the United States....

We condemn the action of the Republican administration in compromising with the Standard Oil Company and the tobacco trust and its failure to invoke the criminal provisions of the antitrust law against the officers of those corporations after the court had declared that from the undisputed facts in the record they had violated the criminal provisions of the law....

Believing that the most efficient results under our system of government are to be attained by the full exercise by the States of their reserved sovereign powers, we denounce as usurpation the efforts of our opponents to deprive the States of any of the rights reserved to them, and to enlarge and magnify by indirection the powers of the Federal government.

We congratulate the country upon the triumph of two important reforms demanded in the last national platform, namely, the amendment of the Federal Constitution authorizing an income tax, and the amendment providing for the popular election of senators, and we call upon the people of all the States to rally to the support of the pending propositions and secure their ratification.

We note with gratification the unanimous sentiment in favor of publicity, before the election, of campaign contributions ... and we commend the Democratic House of Representatives for extending the doctrine of publicity to recommendations, verbal and written, upon which presidential appointments are made, to the ownership and control of newspapers, and to the expenditures made by and in behalf of those who aspire to presidential nominations, and we point for additional justification for this legislation to the enormous expenditures of money in behalf of the President and his predecessor in the recent contest for the Republican nomination for President.

We pledge the Democratic party to the enactment of a law prohibiting any corporation from contributing to a campaign fund and any individual from contributing any amount above a reasonable maximum....

We favor the efficient supervision and rate regulation of railroads, express companies, telegraph and telephone lines engaged in interstate commerce....

We oppose the so-called Aldrich bill or the establishment of a central bank; and we believe our country will be largely freed from panics and consequent unemployment and business depression by such a systematic revision of our banking laws as will render temporary relief in localities where such relief is needed, with protection from control of dominion by what is known as the money trust....

We favor the adoption of a liberal and comprehensive plan for the development and improvement of our inland waterways, with economy and efficiency, so as to permit their navigation by vessels of standard draft.

We repeat our declarations of the platform of 1908, as follows:

'...It is the function of the courts to interpret the laws which the people enact, and if the laws appear to work economic, social or political injustice, it is our duty to change them. The only basis upon which the integrity of our courts can stand is that of unswerving justice and protection of life, personal liberty, and property. As judicial processes may be abused, we should guard them against abuse....

'We pledge the Democratic party to the enactment of a law creating a department of labor, represented separately in the President's cabinet in which department shall be included the subject of mines and mining.'

We pledge the Democratic party, so far as the Federal jurisdiction extends, to an employees' compensation law providing adequate indemnity for injury to body or loss of life....

We believe in encouraging the development of a modern system of agriculture and a systematic effort to improve the conditions of trade in farm products so as to benefit both consumer and producer. And as an efficient means to this end we favor the enactment by Congress of legislation that will suppress the pernicious practice of gambling in agricultural products by organized exchanges or others....

We reaffirm the position thrice announced by the Democracy in national convention assembled against a policy of imperialism and colonial exploitation in the Philippines or elsewhere. We condemn the experiment in imperialism as an inexcusable blunder, which has involved us in enormous expense, brought us weakness instead of strength, and laid our nation open to the charge of abandonment of the fundamental doctrine of self-government. We favor an immediate declaration of the nation's purpose to recognize the independence of the Philippine Islands as soon as a stable government can be established, such independence to be guaranteed by us until the neutralization of the islands can be secured by treaty with other Powers.

Our platform is one of principles which we believe to be essential to our national welfare. Our pledges are made to be kept when in office, as well as relied upon during the campaign, and we invite the co-operation of all citizens, regardless of party, who believe in maintaining unimpaired the institutions and traditions of our country.

More Information

- Auchincloss, Louis. *Woodrow Wilson.* New York: Viking, 2000.
- Chambers, William N. *The Democrats, 1789–1964: A Short History of a Popular Party.* Princeton, NJ: Van Nostrand, 1964.
- Cherny, Robert W. *A Righteous Cause: The Life of William Jennings Bryan.* Boston: Little, Brown, 1985.
- Finan, Christopher M. *Alfred E. Smith, The Happy Warrior.* New York: Hill & Wang, 2002.
- Mink, Gwendolyn. *Old Labor and New Immigrants in American Political Development: Union, Party, and State, 1875–1920.* Ithaca, NY: Cornell University Press, 1986.
- Romero, Francine Sanders (ed.). *Presidents from Theodore Roosevelt through Coolidge, 1901–1929: Debating the Issues in Pro and Con Primary Documents.* Westport, CT: Greenwood Press, 2002.
- Sarasohn, David. *The Party of Reform: Democrats in the Progressive Era.* Jackson: University Press of Mississippi, 1989.
- Schlesinger, Arthur M., Jr. (ed.). *History of U.S. Political Parties,* Vol. III. New York: Chelsea House Publishers, 1973.
- Witcover, Jules. *Party of the People: A History of the Democrats.* New York: Random House, 2003.

On the Web

- American Presidency Project, Political Party Platforms. University of California at Santa Barbara. *http://www.presidency.ucsb.edu/site/docs/platforms.php.*
- Democratic National Committee. *http://www.democrats.org/.*
- Smith, Alfred Emanuel. Encyclopedia Americana online. *http://ap.grolier.com/article?assetid=0359970-00&templatename=/article/article.html.*
- William Jennings Bryan. Nebraskastudies.org. *http://www.nebraskastudies.org/0600/frameset_reset.html?http://www.nebraskastudies.org/0600/stories/0601_0304.html.*
- Woodrow Wilson biography. The White House. *http://www.whitehouse.gov/history/presidents/ww28.html.*
- Woodrow Wilson. Presidents of the United States (links to related pages). *http://www.presidentsusa.net/wilson.html.*

Socialist Party, 1901–

Flash Focus: Socialist Party

Origins

The Socialist Party was founded in 1901 in New York City in order to unite smaller socialist organizations including the Social Democratic Party, Christian Socialists, Social Laborites, and a wing of the Socialist Labor Party. The party attracted populist sympathizers and industrial workers The party was based on the fundamental belief that economic power, like political power, should be shared by all citizens and controlled democratically.

Issues

Democratic control of the economy. Socialists argued that economic power, like political power, should be controlled democratically. In practice, this meant government ownership (the Socialists called it collective ownership) of factories, land, and mines.

Workers' rights. The Socialist Party consistently supported the right of industrial and agricultural workers to strike and to bargain with corporations for better wages and working conditions. It also backed government regulations such as the minimum wage. One of its founders, Eugene Debs, was a leading union leader in the late nineteenth century.

Opposition to war. The Sedition Act of 1918 banning criticism of World War I resulted in several arrests of party members. During World War II, the party split between veteran members who advocated nonviolence and younger members who supported the war against Germany and Japan. The Socialist Party protested U.S. involvement in Vietnam in the 1960s and voiced its opposition to U.S. military operations in Afghanistan and Iraq after 2001.

Civil and human rights. In line with the party's support for workers' rights, Socialists advocated equal rights for African Americans, women, and homosexuals. The party was especially active in the civil rights movement of the 1960s.

Impact

The Socialist Party made an impressive electoral showing in 1912 when its presidential candidate, Eugene Debs, won six percent of the vote. Socialist candidates won many state and local races, including 79 mayoral contests. The Great Depression of 1929 was a boon to the party; in the presidential election of 1932 the Socialist nominee, Norman Thomas, won 900,000 votes. Thereafter, however, Socialist victories dwindled. In 1991, Bernie Sanders of Vermont was elected to the House of Representatives, the first declared Socialist to be elected in decades. Despite its failure to put candidates in office, many of the party's social and economic ideas designed to protect workers' rights were enacted over time.

See also: Socialist Labor Party, p. 95; Social Democratic Party, p. 102; Communist Party, p. 128; Eugene Debs, Vol. 1, p. 110.

Formally organized in 1901, the Socialist Party unified several smaller leftist groups in an era when neither of the two dominant parties, the Democrats and the Republicans, promoted legislation contrary to the interests of large industrial corporations. The Socialist Party was founded by New York attorney Morris Hillquit and railroad union organizer Eugene Debs (see Vol. 1, p. 110). They presided over the merger of the Social Democratic Party (see p. 102) and a wing of the older Socialist Labor Party (see p. 95). Both parties had championed populist causes and the rights of industrial laborers. The new party formally came into existence at a convention in 1901 in Indianapolis, Indiana, Debs's home state.

Debs, a former Democratic city clerk and member of the Indiana legislature, was active in trade unions, eventually becoming the head of the American Railway Union. The union had struck the Pullman Company, which manufactured railroad cars, in 1894, a strike that resulted in a national train stoppage. President Grover Cleveland (see Vol. 1, p. 95) intervened to halt the strike, and Debs was eventually jailed for his involvement. Debs began to read Socialist literature while in prison and emerged as a political leader even as his union collapsed after the rail strike was defeated. Debs first ran as a presidential candidate of the Social Democratic Party in 1900 before that party merged into the Socialist Party the next year.

Early Successes

The Socialist Party enjoyed early success and growth, attracting industrial workers who desired to form unions and gain the right to strike in order to negotiate with their employers for better wages and working conditions. The party drew a variety of political activists from a broad political spectrum that included Marxists, Christian Socialists, and immigrants from a long tradition of socialist parties in Europe. The party's initial strength was great enough that its leaders quickly decided to attempt to make the Socialist Party a major party to compete nationally with Democrats and Republicans.

The party gained strength in many parts of the United States. Jewish immigrants working in the garment industry made up a considerable amount of support in New York, along with many intellectuals. The leader of the Socialist Party in Pennsylvania also served as the state president of the American Federation of Labor. Debs and prominent Socialist Norman Thomas (see p. 117) were from the Midwest, where the movement had been growing in Chicago's trade unions. There was also growing support as a result of previous political parties dedicated to spreading Socialist ideas, in Missouri, Kansas, and Arkansas, as well as California and the Pacific Northwest.

In its first party platform adopted at the initial 1901 Indianapolis convention, the Socialist Party immediately distinguished itself from other socialist political organizations,

FlashFocus: Norman Mattoon Thomas

Born: November 20, 1884, Marion, Ohio
Died: December 19, 1968, Huntington, New York
Political Career: Socialist candidate for president, 1928, 1932, 1936, 1940, 1944, 1948.

Norman Thomas was educated at Bucknell University and at Princeton University, graduating in 1905 as the class valedictorian. After working in New York City and traveling, he became assistant to the pastor at Christ Church in New York, then associate minister at Brick Presbyterian Church. He graduated from the Union Theological Seminary in 1911. Ordained as a Presbyterian minister, he became pastor at the East Harlem Presbyterian Church and served as chairman of the American Parish settlement house.

Like most Socialists, Thomas opposed America's involvement in World War I. In 1916 he joined the Fellowship of Reconciliation, a pacifist group, and became well known as the editor of its newsletter, *The World Tomorrow*. He joined the American Union Against Militarism in 1917 and helped found its Civil Liberties Bureau, which evolved into the American Civil Liberties Union.

Thomas left his position as pastor in 1918 to join the Socialist Party. He became associate editor of *Nation* magazine and codirector of the League for Industrial Democracy, a position he held from 1922 to 1937. He ran on the Socialist ticket for governor of New York in 1924 and for mayor of New York City in 1926. Upon the death of Socialist leader Eugene Debs in 1926, Thomas became head of the Socialist Party. He conducted a string of unsuccessful campaigns for office: New York Senate, 1926; New York City alderman, 1929; mayor, 1929; Manhattan borough president, 1931; and U.S. president every four years from 1928 to 1948.

Because of the Socialist Party's opposition to World War I, the party declined in strength in the years following the war, and Thomas won few votes in his bids for the presidency. During the Great Depression the party experienced a slight revival, but the New Deal of President Franklin Roosevelt incorporated many of the reforms the Socialists advocated, and the party continued to lose strength.

Thomas opposed American involvement during World War II, joining the Keep America Out of War Committee in 1938. As the war progressed, he shifted from opposition to "critical support," but remained outspoken in his criticism, particularly of the internment of Japanese Americans in 1942. Despite the decline of the Socialist Party, he remained politically active until his death in 1968.

such as the Socialist Labor Party, by expanding on merely overthrowing capitalistic society. The Socialist Party favored federal welfare for the elderly, disabled, and unemployed; universal education up to 18 years of age in an era when many children went to work before they were 12; public ownership of utilities such as electric and natural gas companies, and public ownership of transportation. They also promoted public ownership of the means of production, such as factories, and abolition of corporate monopolies. The Socialist Party opposed American involvement in military conflicts abroad.

Debs was nominated as the Socialist Party's presidential candidate in 1904, 1908, and 1912. In the 1912 election (see Vol. 1, p. 121), won by Democrat Woodrow Wilson (see Vol. 1, p. 122), Debs reflected the growing strength of the Socialists, finishing with six percent of the vote, while over 1,200 Socialist Party candidates won state and local elections, including 79 mayoral contests. In the same election, the Socialist Party adopted a list of demands that expanded on the themes of the 1901 document, such as federal relief for the unemployed through public works projects, an eight-hour workday, a minimum wage, and government safety and sanitation inspections of plants and factories. The Socialists advocated government-secured pensions for retirees and unemployment insurance for workers who lost their jobs. Many Socialist demands of 1912 were eventually adopted as part of the New Deal of President Franklin Roosevelt (see Vol. 1, p. 141) after 1932, although the Progressive Party (see p. 121) of Theodore Roosevelt (see Vol. 1, p. 114) in 1912 also supported many Socialist goals.

World War I and the Socialists

The Socialists maintained their strength in the election of 1916, but World War I slowed their momentum. Opposed to the war, party members found themselves the targets of anti-sedition legislation passed by Congress that included the prevention of the use of mail to communicate their antiwar views. Debs was again sent to prison for denouncing the federal government's prosecution of the new laws.

Many trade union members who might otherwise have supported the Socialist Party turned away from it to stand behind the war effort, but the party did not totally lose support. In the 1920 presidential election (see Vol 1, p. 128), Debs won 920,000 votes while sitting in a prison cell, but a major split in the party had already occurred. In the aftermath of the 1917 Russian Revolution, a significant Socialist faction, largely made up of eastern European-born immigrants, began advocating the overthrow of the capitalistic American system by means of a violent revolution and left the Socialists to join the Communist Party (see p. 128).

In 1924, the Socialist Party rallied its support behind Robert La Follette, the Progressive Party candidate (see p. 133 and Vol. 1, p. 132). Four years later, the Socialists nominated Norman Thomas, a minister and social worker from Ohio and the new leader of the party, who won nearly 900,000 votes. Thomas was also a founder of the American Civil Liberties Union which supports freedoms guaranteed by the Bill of Rights to the Constitution.

The economic impact of the Great Depression starting in 1929 increased Socialist Party membership, and Thomas was again nominated as the party's presidential candidate in 1932

A 1904 campaign poster for the Socialist Party with portraits of Eugene Debs, the candidate for president, and Ben Hanford, the candidate for vice president.

(see Vol. 1, p. 140). Thomas won about 884,000 votes. Support for the Socialists gradually decreased as newly elected Democratic President Franklin Roosevelt's New Deal policies implemented many of the programs long advocated by Socialists. The Democratic Party siphoned off support for the Socialists from immigrants living in cities. The severe economic crisis of the Depression persuaded many voters that a more experienced politician like Roosevelt was needed in the White House.

As the 1930s wore on, a new group of leaders emerged from the Socialist Party who began moving the party away from winning elections and toward showing support to the Soviet Union. Dissatisfied veterans of the party broke away in 1936 to form the Social Democratic Federation, and membership in the Socialist Party declined to just 6,500 by 1937. World War II brought further division, as party members struggled to agree on wartime policies. Thomas headed a pacifist faction and continued to run as the Socialist Party's presidential nominee through the 1948 election.

When World War II ended, the Socialist Party again turned its attention to supporting industrial workers and gained some influence in the Congress of Industrial Organizations, one of the two major alliances of labor unions. In the 1950s, the party welcomed parts of the Social Democratic Federation (which had split from the Socialist Party in 1936) back into the fold. Another group, the Independent Socialist League, dissolved for the express purpose of joining the Socialist Party. During the 1950s and early 1960s, the party provided support for movements such as the 1963 civil rights March on Washington (see Vol. 4, p. 122) and the Congress of Racial Equality (see Vol. 4, p. 80).

The party debated whether to field a presidential candidate in 1960, but Thomas (who still had the support within the party to be nominated) opposed the plan, reasoning that a Socialist candidacy would take away votes from Democrat John Kennedy in his contest with Republican Richard Nixon (see Vol. 1, p. 163). The Socialist Party appeared on the presidential ballot in only a few states.

Influence of the Modern Socialist Party

During the 1960s, the Socialists comprised various groups such as the Democratic Socialist Organizing Committee, the New American Movement, and the Students for a Democratic Society. These groups increasingly devoted their energies toward the civil rights movement and, as the decade wore on, to opposing escalation of the Vietnam War, but largely outside the context of elective politics.

The Socialist Party continued into the twenty-first century as a formal organization advocating positions on such issues as government funded health care, a higher minimum wage, and human rights. In 1980, the party was renamed Socialist Party USA. While party membership remained small, the issues on which it focused remained in the forefront of political debate. One party member, Bernie Sanders of Vermont, was elected to the House of Representatives.

After the attacks on the World Trade Center in New York and the Pentagon in Washington on September 11, 2001, the Socialist Party voiced opposition to U.S. military action in Afghanistan and Iraq. A party leader from the 1960s to the 1980s, Michael Harrington, observed that his party's "most significant accomplishments were made indirectly, and not in the party's own name."

Socialist Party Platform, 1912

In 1912, the Socialist Party scored impressive electoral showings in national, state, and local elections. Its candidate for president, Eugene Debs, won six percent of the vote, and nearly 1,200 Socialist candidates won races across the nation, including 79 as mayor. Following is the party's national platform for 1912, adopted in Indianapolis, Indiana.

The Socialist party declares that the capitalist system has outgrown its historical function and has become utterly incapable of meeting the problems now confronting society. We denounce this outgrown system as incompetent and corrupt and the source of unspeakable misery and suffering to the whole working class.

Working Program

As measures calculated to strengthen the working class in its fight for the realization of its ultimate aim, the co-operative commonwealth, and to increase its power against capitalist oppression, we advocate and pledge ourselves and our elected officers to the following program:

Collective Ownership

The collective ownership and democratic management of railroads, wire and wireless telegraphs and telephones, express service, steamboat lines, and all other social means of transportation and communication and of all large scale industries.

The immediate acquirement by the municipalities, the states or the federal government of all grain elevators, stock yards, storage warehouses, and other distributing agencies, in order to reduce the present extortionate cost of living.

The extension of the public domain to include mines, quarries, oil wells, forests and water power.

The further conservation and development of natural resources for the use and benefit of all the people....

The collective ownership of land wherever practicable, and in cases where such ownership is impracticable, the appropriation by taxation of the annual rental value of all the land held for speculation and exploitation.

The collective ownership and democratic management of the banking and currency system.

Industrial Demands

The conservation of human resources, particularly of the lives and well-being of the workers and their families:

By shortening the workday in keeping with the increased productiveness of machinery.

By securing for every worker a rest period of not less than a day and a half in each week.

By securing a more effective inspection of workshops, factories and mines.

By forbidding the employment of children under sixteen years of age.

By the co-operative organization of the industries in the federal penitentiaries for the benefit of the convicts and their dependents.

By forbidding the interstate transportation of the products of child labor, of convict labor and of all uninspected factories and mines.

By abolishing the profit system in government work and substituting either the direct hire of labor or the awarding of contracts to co-operative groups of workers.

By establishing minimum wage scales.

By abolishing official charity and substituting a non-contributary system of old age pensions, a general system of insurance by the State of all its members against unemployment and invalidism and a system of compulsory insurance by employers of their workers, without cost to the latter, against industrial diseases, accidents and death.

Political Demands

The absolute freedom of press, speech and assemblage.

The adoption of a graduated income tax and the extension of inheritance taxes, graduated in proportion to the value of the estate and to nearness of kin – the proceeds of these taxes to be employed in the socialization of industry.

The abolition of the monopoly ownership of patents and the substitution of collective ownership, with direct rewards to inventors by premiums or royalties.

Unrestricted and equal suffrage for men and women.

The adoption of the initiative, referendum and recall and of proportional representation, nationally as well as locally.

The abolition of the Senate and of the veto power of the President.

The election of the President and Vice-President by direct vote of the people.

The abolition of the power usurped by the Supreme Court of the United States to pass upon the constitutionality of the legislation enacted by Congress. National laws to be repealed only by act of Congress or by a referendum vote of the whole people.

Abolition of any federal district courts and the United States circuit court of appeals. State courts to have jurisdiction in all cases arising between citizens of several states and foreign corporations. The election of all judges for short terms.

More Information

▶ Hesseltine, W.B. *The Rise and Fall of Third Parties.* Washington, D.C: Public Affairs Press, 1957.
▶ Judd, R.W. *Socialist Cities: Municipal Politics and the Grass Roots of American Socialism.* Albany: State University of New York Press, 1989.
▶ Kipnis, Ira. *The American Socialist Movement, 1897–1912.* New York: Monthly Review Press, 1972.
▶ Nash, H. Jr., *Third Parties in American Politics.* Washington, DC: Public Affairs Press, 1959.
▶ Shannon, David. *The Socialist Party of America.* New York: Macmillan, 1967.

- Weinstein, James. *The Decline of Socialism in America, 1912–1925.* New Brunswick, NJ: Rutgers University Press, 1967.

On the Web
- Socialist Party USA. *http://sp-usa.org/.*
- Socialism. Internet Modern History Sourcebook (links to online primary sources). *http://www.fordham.edu/halsall/mod/modsbook33.html.*
- Thomas, Norman. Address to the Socialist Party, 1948. The History Channel online audio file. *http://www.historychannel.com/speeches/archive/speech_297.html.*
- "Why Did the Socialist Movement Fail in the United States?" Digital History. *http://www.digitalhistory.uh.edu/historyonline/con_socialism.cfm.*

Progressive ("Bull Moose") Party, 1912–16

FlashFocus: Progressive Party, 1912

Origins

In 1912, former Republican President Theodore Roosevelt decided that the policies of his hand-picked successor, William Howard Taft, were too conservative and had failed to follow through on the reforms initiated by Roosevelt. Thwarted by party leaders from getting the Republican nomination for the 1912 election, Roosevelt ran on his own ticket, the Progressive Party, popularly known as the Bull Moose Party after Roosevelt declared that he felt as "fit as a bull moose."

Issues

Business regulation. As president, Roosevelt had worked to break up business monopolies (such as Standard Oil) and believed that government regulations were needed to insure fair competition. Roosevelt proposed a new federal agency to regulate all large corporations engaged in interstate commerce.

Protection of workers. The Progressive Party supported mandated minimum occupational standards to insure safe working conditions for laborers, strict laws against child labor, and a fair minimum wage (what Roosevelt termed a "living wage").

Political reforms. Roosevelt had won most primary elections over Taft, only to see party powerbrokers give the presidential nomination to Taft. The Progressives urged reform of the presidential nominating process by giving more weight to the outcome of primaries.

Women's suffrage. The party supported the right of women to vote.

Judicial reform. The Progressive Party proposed that the people be able to vote directly on a law after it has been deemed unconstitutional by the federal courts.

Taxation. The party supported a graduated inheritance tax and supported legislation to amend the Constitution, granting the federal government the ability to tax an individual's income.

Conservation. The Progressive Party wanted to amplify the work Roosevelt had done for the environment in areas such as soil protection, government game reserves, and development of the Mississippi River.

Impact

Roosevelt and his running mate, California Governor Hiram Johnson, won 27.4 percent of the vote, the highest ever for a third-party candidate in American history. They carried six states and won 4.1 million votes. The Bull Moose Party effectively split the Republican vote, allowing Democrat Woodrow Wilson to win the White House. Progressive Party candidates also won 13 seats in the U.S. House of Representatives in 1912. Four years later, Roosevelt declined the Progressive Party nomination and supported the Republican candidate. With Roosevelt gone, the party organization fell apart and disbanded.

See also: Republican Party, 1900–32, p. 105; People's Party (Populist), p. 98; Progressive Party, 1924, p. 132; Democratic Party, 1932–68, p. 141.

The Bull Moose Party (formally called the Progressive Party, a name shared with unrelated later parties) proved to be a one-time vehicle for one politician, Theodore Roosevelt (see Vol. 1, p. 114), in the presidential race of 1912 (see Vol. 1, p. 121). Many of the party's principles, on the other hand, had earlier been advocated by the People's Party (often called the Populist Party, see p. 98) and continued to find representation in other parties, including a later Progressive Party in the 1920s (see p. 132).

The Progressive Party reflected Roosevelt's philosophy of government in the new industrial age, a philosophy Roosevelt called "New Nationalism." The party advocated government oversight of industry, legal protection of the rights of workers in factories and on farms, and extension of environmental protection programs begun by Roosevelt when he was president from 1901 to 1909.

Roosevelt's Progressive Party sought to achieve through government regulation what more radical groups like the Socialists (see p. 116) sought to achieve by actual government ownership of industrial corporations. Many of the goals of the Bull Moose Progressives were later taken over by the Progressives of 1924 and the Democratic Party under President Franklin Roosevelt (see p. 141 and Vol. 1, p. 141).

Origins of the Progressive Party

Returning to the national political scene three years after leaving the White House, Roosevelt effectively rallied the support of the growing progressive movement within the United States and altered the shape and outcome of the 1912 presidential race, though not in the way he envisioned.

As president Roosevelt had championed aggressive government intervention in the affairs of the economy, the nation's working class, and the environment. Roosevelt succeeded in pushing through his "Square Deal" for the American people that had included legislation creating government inspection of meat and regulation and dismantling of monopolistic business combinations. Roosevelt also moved to give the federal government a prominent role in the conservation of the nation's national resources by issuing executive orders protecting land and creating and maintaining valuable agricultural soil.

Some of Roosevelt's policies as president had been advocated by the Progressive Party (sometimes called the Populist Party) in the 1890s and were strongly opposed by business owners used to operating without government interference. Although Republicans had been generally sympathetic to protecting business interests, Roosevelt was well pleased with his record when he finished his term in 1909. He left office expecting that his former vice president and handpicked successor, William Howard Taft (see Vol. 1, p. 118 and Vol. 3, p. 95), would carry on with his policies. But Taft did not share Roosevelt's en-

FlashFocus: Hiram Johnson

Born: September 2, 1866, Sacramento, California
Died: August 6, 1945, Bethesda, Maryland
Career: Governor of California, 1911–17; vice presidential candidate, Progressive Party, 1912; U.S. Senator, 1917–45.

Hiram Johnson had already established his reputation as a progressive Republican when Theodore Roosevelt asked him to run as vice president on the Progressive ("Bull Moose") Party ticket in 1912. Johnson, the son of a lawyer and politician, initially gained fame prosecuting corrupt politicians in San Francisco. He was elected governor on the slogan "Kick the Southern Pacific out of politics," a reference to the large and politically active railroad company. As the candidate of the Lincoln-Roosevelt League, a reform group inside the California Republican Party, Johnson captured the gubernatorial nomination and was narrowly elected governor on a ticket that included other reform-oriented Republicans. Johnson and his colleagues pushed through a broad range of reforms, including establishment of public utilities and railroad commissions to regulate those two industries, a conservation commission, restrictions on child labor, and direct primary elections.

In 1911, Johnson was a charter member of the National Progressive Republican League that opposed nomination of President William Taft (see Vol. 1, p. 118) for a second term. In early 1912, when former President Theodore Roosevelt announced he would run for the Republican nomination, Johnson immediately supported him. After the Republican Party nominated Taft, Roosevelt decided to run as the candidate of the new Progressive Party (often called the Bull Moose Party) and chose Johnson as his vice presidential running mate.

Although the defeat of the Progressives in the presidential contest marked the end of Roosevelt's days as a candidate, Johnson's career was far from over. In 1914 Johnson was reelected governor, running as a Progressive, and in 1916 he was elected to the U.S. Senate as a Republican. He served in the Senate from 1917 until his death in 1945. Johnson continued to promote progressive legislation in domestic affairs while becoming an isolationist in foreign affairs. He opposed participation in World War I and later opposed both the Versailles Peace Treaty and U.S. entry into the World Court. In 1932 and 1936, Johnson, nominally a Republican, supported Democrat Franklin Roosevelt and most of Roosevelt's legislation under the New Deal. In foreign affairs, however, Johnson stuck with his isolationism, even in the face of World War II, and those views came to isolate him politically in the years preceding his death.

thusiasm for reform, and Roosevelt grew increasingly dissatisfied with what he and other progressive Republicans viewed as Taft's conservatism and slow pace of reform. Roosevelt's decision to challenge Taft for the Republican nomination in 1912 came after Taft's attorney general sued to dissolve the U.S. Steel Corporation. In the suit, the government specifically mentioned U.S. Steel's acquisition of the Tennessee Coal and Iron Company—an acquisition approved by Roosevelt as part of a plan to end the Panic (economic depression) of 1907. Roosevelt regarded the government suit as a personal insult and announced in February that he was running for president.

His decision to run for the Republican nomination infuriated many Republicans who realized that his entrance into the race would split the party. Competing in presidential primaries, Roosevelt outpolled Taft, but at the party convention, conservatives controlled enough delegates to nominate Taft for reelection. Roosevelt, upset at what he thought was a prearranged affair, left the Republican Party. Two months later, the Progressive Party was organized as his vehicle to return to the White House. When Roosevelt was quoted as saying he felt as "fit as a bull moose," the party had its symbol and nickname.

The progressives held their own convention in Chicago. While most of the Republican Party leadership remained committed to Taft, many middle- and upper-class delegates were attracted to Roosevelt's message of reform and his magnetic personal appeal. Wisconsin Republican Senator Robert LaFollette (see p. 133), the leader of the National Progressive Republican League, hoped to win the presidential nomination of the new party, but the delegates chose Roosevelt instead, whereupon LaFollette and his supporters withdrew support for the Bull Moose effort.

Roosevelt based his campaign on what he coined "New Nationalism," the utilization of government to enhance the productivity and tranquility of the society at large. The philosophy of the Progressive Party seemed the polar opposite of Thomas Jefferson's principles of limited government and the absence of governmental interference in the economy and the affairs of private enterprise (see p. 15 and Vol. 1, p. 13).

The party supported women's right to vote, legislation to expose and remedy corrupt business practices, the registration of lobbyists, and the general reform of legal practices. Roosevelt called for the establishment of a department of labor and more power for the Interstate Commerce Commission. In many respects, Roosevelt's New Nationalism foreshadowed the New Deal proposals of his cousin, Franklin Roosevelt (see Vol. 1, p. 141), who was elected president as a Democrat in 1932.

End of the Progressive Party

True to his personality, Roosevelt campaigned with an indomitable spirit, even surviving a gunshot wound by a would-be assassin in Milwaukee, Wisconsin, in October. After being shot and determining that there was no internal bleeding by coughing into his hand, he delivered a scheduled speech to an astonished and hushed crowd.

In November, Roosevelt and the Progressive Party won more than 4 million votes, carried six states, and won 88 electoral votes. Much of Roosevelt's support was siphoned from the Republican Party candidate, Taft. The result was that Democrat Woodrow Wilson (see Vol. 1, p. 122) collected 435 electoral votes (but just 41.8 percent of the popular vote) to

In this 1912 cartoon from *Harper's Weekly*, Theodore Roosevelt, shown as a moose, grins while the Democratic donkey and Republican elephant watch in alarm from behind a wall.

become the first Democrat since Grover Cleveland (see Vol. 1, p. 95) in 1892 to win the presidency.

The success of the Progressive candidates on the presidential ticket failed to benefit the party's candidates for legislative offices. Progressive Party candidates won only a few seats in the House of Representatives, none in the Senate, and won no victories in governor's races.

In 1916, Roosevelt declined the nomination of the Progressive Party, choosing to realign himself with the Republican Party. His rift with the party in 1912 had come at great personal cost, and he did not wish to campaign again. Roosevelt's refusal to run left the upstart party adrift, and without an effective organization, the Progressive Party faded away.

Platform of the Progressive ("Bull Moose") Party, 1912

"New Nationalism" was the label used by Theodore Roosevelt to describe his ideas for government participation in the growing industrial economy of the United States. It was summarized in the 1912 platform of his Progressive Party, sometimes dubbed the Bull Moose Party to distinguish it from other Progressive Parties. Excerpts:

> We of the Progressive Party here dedicate ourselves to the fulfillment of the duty laid upon us by our fathers to maintain the government of the people, by the people and for the people whose foundations they laid.

The Old Parties

> The deliberate betrayal of its trust by the Republican Party, the fatal incapacity of the Democratic Party to deal with the new issues of the new time, have compelled the people to forge a new instrument of government through which to give effect to their will in laws and institutions.
>
> Unhampered by tradition, uncorrupted by power, undismayed by the magnitude of the task, the new party offers itself as the instrument of the people to sweep away old abuses, to build a new and nobler commonwealth.
>
> *Equal Suffrage:* The Progressive party, believing that no people can justly claim to be a true democracy which denies political rights on account of sex, pledges itself to the task of securing equal suffrage to men and women alike.
>
> *Corrupt practices:* We pledge our party to legislation that will compel strict limitation of all campaign contributions and expenditures, and detailed publicity of both before as well as after primaries and elections.
>
> *Publicity and public service:* We pledge our party to legislation compelling the registration of lobbyists; publicity of committee hearings except on foreign affairs, and recording of all votes in committee; and forbidding federal appointees from holding office in state or national political organizations, or taking part as officers or delegates in political conventions for the nomination of elective State or National officials.
>
> *The courts:* The Progressive party demands such restriction of the power of the courts as shall leave to the people the ultimate authority to determine fundamental questions of social welfare and public policy. To secure this end, it pledges itself to provide:
>
> 1. That when an act, passed under the police power of the state, is held unconstitutional under the state Constitution, by the courts, the people, after an ample interval for deliberation, shall have an opportunity to vote on the question whether they desire the act to become law, notwithstanding such decision.
>
> 2. That every decision of the highest appellate court of a state declaring an act of the legislature unconstitutional on the ground of its violation of the federal Constitution shall be subject to the same review by the Supreme Court of the United States as is now accorded to decisions sustaining such legislation.
>
> *Social and industrial justice:* We pledge ourselves to work unceasingly in State and Nation for:
>
> Effective legislation looking to the prevention of industrial accidents, occupational diseases, overwork, involuntary unemployment, and other injurious effects incident to modern industry;
>
> The fixing of minimum safety and health standards for the various occupations, and the exercise of the public authority of State and Nation, including the Federal Control over interstate commerce, and the taxing power, to maintain such standards;
>
> The prohibition of child labor;
>
> Minimum wage standards for working women, to provide a "living wage" in all industrial occupations;

The general prohibition of night work for women and the establishment of an eight-hour day for women and young persons;

One day's rest in seven for all wage workers;

The eight-hour day in continuous twenty-four-hour industries.

Business: We demand a strong national regulation of interstate corporations. The corporation is an essential part of modern business.... But the existing concentration of vast wealth under a corporate system, unguarded and uncontrolled by the nation, has placed in the hands of a few men enormous, secret, irresponsible power over the daily life of the citizen— a power insufferable in a free government and certain of abuse.

We favor strengthening the Sherman Law by prohibiting agreement to divide territory or limit output; refusing to sell to customers who buy from business rivals; to sell below cost in certain areas while maintaining higher prices in other places; using the power of transportation to aid or injure special business concerns; and other unfair trade practices.

More Information

- Brands, H.W. *T.R.: The Last Romantic.* New York: Basic Books, 1997.
- Gable, John Allen. *The Bull Moose Years: Theodore Roosevelt and the Progressive Party.* Port Washington, NY: Kennikat Press, 1978.
- Graff, Henry F., ed. *The Presidents: A Reference History.* 3rd ed. New York: Macmillan, 2002.
- Miller, Nathan. *Theodore Roosevelt: A Life.* New York: Morrow, 1994.
- Morris, Edmund. *Theodore Rex.* New York: Random House, 2001.
- Mowry, George E. *The Era of Theodore Roosevelt, 1900–1912.* New York: Harper, 1958.

On the Web

- Almanac of Theodore Roosevelt. *http://www.theodore-roosevelt.com/trarmageddon.html.*
- Bull Moose Years of Theodore Roosevelt. *http://www.theodoreroosevelt.org/life/bullmoose.htm.*
- Progressive Movement. U-S-History.com. *http://www.u-s-history.com/pages/h1061.html.*
- Progressive Party. Encyclopedia Americana. *http://ap.grolier.com/article?assetid=0322300-00&templatename=/article/article.html.*

Farmer-Labor Party, 1918–44

FlashFocus: Farmer-Labor Party

Origins

The Farmer-Labor Party represented an unusually successful alliance between hard-pressed farmers and urban industrial workers at a time when both groups were suffering economic hardships. The party came together in 1918 as an amalgamation of three groups: the Non-Partisan League (an outgrowth of the Populist Party) of the 1890s, the Socialist Party, and the Minnesota Federation of Labor. It was active on the Minnesota state level from the early 1920s until the mid-1940s, pursuing a variety of causes important to poor grain farmers and industrial workers.

Issues

Unions. In an era when many conservative state governments used the police and state militia to crack down on unions to prevent them from striking, the Farmer-Labor Party used state forces to protect union organizing among miners in the state's Iron Range and among industrial workers in Minneapolis and St. Paul—including unions whose leaders had strong communist involvement.

Farm foreclosures. For many farmers, the 1930s were a time of bank foreclosures on loans (forced sale of property to repay loans). The first Farmer-Labor governor of Minnesota, Floyd Olsen, arranged a one-year moratorium on farm foreclosures.

Impact

The Farmer-Labor Party elected three Minnesota governors, four U.S. Senators, and controlled the state legislature during the 1930s. It was one of the most radical political parties ever elected to power in the United States. Once it gained power over the state government in the election of 1930, the party largely turned the tables on industrialists and bankers by using the state militia (National Guard) to protect the right of workers to organize unions and to strike, and suspending farm foreclosures for a year during the Great Depression—roles that were just the opposite of those assigned to militias of other states. In 1944, the party merged with the state Democratic Party, forming the Democratic-Farm-Labor Party.

See also: People's Party (Populists), p. 98; Progressive Party, 1924, p. 132; Socialist Party, p. 116; Democratic Party, 1932–68, p. 141.

Many farmers in the upper Midwest were suffering economically during World War I, caught in a squeeze between low prices for their crops and high costs for shipping and storage after harvest. The Farmer's Non-Partisan League had begun organizing in North Dakota in 1916 with five principal objectives: public ownership of grain elevators, flour mills, packing houses, and cold storage plants; exempting farm improvements from taxes; state inspection of grain; state hail insurance; and establishment of state-owned nonprofit banks to make low-cost loans to farmers. The Farmer's Non-Partisan League was effectively advocating socialist programs without socialism—that is, while the Socialist Party (see p. 116) also advocated government ownership of key economic institutions, the Non-Partisan League did not support public ownership of land (and other means of production, such as factories). Independent farmers were enthusiastic about the goals of the Farmer's Non-Partisan League while they rejected the same proposals from others as leading toward full-fledged socialism. In North Dakota, the Farmer's Non-Partisan League sought to implement its programs by competing in Republican primary elections (Democrats were not a competitive party in either North Dakota or Minnesota at the time). In 1916, the league captured control of North Dakota's Republican Party and went on to win the governorship and state house of representatives in the general election.

The next year, 1917, the Farmer's Non-Partisan League sent organizers east into neighboring Minnesota to try to duplicate their success. In Minnesota, the league was vigorously opposed by the Republican establishment, from the governor down to Republican professionals and local businessmen in small towns. League organizers were often beaten, tarred and feathered, or threatened with lynching. Many of their meetings were simply banned. The state government was also active in discouraging the Non-Partisan League. In April 1917, shortly after the United States entered World War I, the state legislature established the Public Safety Commission which had the power to "do and perform all acts and things necessary or proper so that the resources of the state may most efficiently be applied toward the successful prosecution" of the war. The chairman of the commission, John McGee, was chairman of the Minneapolis Grain Exchange and had fought with both farmers and labor unions. McGee and Governor Joseph Burnquist effectively declared that any opposition to American involvement in the war, and any left-wing organizing efforts, were unpatriotic and should be suppressed.

Nevertheless, the Non-Partisan League continued organizing, and by 1918 its candidate came within 50,000 votes of unseating Burnquist for the Republican nomination for governor. Organizing efforts continued after the war, and in 1924 the Farmer's Non-Partisan League and the Worker's Non-Partisan League merged into the Farmer-Labor Federation, renamed the Farmer-Labor Association in 1925.

Election Success

The Farmer-Labor Association was effectively the second largest party in Minnesota, behind the Republicans, until the stock market crash of 1929 led to the Great Depression. In 1930, the Farmer-Labor Association candidate for governor,

FlashFocus: Floyd Bjerstjerne Olson

Born: November 13, 1891, Minneapolis, Minnesota
Died: August 22, 1936, Rochester, Minnesota
Political Career: Prosecutor, Hennepin County, Minnesota, 1920–30; governor of Minnesota, 1930–36.

Floyd Olson was born in Minneapolis, Minnesota, to a Norwegian father and a Swedish mother. When his parents fought, Olson would escape to the homes of poor Jews in the neighborhood, and he developed an awareness of the effect poverty had on others. He attended the University of Minnesota, leaving after one year to travel west. He went to Alaska in search of gold before becoming a dock worker in Seattle, where he joined the International Workers of the World, a radical organization. He then returned to Minneapolis and studied law at Northwestern Law College. After graduating in 1915, he worked as a defense attorney.

Although many of Olson's ideas were radical, he began his political career as a moderate, joining the Democratic Party and running unsuccessfully for Congress as a Democrat in 1918 and 1920. Despite this affiliation with the Democrats, he was elected assistant attorney of Hennepin County in 1919 and county attorney in 1920 as a Republican, winning reelection as county attorney in 1922 and 1926. In addition, he aligned himself with the Farmer-Labor Association to run for governor of Minnesota; he lost in 1924, but ran again in 1930 and was elected. During his first term, his positions were more moderate than those of the Farmer-Labor Association.

As the Great Depression took hold across America, progressive measures became more popular, enabling Olson to become more outspoken about his position on reforms such as government ownership of utilities and unemployment benefits during his reelection campaign and after his reelection in 1932. His second term was decidedly more radical than his first, and he was highly popular with unions for his prolabor stance. Olson was reelected to a third term as governor in 1934 and continued to press for reforms. He campaigned for a seat in the Senate in 1936, but fell ill with cancer before the election. He died in Rochester, Minnesota, in 1936.

Floyd Olson (see above), was elected governor with 59.3 percent of the popular vote. Olson was a gifted speaker who reached out to farmers angry with falling prices and threats of bank foreclosures, and urban laborers denied the right to join unions and stage strikes for higher wages. He also had been an early supporter of the American Civil Liberties Union, founded to protect the constitutional rights of American citizens, especially those mentioned in the Bill of Rights.

The election successes of the Farmer-Labor Association were echoed in other ways. Farmers helped thwart foreclosure auctions by forcing artificially low bids so that a defaulting borrower could easily "buy" his farm from the bank; the Teamsters Union won a large-scale strike in Minneapolis, opening the way to widespread union organizing. The Congress of Industrial Organizations, a newly formed alliance of labor unions, launched organizing campaigns among lumberjacks and miners in the Iron Range region of the state.

Workers and farmers established cooperatives to compete with merchants in providing food, hardware, gasoline, and grain elevator storage. Many of these activities were tied, either informally or formally, to the Farmer-Labor Association, which went beyond being a political party to become part of a widespread social movement that included popular adult education programs.

As governor, Olson proceeded cautiously during his first term (1931 to 1933). In 1932, however, a widespread farmer's strike in Minnesota resulted in farmers holding their crops off the market in hopes of receiving higher prices. Olson endorsed the strike, as well as a wide variety of relief measures, including a moratorium on farm foreclosures. Although the farm strike eventually failed, it did lead to Olson's reelection by a wide margin in 1932, and the following April the governor threatened to impose martial law if the Republican-dominated state senate did not pass his proposed social relief measures.

Olson's move in the spring of 1933 coincided with the inauguration of Democrat Franklin Roosevelt (see Vol. 1, p. 141) as president. The social welfare programs proposed in Minnesota were similar in many ways to aspects of Roosevelt's New Deal. But Olson's programs preceded the New Deal, and the Minnesota governor became a national figure.

Olson was elected a third time in 1934. At its 1934 state convention, the Farmer-Labor Association passed a resolution that said: "We declare that capitalism has failed and that immediate steps must be taken by the people to abolish capitalism in a peaceful and lawful manner, and that a new, sane, and just society must be established, a system in which all the natural resources, machinery of production, transportation, and communications shall be owned by the government and operated democratically for the benefit of all the people, and not for the benefit of the few." The statement also demanded "public ownership of all mines, water power, transportation and communications systems, banks, packing plants, factories, and all public utilities," as well as the state takeover of idle factories. It promised state support for consumer cooperatives, state operated insurance programs, a two-year extension of the mortgage moratorium, free textbooks to all students (to be produced by a state-owned publishing operation), and a steep tax on large incomes and large inheritances. In all, it was perhaps the most radical declaration ever adopted by a party that controlled the governor's office and the state house of representatives (though not the state senate).

The Minneapolis Teamster's Strike

A few weeks after the Farmer-Labor Association passed its resolution, the Teamsters Union local chapter in Minneapolis voted to strike trucking companies that served the commercial and industrial companies in the city. The union was notable because its leaders were also members of the Communist League (a rival to the Communist Party, see p. 128) as well as being skilled organizers.

The strikers meant business. They organized patrols to block trucks driven by nonstriking teamsters from entering Minneapolis. They ran their own hospital, lest injured strikers be detained in hospitals controlled by private interests. The truckers were supported by 35,000 construction workers who walked off their jobs, as well as by striking farmers who made their produce available to the teamsters.

On May 20 and 21, 1934, violence erupted between striking teamsters and the police, as well as civilian volunteers, among whom were upper-class gentlemen dressed in stylish safari outfits. Two pitched battles ensued over two days, which the striking teamsters won. At least one antiunion combatant, a lawyer, was killed. The strikers overwhelmed the police and their allies, and seized control of the streets while the police were in hiding. Governor Olson intervened to arrange a truce without actually suppressing the strikers.

Two months later, on July 20, the two sides had a return engagement. Police drove a truck toward a line of teamster pickets in downtown Minneapolis. When the pickets moved to block the truck, police inside the truck opened fire, wounding 67 picketers and killing two. The teamsters were infuriated, and at a mass meeting, they called on the union to march on city hall to lynch the mayor and police chief. The union's leaders resisted the proposal to take over the city by force.

Three days later, federal mediators suggested a settlement of the strike—a small raise for the truckers—which the union accepted but the employers rejected. In response, Olson called out the National Guard to protect the strikers—an unprecedented use of the state militia to protect strikers against the police. Olson used the same technique at a later strike involving a flour mill.

Olson endorsed Roosevelt's reelection in 1936 (see Vol. 1, p. 144), and he was nominated to run for the U.S. Senate. But the governor died of stomach cancer before the election. He was succeeded by another Farmer-Labor candidate for governor, Elmer Benson, who was easily elected along with Farmer-Labor candidates who captured five of Minnesota's eight seats in Congress, the U.S. Senate seat that Olson was running to fill, and a solid majority in the state house of representatives, as well as many local offices.

Decline of the Farmer-Labor Association

In 1938, Benson was defeated by a Republican, Harold Stassen. The decline of the Farmer-Labor Association was largely attributed to its inability to solve the larger problems of the Great Depression and a general weariness with confrontations over the past eight years.

America's entry into World War II in 1941 further sealed the political fate of the Farmer-Labor Association as an independent political entity. In 1944, the association merged with the Minnesota Democratic Party to become the Democratic-Farmer-Labor (DFL) Party, which is the name still used in the twenty-first century.

The last struggle of the Farmer-Labor branch of the party was waged in 1948. The Farmer-Labor members of the new party wanted to endorse the Progressive Party candidacy of Henry Wallace (see p. 161) for president against Democrat Harry Truman (see Vol. 1, p. 154). The Democrats, led by Minneapolis Mayor Hubert Humphrey (see Vol. 1, p. 175), fought to endorse Truman. After six months of intense political warfare, Humphrey and the Democratic faction prevailed, effectively marking the end of the Farmer-Labor faction. Thereafter, the party was a branch of the national Democratic Party in all but name.

More Information

▶ Gieske, Millard. *Minnesota Farmer-Laborism: The Third Party Alternative.* Minneapolis: University of Minnesota Press, 1979.
▶ Haynes, John Earl. *Dubious Alliance: The Making of Minnesota's DFL Party.* Minneapolis: University of Minnesota Press, 1984.
▶ Valley, Richard M. *Radicalism in the States: The MFL Party and the American Political Economy.* Chicago: University of Chicago Press, 1989.

On the Web

▶ Kucera, Barb. "Farmer-Labor movement owes much to Mahoney." *http://www.workdayminnesota.org/permanent/ working_life/history/advocate_series/farmerlabor2.php.*
▶ The Non-Partisan League. Minnesota Historical Society. *http://www.mnhs.org/library/tips/history_topics/102nonpartisan .html.*
▶ O'Connell, Thomas G. Toward the Cooperative Commonwealth: An Introductory History of the Farmer-Labor Movement in Minnesota, 1917–1949. Ph.D. thesis. *http://www.mtn.org/~fholson/fla0hist.htm.*

Communist Party, 1919–

FlashFocus: Communist Party

Origins
Leaders of the 1917 Bolshevik Revolution in Russia called on left-wing parties abroad to form communist parties and to support their new government. In the United States, two such parties were formed but kept low profiles under intense government scrutiny. The two groups later merged into the Communist Party of the United States, led by labor organizers William Foster and Earl Browder. The active involvement of Russians in party affairs gave American communists the aura of being agents for a foreign country.

Issues
Revolution. The Communist Party advocated the revolutionary overthrow of the government in favor of a communist system based on a hierarchical, central leadership in which the government owned the means of production, i.e., factories, farms, and mines.
Workers' rights. The Communist Party in the United States supported workers' right to unionize, especially during the economic depression of the 1930s. Communist strategy was to work from inside labor unions to gain political clout.
Workers' rule. The party argued that the only way for workers to end exploitation was by the establishment of a government in which the working class was also the ruling power. This included abolishing privately owned corporations.
Support for the Soviet Union. The Communist Party in the United States often subordinated itself to direction from the Soviet Union, especially in foreign affairs. This laid the party open to accusations of treason, especially when American foreign policy conflicted with that of the U.S.S.R.
Civil rights. The Communist Party in the United States made a concerted effort to appeal to black Americans. It argued that African Americans were a national minority, not just a racial minority, and deserved their own country carved out of the southern states.

Impact
Communist Party membership rose during the economic depression of the 1930s, but the party's political and economic positions kept it from becoming a significant factor in American politics. Communists ran presidential candidates from 1924 to 1940 and from 1968 to 1984. Their best showing was in 1932, when Foster collected 103,253 votes (0.3 percent). Despite not running candidates for office, the Communist Party continued to function after 1984, helping organize protest demonstrations and publishing a weekly newspaper and monthly magazine. The fall of communism in the Soviet Union in 1991 diminished the already slight support for the party in the United States.

See also: Socialist Party, p. 116; American Labor Party, p. 152.

The Communist Party in the United States formed in 1919, just shortly after the Bolshevik Revolution in Russia and in the aftermath of World War I. Russian communists, confronted by civil war and invasion by British, French, and American forces, desperately sought support from left-wing sympathizers abroad. They urged American socialists to leave the Socialist Party and regroup as communists. Two major communist groups formed as a result: the larger Communist Party of America and the smaller Communist Labor Party. Both organizations wished to emulate the model of the Russian Communist Party as presided over by Vladimir Lenin—a close-knit, secretive organization that followed orders from its leaders. It was the same dictatorial organizational model followed by the new Soviet state under Lenin and later under Joseph Stalin. The main distinction between socialists and communists thus became one of organization rather than of abstract goals, such as democratic control of economic power (the means of production) as well as government power.

In the United States, Lenin's theory of how to organize a party in order to seize power—formulated in response to the antidemocratic pursuit by the Russian czars' secret police—proved to be the undoing of the Communist Party. The dictatorial reality of the Soviet government seemed entirely inappropriate for the open society of the United States and provided ammunition for right-wing opponents of socialism to brand the Communist Party—and by implication, all socialists—an agent of political oppression.

Early Days of the Communist Party

The administration of Woodrow Wilson (see Vol. 1, p. 121) and his attorney general, A. Mitchell Palmer, was highly sensitive to the prospect that the Bolshevik Revolution could spread to the United States. Federal agents conducted numerous raids in the period 1919–21 (called the Palmer raids) looking for communists and deporting noncitizen immigrants deemed to be subversive. It was just the first of many instances in which antisocialists evoked fears of revolution—what Palmer called the "tongues of revolutionary heat licking the altars of the churches, leaping into the belfry of the school bell, crawling into the sacred corners of American homes, seeking to replace marriage vows with libertine laws, burning up the foundations of society"—to justify suppression of civil liberties. In some respects, this early overreaction to the Communist Party foreshadowed the party's most significant impact in the long run—the inspiration of attacks on civil liberties by its opponents.

During this period, the Soviet government-controlled organization Comintern (Communist International) strongly urged disparate American communist groups to unify. The re-

Several Communist leaders pose for a picture at their 1948 arraignment for violation of the Smith Act. From left to right: William Foster, Jack Stachel, Henry Winston, Benjamin Davis, Eugene Dennis, and John Williamson.

sult was a new Communist Party formed in the mid-1920s with the goal of implementing the revolutionary vision of the Soviet Union in America by working through established labor organizations. Labor organizers William Foster and Earl Browder (see p. 130) directed the party's efforts.

The Communists ran their first presidential ticket in 1924 under the name of the Workers' Party. Foster was the presidential nominee, collecting just 38,669 votes (the winner that year, Republican Calvin Coolidge, had 15,723,789 votes; see Vol. 1, p. 132).

For the rest of the decade, the Communist Party tried unsuccessfully to increase its influence by courting the farmer-labor movement. Farmer-labor leaders such as Senator Robert La Follette of Wisconsin (see p. 133) blocked attempts by the Communists to become a leading voice of the Progressive movement. The party also led unsuccessful strikes among textile workers in New England and garment workers in New York. The failure of the strikes made it difficult to make inroads in the labor movement. In 1929, the faction of the party run by Foster and Browder was officially recognized by the Comintern, and the group was renamed the Communist Party of the United States of America.

Depression Era Growth

The severe economic depression arising from the stock market crash of 1929 presented the Communist Party with its best chance for growth. The party participated vigorously in unemployment relief movements, called for the equal rights of African Americans (and for establishment of a separate black republic in the South), and campaigned for the right of workers to join unions. The Communists also attacked socialists for supposedly being in league with capitalists after the socialists publicly opposed a violent revolution and opposed the Soviet system. The attacks isolated the Communists from actual political influence, even though party membership grew in the early 1930s.

In 1932, the Communists enjoyed their greatest electoral success. Campaigning on the theme that the Communist Party USA best represented the American underclass—African Americans, industrial workers, and farmers—the party won 103,311 votes (out of 40 million cast), which represented 0.3 percent of the popular vote. After the overwhelming victory of Democrat Franklin Roosevelt (see Vol. 1, p. 140), the Communists began working with noncommunist groups, dropped their opposition to New Deal programs, and gained influence among union movements. In 1940, after previously opposing German expansion in Europe, the Communist Party suddenly dropped that part of its platform following signing of a Soviet-German nonaggression pact. That change seemed to underscore the Communist Party's willingness to take orders from Moscow, and the party lost popular support.

During World War II, Browder dissolved the party, deciding instead to operate from inside the established parties. In 1944, the Communists supported Roosevelt for a fourth term (Roosevelt rejected their endorsement). The party had respect

FlashFocus: Earl Russell Browder

Born: May 20, 1891, Wichita, Kansas
Died: June 27, 1973, Princeton, New Jersey
Political Career: Secretary, Communist Party USA, 1929–44.

Browder's formal education ended after the third grade, when he went to work to help support his family. At age 15, Browder joined the Socialist Party and later joined the Syndicalist League of North America, where he headed a local trade union chapter. Upon finishing a correspondence course in law in 1914, Browder managed a farmers' cooperative store in Olathe, Kansas.

Like many leftists, Browder opposed U.S. participation in World War I and refused to be drafted into the army. He was jailed for 16 months, after which he joined the Communist Party, then fixated on the 1917 Bolshevik Revolution that had put communists in power in Russia. In 1921, he attended the first Congress of the Red International of Labor Unions in Moscow representing the Trade Union Educational League. When the Communist Party merged with the Workers Party to form the Communist Party of the USA, Browder became the top aide to party secretary William Foster.

After attending another conference in Moscow in 1926, Browder went to China as part of a Communist delegation. He stayed there for three years as the secretary of the Pan-Pacific Trade Union Secretariat and editor of an underground newspaper. When he returned to the United States in 1929, Browder took over as secretary of the Communist Party, a position he held for the next 15 years.

Under Browder, Communist Party membership grew, and the party gained respect among intellectuals. Browder tried to create a broader alliance of reformers and changed the name of the Communist Party to the Communist Political Association as a patriotic gesture. Browder ran for president as a Communist in 1936 and 1940. However, Communist leaders in Moscow, feeling that Browder had deviated from the principles of communism, dissolved the association in 1945, and the Communist Party was reestablished. Browder was expelled from the party soon afterward, ending his political career. He died in Princeton, New Jersey, in 1973.

and membership after it stopped opposing American involvement in World War II, and it even began to argue there was no longer a need for an international revolutionary organization and that it was now loyal to the United States.

But after World War II, when the U.S.-Soviet wartime alliance ended and the Cold War began, Communists in the United States became suspect in the eyes of voters and the government alike. Browder was removed as the leader of the party after being denounced by the Kremlin and stripped of his party membership. The party now returned to its role of endorsing the principles and edicts of the Soviet Union, opposing the Marshall Plan and the establishment of the North American Treaty Organization among American allies.

The federal government investigated and prosecuted Communists who had gained leadership positions in labor unions and the federal government. Eleven Communist leaders were convicted of attempting to overthrow the government of the United States in 1949, in violation of the Smith Act of 1940. The next year, Congress passed legislation (the Taft-Hartley Act) requiring Communists to register with the federal government and to reveal the names of any contributors to the movement. In addition, Senator Joseph McCarthy of Wisconsin conducted widely publicized congressional hearings, nominally to identify Communists who might be working in the federal government. Restrictions placed on the Communists during the years after World War II basically outlawed the party.

The government crackdown and the McCarthy hearings resulted in a massive loss of members. The party did not resume electoral politics until 1968, a tumultuous year in which the United States was sharply divided over the Vietnam War and civil rights. The party's candidate, Charlene Mitchell, won just 1,077 votes. Four years later, Communist Gus Hall won 25,597 votes (compared to over 47 million votes for winner Richard Nixon; see Vol. 1, p. 173) after the party returned to its traditional calls for the end of minority oppression, decreasing the strength of the American military, and better wages for workers.

The Communists stopped running presidential candidates after 1984.

Communist Party Platform, 1924

In 1924, the Communist Party of the United States mounted its first campaign for president. Following are excerpts from its platform that year.

The workers and exploited farmers of the United States face the question of how to organize and use their political power in the coming election. Before deciding this question every industrial worker, agricultural worker, and exploited farmer should give fundamental consideration to the situation which exists in this country.

In the Grip of the Exploiters

The United States is the wealthiest country in the world. We have natural resources which supply us with raw materials and a great industrial organization which can turn these raw materials into the finished products which satisfy human needs. With the raw materials available and the tremendous machinery of production we have the means of giving a high standard of life – good food, good clothing, good homes, the opportunity for education and recreation – to every person in this country. This high standard of life is denied the workers and exploited farmers of the United States. Millions of these producers of wealth are able to secure for their labor only the means for a bare existence. Millions of workers must work long hours, under bad working conditions, for low wages. Millions are periodically unemployed, as at present, with all the consequent misery and suffering for themselves and their families. In order to keep these conditions from growing worse, millions of industrial workers are periodically compelled to go on strike to fight back the greedy employers. Millions of farmers have been driven into bankruptcy and from the land because of inability to earn enough for a living. These conditions prevail in a country in which we have the means of supplying a high standard of life to every person because a relatively small class has fastened its grip upon the raw materials and industries and uses these to enrich itself at the expense of the producers. Through theft, fraud, corruption, bribery and the capitalist system of profit taking, this capitalist class has become the owner of the land, raw material and machinery of production upon which the workers and farmers are dependent for a livelihood. The raw materials and industries of the United States are owned by the Garys, Morgans, Rockefellers, Fords, McCormicks, and other great capitalists. The workers and farmers alike pay tribute to these capitalists. They are compelled to accept a low standard of living in order that the capitalists may amass even greater fortunes for themselves. It is this system of capitalist ownership of industry which gives the wealth produced to the few, that denies the millions of industrial workers, agricultural workers and exploited farmers the enjoyment of that high standard of life which their labor and the wealth they produce make possible in this country. It is this system of capitalist ownership of industry which is the basis of the class struggle between the workers, fighting for more of what they produce, and the capitalists, ever bent on securing greater and greater profits for themselves.

How the Capitalists Use the Government

The government of the United States is and has been a government of, by, and for the capitalists. It is through the government and use of the governmental power that the capitalists maintain their grip on the industries and their power to rob the industrial workers, agricultural workers, and farmers. During the war, with the connivance of government officials, the capitalists looted the country of billions of wealth. Since the war the shipping board deals, the war veterans' board corruption, the Teapot Dome exposures have shown how the capitalists fill their pockets at the expense of the working and farming masses.... The government is a dictatorship of the capitalists and their instrument for the oppression and exploitation of the workers. Although the workers are permitted to vote, the capitalists are able, through their control of the means of information and through their economic power, to completely dominate the government, national, state and local.

The Workers Must Rule

There is only one way in which the exploitation of the workers and farmers of this country can be ended. That is through the workers organizing their mass power, ending the capitalist dictatorship and establishing the Workers' and Farmers' Government....

More Information

▶ Isserman, Maurice. *Which Side Were You On? The American Communist Party during the Second World War.* Champaign-Urbana: University of Illinois Press, 1994.
▶ Klehr, Harvey and John E. Haynes. *The American Communist Movement: Storming Heaven Itself.* New York: Twayne, 1992.
▶ Marx, Karl and Friedrich Engels. *The Communist Manifesto.* New York: Signet reprint edition, 1998 (first published 1848).
▶ Ottanelli, F. M. *The Communist Party of the United States from the Depression to World War II.* New Brunswick, N.J.: Rutgers University Press, 1991.

On the Web

▶ Communist Party in the United States. *http://www.infoplease.com/ce6/history/A0857499.html.*
▶ Communist Party in the United States. *http://www.bartleby.com/65/co/CommunisUS.html.*
▶ CPUSA Online. *http://www.cpusa.org/.*
▶ Socialist Party of America. *http://www.spartacus.schoolnet.co.uk/USAsocialismP.htm.*
▶ Workers' Party Platform 1924. *http://www.geocities.com/*

Progressive Party, 1924

FlashFocus: Progressive Party, 1924

Origins

The Progressive Party of 1924 was a coalition of railway union leaders, stragglers from Theodore Roosevelt's Progressive ("Bull Moose") Party of 1912, and socialists. The party decided to field only a presidential ticket in 1924, headed by Wisconsin Senator Robert LaFollette.

Issues

Monopolies. The party advocated federal intervention to destroy monopolies and large corporations, as well as public ownership of railroads.
Tax policy. The Progressive Party favored reducing taxes on moderate incomes and increasing taxes on the wealthy, including taxes on inheritance, large estates, and "excess" profits.
Working conditions. The Progressive Party advocated federal regulation of industries, including a "fair wage," safe working conditions, an end to child labor, and regulations to protect women in the workplace.
Election of federal judges. Progressives objected to federal court injunctions against strikes and proposed that federal judges be popularly elected rather than appointed by the executive branch.
Arms reduction. La Follette made himself a national figure by opposing American participation in World War I, and the party called for a reduction of the size of the U.S. military.
National referendums. The Progressive Party called for amendments to the Constitution that would provide for the direct nomination and election of the president, rather than the electoral college system, and also referendums to decide questions of war in the absence of a direct invasion of United States soil.

Impact

Robert La Follette received 4.8 million votes (16.6 percent), but carried only one state, Wisconsin. The party fell apart as a national entity after the death of La Follette in 1925; his sons revived the party at the state level in Wisconsin in the mid-1930s.

See also: Progressive ("Bull Moose") Party, p. 121; Progressive Party 1948, p. 160; Election of 1924, Vol. 1, p. 132.

As with the Progressive Party organized by Theodore Roosevelt (see Vol. 1, p. 114) for the 1912 election (popularly called the Bull Moose Party; see p. 121), the Progressive Party of the mid 1920s was a reform effort shaped by a Republican in response to a trend toward conservative policies. Senator Robert La Follette (see p. 133) of Wisconsin was the leader of this new iteration of the Progressive Party, which had its greatest appeal among organized labor and farmers.

Origins of the Progressive Party

Leaders of railroad and machinist unions came together to form the Conference for Progressive Political Action (CPPA) in 1922. La Follette was an early supporter of the effort, and the organization was joined by several more groups such as the Farmer-Labor Party (see p. 125), the Socialist Party (see p. 116), and the American Federation of Labor. Encouraged by the victories of over 100 progressive candidates throughout the United States in 1922, and particularly La Follette's reelection to the Senate from Wisconsin, the group looked to stage a national effort in 1924. Throughout 1923, the socialist and labor union factions of the group squabbled over whether or not to establish a full-fledged political party. The final decision was made to run an independent presidential candidate in 1924 but to stay out of state and local elections.

The CPPA met in July 1924 to nominate a presidential ticket, although it was understood at the outset that the candidate would be La Follette. He in turn chose Democratic Senator Burton Wheeler of Montana as his vice presidential running mate. When La Follette predicted that the results of the election would bring about the need for a new political party dedicated to the progressive cause, American socialists gave him their support.

La Follette was well-known throughout the nation for his opposition to American involvement in World War I and his defense of freedom of speech during wartime. As governor of Wisconsin, La Follette had advocated reform policies such as workers' compensation (continuing-pay in case of illness or injury), progressive taxation (higher-paid people pay a higher percentage of their income in taxes), and a reduction in railroad freight rates (a favorite topic for farmers). These programs taken together became known as the "Wisconsin Idea."

The 1924 Progressive Party platform, most of which was taken from a variety of speeches given by La Follette, reflected the desires of the various constituencies that shaped the party. Agricultural interests were represented in the party's call for abolishing corporate monopolies, as well as provisions for farm credit and government assurance of fair market prices. Socialists were mollified by the party's stance on public ownership of railroads and the electric power system, while labor unions endorsed proposed legislation to eliminate the use of court-ordered injunctions to halt labor disputes.

In addition to these bows to internal interest groups, the party advocated the popular election of, and term limits on, federal judges (who, under the Constitution, were appointed by the president for life terms) and holding a referendum before going to war. The party also endorsed a constitutional amendment to eliminate the electoral college in presidential elections and instead to choose presidents by popular majority.

The Election and the Party's End

In 1924, both the Democratic and Republican presidential nominees were viewed as quite conservative, especially in comparison to La Follette. The Democrats nominated corporate attorney John Davis (see Vol. 1, p. 134), who would later argue the losing side of *Brown v. Board of Education* in front of the Supreme Court in 1954 (see Vol. 3, p. 141). Republican Calvin Coolidge (see Vol. 1, p. 133) was the incumbent (he had succeeded President Warren Harding—see Vol. 1, p. 129—after Harding's death) who was well-known for his hands-off approach to government and business relations. The 1924 campaign was rough, and Republicans enthusiastically attacked La Follette for his previous isolationism and antiwar stance, accusing him of sympathizing with Germany.

The Progressive Party was at a disadvantage organizationally, even compared with other third parties of the past. Because the party advertised the fact that it was not necessarily going to remain a permanent fixture on the political scene, it could not generate support from candidates running for lesser offices around the nation. Outside Wisconsin and its surrounding states, a campaign staff of nonprofessionals proved to be a hindrance going up against the well-organized and well-funded major parties.

La Follette and Burton picked up just under 5 million votes (16.6. percent), but carried only La Follette's home state of Wisconsin. Coolidge won the election with 15.7 million votes (54 percent). Still, La Follette won a higher percentage of the vote than any previous third party with the exception of Theodore Roosevelt in 1912 (see Vol. 1, p. 121). The Progressive Party ran second to Coolidge in California, Idaho, Iowa, Minnesota, Montana, Nevada, North Dakota, Oregon, South Dakota, Washington, and Wyoming.

The Progressive Party ceased to be a national force after La Follette's death in 1925. It was revived in Wisconsin by La Follette's sons in the 1930s when Robert La Follette, Jr., became a United States senator and Philip La Follette became governor of Wisconsin, but the "La Follette movement" did not extend beyond Wisconsin.

Platform of the Progressive Party, 1924

Excerpts from the 1924 platform of the Progressive Party headed on the national ticket by Robert M. La Follette.

The great issue before the American people today is the control of government and industry by private monopoly.

For a generation the people have struggled patiently, in the face of repeated betrayals by successive administrations, to free themselves from this intolerable power which has been undermining representative government.

Through control of government, monopoly has steadily extended its absolute dominion to every basic industry.

In violation of law, monopoly has crushed competition, stifled private initiative and independent enterprise…

The equality of opportunity proclaimed by the Declaration of

FlashFocus: Robert La Follette

Born: June 14, 1855, Primrose, Wisconsin
Died: June 18, 1925, Washington, D.C.
Political Career: District attorney, Dane County, Wisconsin, 1880-84; U.S. Representative from Wisconsin, 1884-90; governor of Wisconsin, 1900-06; U.S. Senator from Wisconsin, 1906-24; Progressive candidate for president, 1924.

In an era when both the Republican and Democratic Parties were essentially conservative institutions, Robert La Follette carried the banner of the progressive wing of the Republicans for two decades, finally running for president on the ticket of a revived Progressive Party in 1924.

La Follette, the son of a small farmer, was a practicing attorney before becoming district attorney of Dane County, Wisconsin, at age 25. Four years later he was elected to the U.S House of Representatives as a Republican. La Follette was reelected twice before losing his seat in 1890, mainly due to his vote in favor of the Tariff Act of 1890.

La Follette resumed his law practice and was elected governor of Wisconsin in 1900 after two unsuccessful campaigns for the office. As governor, La Follette favored government reform, workers' compensation (continued pay in case of illness or injury), popular election of U.S. senators, and progressive taxation. Together, these positions became known as the "Wisconsin Idea."

La Follette resigned as governor in 1906 to take his seat in the U.S. Senate, which he had won in a special election the year before. He was eventually reelected to the Senate three times. In 1912, La Follette was a leading candidate for the newly formed Progressive Party until former President Theodore Roosevelt decided to head the ticket instead. La Follette then resigned from the new party, only to revive it a dozen years later. La Follette supported Democrat Woodrow Wilson for president in 1912.

In the Senate, La Follette was an outspoken opponent of military build-up and American entry into World War I. After the war, he led a Senate investigation into corruption in the administration of his fellow Republican, President Warren Harding.

Frustrated with the political climate, La Follette founded the National Progressive Republican League to try to move his party toward a more liberal stance on various issues. La Follette and his wife, Belle, founded a magazine in 1909 that is still published today as *The Progressive*.

Faced with solidly conservative candidates for president in 1924, La Follette revived the Progressive Party, which nominated him for president. La Follette finished a distant third behind President Calvin Coolidge and Democratic candidate John W. Davis. La Follette died the next year and was succeeded in the Senate by his son, Robert La Follette, Jr.

Independence and asserted and defended by Jefferson and Lincoln as the heritage of every American citizen has been displaced by special privilege for the few, wrested from the government of the many…

We pledge a complete housecleaning in the Department of Justice, the Department of the Interior, and the other executive departments. We demand that the Federal Government be used to crush private monopoly, not to foster it.

We favor…the fixing of railroad rates upon the basis of actual, prudent investment and cost of service. We pledge speedy enactment of the Howell-Barkley Bill for the adjustment of controversies between railroads and their employees, which was held up in the last Congress by joint action of reactionary leaders of the Democratic and Republican parties. We declare for public ownership of railroads with definite safeguards against bureaucratic control, as the only…solution of the transportation problem.

We…favor a taxation policy providing for immediate reductions of moderate incomes, large increases in the inheritance tax rates upon large estates to prevent the indefinite accumulation by inheritance of great fortunes in few hands, taxes upon excess profits to penalize profiteering, and complete publicity, under proper safeguards, of all Federal tax returns…

We favor submitting to the people, for their considerate judgment, a constitutional amendment providing that Congress may by enacting a statute make it effective over a judicial veto.

We favor such an amendment to the constitution as may be necessary to provide for the election of all Federal Judges, without party designation, for fixed terms, not exceeding ten years, by direct vote of the people.

We favor abolition of the use of injunctions in labor disputes and declare for complete protection of the right of farmers and industrial workers to organize, bargain collectively through representatives of their own choosing, and conduct without hindrance cooperative enterprises.

We demand that the Interstate Commerce Commission proceed forthwith to reduce by an approximation to pre-war levels the present freight rates on agricultural products, including live stock, and upon the materials required upon American farms for agricultural purposes.

We favor prompt ratification of the Child Labor amendment, and subsequent enactment of a Federal law to protect children in industry.

Over and above constitutions and statutes and greater than all is the supreme sovereignty of the people and with them should rest the final decision of all great questions of national policy. We favor such amendments to the Federal Constitution as may be necessary to provide for the direct nomination and election of the President, to extend the initiative and referendum to the federal government, and to insure a popular referendum for or against war except in cases of actual invasion.

We denounce the mercenary system of foreign policy under recent administrations in the interests of financial imperialists, oil monopolists and international bankers, which has at times degraded our State Department from its high service as a strong and kindly intermediary of defenseless governments to a trading outpost for those interests and concession-seekers engaged in the exploitations of weaker nations, as contrary to the will of the American people, destructive of domestic development and provocative of war. We favor an active foreign policy to bring about a revision of the Versailles treaty in accordance with the terms of the armistice, and to promote firm treaty agreements with all nations to outlaw wars, abolish conscription, drastically reduce land, air, and naval armaments, and guarantee public referendum on peace and war.

More information

- Greenbaum, Fred. *Robert M. La Follette.* Boston: Twayne, 1975.
- Maxwell, Robert S. *La Follette and the Rise of Progressives in Wisconsin.* Madison: University of Wisconsin Press, 1956.
- Thelen, David. *Robert M. La Follette and the Insurgent Spirit.* Madison: University of Wisconsin Press, 1976.
- Unger, Nancy. *Fighting Bob La Follette: The Righteous Reformer.* Chapel Hill: University of North Carolina Press, 2000.
- Weisberger, Bernard A. *The La Follettes of Wisconsin: Love and Politics in Progressive America.* Madison: University of Wisconsin Press, 1994.

On the Web

- La Follette Progressives, U-S-History.com. *http://www.u-s-history.com/pages/h1440.html.*
- Progressive Party. *http://gi.grolier.com/presidents/ea/side/progress.html.*
- Robert M. La Follette. *http://www.msys.net/cress/ballots2/lafoll.htm.*

Republican Party, 1932–68

FlashFocus: Republican Party, 1932–68

Origins
The Republican Party suffered devastating losses in 1932, marking the end to over seven decades of domination of national politics. The party could do little but look on as Democratic President Franklin Roosevelt ushered in a new era of government involvement in the economy during the Great Depression, then presided over all but the last few months of World War II. Throughout the middle third of the twentieth century, Republicans held onto the essentially conservative beliefs enunciated by President William Taft and continued by his son, Senator Robert "Mr. Republican" Taft of Ohio.

Issues
Foreign policy. In the years before American entry into World War II, Republicans pursued an isolationist foreign policy, opposing U.S. involvement in another European conflict. After World War II, Republicans supported containment of Soviet influence.

Taxes. A fundamental principle of the modern Republican Party was the belief that lower taxes would spur economic growth. The party supported tax reductions and also argued for simplifying the federal tax code.

Welfare reform. Reducing federal involvement in federal welfare was a hallmark of the party during the era of the New Deal under President Franklin Roosevelt and under President Lyndon Johnson's Great Society (1964–68). During the presidency of Republican Dwight Eisenhower (1953–61), Republicans constantly resisted welfare programs favored by Democrats who controlled Congress for all but four years in the period 1931 to 1981.

Government regulation. The Republican Party argued that excessive federal regulation of business caused increased costs and excessive government influence in private enterprise. Republicans consistently supported laws to reduce governmental regulations.

Impact
In the 36 years between 1933 and 1969, Republicans held the White House for just eight years (1953 to 1961). Of the 18 Congresses that met during that period, Republicans held majorities in both houses just twice (1947–49 and 1953–55) and failed to capture a majority in either house of Congress in the other 16 Congresses. The party was largely reduced to foot-dragging, resisting, or trying to dilute Democratic programs that made the federal government an important force in protecting citizens from economic downturns and extending full rights to minorities. In foreign affairs, Republicans were isolationists up to the eve of World War II (1941–45), but were enthusiastic supporters of the Cold War (1945–91).

See also: Republican Party, 1900–32, p. 105; Republican Party, 1968–2004, p. 163; Democratic Party 1932–68, p. 141.

The stock market crash of 1929 presaged the end to over 70 years of Republican domination of national politics. Herbert Hoover's election as president in 1928 was the last Republican victory until 1952, and the 71st Congress of 1928–31 marked the last time Republicans controlled both the House of Representatives and the Senate for the next 64 years, with two exceptions (the 80th Congress, 1947–49, and the 83rd Congress, 1953–55. The period from 1932 to 1968 falls into four distinct parts in the life of the Republican Party and the nation as a whole: the Great Depression (1930–40); World War II (1941–45); the Cold War (1945–91); and the Sixties, a decade that saw enormous cultural and social changes sweep across the country during the Vietnam War.

Throughout these tumultuous decades, the Republican Party held firm on principles that had governed it since the late 1800s: belief in limited government, confidence that business should be largely left alone, and strong support for the conservative social positions shared by the white, Protestant, upper-middle and middle classes. While the party continued to be torn between a more liberal eastern wing and a conservative Midwestern and western wing, the ultranationalist support for American overseas expansion that characterized parts of the party earlier in the twentieth century gave way to a conservative isolationist streak in the years leading up to World War II.

Depression and the Republicans

The magnitude of the economic depression touched off by the stock market crash of 1929—and a subsequent, even greater crash in 1930—was unprecedented in the United States. A fourth of the working population was out of work, often with no way of obtaining food short of charity. To make matters worse, a severe drought hit the nation's midsection, making it impossible for many farmers to grow crops, much less keep up payments on loans. In the middle of the decade, both the industrial economy and the agricultural economy lay in ruins.

In 1932, Republicans nominated President Herbert Hoover (see Vol. 1, p. 137) for reelection. Hoover had already spent two years trying to alleviate the worst effects of the depression, with very limited success. Hoover, like the rest of his party, firmly believed that the Constitution limited his freedom of action and that he lacked constitutional authority to take more dramatic measures. Hoover speeded up federal construction projects and urged state governments to do the same. He tried to organize efforts to relieve potential starvation of unemployed workers, but his efforts fell far short of what was needed. Hoover lost the election with just 39.6 percent of the vote to 57.4 percent for Democrat Franklin Roosevelt (see Vol. 1, p. 141), a margin of nearly seven million votes.

In Roosevelt, the Republicans faced the most formidable political opponent they had ever faced, or ever faced again. The former New York governor exuded optimism in an era of deep pessimism, campaigning on the tune "Happy Days Are Here Again" even though that was far from the truth. Unlike the cautious, conservative Republicans, Roosevelt was willing to try nearly anything to relieve misery while trying to restart the economy. Outnumbered in the House of Representatives 310 to 117 and in the Senate 60 to 35 during the 73rd Congress from 1933 to 1935, and by even greater margins in 74th and 75th Congresses, the Republicans were helpless to affect Roosevelt's New Deal program of federal intervention in the economy.

In 1936, Republicans nominated Governor Alf Landon (see Vol. 1, p. 145) of Kansas, a moderate conservative, for president. He lost to Roosevelt by a margin of 36.5 percent to 60.8 percent, an even worse showing than Hoover's loss in 1932 (39.6 percent to 57.4 percent).

The only brake on Roosevelt was the Supreme Court, where four justices—Willis Van Devanter (see Vol. 3, p. 85), James McReynolds (see Vol. 3, p. 87), George Sutherland (see Vol. 3, p. 95), and Pierce Butler (see Vol. 3, p. 96)—all but one of whom had been appointed by a Republican president—consistently declared New Deal programs to be unconstitutional. (Called the "Four Horsemen," these justices were joined on different cases by a fifth justice to create a majority in finding laws unconstitutional.) The Supreme Court's deliberations were not overtly political, but the positions taken by the Four Horsemen were consistent with the positions of Republicans in Congress. Even this restraint was finally removed in 1937, after Roosevelt proposed adding up to six new justices to overcome the conservatives' opposition. His plan was thwarted, but proved effective as Chief Justice Charles Hughes (see Vol. 1, p. 126, and Vol. 3, p. 104) intervened to clear the way for the president's legislation.

Throughout the 1930s, Republican leadership in Congress was consistently more conservative than the party's rank-and-file members. This division between die-hard opponents of the New Deal in Congress and more moderate Republicans in the field was reflected in the party's 1936 presidential nomination. Landon was the candidate of the moderate wing, even as hidebound conservatives continued to dominate the actions of the Republican minority in Congress. It was a division that continued to split Republican ranks until 1944.

The conservative wing of the party was led by Senator Robert Taft of Ohio, son of the late president and Supreme Court Chief Justice William Howard Taft (see Vol. 1, p. 118 and Vol. 3, p. 95). In foreign policy, the Taft conservatives advocated isolationism, opposing aid to Great Britain before World War II and aid to rebuild Europe after the war. Domestically, Taft and his supporters were devoted enemies of the New Deal, arguing that the policies and executive actions taken by Roosevelt lay outside the constitutional authority of the president—virtually the same position taken by Taft's father during his administration and by Herbert Hoover from 1929 to 1932. The Taft conservatives were convinced that expanding social programs, and even the war effort itself, would erode individual freedoms by creating a stronger central government.

World War II

The Great Depression yielded to economic recovery only with the onset of war in Europe after 1939. Manufacturing of armaments to provide to Britain under the Lend Lease program initiated by Roosevelt helped stimulate a recovery in the industrial sector, even as the effects of drought eased for the agricultural sector. Republicans nominated a moderate former Democrat, corporate lawyer Wendell Willkie, for president in 1940. He lost to Roosevelt, but gained 44.8 percent of the vote, the Republicans' best showing since 1928. (Roosevelt was re-elected with 54.7 percent of the vote, down from 60.8 percent in 1936.)

American entry into the war was by no means a foregone conclusion in 1940 and 1941. Roosevelt, persuaded that American interests lay in saving Britain from the assault by Germany, had maneuvered ways to provide military aid to the British while remaining officially neutral. Congressional Republicans were led by midwesterners who were outspokenly isolationist, resisting any steps that might involve the United States in another war after World War I. Their position became untenable on the morning of December 7, 1941, when the Japanese Navy attacked the U.S. Pacific fleet lying at anchor at Pearl Harbor, Hawaii. From that moment, the political equation changed sharply. The surprise attack instantly united the nation behind a gargantuan, all-consuming effort to win the war, with Roosevelt as commander-in-chief.

Nevertheless, despite the war, Republicans made gains in the Congressional elections of 1942, adding 46 seats to their total in the House of Representatives and nine seats in the Senate. Two years later, with war still raging in Europe and Asia, Roosevelt's margin of victory for an unprecedented fourth term fell to 53.4 percent to 45.9 percent for Republican Thomas Dewey (see Vol. 1, p. 152) of New York, representative of the eastern liberal wing of the party, although the choice was distasteful to conservative Republicans from the Midwest led by the outspoken Senator Taft of Oho. In the 1944 Congressional races, Republicans gained one seat in the Senate but lost 18 seats in the House.

On April 12, 1945, Franklin Roosevelt died suddenly of a cerebral hemorrhage, just five months after his fourth presidential election victory. He was replaced by Vice President Harry Truman of Missouri, opening a fresh opportunity for the Republicans.

The Cold War

Five months after Truman took office, World War II ended with the unconditional surrender of Japan on September 2, 1945 (Germany had surrendered on May 7, 1945). But already, the shape of the war in Europe had set the stage for another conflict, the Cold War. The Soviet Union, ruled by the Communist Party since 1917, had occupied the eastern half of

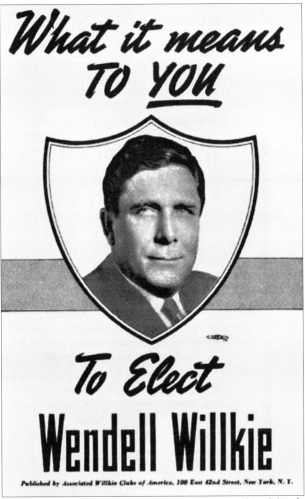

Fliers such as this one distributed by the Associated Willkie Clubs of America during Wendell Willkie's presidential campaign were the primary means of advertising before television.

Europe, driving back German troops to Berlin, while American forces, allied with Britain, had largely occupied the western half of the continent. As the Soviets advanced, they set up and supported domestic communists, even as the United States launched programs to help reconstruct western Europe under the rule of noncommunist parties.

In the life of the Republican Party, the end of World War II led to victories in Congressional elections of 1946 that gave the party control of both houses of Congress for the first time since 1928. Republicans gained 55 House seats and 13 Senate seats, but managed to turn their victory into defeat by overstretching. Eager to make up for nearly a decade and a half of powerlessness, the Republicans managed to alienate nearly every bloc of voters, even while failing to achieve their program because they could not overcome presidential vetoes. And they handed Truman a campaign slogan for 1948, when he ran against the "do nothing" Republican 80th Congress.

Nevertheless, Democrats handed Republicans a seemingly golden opportunity in 1948 when they split into three factions: southern conservatives, enraged over a civil rights plank in the Democratic platform, bolted and formed the Dixiecrats (see Vol. 4, p. 87), nominating South Carolina Governor Strom Thurmond, while liberals followed former cabinet secretary Henry Wallace (see p. 161) into a fourth manifestation of the Progressive Party (see p. 160). So convinced were Republicans that the Democrats were fatally split and that their nominee, Thomas Dewey of New York (see Vol. 1, p. 152), would win, that on election eve an early edition of the *Chicago Daily Tribune* printed a bold headline: "Dewey Defeats Truman." Later, it was Truman's pleasure to hold up the newspaper after the final results were in: Truman 49.6 percent, Dewey 45.1 percent. Even that margin of victory understates the Republican loss, since the two breakaway Democratic factions, Dixiecrats and Progressives, together polled 4.8 percent of the vote, which might have been expected to go to the Democrats. Republicans also lost control of both the House and Senate.

At the same time, however, the Cold War was having a different sort of impact. Conservatives in Congress began delving into alleged communist influence in the government during the Roosevelt years, a period in which the official policy of the American Communist Party (see p. 128) was to operate inside other parties and inside the government. In August 1948, a former communist, Whittaker Chambers, testified before the Republican-controlled House Un-American Affairs Committee that a former State Department official in the Roosevelt administration, Alger Hiss, had been a member of the Communist Party. Hiss denied the allegation, and the testimony had little impact on the 1948 elections.

But a young Republican congressman (and later senator) from California, Richard Nixon (see Vol. 1, p. 174), took the Chambers allegations and ran with them after Hiss was convicted of perjury two years later. So too did a previously obscure Republican senator from Wisconsin, Joseph McCarthy, who claimed he had a list of 255 communists working for the State Department. Did the Democrats knowingly permit communists to work in the government? Such was the allegation of Nixon and McCarthy in a series of hearings that lasted into the early 1950s—hearings that helped propel Nixon onto the Republican ticket as the vice presidential nominee in 1952 and McCarthy into being censured by the Senate in 1954.

In foreign affairs, Truman had intervened in Korea after communist North Koreans invaded the southern half of the country. Fighting under the flag of the United Nations, the war rapidly bogged down, giving the Republicans a campaign theme in 1952. At the 1952 Republican convention, the commander of U.S. and British forces in Europe at the end of World War II, General Dwight Eisenhower (see Vol. 1, p. 159), was nominated after defeating Taft by a small majority on the first ballot. Eisenhower immediately sought to bring the Republicans together by signing a statement of principles drafted by Taft and asking California's now-Senator Nixon to be his vice presidential running mate. Eisenhower also promised to go to Korea to find a way out of a military stalemate.

FlashFocus: Robert Alphonso Taft

Born: September 8, 1889, Cincinnati, Ohio
Died: July 31, 1953, New York, New York
Political Career: Ohio house of representatives, 1920–26; Ohio state senate 1931–33; U.S. Senator from Ohio, 1938–53.

Robert Taft was "Mr. Republican" during his tenure in the U.S. Senate, a widely respected spokesman for the quintessential midwestern conservatism of the Republican Party.

The son of president and Supreme Court Justice William Taft, Robert Taft attended the Taft School, founded by his uncle, Yale University, and Harvard Law school, receiving his law degree in 1913. He practiced law in Cincinnati until U.S. entry into World War I in 1917, when he was rejected from the army for poor vision. Instead, he served as assistant counselor to the U.S. Food Administration. After the war, he was a legal advisor to the American Relief Administration, where he caught the attention of Herbert Hoover, who named Taft to the administration's executive board.

Taft's political career began in 1920, when he was elected to the Ohio state legislature, becoming speaker of the state house of representatives in 1926. He left the legislature in 1931, when he was elected to one term as state senator.

In 1938, Taft was elected to the U.S. Senate, where he would serve until his death in 1953. He was an outspoken critic of the New Deal and U.S. involvement in the war that engulfed Europe in 1939, although once the U.S. entered World War II in 1941, he supported the war effort. After World War II, he opposed the trials and sentences of Nazi leaders because he believed their civilian trials were unconstitutional and were motivated by vengeance, not justice. Taft supported U.S. participation in the U.N., but otherwise remained an isolationist, discouraging the country from entering into military alliances. Although he had opposed drafting striking workers, he coauthored the Taft-Hartley Act of 1947, which sought to limit the power of organized labor. Taft also supported limited government aid to the underprivileged through public housing, health care, and education measures.

Taft wanted to be president and sought the Republican nomination several times, but he was never nominated. He died of cancer in 1953.

Eisenhower defeated Democrat Adlai Stevenson of Illinois (see Vol. 1, p. 160), and Republicans regained control of the House and Senate, thereby controlling Congress and the White House for the first time since Herbert Hoover's election in 1928. But from the party's standpoint, the dual victory was slightly misleading. Eisenhower, a career military officer, was not an avid Republican (he had been courted as a presidential candidate by both Republicans and Democrats) and had a strong aversion to becoming embroiled in party politics. Had he done so, it is possible he could have eased the strains between the party's conservative and liberal wings.

Instead, Eisenhower acted more like a nonpartisan president. This worked both ways for the Republicans. On the one hand, it enabled Eisenhower to attract traditionally Democratic voters—for example, he drew 45 percent of northern, urban blue-collar workers in 1952 and 50 percent in 1954—while also appealing to the rapidly growing, moderately conservative white suburban electorate. He also made inroads into the conservative South, where Democrats had long dominated but where the growing issue of civil rights was beginning to erode Democratic support among the white majority. Eisenhower's ability to maintain this broad appeal increased his margin of victory from 55.1 percent in 1952 to 57.4 percent in 1956.

On the other hand, Eisenhower's approach undercut Republican arguments in favor of a single party controlling both the White House and Congress. Democrats regained control of both the House and Senate in 1954 and continued to gain seats in 1956 and 1958. Eisenhower, unmoved by a strong desire to establish party dominance and faced with a Democratic majority in Congress for six of his eight years as president, worked willingly with the other party, which continued its control of Congress until 1981.

Eisenhower's second term (1957–61) was complicated by three factors: his decision to send federal troops to Little Rock, Arkansas, to enforce federal orders to integrate Central High School (see Vol. 4, p. 101); a sharp recession starting in 1957; and the president's own slight stroke in 1957, which temporarily impaired his speech and raised questions about his continued fitness for office. In the elections of 1958, Republicans lost more seats in Congress (47 seats in the House and 12 in the Senate), leaving the party even more heavily dependent on a lame duck and possibly ailing president.

The Sixties

In 1960, there was little challenge to Vice President Richard Nixon as the Republican presidential nominee. Nixon, from California, represented the party's conservative western wing. More important, however, Nixon had been a strongly partisan Republican during eight years of Eisenhower's *de facto* bipartisanship. After the death of Taft, Nixon inherited the informal title "Mr. Republican." His only real rival for the nomination was New York's Governor Nelson Rockefeller, but Rockefeller took himself out of the running on December 24, 1959, leaving Nixon with a clear shot for the nomination.

Nixon came within a hair's breadth of winning the election. The final vote tally was John Kennedy, the Democrat, 34,226,731 votes (49.7 percent) to Nixon's 34,108,157 (49.5 percent). Republicans picked up 21 seats in the House but were still in the minority. Two years later, Nixon ran for governor of California, but lost. After that election, he declared bitterly to reporters, "You won't have Nixon to kick around any more"— an outburst that seemed to take Nixon out of politics for good.

Nixon's withdrawal helped prepare the way for the ascent of Arizona Republican Barry Goldwater (see Vol. 1, p. 171) as the party's presidential candidate in 1964. Goldwater was an exceptionally conservative Republican who won the nomination over Rockefeller of New York, representative of the party's liberal wing. The bitter contest between the two men for the nomination was the first sign of a significant shift in the party's ideological alignment, a shift that only became apparent in 1980 (see p. 169).

Goldwater opposed expansion of the federal government in belief that social programs were better administered by state and local governments. Some party members interpreted Goldwater's support for state governments as a veiled opposition to the civil rights movement, since many southern politicians argued that federal civil rights legislation violated states' rights to control their own affairs. Goldwater also believed federal welfare programs were too costly. In foreign affairs, Goldwater supported American intervention to preserve an anticommunist government in South Vietnam and gave thinly veiled threats to use nuclear weapons to fight communism around the world. These threats frightened many moderate voters, and Goldwater went down to a crushing defeat, collecting just 38.5 percent of the vote to Democrat Lyndon Johnson's 61.1 percent (see Vol. 1, p. 169). Despite Goldwater's defeat, the conservative wing found a new voice in the person of Ronald Reagan (see Vol. 1, p. 186), a film actor, television show host, spokesman for the General Electric company—and future governor of California and president of the United States.

At the same time the 1964 election was unfolding, a major cultural and social upheaval was getting underway. In the South, the civil rights campaign led by Dr. Martin Luther King (see Vol. 4, p. 97) was upsetting the traditional balance of power and traditional social mores as African Americans demanded an end to racial segregation and enforcement of their equal rights guaranteed by the Fourteenth Amendment (see Vol. 4, p. 51). President Johnson (see Vol. 1, p. 170), the former Democratic majority leader in the Senate who as vice president succeeded John Kennedy after the latter's assassination in November 1963, effectively abandoned decades of southern Democratic resistance to African American rights by endorsing the most sweeping civil rights legislation in a century, culminating with the Voting Rights Act of 1965 (see Vol. 4, p. 132). Democratic support for civil rights legislation started a migration of southern whites from the Democratic Party to the Republicans (and a shift of African American support from the Republicans to the Democrats), a change that became manifest in 1968 (see Vol. 1, p. 173) with a dramatic realignment of both parties.

Simultaneously, American involvement in the Vietnam War created a strong antiwar movement, especially among white college students, accompanied by sometimes violent protests. Violence also spread into civil rights protests—and still later into urban rioting in black ghettos—which were deeply disturbing to conservative whites, as was a dramatic liberalization of attitudes among college students toward sex, illegal drugs like marijuana, and rock-'n'-roll. A generation raised in the era of "Jim Crow," listening to the dulcet dance tunes of Glenn Miller's orchestra and accustomed to the feeling of national unity during World War II, recoiled at the seemingly chaotic, sex-crazed cacophony of the late 1960s—and was only too glad to turn away from the ruling Democratic party to the conservative from California, Richard Nixon, in 1968.

Republican Party Platform, 1940

The Republican platform of 1940 sounded three major themes: an attack on the New Deal social policies of the Democratic administration of President Franklin Roosevelt; a determination to avoid involvement in the war that was then engulfing Europe; and reliance on private business to solve the nation's social problems. Excerpts:

The record of the Roosevelt Administration is a record of failure....

Instead of leading us into More Perfect Union, the Administration has deliberately fanned the flames of class hatred.

Instead of the Establishment of Justice the Administration has sought the subjection of the Judiciary to Executive discipline and domination.

Instead of insuring Domestic Tranquility the Administration has made impossible the normal friendly relation between employers and employees and has even succeeded in alienating both the great divisions of Organized Labor.

Instead of Providing for the Common Defense the Administration, notwithstanding the expenditure of billions of our dollars, has left the Nation unprepared to resist foreign attack.

Instead of promoting the General Welfare the Administration has Domesticated the Deficit, Doubled the Debt, Imposed Taxes where they do the greatest economic harm, and used public money for partisan political advantage.

Instead of the Blessings of Liberty the Administration has imposed upon us a Regime of Regimentation which has deprived the individual of his freedom and has made of America a shackled giant.

Wholly ignoring these great objectives, as solemnly declared by the people of the United States, the New Deal Administration has for seven long years whirled in a turmoil of shifting, contradictory and overlapping administrations and policies. Confusion has reigned supreme. The only steady undeviating characteristic has been the relentless expansion of the power of the Federal government over the everyday life of the farmer, the industrial worker and the business man. The emergency demands organization—not confusion. It demands free and intelligent cooperation—not incompetent domination. It demands a change. The New Deal Administration has failed America.

It has failed by seducing our people to become continuously dependent upon government, thus weakening their morale and quenching the traditional American spirit.

It has failed by viciously attacking our industrial system and sapping its strength and vigor.

It has failed by attempting to send our Congress home during the world's most tragic hour, so that we might be eased into the war by word of deed during the absence of our elected representatives from Washington....

The Republican Party is firmly opposed to involving this Nation in foreign war. We are still suffering from the ill effects of the last World War: a war which cost us a twenty-four billion dollar increase in our national debt, billions of uncollectible foreign debts, and the complete upset of our economic system, in addition to the loss of human life and irreparable damage to the health of thousands of our boys....

The New Deal's failure to solve the problem of unemployment and revive opportunity for our youth presents a major challenge to representative government and free enterprise. We propose to recreate opportunity for the youth of America and put our idle millions back to work in private industry, business, and agriculture. We propose to eliminate needless administrative restrictions, thus restoring lost motion to the wheels of individual enterprise....

We shall remove waste, discrimination, and politics from relief—through administration by the States with federal grants-in-aid on a fair and nonpolitical basis, thus giving the man and woman on relief a larger share of the funds appropriated....

We believe in tariff protection for Agriculture, Labor, and Industry, as essential to our American standard of living. The measure of the protection shall be determined by scientific methods with due regard to the interest of the consumer....

The Congress should reclaim its constitutional powers over money, and withdraw the President's arbitrary authority to manipulate the currency, establish bimetallism, issue irredeemable paper money, and debase the gold and silver coinage....

Public spending has trebled under the New Deal, while tax burdens have doubled. Huge taxes are necessary to pay for New Deal waste and for neglected national defense. We shall revise the tax system and remove those practices which impede recovery and shall apply policies which stimulate enterprise. We shall not use the taxing power as an instrument of punishment or to secure objectives not otherwise obtainable under existing law....

Millions of men and women still out of work after seven years of excessive spending refute the New Deal theory that 'deficit spending' is the way to prosperity and jobs. Our American system of private enterprise, if permitted to go to work, can rapidly increase the wealth, income, and standard of living of all the people. We solemnly pledge that public expenditures, other than those required for full national defense and relief, shall be cut to levels necessary for the essential services of government....

We vigorously condemn the New Deal encouragement of various groups that seek to change the American form of government by means outside the Constitution. We condemn the appointment of members of such un-American groups to high positions of trust in the national Government. The development of the treacherous so-called Fifth Column, as it has operated in war-stricken countries, should be a solemn warning to America. We pledge the Republican Party to get rid of such borers from within....

The New Deal policy of interference and arbitrary regulation has injured all business, but especially small business. We promise to encourage the small business man by removing unnecessary bureaucratic regulation and interference....

To insure against the overthrow of our American system of government we favor an amendment to the Constitution providing that no person shall be President of the United States for more than two terms....

More Information

▶ Blum, John Morton. *V Was for Victory: Politics and American Culture During World War II*. New York: Harcourt Brace Jovanovich, 1976.

▶ Dunar, Andrew J. *The Truman Scandals and the Politics of Morality*. Columbia: University of Missouri Press, 1984.

▶ Morris, Richard. *Richard Milhous Nixon: The Rise of an American Politician*. New York: Henry Holt, 1990.

▶ Neal, Steve. *Harry and Ike: The Partnership That Remade the Postwar World*. New York: Scribner, 2001.

▶ Patterson, James T. *Mr. Republican: A Biography of Robert A. Taft*. Boston: Houghton Mifflin. 1972.

▶ Pickett, William B. *Eisenhower Decides to Run: Presidential Politics and Cold War Strategy*. Chicago: Ivan R. Dee, 2000.

▶ Reeves, Richard. *President Nixon: Alone in the White House*. New York: Simon and Schuster, 2001.

▶ Romasco, Albert U. *The Poverty of Abundance: Hoover, the Nation, the Depression*. New York: Oxford University Press, 1965.

▶ Schlesinger, Arthur M., Jr. *History of U.S. Political Parties*, Vol. III and IV. New York: Chelsea House Publishers, 1973.

▶ Sundquist, James L. *The Decline and Resurgence of Congress*. Washington, D.C.: Brookings Institute, 1981.

On the Web

▶ Ambrose, Stephen. "Dwight D. Eisenhower." PBS. http://www.pbs.org/newshour/character/essays/eisenhower.html.

▶ Eisenhower, Dwight. Inauguration speeches, 1953 and 1957. The American Presidency Project, University of California at Santa Barbara. http://www.presidency.ucsb.edu/.

▶ Frederickson, Kari. *The Dixiecrat Revolt and the End of the Solid South, 1932–1968* (excerpts). University of North Carolina Press. http://uncpress.unc.edu/chapters/frederickson_dixiecrat.html.

▶ Hayes, Michael T. "The Republican Road Not Taken: The Foreign-Policy Vision of Robert A. Taft." http://www.independent.org/tii/content/pubs/review/tir84_hayes.html#4b.

▶ Republican Party Platforms, 1932–1968. The American Presidency Project, University of California at Santa Barbara. http://www.presidency.ucsb.edu/.

▶ Republican Party. http://gi.grolier.com/presidents/ea/side/rparty.html.

▶ Wicker, Tom. "Richard M. Nixon." PBS. http://www.pbs.org/newshour/character/essays/nixon.html.

Democratic Party, 1932–68

FlashFocus: Democratic Party, 1932–68

Origins
The Democratic Party came to power in 1932 during the Great Depression, the worst economic downturn in American history. Franklin Roosevelt's New Deal, which in the end proved largely ineffective in ending the Depression, nevertheless gave hope to the unemployed and desperate and helped forge a new coalition of northern, urban, industrial workers allied with conservative southern Democrats that made the Democrats the dominant political party for nearly 50 years.

Issues
Social welfare. Federal intervention in the economy to relieve the suffering of the Great Depression was a hallmark of the party's New Deal legislation from 1932 to 1938, but remained controversial, especially among conservative Democrats from the South. In 1964, Democratic President Lyndon Johnson launched the Great Society, a program of social welfare legislation that effectively was intended to complete the work of Franklin Roosevelt's New Deal 30 years earlier.

Class warfare. While never openly declaring class warfare, the Democratic Party came to represent the poor, the unemployed, the undereducated, and African Americans to a greater extent than ever before. Conservative rural interests supported the party during the Roosevelt New Deal era, but later retreated to the more conservative Republican Party in the North, while southern Democrats always remained the party of conservative rural interests.

World War II, Cold War, Vietnam War. The United States engaged in three conflicts under Democratic presidents. To a large extent, the first two conflicts were conducted outside the realm of politics, but the Vietnam War became highly politicized and helped lead to a resurgence of the Republican Party in 1968.

Impact
Between 1932 and 1968, Democrats controlled the White House for all but eight years and both houses of Congress for all but four years. Starting with the New Deal, Democrats oversaw a dramatic change in the role of the federal government in the national economy, welfare, and civil rights. But throughout the period, Democrats remained primarily a party of alliances between factions that were quite different—conservative southerners representing largely rural interests, and northern, urban liberals. Consequently, while presidents like Roosevelt and John Kennedy were able to bring together the party through force of personality, the Congressional wing of the party remained sharply divided between North and South.

See also: Democratic Party, 1900–32, p. 111; Democratic Party, 1968–2004, p. 163; Republican Party, 1932–68, p. 135; Farmer-Labor Party, p. 125; Union Party, p. 149.

The election of Democrat Franklin Roosevelt (see Vol. 1, p. 141) as president in 1932 set the stage for a tectonic shift in American political power away from rural, agricultural domination and toward urban, industrial domination. The engine that created the shift was not inside the Democratic Party; rather it was the worst economic depression suffered by the U.S. economy, a downturn that started with a stock market crash in 1929 and grew steadily worse. In 1932, there were about 13 million unemployed men in the United States. Counting the dependents of the unemployed, about 40 million people out of a total population of 123 million had no income and could find no way to earn money for food, housing, and clothing. Efforts by the Republican administration of President Herbert Hoover (see Vol. 1, p. 137) were a case of being too little too late. The needs of the unemployed overwhelmed humanitarian relief efforts launched by Hoover, and his innate conservatism—and his conviction that private enterprise would eventually lead the way to economic recovery—made it inevitable that a Democrat, perhaps any Democrat, would win the presidential election of 1932.

The Roosevelt Era: 1933–45

The Franklin Roosevelt era lasted 12 years, from his inauguration in March 1933 to his death in April 1945. It represented a major change in the role of the federal government. Within 100 days of taking office, the administration pushed through Congress 15 landmark bills that included programs for direct federal aid to the unemployed, agricultural and industrial planning, public works to create new jobs, and federal insurance for securities, bank deposits, and mortgages—a collection of programs and government agencies collectively known as the New Deal, a name taken from Roosevelt's 1932 campaign. Many programs were passed with Republican cooperation in a time of unprecedented national malaise. Millions of Americans were unable to find any work and provide for their families. Many of them were deeply angry, ready to turn to radical solutions proposed by communists, among others. Roosevelt, who displayed an upbeat attitude in public despite a personal history of overcoming hardship (he contracted poliomyelitis at age 39, which left his legs paralyzed), declared in his inauguration speech in March 1933: "The only thing we have to fear is fear itself."

Nevertheless, not all Republicans—or Democrats—bought into Roosevelt's program of a much bigger federal government and much bigger government deficits. The party standard-bearer of 1928, Al Smith of New York, joined other dissident Democrats and businessmen in August 1934 in forming the Liberty League to attack Roosevelt's programs. And indeed, there was scant evidence that the New Deal was working. Unemployment numbers edged down to 10.6 million in 1935, even as businessmen hardened their opposition to the New Deal.

For labor unions, however, the New Deal was viewed as a godsend. Union membership had soared with the onset of the Great Depression. In 1935, labor leader John L. Lewis organized the Congress of Industrial Organizations (CIO) to bring together unions organized by industry (rather than by skills, as in the case of the older American Federation of Labor, or AFL). Strikes became widespread, including a general strike in Minneapolis that seemed poised to end in an outright rebellion (see Farmer-Labor Party, p. 125). Political figures ranging from Governor Floyd Olson of Minnesota (see p. 126) to radio priest Father Charles Coughlin and Louisiana Governor Huey Long threatened to organize a political movement to the left of the Democrats.

Low-Income Coalition

In 1935, Roosevelt abandoned efforts to sustain the cooperation of industry and turned to creating a coalition of labor unions, tenant farmers, and other Americans with low incomes. Early the next year, Roosevelt vowed that his reelection campaign would wage a "crusade" against what he called "economic royalists." He was reelected by an even bigger margin than in 1932 (60.8 percent of the popular vote in 1936, up from 57.4 percent in 1932; see Vol. 1, pp. 140 and 144). For most voters, the Democrat had no viable alternative. Republicans had nominated Kansas Governor Alf Landon (Vol. 1, p. 145), a mild progressive, but saddled him with a Hoover-era platform advocating reliance on private enterprise to pull the economy back on track.

Roosevelt and the Democrats, on the other hand, had something for nearly everyone. In the South, which had been a virtual one-party region since the end of Reconstruction, there were programs to help cotton and tobacco farmers and the massive Tennessee Valley Authority public works project. For farmers on the plains, hard hit by both the Great Depression and by drought, prices had risen, and the New Deal provided new help for crops and mortgage insurance. Most importantly, urban workers appreciated the Wagner Act, which strengthened the hand of labor unions over management. New in 1936 was a tremendous shift of the African American vote from the Republicans to the Democrats; in northern states, 76 percent of African Americans voted Democratic in 1936. Roosevelt had also taken care to appoint a significant number of Catholic and Jewish judges.

But in another sense, Roosevelt's victory of 1936 had much more to do with the personality of the president than with either the New Deal or the Democratic Party. Roosevelt exuded confidence. His wife Eleanor had taken care to listen to the concerns of tenant farmers and especially African Americans. Americans at the bottom of the economic heap felt that someone was listening to them and representing their interests. In 1936, 60 percent of middle-income voters went for Roosevelt, 76 percent of lower-income groups, 80 percent of unskilled workers, 84 percent of those on welfare, and 80 percent of labor union members. For the Democratic Party, 1936 saw repeal of the rule that had required a two-thirds majority to win the presidential nomination, a rule that helped ensure candidates acceptable to the conservative South. Although the South remained solidly Democratic for the next 30 years, the seeds had been sown for a later shift in electoral politics.

Split in the Party

The split between conservative southern Democrats and their more liberal northern counterparts became evident in 1937. Roosevelt had proposed expanding the number of Supreme Court justices in order to overcome opposition to his programs by the Supreme Court, particularly from the notorious "Four Horsemen"—four conservative justices who consistently voted to declare New Deal programs unconstitutional. Southern Democrats and Republicans joined to defeat Roosevelt's proposal in August 1937. That autumn, a new economic downturn struck, suggesting that the New Deal had not been effective after all.

By 1938, the era of the New Deal was over. No new programs were enacted, and Roosevelt abandoned plans for universal medical insurance. He campaigned for liberals in Democratic primaries, including several in the South, in 1938, but his candidates were not nominated. The president considered an "exclusion" program to drive conservatives out of the Democratic Party and replace them with liberals. This, he reasoned, would make a more rational system of political parties: the liberal, progressive Democrats and the conservative Republicans. But his heart was not in the project, and he soon abandoned it, leaving the Democratic Party as it had long been: a sometimes shaky Congressional coalition of southern conservatives and northern liberals. On the local level, the Democratic Party was a coalition of largely independent state organizations that operated with little regard for directions from the national chairman. In the South, party primaries largely dictated who would be elected (Republicans were seldom a factor), and only a small minority of voters (around 15 percent typically), almost always white, participated. In the cities, the other center of Democratic support, local party organizations (called "machines") still chose candidates and got voters to the polls on election day. Little about either structure changed during Roosevelt's 12 years in office.

Onset of War

In 1940, although unemployment remained high (about nine million), attention was focused on the prospect of war. Germany had invaded and quickly overrun France in 1939, the Battle of Britain was in full swing, and the Soviet Union had been brought into the conflict with Germany's attack on Russia on June 21, 1941. Roosevelt, clearly sympathetic with the British, had arranged to help arm Britain through a program called Lend Lease—which helped stimulate industrial production of armaments in the United States—but was faced with

Republican isolationist opposition to involvement in the war. Roosevelt won an unprecedented third term in 1940, running largely because the Democrats did not have another clear winner to put on the ballot. His percentage of the popular vote was 54.7 percent, and the Democrats lost six prairie states, but his margin of victory was still over five million votes. Significantly, while Roosevelt fared well against the moderate utilities lawyer Wendell Willkie (see Vol. 1, p. 148), conservatives made some gains in the Congressional races. There were, in effect, two votes in 1940: one for a liberal in the White House, the other for conservatives to go to Congress.

World War II Era

After the United States entered World War II on December 8, 1941, the day after the Japanese attack on Pearl Harbor, Roosevelt faced a political dilemma. On one hand, his liberal advisors urged him to link the war with his domestic battle with conservatives, making the case that the United States was fighting fascism, which combined tyranny with elitist control of the economy, and racism. On the other hand, Roosevelt was tempted to appeal to the national unity created by the Japanese attack on Pearl Harbor, presenting the war as an all-class struggle. Liberals objected that this would enable businessmen to regain some of the power and influence they had lost during the New Deal era. Roosevelt never clearly came down on one side or the other of this argument. In 1942, he argued for an "end to politics" in fighting the war, but in his State of the Union speech of 1944, he presented a new Economic Bill of Rights, arguing that it was "essential to peace" to provide Americans with "a second Bill of Rights under which a new basis of security and prosperity can be established for all—regardless of station, race, or creed." These rights included the right to a job, to an income sufficient to provide food, clothing, and recreation, the right of farmers to sell crops at a price high enough to provide a decent living, the right to a decent home, the right to medical care, the right to a good education, and the right to adequate protection from "the economic fears of old age, sickness, accident, and unemployment."

In laying out these rights, Roosevelt set the groundwork for President Lyndon Johnson's (see Vol. 1, p. 170) Great Society program 20 years later.

In 1944, with victory in World War II within sight, there was little question that Roosevelt would run for a fourth term, despite his poor health. But this did not mean he fully controlled the party. Conservatives insisted on dumping the liberal Vice President Henry Wallace (see Vol. 1, p. 147) and substituting the relatively unknown Senator Harry Truman (see Vol. 1, p. 155) of Missouri. The nomination of Truman marked a distinct turn to the right by the Democrats.

After FDR

Roosevelt died in April 1945, just a month after his inauguration. His death brought to a close an era in which the Democratic Party became more nationally oriented, more vigorous, more inventive, more cosmopolitan. It had achieved a majority by uniting society's underdogs—those without property, without education, without a job. It had built a strong advantage in rapidly growing cities.

Against this trend, southern Democrats remained largely rural and agricultural and resistant to letting African Americans participate in political power. This division in the party—between northern, urban liberals representing organized labor and southern conservatives—would break out into the open in the election of 1948.

Roosevelt had also served as a strong force keeping the Democratic Party together, with a focus on the White House. His successor as president, Harry Truman, lacked Roosevelt's charismatic personality. He was, moreover, confronted by a new set of challenges brought on by the end of World War II.

With the end of fighting and Japan's surrender in September 1945, Truman faced domestic discontent over rising prices and a series of labor strikes, reflecting pent-up demand that had been put on hold by four years of war. Even though labor unions had become a bulwark of the Democratic Party, Truman nevertheless reacted to a rail strike in May 1946 by seizing struck railroads and trying to draft the strikers into the Army to keep the country's freight transportation system going. Popular discontent with both inflation and labor unrest resulted in sharp gains for Republicans in Congressional races in 1946. For the first time since 1928, Republicans won control of both the Senate and House of Representatives.

Over the next two years, leading up to the presidential election in 1948, strains between the party's northern liberal stream and its southern conservatives broke into the open. Truman's commerce secretary, former vice president Henry Wallace, challenged Truman's tough stance against the Soviet Union and urged a more conciliatory posture. Truman removed Wallace from his cabinet post, which led Wallace to break with the Democrats to run as the Progressive Party (see p. 160) candidate.

Move to the Left

Truman, alarmed at the possible loss of liberal support, made a strategic decision to move to the left. He moved to support civil rights for African Americans, advocated housing reforms, and pushed for protection of labor rights by attacking the Taft-Hartley Act, passed by the Republican 80th Congress, that had banned closed shops (mandatory union membership), strikes over union jurisdictional issues, mass picketing, and union political contributions.

At the same time, in international affairs Truman adopted a new get-tough attitude toward communism. In 1947, he put forward what came to be known as the Truman Doctrine, a policy to supply aid (initially to Greece and Turkey) to countries as one means of fending off domestic communist takeovers. After a period of increasingly difficult relations with the Soviet Union, an ally during World War II, the Truman Doctrine effectively signaled the start of the Cold War—a prolonged ideological struggle with the Soviet Union that lasted until the collapse of Russian communism in 1991.

In February 1948, Truman sent a message to Congress calling for action to guarantee the civil rights of African Americans, a message resisted by southern Democrats. This commitment to civil rights was later reinforced by a plank in the 1948 platform (see Vol. 4, p. 85) and led southern Democrats to stalk out of the convention to form their own party, the "Dixiecrats" (see Vol. 4, p. 87).

Truman thus entered the 1948 election with challenges on the right (the Dixiecrats) and the left (the Progressive Party of Henry Wallace). Wallace's campaign soon faltered amid charges it was dominated by communists. And while the Dixiecrats collected 39 electoral votes in 1948, Truman and the Democrats won the election with 303 electoral votes (to 189 for Republican Thomas Dewey) and regained their majorities in both the House and Senate. Seemingly, the Roosevelt coalition had held together one more time. But the election also showed internal weaknesses in the party that would cost it the White House in 1952 and 1956.

Truman's last four years in office were wracked by political scandals at home and setbacks abroad. Overseas, Chinese communists attacked Beijing and eventually drove the anti-communist nationalists out of the country. Communist North Koreans crossed the 50th parallel and invaded the southern half of the peninsula, prompting the United States, under the banner of the United Nations, to become involved in the Korean War—a war that became particularly controversial after Truman recalled U.S. General Douglas MacArthur in 1951 for failing to follow a direct order that he halt his advance against the North Koreans. The United States organized the North Atlantic Treaty Organization to combat a perceived Soviet military threat, even as the Russians exploded an atomic weapon, ending the American atomic monopoly.

Loss of the White House

Thus, the Democrats entered the 1952 elections forced to defend government corruption, continuing allegations of communist subversion of government offices, and a weak economy. The Republicans nominated World War II General Dwight Eisenhower (some southern Democrats had also approached Eisenhower about running as a Democrat), who vowed to go to Korea to end the conflict. The Democratic nominee, Illinois Governor Adlai Stevenson (see Vol. 1, p. 160), lost in a landslide. In Congressional elections, Democrats lost their majorities in both the Senate and the House. In Congress, two Texans became the minority leaders: Lyndon Johnson (see Vol. 1, p. 170) in the Senate and Sam Rayburn in the House.

Two years into Eisenhower's administration, Democrats regained their majorities in both houses of Congress—dual majorities they held until 1981. These majorities gave continuing influence to the Congressional wing of the party that was largely dominated by conservative southerners. Although Eisenhower was reelected president in 1956 (with 57.4 percent of the popular vote, the second largest popular majority ever), he had short political coattails. Democrats continued to benefit from voters who split their votes between the president and Congress.

In the last four years of Eisenhower's administration, civil rights began to emerge as a major issue. The Supreme Court in 1954 had ruled (in *Brown v. Board of Education,* see Vol. 3, p. 141) that school desegregation was unconstitutional. In response, 83 southern Democrats signed the Southern Manifesto (see Vol. 4, p. 99) in 1956 vowing to resist racial integration. Nevertheless, when Eisenhower proposed the Civil Rights Act of 1957 (see Vol. 4, p. 104), majority leader Johnson strongly supported the law, and it passed. This act, plus Eisenhower's decision to send troops to enforce court-ordered integration of the Little Rock, Arkansas, Central High School in 1957 (see Vol. 4, p. 101), cost Republicans the support of whites in the South and helped guarantee continuing Democratic domination of Congress in the election of 1958. A short but sharp recession toward the end of 1957 lasting into 1958 also harmed the Republicans, who lost 47 seats in the House of Representatives.

The election of 1960 presented the Democratic Party a new calculus. Some elements of the Roosevelt coalition were intact—labor unions, African Americans, and urban immigrants (some of whom had migrated not from overseas but from rural areas to big cities). On the other hand, by 1960 suburbs had grown significantly and were inclined to vote Republican (with some notable exceptions, such as Catholic voters), an echo of Republican strength among white, Protestant, middle- and upper-middle-class voters exhibited before 1932. The fact that the 1960 Democratic nominee, Senator John Kennedy of Massachusetts (see Vol. 1, p. 166), was himself Catholic helped Democrats carry central cities and cut into Republican strength in the suburbs just enough to squeeze out a razor-thin victory margin of just 118,574 votes out of 68 million cast.

Kennedy, like Roosevelt, exhibited the importance of personal style in determining political loyalty toward the White House wing of the Democratic Party. He exuded youth, confidence, vitality, and glamour (aided by his wife Jacqueline and their two young children, Caroline and John). In the 1962 Congressional elections, Democrats held their majorities in Congress—the first time since 1934 that the party in charge of the White House had not lost seats in an off-year election. But to a large extent, Kennedy's liberal New Frontier legislative initiatives were stalled by the conservative southern Democratic majority—another demonstration, if one were needed, of the fundamental difference between holding the White House and dominating Congress.

LBJ Era

It was only after Kennedy's assassination in November 1963 in Dallas, Texas, that Lyndon Johnson, who as vice president

"There's Money Enough To Support Both Of You — Now, Doesn't That Make You Feel Better?"

This 1968 cartoon criticizes President Lyndon Johnson for neglecting domestic, and in particular urban, interests while continuing to fund U.S. efforts in Vietnam.

succeeded Kennedy, turned his legendary skill at legislative manipulation to enact the Kennedy program under a new rubric: the Great Society.

The Republican Party in 1964 had entered a new era, although it was not evident at the time, by nominating Senator Barry Goldwater of Arizona for president (see Vol. 1, p. 171). Goldwater was an archconservative for whom ideology played a more important role than practical politics. In effect, he would rather be right than be elected. Johnson overwhelmed Goldwater, winning all but 6 states, with 61.1 percent of the popular vote and 486 electoral votes to Goldwater's 52. So one-sided was the outcome of the 1964 elections that some commentators at the time wondered whether the Republican Party was destined to follow the Whigs (see p. 27) into political obscurity. But Goldwater's poor showing was misleading, failing to predict the impact of the Vietnam War and urban violence over the next four years. Nor did commentators foresee that Goldwater's candidacy was a seed from which would grow a strong right-wing crusade that took over the party in 1980 (see p. 169).

Faced with veto-proof majorities in both the Senate and House, Johnson proceeded on a program of legislative activism second only to that of Franklin Roosevelt 30 years earlier. Johnson's Great Society programs in effect finished the work of the New Deal by offering medical care to the elderly, a host of new welfare benefits, and dramatic improvements in civil rights. The Voting Rights Act of 1965 (see Vol. 4, p. 132) for the first time delivered on promises to African Americans made a century earlier for a place at America's political table. This legislation brought into focus as never before the long-standing strains between southern, white, conservative Democrats and liberal Democrats of the North. In the next election, Republican presidential candidate Richard Nixon (see Vol. 1, p. 174) initiated a "southern strategy" to capture white voters resentful of civil rights—and recapture the White House from a deeply divided Democratic Party.

Civil rights was not the only topic dividing the Democrats from 1965 to 1968. The war in Vietnam had become deeply unpopular, especially among college-age youths. When Minnesota Senator Eugene McCarthy reluctantly launched a challenge to Johnson for the 1968 nomination, college students flocked to help his campaign. The result was that although McCarthy lost to Johnson in the New Hampshire primary in March 1968, the margin was surprisingly thin. McCarthy's showing encouraged New York Senator Robert Kennedy, brother of the slain President John Kennedy, to enter the presidential sweepstakes—and by the end of March, Johnson declared that he would not be a candidate for reelection.

Democratic Party Platform – 1932

In the midst of the Great Depression, the Democratic Party promised to improve the economic situation that had brought the nation to its knees. The Democratic Party platform from 1932, excerpts of which follow, outlined their plan.

In this time of unprecedented economic and social distress the Democratic Party declares its conviction that the chief causes of this condition were the disastrous policies pursued by our government since the World War, of economic isolation, fostering the merger of competitive businesses into monopolies and encouraging the indefensible expansion and contraction of credit for private profit at the expense of the public.

Those who were responsible for these policies have abandoned the ideals on which the war was won and thrown away the fruits of victory, thus rejecting the greatest opportunity in history to bring peace, prosperity, and happiness to our people and to the world.

They have ruined our foreign trade; destroyed the values of our commodities and products, crippled our banking system, robbed millions of our people of their life savings, and thrown millions more out of work, produced wide-spread poverty and brought the government to a state of financial distress unprecedented in time of peace.

The only hope for improving present conditions, restoring employment, affording permanent relief to the people, and bringing the nation back to the proud position of domestic happiness and of financial, industrial, agricultural and commercial leadership in the world lies in a drastic change in economic governmental policies.

FlashFocus: Richard J. Daley

Born: May 15, 1902, Chicago, Illinois
Died: December 20, 1976, Chicago, Illinois
Political career: Mayor of Chicago, 1955–76.

Richard J. Daley was one of the last urban Democrats who controlled an effective "machine" that was pivotal in determining the outcome of an election.

Born in the south side Chicago neighborhood of Bridgeport in 1902, Daley worked his way up in the Democratic Party machine that dominated city politics to be elected mayor in 1955. He soon established himself as the boss of the Democratic Party in Chicago. Daley and his administration were often accused of using less-than-ethical strategies to deliver Democratic votes, although Daley himself was never successfully challenged.

Daley used his position as leader of the Democratic Party in Illinois to further the progress of the city of Chicago. Like many large cities during the 1950s and 1960s, Chicago faced an increase in areas of concentrated poverty, which meant an increase in the need for revenue to deal with social problems. Rather than raise taxes, Daley was able to defray many of the costs of such programs using tactics such as consolidating services between city and county, enabling Chicago to avoid many of the fiscal and social problems that plagued other major U.S. cities.

Race relations, however, proved to be a problem for Daley, who worked to keep the city segregated for fear that "white-flight"—movement of whites to the suburbs—could destroy his political coalition. In 1967, civil rights leader Martin Luther King launched an open (nonsegregated) housing campaign in Chicago that met staunch opposition from whites. Daley conceded only vague promises to alleviate the difficulties many blacks had in obtaining fair housing.

Daley came under further national scrutiny in 1968 during the upheaval in African American neighborhoods following the assassination of King by issuing "shoot-to-kill" orders to the police to quell the riots. That summer, antiwar demonstrations outside the Democratic National Convention site in Chicago were met by police violence; a national committee later described the melee as a "police riot."

Despite the controversies, Daley served as mayor until his death in 1976. Reforms in national and local politics soon swept aside the influence and power of the machine system.

We believe that a party platform is a covenant with the people to have [sic] faithfully kept by the party when entrusted with power, and that the people are entitled to know in plain words the terms of the contract to which they are asked to subscribe. We hereby declare this to be the platform of the Democratic Party:

The Democratic Party solemnly promises by appropriate action to put into effect the principles, policies, and reforms herein advocated, and to eradicate the policies, methods, and practices herein condemned. We advocate an immediate and drastic reduction of governmental expenditures by abolishing useless commissions and offices, consolidating departments and bureaus, and eliminating extravagance to accomplish a saving of not less than twenty-five per cent in the cost of the Federal Government. And we call upon the Democratic Party in the states to make a zealous effort to achieve a proportionate result.

We favor maintenance of the national credit by a federal budget annually balanced on the basis of accurate executive estimates within revenues, raised by a system of taxation levied on the principle of ability to pay.

We advocate a sound currency to be preserved at all hazards and an international monetary conference called on the invitation of our government to consider the rehabilitation of silver and related questions.

We advocate a competitive tariff for revenue with a fact-finding tariff commission free from executive interference, reciprocal tariff agreements with other nations, and an international economic conference designed to restore international trade and facilitate exchange.

We advocate the extension of federal credit to the states to provide unemployment relief wherever the diminishing resources of the states makes it impossible for them to provide for the needy; expansion of the federal program of necessary and useful construction effected [sic] with a public interest, such as adequate flood control and waterways.

We oppose cancellation of the debts owing to the United States by foreign nations…

And in conclusion, to accomplish these purposes and to recover economic liberty, we pledge the nominees of this convention the best efforts of a great Party whose founder announced the doctrine which guides us now in the hour of our country's need: equal rights to all; special privilege to none.

Inaugural Address of John Kennedy, January 20, 1961

President John Kennedy's inaugural address captured the spirit of the young president succeeding the aging Dwight Eisenhower and offered the promise of a new Democratic era that would succeed the Roosevelt era of 1932–45. It also captured the principal themes of the 1960 election: renewed dedication to the Cold War while offering the olive branch of peace; support for the United Nations; a new American role overseas; and proposals to revitalize the domestic economy.

We observe today not a victory of party but a celebration of freedom—symbolizing an end as well as a beginning—signifying renewal as well as change. For I have sworn before you and Almighty God the same solemn oath our forebears prescribed nearly a century and three quarters ago.

The world is very different now. For man holds in his mortal hands the power to abolish all forms of human poverty and all forms of human life. And yet the same revolutionary beliefs for which our forebears fought are still at issue around the globe—the belief that the rights of man come not from the generosity of the state but from the hand of God.

We dare not forget today that we are the heirs of that first revolution. Let the word go forth from this time and place, to friend and foe alike, that the torch has been passed to a new generation of Americans—born in this century, tempered by war, disciplined by a hard and bitter peace, proud of our ancient heritage—and unwilling to witness or permit the slow undoing of those human rights to which this nation has always been committed, and to which we are committed today at home and around the world.

Let every nation know, whether it wishes us well or ill, that we shall pay any price, bear any burden, meet any hardship, support any friend, oppose any foe to assure the survival and the success of liberty.

This much we pledge—and more.

To those old allies whose cultural and spiritual origins we share, we pledge the loyalty of faithful friends. United, there is little we cannot do in a host of cooperative ventures. Divided, there is little we can do—for we dare not meet a powerful challenge at odds and split asunder.

To those new states whom we welcome to the ranks of the free, we pledge our word that one form of colonial control shall not have passed away merely to be replaced by a far more iron tyranny. We shall not always expect to find them supporting our view. But we shall always hope to find them strongly supporting their own freedom—and to remember that, in the past, those who foolishly sought power by riding the back of the tiger ended up inside.

To those peoples in the huts and villages of half the globe struggling to break the bonds of mass misery, we pledge our best efforts to help them help themselves, for whatever period is required—not because the communists may be doing it, not because we seek their votes, but because it is right. If a free society cannot help the many who are poor, it cannot save the few who are rich.

To our sister republics south of our border, we offer a special pledge—to convert our good words into good deeds—in a new alliance for progress—to assist free men and free governments in casting off the chains of poverty. But this peaceful revolution of hope cannot become the prey of hostile powers. Let all our neighbors know that we shall join with them to oppose aggression or subversion anywhere in the Americas. And let every other power know that this Hemisphere intends to remain the master of its own house.

To that world assembly of sovereign states, the United Nations, our last best hope in an age where the instruments of war have far outpaced the instruments of peace, we renew our pledge of support—to prevent it from becoming merely a forum for invective—to strengthen its shield of the new and the weak—and to enlarge the area in which its writ may run.

Finally, to those nations who would make themselves our adversary, we offer not a pledge but a request: that both sides begin anew the quest for peace, before the dark powers of destruction unleashed by science engulf all humanity in planned or accidental self-destruction.

We dare not tempt them with weakness. For only when our arms are sufficient beyond doubt can we be certain beyond doubt that they will never be employed.

But neither can two great and powerful groups of nations take comfort from our present course—both sides overburdened by the cost of modern weapons, both rightly alarmed by the steady spread of the deadly atom, yet both racing to alter that uncertain balance of terror that stays the hand of mankind's final war.

So let us begin anew—remembering on both sides that civility is not a sign of weakness, and sincerity is always subject to proof. Let us never negotiate out of fear. But let us never fear to negotiate.

Let both sides explore what problems unite us instead of belaboring those problems which divide us.

Let both sides, for the first time, formulate serious and precise proposals for the inspection and control of arms—and bring the absolute power to destroy other nations under the absolute control of all nations.

Let both sides seek to invoke the wonders of science instead of its terrors. Together let us explore the stars, conquer the deserts, eradicate disease, tap the ocean depths and encourage the arts and commerce.

Let both sides unite to heed in all corners of the earth the command of Isaiah—to "undo the heavy burdens ... (and) let the oppressed go free."

And if a beach-head of cooperation may push back the jungle of suspicion, let both sides join in creating a new endeavor, not a new balance of power, but a new world of law, where the strong are just and the weak secure and the peace preserved.

All this will not be finished in the first one hundred days. Nor will it be finished in the first one thousand days, nor in the life of this Administration, nor even perhaps in our lifetime on this planet. But let us begin.

In your hands, my fellow citizens, more than mine, will rest the final success or failure of our course. Since this country was founded, each generation of Americans has been summoned to give testimony to its national loyalty. The graves of young Americans who answered the call to service surround the globe.

Now the trumpet summons us again—not as a call to bear arms, though arms we need—not as a call to battle, though embattled we are—but a call to bear the burden of a long twilight struggle, year in and year out, "rejoicing in hope, patient in tribulation"—a struggle against the common enemies of man: tyranny, poverty, disease and war itself.

Can we forge against these enemies a grand and global alliance, North and South, East and West, that can assure a more fruitful life for all mankind? Will you join in that historic effort?

In the long history of the world, only a few generations have been granted the role of defending freedom in its hour of maximum danger. I do not shrink from this responsibility—I welcome it. I do not believe that any of us would exchange places with any other people or any other generation. The energy, the faith, the devotion which we bring to this endeavor will light our country and all who serve it—and the glow from that fire can truly light the world.

And so, my fellow Americans: ask not what your country can do for you—ask what you can do for your country.

My fellow citizens of the world: ask not what America will do for you, but what together we can do for the freedom of man.

Finally, whether you are citizens of America or citizens of the world, ask of us here the same high standards of strength and sacrifice which we ask of you. With a good conscience our only sure reward, with history the final judge of our deeds, let us go forth to lead the land we love, asking His blessing and His help, but knowing that here on earth God's work must truly be our own.

More Information

- Abbott, Philip. *The Exemplary Presidency; Franklin D. Roosevelt and the American Political Tradition.* Amherst: University of Massachusetts Press, 1989.
- Badger, Anthony J. *The New Deal: The Depression Years, 1933–40.* New York: Macmillan, 1989.
- Bernstein, Irving. *Guns or Butter: The Presidency of Lyndon Johnson.* New York: Oxford University Press, 1996.
- Davis, Kenneth S. *FDR: The War President, 1940–1943.* New York: Random House, 2000.
- Freedman, Lawrence. *Kennedy's Wars: Berlin, Cuba, Laos, and Vietnam.* New York: Oxford University Press, 2000.
- Gullan, Harold I. *The Upset That Wasn't: Harry S. Truman and the Crucial Election of 1948.* Chicago: Ivan R. Dee, 1998.
- Kearns, Doris. *Lyndon Johnson and the American Dream.* New York: St. Martin's Press, 1991.
- Matusow, Allen J. *The Unraveling of America: A History of Liberalism in the 1960s.* New York: Harper & Row, 1984..
- McCullough, David. *Truman.* New York: Simon and Schuster, 1992.
- Reeves, Richard. *President Kennedy: Profile of Power.* New York: Simon & Schuster, 1993.
- Ward, Geoffrey C. *A First-Class Temperament: The Emergence of Franklin Roosevelt.* New York: Harper and Row, 1989.

On the Web

- Democratic National Committee. *http://www.democrats.org/.*
- Democratic Party History. CNN.com. *http://www.cnn.com/ELECTION/2000/conventions/democratic/features/history/.*
- Papers of Franklin Roosevelt. Avalon Project at Yale Law School. *http://www.yale.edu/lawweb/avalon/presiden/roospap.htm.*
- Papers of Harry Truman. Avalon Project at Yale Law School. *http://www.yale.edu/lawweb/avalon/presiden/trumpap.htm.*
- The American Presidency Project. University of California at Santa Barbara. Links to party platforms. *http://www.presidency.ucsb.edu/.*

Union Party, 1936–39

FlashFocus: Union Party

Origins

In 1936, a group of Democrats from the populist tradition broke with President Franklin Roosevelt to advocate a more aggressive plan to alleviate the woes of the Great Depression. The party comprised a variety of political activist groups such as the National Union for Social Justice, groups advocating government-funded pensions for the elderly, and the "share-the-wealth" program of Senator Huey Long of Louisiana.

Issues

Living wage and protection. The Union Party pledged to introduce and sign legislation that would establish a legal minimum living wage for all workers within the United States who were able and willing to work. In addition, the party advocated a federal assurance that agricultural production would yield a profit for farmers.

Protectionism. The party vowed to protect American commercial, industrial, and agricultural markets from foreign competition and from all materials and processed goods produced overseas below a determined living wage.

Break up monopolies. The Union Party advocated federal control and decentralization of monopolistic corporations in the hopes of encouraging small businesses to prosper in a more favorable competitive atmosphere.

Income limits. The Union Party wanted to place a limit on the allowable annual income of individuals after taxes. It also favored limiting the size of inheritance and gifts. Both goals would be achieved through taxation.

Defense and foreign policy. The Union Party pledged itself to defending the United States from attack on its own shores, but with the caveat that U.S. armed forces would not be used in foreign lands or waters by themselves or in alliance with any foreign nations.

Retirement of debts. The party supported the establishment of a federal bank through which the government would retire federal debts and refinance farm and home debts. This plan also called for the new bank to issue currency and to regulate credit.

Impact

The fledgling party's goal was to defeat Roosevelt in the 1936 election, but lack of funding and organization, plus anti-Semitic rhetoric on the part of some of its leaders, doomed the party to failure. Roosevelt won in a landslide, and the Union nominee, William Lemke of North Dakota, failed to win a single electoral vote. The disastrous presidential campaign of 1936, marked by disorganization and undisciplined campaigning by prominent members of the party, resulted in the dissolution of the party after a single outing.

See also: Democratic Party, 1932–68, p. 141; American Labor Party, p. 152; American First Party, p. 155.

The Great Depression of the 1930s was the worst economic crisis ever faced by the United States. In 1932, the nation had elected New York Governor Franklin Roosevelt to the White House. By the time he was inaugurated in March 1933, the banking and credit structure of the nation was crumbling. In his first hundred days in office, Roosevelt extended federal aid to private banks, rammed relief programs through Congress, and created government programs to refinance private debts. Nevertheless, some Democrats insisted on more.

Origins of the Union Party

Several supporters of Roosevelt felt that the president's new economic program did not go far enough to alleviate the problems caused by the Depression. This group was led by the Reverend Charles Coughlin, a Catholic priest who headed the National Union for Social Justice; Dr. Francis E. Townsend, an advocate for federal aid for senior citizen pensions; and Gerald L. K. Smith of the "Share-the-Wealth" program. Their plan was to challenge both the Democratic and Republican parties in the 1936 national elections with a more aggressive relief program.

Coughlin, from suburban Detroit, gained fame as a fiery public speaker, and he reached a wide audience through speeches broadcast on the radio. He criticized such diverse interests as bankers, communists, and members of trade unions. In 1934, Coughlin (who had vigorously supported Roosevelt in 1932) organized the National Union for Social Justice and urged Roosevelt to expand the New Deal policy by nationalizing banks, natural resources, and utilities. When it was clear that Roosevelt would not go that far, Coughlin and his backers formed the Union Party. Coughlin's rousing addresses appealed to the emotions of potential voters.

Coughlin figured prominently in both the organization of the party and the selection of its presidential ticket. In June 1936, the party nominated Republican Representative William Lemke of North Dakota for president and railroad union attorney Thomas O'Brien of Massachusetts for vice president. Lemke was chosen primarily because out of all the candidates considered by Coughlin and his supporters, he was the only one with significant political experience and a proven electoral track record.

Lemke, O'Brien, and Coughlin wrote a party platform that included additional reforms in banking and currency, a guaranteed income for workers, restrictions on the accumulation of wealth, and a strict isolationist foreign policy. The party differed from Socialists in that the Union Party did not believe in governmental seizure of private property. No formal party convention was held, although a gathering of Coughlin's National Union for Social Justice endorsed the platform by a vote of 8,152 to 1.

FlashFocus: William Lemke

Born: August 13, 1878, Albany, Minnesota
Died: May 30, 1950, Fargo, North Dakota
Political Career: Cofounder, Non-Partisan League, 1915; U.S. House of Representatives, 1932–50; presidential candidate, Union Party, 1936.

The son of a farmer, William Lemke experienced firsthand the struggles of farmers and the successes of farmers' organizations such as the Farmers' Alliance and the populist movement. He remained sympathetic to farmers' causes throughout his political career. After graduating from public high school in Dakota Territory, he enrolled at the University of North Dakota, graduating in 1902 and pursuing law studies there before completing his legal education at Georgetown University and Yale University. After graduating from Yale in 1905, he returned to North Dakota to open his own law practice in Fargo.

Soon afterwards, Lemke became active in agrarian politics. He was an attorney for the Society of Equity (a group of discontented farmers in North Dakota) and helped to found the Non-Partisan League in 1915, soon rising to a position of leadership. He served as chairman of the Republican state committee from 1916 to 1920, as well as serving on the national executive committee of the Non-Partisan League from 1917 to 1921, and was the primary author of the league's legislative program of 1919. Lemke was elected attorney general of North Dakota in 1920.

By the early 1920s, however, the Nonpartisan League was losing power, in part due to its opposition to U.S. involvement in World War I. Allegations that Lemke had misused state funds for his own personal use, though never proven, did result in a recall election that removed him from office. He ran for governor of North Dakota in 1922 but was defeated. He ran for the U.S. senate in 1926 on the Farmer-Labor Party (see p. 125) ticket, but was again defeated. In 1932, after successfully campaigning on behalf of President Roosevelt, Lemke was elected to the House of Representatives. While serving in the House, he continued to work on behalf of farmers, authoring and supporting reform legislation. However, when President Roosevelt would not support some of his reforms, Lemke accepted the presidential nomination of the Union Party in 1936. The Union Party never broke into the mainstream, and Lemke's candidacy was unsuccessful. He continued to serve in Congress, supporting environmental causes, until his death in 1950.

The absence of a formal convention illustrated a lack of organization. Without a strong base, the party suffered financially. In addition, Coughlin was an outspoken supporter of the Nazi regime of Adolf Hitler and often directly smeared Wall Street bankers of the Jewish faith during his radio broadcasts.

Problems of organization and image doomed the party's goal of ousting Roosevelt. Lemke did not qualify for the ballot in every state and ended up with only 882,000 votes, less than two percent of the total, and no electoral votes. Roosevelt was reelected with 60.8 percent of the popular vote and 523 electoral votes, to 36.5 percent of the popular vote and eight electoral votes for the Republican candidate, Alfred Landon.

Roosevelt's New Deal policies made the Union Party seem redundant to many voters, and others were turned away by Coughlin's fiery rhetoric. Lemke's support was primarily rooted in German immigrants and Catholics, as well as elderly voters who were drawn to the party's message of federal protection of retirement benefits. The Union Party as a whole failed to win any gubernatorial or congressional elections, though Lemke was reelected to Congress running as a both a Republican and a Unionist in his district.

After the election, the party quickly began to break apart. The Union Party attempted to make inroads at the local level, but did not meet with success and vanished completely in 1939.

Union Party Platform, 1936

The Union Party's single platform was adopted in 1936. It reflected both the economic depression and rising tensions in Europe brought about by the rise of the Nazis in Germany and the Fascists in Italy.

America shall be self-contained and self-sustained – no foreign entanglements, be they political, economic, financial or military.

Congress and Congress alone shall coin and issue the currency and regulate the value of all money and credit in the United States through a central bank of issue.

Immediately following the establishment of the central bank of issue Congress shall provide for the retirement of all tax-exempt, interest-bearing bonds and certificates of indebtedness of the Federal Government and shall refinance all the present agricultural mortgage indebtedness for the farmer and all the home mortgage indebtedness for the city owner by the use of its money and credit which it now gives to the private bankers.

Congress shall legislate that there will be an assurance of a living annual wage for all laborers capable of working and willing to work.

Congress shall legislate that there will be assurance of reasonable and decent security for the aged, who, through no fault of their own, have been victimized and exploited by an unjust economic system which has so concentrated wealth in the hands of a few that it has impoverished great masses of our people.

Congress shall legislate that American agricultural, industrial, and commercial markets will be protected from manipulation of foreign moneys and from all raw material and processed goods produced abroad at less than a living wage.

Congress shall establish an adequate and perfect defense for our country from foreign aggression either by air, by land, or by sea, but with the understanding that our naval, air, and military forces must not be used under any consideration in foreign fields or in foreign waters either alone or in conjunction with any foreign power. If there must be conscription, there shall be a conscription of wealth as well as a conscription of men.

In this 1936 meeting, Gerald L.K. Smith, Francis Townsend, and William Lemke take steps toward organizing the new Union Party.

Congress shall so legislate that all Federal offices and positions of every nature shall be distributed through civil-service qualifications and not through a system of party spoils and corrupt patronage.

Congress shall restore representative government to the people of the United States to preserve the sovereignty of the individual States of the United States by the ruthless eradication of bureaucracies.

Congress shall organize and institute Federal works for the conservation of public lands, waters, and forests, thereby creating billions of dollars of wealth, millions of jobs at the prevailing wage, and thousands of homes.

Congress shall protect small industry and private enterprise by controlling and decentralizing the economic domination of monopolies to the end that these small industries and enterprises may not only survive and prosper but that they may be multiplied.

Congress shall protect private property from confiscation through unnecessary taxation with the understanding that the human rights of the masses take precedence over the financial rights of the classes.

Congress shall set a limitation upon the net income of any individual in any one year and a limitation of the amount that such an individual may receive as a gift or as an inheritance, which limitations shall be executed through taxation.

Congress shall reestablish conditions so that the youths of the Nation, as they emerge from schools and colleges, will have the opportunity to earn a decent living while in the process of perfecting and establishing themselves in a trade or profession.

More Information:

▶ Brinkley, Alan. *Voices of Protest: Huey Long, Father Coughlin, and the Great Depression.* New York: Vintage Books, 1982.

▶ Bennett, D.H. *Demagogues in the Depression.* New Brunswick, NJ: Rutgers University Press, 1969.

▶ Fried, Albert. *FDR and His Enemies.* New York: Palgrave, 2001.

▶ Graff, Henry F. (ed.) *The Presidents: A Reference History.* New York: Macmillan, 2002.

On the Web:

▶ Father Coughlin's Speeches.
http://www.ssa.gov/history/fcspeech.html.

American Labor Party, 1936–56

FlashFocus: American Labor Party

Origins

The American Labor Party was organized in New York in 1936 by liberals and labor leaders to support the New Deal policies of Democratic President Franklin Roosevelt, as well as other candidates who championed Roosevelt's policies. The party never ran its own separate candidate for president but was content to help Roosevelt remain in office. In 1948, the party supported Progressive Henry Wallace.

Issues

Support for the New Deal. The party backed Roosevelt's efforts to transform the nation's Depression economy through various legislation and programs that gave economic relief to banks and benefits to citizens. Programs such as Social Security, the establishment of the National Labor Relations Board, and the Public Works Administration were reforms that many Socialists who made up the American Labor Party had long-advocated.
Civil rights. The party supported civil rights for black Americans suffering from discriminatory practices in education, voting, and employment.
Soviet Union. The American Labor Party supported the candidacy of Henry Wallace in 1948, largely based on his view that the U.S. should pursue peaceful coexistence and negotiation with the Soviet Union, rather than the arms build-up and containment policies of the Cold War.

Impact

The American Labor Party's initial role was to help assure the reelection of Franklin Roosevelt in 1936. The party generated over 300,000 votes for Roosevelt that year and nearly 500,000 in 1940 and 1944. Without that support, it is doubtful that Roosevelt would have won New York's electoral votes in those elections. The party endorsed Progressive Party candidate Henry Wallace in 1948, helping him win more than 509,000 votes in New York. The increasing influence of Communists in the party caused internal arguments over the party's position on American relations with the Soviet Union. The dispute caused a group of party members to split off in 1944 and form the Liberal Party, and the American Labor Party steadily declined until its executive committee voted itself out of existence in 1956.

See also: Democratic Party, 1932–68, p. 141; Liberal Party, p. 157; Progressive Party, 1948, p. 160.

The Great Depression in the United States created economic and spiritual despair in the 1930s. President Franklin Roosevelt (see Vol. 1, p. 141), a Democrat, was elected president in 1932 on the promise of a "New Deal" and a better day. His program of economic and social relief programs was aimed at jumpstarting the economy and improving public morale. Before Roosevelt, the Democratic Party—largely dominated by southern politicians—had not been appreciably more liberal than the Republicans. The New Deal marked a change in direction for Democrats and also attracted political activists who had long argued for government intervention in economic affairs, often from within more left-wing parties like the Socialists (see p. 116) or even the Communists (see p. 128).

Origins of the American Labor Party

The American Labor Party was founded in 1936 when a group of influential socialists in New York recognized that Roosevelt's New Deal contained much of the legislation and reform that they had championed for many years. At the same time, many socialists believed that the Socialist Party's presidential nominee that year, Norman Thomas (see p. 117), was a weak candidate who would only help bring votes to Republican Party (see p. 135) candidate Alf Landon (see Vol. 1, p. 145). The American Labor Party provided a home for dissident socialists and union members to vote for Roosevelt while at the same time not being required to endorse the state Democratic Party.

The American Labor Party was led by David Dubinsky (see p. 158), president of the International Ladies' Garment Workers' Union, and Emil Rieve, head of the American Federation of Hosiery Workers. Dubinsky, a Polish immigrant, rose rapidly to the leadership of his union after arriving in the United States in 1911. He also served as vice president of the American Federation of Labor and played a vital role in linking that organization with the Congress of Industrial Organizations.

The American Labor Party's activities were largely centered in New York City, where it was effective in electing Fiorello La Guardia, himself a Republican, as mayor in 1937 and 1941, and liberal Vito Marcantonio as a congressman in 1938.

In presidential affairs, the party initially hoped to bring about 100,000 New York votes for Roosevelt in 1936. After prominent socialists and union leaders began to join the party, that estimate turned out to be conservative. In November, over 275,000 votes came in for Roosevelt on the American Labor Party ballot line. The vote proved vital in helping Roosevelt win New York and retain the presidency.

The American Labor Party continued to support Roosevelt despite the president's difficulties in getting more New Deal legislation passed by Congress and dealing with Supreme Court decisions declaring New Deal laws unconstitutional. Roosevelt pressed on, and legislation such as the Fair Labor Standards Act, which guaranteed a minimum wage, a maximum workweek, and the abolition of child labor, further appealed to groups like the American Labor Party.

The party's support again proved critical for Roosevelt in his 1940 (see Vol. 1, p. 147) and 1944 (see Vol. 1, p. 151) reelection efforts. In both elections, the American Labor Party line came in with around 500,000 votes for Roosevelt. Without this support, it is unlikely Roosevelt would have been reelected in either year since he might not have carried New York.

The party continued to flex its muscles locally as well. In 1936 and 1938, the party endorsed the Democratic nominee for governor of New York, Herbert Lehman, and this support provided the margin of victory.

End of the party

In 1944, the American Labor Party split when some of its more prominent members abandoned the party because of the increasing influence of communists. In 1944, Dubinsky had been defeated for the position of state party chairman by Sidney Hillman, a Lithuanian garment worker who, during his rise to union leadership in that industry, was often branded as a communist sympathizer (although he himself was not a communist). Dubinsky became convinced that the American Labor Party was becoming dominated by communists, and he and many other longtime members helped to form the new Liberal Party in New York (see p. 157). Both the American Labor Party and the new Liberal Party backed Franklin Roosevelt in 1944.

In 1948, the American Labor Party supported Progressive Party candidate Henry Wallace (see p. 161), the former vice president and member of the President Harry Truman's cabinet. Truman (see Vol. 1, p. 155) had fired Wallace from the cabinet for his aggressive arguments in favor of cooperating with the Soviet Union, though it would be difficult to argue that Wallace was procommunist. The Progressives did not gain access to the New York ballot in 1948, so all of Wallace's votes in New York—over 509,000—came on the American Labor Party line. This support for Wallace took votes away from Truman and helped deny him New York's electoral votes against the Republican candidate, New York's Republican Governor Thomas Dewey (see Vol. 1, p. 152). Truman nevertheless won the election (see Vol. 1, p. 154).

After the 1948 election, the American Labor Party began to decline. The party supported Progressive Party candidate Vincent Hallinan of California for president in 1952, but Hallinan gathered just over 140,000 votes out of more than 61.3 million cast. In 1954, the American Labor Party's New York gubernatorial candidate gathered only 47,000 votes. At the time, New York law required that a party gain at least 50,000 votes to maintain its status and access to the ballot. Identifying the downward trend of the party membership and its dim prospects for future recruitment and support, the executive committee of the American Labor Party voted itself out of its existence in 1956.

More Information

▶ Badger, Anthony J. *The New Deal: The Depression Years, 1933–40.* New York: Macmillan, 1989.

FlashFocus: Fiorello La Guardia

Born: December 11, 1882, New York, New York

Died: September 20, 1947, New York, New York

Political Career: U.S. Representative from New York, 1917–19 (with a break while serving as an aviator in World War I), 1923–32; New York board of aldermen, 1919–21; mayor of New York City, 1934–45.

Fiorello ("Little Flower" in Italian) La Guardia, three times mayor of New York City, was one of the most colorful politicians of his era. A slightly rotund figure standing five feet two inches tall, La Guardia presided over city government during the Great Depression. He was an irrepressible bundle of energy who launched public welfare programs and public housing projects, and built the two airports (one of which is named after him) while still making time to rush to fires and read the Sunday comics to children during a newspaper strike.

The son of immigrants, La Guardia was born in New York City, grew up in South Dakota and Arizona where his father was an Army bandmaster, then moved to Austria. At age 17, he began working for the U.S. Consular Corps in Hungary. In 1906, he returned to New York, graduated from high school, and became a translator at the Ellis Island immigrant reception center.

He was elected U.S. representative in 1917 as a progressive Republican from a Democratic working-class district of Manhattan, beginning a political career that defied party labels. He was reelected to Congress from two different districts, running variously as a "fusion" candidate (Republicans and Democrats united against a Socialist), then as a Socialist and Progressive candidate. He became mayor as a Republican and City Fusion candidate in 1934 and was twice reelected, in 1937 and 1941, running on three tickets: Republican, City Fusion, and American Labor Party.

La Guardia was the prototype of an activist political leader during the Great Depression, when radical left-wing parties, including the Communist Party, were gaining influence. The American Labor Party was organized specifically to woo such leftists in New York State into voting for President Franklin Roosevelt (see Vol. 1, p. 141) on a ballot line other than the Democrats since that party's southern wing was highly conservative.

La Guardia's ambition to become Roosevelt's war secretary at the outset of World War II was thwarted. He served as director general of the United Nations Relief and Rehabilitation Administration in 1946. He died in New York in 1947.

▶ Culver, John C. *American Dreamer: The Life and Times of Henry A. Wallace.* New York: Norton, 2000.

▶ Hawley, Ellis W. *The New Deal and the Problem of Monopoly: A Study in Economic Ambivalence.* Princeton, NJ: Princeton University Press, 1966.

▶ Kessner, Thomas. *Fiorello H. La Guardia and the Making of Modern New York.* New York: McGraw-Hill, 1989.

- La Guardia, Fiorello. *The Making of an Insurgent: An Autobiography.* Philadelphia: Lippincott, 1948.
- Markowitz, Norman D. *The Rise and Fall of the People's Century: Henry A. Wallace and American Liberalism, 1941–1948.* New York: Free Press, 1973.

On the Web
- American Labor Party. *http://www.msys.net/cress/ballots2/alp.htm.*
- Wallace, Henry A. "Tell the People Who We Are." *http://newdeal.feri.org/wallace/haw31.htm.*

America First Party, 1943–47

FlashFocus: America First Party

Origins

The America First Party was largely the vehicle for its founder, Gerald L. K. Smith, and there was little distinction between the man and the party. It was an indirect outgrowth of the America First Committee, a generally right-wing organization strongly opposed to American involvement in the war in Europe after 1939. After the committee disbanded following the attack on Pearl Harbor in December 1941, Gerald L. K. Smith borrowed the name for a similarly isolationist political party to run against President Franklin Roosevelt in 1944.

Issues

Isolationism. Despite the attack on Pearl Harbor and declaration of war by Germany against the United States, Smith continued to oppose American involvement in the European war. He asserted that American foreign policy was controlled by Britain and was designed to save the fading British Empire.

Franklin Roosevelt. Smith detested Roosevelt, whom he accused of plotting the 1935 assassination of Louisiana Governor Huey Long in order to prevent Long from running against Roosevelt in 1936. Smith circulated a fake genealogy of Roosevelt, claiming he was of Jewish descent (in fact, Roosevelt descended from Protestant Dutch settlers in New York).

Religion. Smith campaigned on the idea of "preserving" the United States as "a Christian nation." His speeches were laced with anti-Semitic remarks, blaming Jews for conspiring to enlist the United States on the side of Britain in its war against Nazi Germany. In Smith's views, German dictator Adolf Hitler was the victim of persecution by Jews, rather than the other way around.

Impact

Smith appeared on the ballot in just two states, Michigan and Texas, in 1944 and collected a mere 1,581 votes. He also collected a handful of write-in votes in other states, but his isolationist policies had little appeal during World War II. In 1947, Smith dropped the name America First Party and formed another organization, the Christian Nationalist Crusade. Smith had no lasting impact on American politics except, perhaps, to illustrate the abject failure of extremist, conspiracy-oriented figures in American elections.

See also: Democratic Party, 1932–68, p. 141; American Labor Party, p. 152; Union Party, p. 149.

The America First Party was an example of a small political movement centered around a charismatic public speaker who offered a conspiratorial explanation for the nation's ills. The party was also a case study on how such parties may collect publicity but few votes. In the one presidential election contested by America First, its candidate-founder collected fewer than 2,000 votes.

Organized during World War II, the America First Party advocated isolationism—an idea that had gained popularity before the Japanese attack on Pearl Harbor—and blamed a conspiracy of Jews and backers of the British Empire for getting the United States into the war. The party borrowed its name from the America First Committee, an isolationist organization formed in 1940 to try to keep the United States out of the war in Europe that started with Germany's invasion of Holland, Belgium, and France in September 1939. The America First Committee attracted several well-known names, notably Charles Lindbergh, who became famous as the first person to fly solo across the Atlantic Ocean.

The heyday of the America First Party's ideas had already passed by the time of its organizing convention, held in January 1943 in Detroit, Michigan. The America First Party was the creation of one man, Gerald L. K. Smith, a radical evangelical preacher for the Disciples of Christ whose political ideas were centered around anticommunism, anti-Semitism, and hatred of President Franklin Roosevelt (see Vol. 1, p. 141). Smith began his political life as a follower of Louisiana governor and Senator Huey Long, for whom Smith worked as a national organizer of the "Share Our Wealth" organization in the early 1930s. The essence of Long's program was a guaranteed annual income for all Americans. Long was highly critical of President Franklin Roosevelt's New Deal economic recovery program during the Great Depression and hoped to replace Roosevelt as the Democratic Party's nominee in 1936. But in 1935, Long was fatally wounded in a hail of gunfire exchanged between his bodyguards and a would-be assassin. Smith became convinced the incident was a plot hatched by Roosevelt to prevent Long from gaining the 1936 Democratic presidential nomination (in fact, the assassin, Carl Weiss, was a doctor who had a personal grudge against Long).

After Long's death in 1935 and Roosevelt's reelection in 1936, Smith organized the Committee of One Million, a group he used to warn that the country was about to be taken over by a communist revolution. Smith attracted the support of some congressmen and from Horace Dodge, the car manufacturer. Smith used radio and direct mail campaigns, as well as personal appearances, to raise funds. He was by all accounts a skilled orator. Smith also was associated with the Union Party (see p. 149), although Smith's radical ideas were not widely welcomed.

A fondness for conspiracy theories as the explanation for important events became Smith's hallmark. Four days after Japan's attack against the U.S. Pacific fleet at Pearl Harbor on December 7, 1941, the America First Committee disbanded as popular opinion swung behind the American war effort. But in Smith's eyes, Pearl Harbor was a plot by President Roosevelt to involve the United States in World War II in an effort to save

FlashFocus: Gerald Lyman Kenneth Smith

Born: February 27, 1898, Pardeeville, Wisconsin
Died: April 15, 1976, Glendale, California

Gerald L.K. Smith was the son of a minister in rural Wisconsin. As a student he won school contests for public speaking. He attended Valparaiso University in Indianapolis, Indiana, where he studied literature, theater, and Biblical history. After graduating, he was ordained as a minister in the Christian Church (also called the Disciples of Christ) and worked in several small churches in Indiana for the next decade. In 1928, Smith moved to Shreveport, Louisiana, to serve the church there. He became involved in populist politics and used radio broadcasts of his sermons to spread his political message and to attack Shreveport's business leaders. After brief membership in William Dudley Pelley's Silver Shirts organization in 1933, Smith joined Huey Long's "Share Our Wealth" movement, which advocated redistribution of wealth and tax increases for the wealthy. He left his position in the church in 1934 so that he could travel and work on behalf of the movement, becoming its national organizer. After the assassination of Huey Long in 1935, Smith attempted to assume leadership of the movement. However, a split in the movement greatly weakened it, and Smith found himself marginalized.

Hoping to regain political prominence, Smith aligned himself with Dr. Francis Townsend and helped his Old Age and Revolving Insurance Plan movement merge with Charles Coughlin's Social Justice movement. This coalition worked to support the presidential candidacy of William Lemke in 1936. When Lemke's campaign failed, these movements faded, and Smith was once again on the sidelines. This time he formed his own organization, the Committee of One Million, an anti-communist group. He also worked against organizations such as the Congress of Industrial Organizations, which he believed was infiltrated by communists, and began publishing his own periodical, *The Cross and the Flag*. Smith also became a determined anti-Semite. He helped start the Christian Nationalist Crusade in 1947, a successor to the Committee of One Million. The crusade adopted *The Cross and the Flag* as its newsletter. In it, Smith continued to attack Communists, Jews and blacks until his death in 1976.

---

the British Empire. Smith absconded with the America First Committee's name and organized the America First Party the next year, albeit without the support of prominent isolationists such as Charles Lindbergh, who had become a prominent member of the America First Committee. Former members of the committee objected to Smith's use of the name, and Smith apparently had been rejected for membership in the group.

Although Smith never gained significant political support, either as a write-in candidate for the Senate in Michigan in 1942 or as a presidential candidate in 1944, his name was well known through his radio broadcasts, direct mail appeals, and personal appearances. One writer described him as "a disseminator of total fabrications that he apparently believed with full sincerity as soon as he invented them."

Smith's 1944 platform covered 10 points: preserving the United States as a "Christian nation," exposing and fighting communism, guarding the United States against the "menace of bureaucratic fascism," maintaining a government by the majority, protecting national resources "for our citizenry first," maintaining a foreign policy of trade with all countries and alliances with none, opposition to world government, "prov[ing] that the workman, the farmer, the businessman, the veteran, the unemployed, the aged, and the infirm can enjoy more abundance under the true American system than any alien system now being proposed by foreign propagandists," halting immigration until all veterans were employed, and abolishing "the corrupt money system."

The platform was written by Smith and published in his magazine *The Cross and the Flag* in advance of the party convention held in August 1944 in Detroit. The convention was attended by a small group of Smith supporters, many of whom were elderly women. Smith's popularity as an evangelical speaker had peaked years before, in 1935, and had steadily waned since Long's death.

The 1944 campaign was the America First Party's last. Smith went on to form another group in 1947, the Christian Nationalists Crusade, and continued to publish his magazine, *The Cross and the Flag*. In 1952, the name America First Party was adopted by Lar Daly of Chicago, who campaigned for president dressed in an Uncle Sam costume.

More Information

- Bennett, David. *Demagogues in the Depression: American Radicals and the Union Party, 1932–1936.* New Brunswick, NJ: Rutgers University Press, 1969.
- Jeansonne, Glen. *Gerald L. K. Smith, Minister of Hate.* New Haven: Yale University Press, 1988.
- Ness, Immanuel and James Ciment (eds.). *The Encyclopedia of Third Parties in America.* Armonk, NY: Sharpe Reference, 2000.
- Ribuffo, Leo P. *The Old Christian Right: The Protestant Far Right from the Great Depression to the Cold War.* Philadelphia: Temple University Press, 1983.
- Smith, Elna M. and Charles F. Robertson (eds.) *Besieged Patriot: Autobiographical Episodes Exposing Communism, Traitorism, and Zionism from the Life of Gerald L.K. Smith.* Eureka Springs, AR: Elna M. Smith Foundation, 1978.

On the Web

- "Huey Long Is a Superman": Gerald L. K. Smith Defends the Kingfish. History Matters, City University of New York and George Mason University. http://historymatters.gmu.edu/d/5107/.
- Jeansonne, Glen. "Gerald L. K. Smith, From Wisconsin Roots to National Notoriety." Wisconsin History. http://www.wisconsinhistory.org/wmh/pdf/wmh_winter02_jeansonne.pdf.

Liberal Party, 1944–

FlashFocus: Liberal Party

Origins

The Liberal Party was founded in 1944 by union leaders opposed to what they regarded as communist influence in the American Labor Party and corruption in the Democratic Party "machine." Although the Liberal Party is active only in New York State, it nevertheless helped determine the outcome of several national presidential elections, notably in 1944 and 1960, when votes collected on the Liberal Party line enabled Democrats to win New York's electoral college votes, which were critical to winning the White House.

Issues

Anticommunism. Toward the end of World War II, the issue of communist influence over the American Labor Party and some trade unions prompted a group of anticommunist labor leaders to form the Liberal Party in New York State.

United Nations. One of the Liberal Party's initial causes was promotion of a strong United Nations to help establish a new world order after World War II.

Civil rights. Equal rights for minorities was an early hallmark of the Liberal Party a full decade before the civil rights movement began to flourish in the 1950s.

Education. The party advocates increased spending on public schools and opposes tax credits to help families pay for private or religious schools. Teachers' unions have long been a backbone of the party's support.

Impact

The Liberal Party, like the American Labor Party before it, was always viewed as a means of nudging the Democratic Party in New York State toward the left. In most cases, the Liberal Party has endorsed Democratic candidates, hoping that the combination of votes on the Liberal and Democratic lines would elect their common candidate (referred to as a fusion candidate). Although the party has been active only in New York, it has been critical in several national races. Its support of Franklin Roosevelt in 1944 and John Kennedy in 1960 proved crucial to winning New York's electoral votes—and consequently the White House—for the Democratic candidate. The party has also been influential in local elections, such as the victory of John Lindsay in the contest for mayor of New York in 1969. Although its influence declined after 1980, the Liberty Party continued to portray itself as an alternative to a corrupt Democratic Party in New York and a Republican Party too closely tied to business interests.

See also: American Labor Party, p. 152; Democratic Party, 1932–68, p. 141; Progressive Party, 1948, p. 160.

The Liberal Party of New York State is an example of how state or regional parties have influenced national politics. Founded in New York in 1944 in reaction to perceived communist influence over the American Labor Party (see p. 152), the Liberal Party was always intended to influence the much larger Democratic Party, rather than elect large numbers of its own candidates. The party did this by endorsing some of the same candidates who were running as Democrats, in hopes that the combined vote totals on the Democratic and Liberal lines of the ballot would put those candidates into office. Among successful candidates endorsed by the Liberal Party were Presidents Franklin Roosevelt (see Vol. 1, p. 141) and John Kennedy (see Vol. 1, p. 166); New York Governors Averell Harriman, Hugh Carey, and Mario Cuomo; U.S. Senators Robert Wagner, Sr., Herbert Lehman, Jacob Javits, Robert Kennedy, and Daniel Patrick Moynihan; and New York City Mayors Fiorello LaGuardia (see p. 153), Robert Wagner, and John Lindsay. In a few instances, Liberal Party candidates were elected over rival Democrats in local races, as in John Lindsay's victory in New York City's mayoral race in 1969.

Origins

In May 1944, a group of anticommunist union leaders and liberal politicians left the American Labor Party out of concern that communists were exerting undue influence. They founded the Liberal Party as a means of persuading the Democratic Party to support liberal policies like those of President Franklin Roosevelt's New Deal—government funded programs to address social problems—as well as post–World War II policies like support for the proposed United Nations.

The interaction between liberals and socialists or communists during the 1930s and '40s was complex. In general, liberals favored government programs and policies that would help correct social problems, such as unemployment and poverty, without upsetting the established system of private ownership of land and factories. Socialists and communists favored government takeovers of the means of production in order to exert democratic control over economic power as well as political power. Socialists and communists, in turn, were split over tactics to achieve their objectives and, after the Bolshevik Revolution in Russia in 1917, over the influence of the Soviet government, with many communist parties subservient to orders from Moscow.

From the outset, the Liberal Party did not have in mind to choose and elect its own candidates. Rather, the party was designed to act as a kind of party within a party, endorsing those Democrats who agreed with the Liberal Party platform in the expectation that the combination of votes cast on the Democratic line and the Liberal line would propel these candidates into office. The calculation was that Democratic candidates

FlashFocus: David Dubinsky

Born: February 22, 1892, Brest-Litovsk, Poland
Died: September 17, 1982, New York City
Political Career: David Dubinsky was born into a poor Jewish family in Russian Poland. His father owned a bakery in the city of Lodz; and when Dubinsky was 11 years old, he went to work there, becoming a master baker by age 14. He joined the Bakers' Union but was arrested in 1907 for being a union member. Upon his release from jail, he became increasingly active in union affairs. After leading a bakers' strike, he was arrested again and expelled from Lodz to Brest-Litovsk. He returned to Lodz illegally, but was discovered and expelled again, this time to Siberia. During the journey to Siberia, Dubinsky escaped and made his way to New York, arriving in 1911 at age 19.

Soon after arriving in New York, Dubinsky joined the Socialist Party. He found work as a garment cutter and joined the International Ladies' Garment Workers' Union (ILGWU). He quickly rose through the ranks of the local chapter as well as the national organization and was the union's most powerful leader by 1924. When the union split over the issue of communism, Dubinsky and his anticommunist faction prevailed, but the organization was weakened. Dubinsky continued to hold positions of power in the union, serving as both secretary-treasurer and president of the ILGWU from 1932 until 1959.

Dubinsky was elected to the executive council of the American Federation of Labor (AFL) in 1934; but two years later, when the AFL did not want to allow nonskilled laborers to join, Dubinsky resigned and helped form the Congress of Industrial Organizations (CIO) for nonskilled workers. However, he believed that unity was important in the labor movement, and in 1940 he returned to the AFL and regained his position on the executive countil in 1945.

Although Dubinsky had been a strong supporter of President Franklin Roosevelt, many Jewish workers did not trust the Democratic Party. In response, Dubinsky helped found the American Labor Party; but when he felt that the party had been infiltrated by communists, he broke away and formed the Liberal Party, representing the anticommunist wing of the labor movement. He continued to hold union office until his retirement in 1966. He died in 1982 after a long illness.

would adopt positions on issues that would make it possible for them to gain the Liberal Party nomination.

This strategy worked almost immediately. In 1944, Franklin Roosevelt appeared on New York ballots as the presidential nominee of the Democratic, Liberal, and American Labor parties. His Republican opponent was the governor of New York, Thomas Dewey (see Vol. 1, p. 152). The Liberal line delivered over 300,000 votes to Roosevelt's total vote count, helping guarantee New York's 43 electoral votes would go to Roosevelt (see Vol. 1, p. 151). The Liberals delivered a similar outcome for Democrat John Kennedy in 1960 (see Vol. 1, p. 165).

One prominent founder of the Liberal Party was theologian and political activist Reinhold Niebuhr, who wrote about the relationship between Christianity and politics. Niebuhr argued that society is ruled by self-interest, and that the study of Christianity is best described as the struggle between good and evil within the human race. Other significant figures in the formation of the Liberal Party included David Dubinsky (see biography on this page), president of the International Ladies' Garment Workers' Union; Alex Rose of the United Hatters, Cap, and Millinery Workers International Union; and Adolf Berle, an adviser to Franklin Roosevelt.

New York and National Politics

The Liberal Party's national influence long reflected New York State's large number of electoral votes in presidential elections and the ability of the Liberal Party to swing the balance between Democrats and Republicans. Many political historians argue that both Roosevelt and Kennedy owed a great deal to the Liberal Party for its help in winning New York's electoral votes, which propelled them both to national victory. The party also played an important role in the 1948 presidential election (see Vol. 1, p. 154), when it endorsed incumbent Democratic President Harry Truman (see Vol. 1, p. 155) in an election that also saw a more liberal candidate, Henry Wallace (see p. 161), running under the Progressive Party banner (see p. 160). The Liberals helped combat the apathy of many Democratic Party operatives that year and organized a rally for Truman at New York City's Madison Square Garden that was crucial in pushing him over the top against the Republican candidate, Governor Dewey.

The Liberal Party has also endorsed Republicans, such as New York Senator Jacob Javits and New York City's Mayor John Lindsay. Conversely, in 1980 the party declined to endorse Democrat Jimmy Carter (see Vol 1, p. 183) for president, instead backing independent John Anderson.

The Liberal Party began losing votes and membership after 1980. In 1998, the party's gubernatorial nominee managed fewer than 80,000 votes, though Hillary Rodham Clinton won the Liberal line in her successful bid for United States senator from New York in 2000.

Liberal Party Platform, 1944

The Liberal Party was organized in May 1944 and adopted a platform at its organizing convention. The platform endorsed 11 planks:

The achievement of full employment for all.

The right of workers to join free and independent trade unions, and the right to bargain collectively.

Health insurance, education, and cultural services for all.

The promotion of conditions favorable to small businesses.

The abolition of poverty & depressed areas in the city and nation.

The conservation and rational use of national resources.

The maintenance of civil and political liberty for all, regardless of race, color, or creed.

Increased extension of unemployment benefits.

An authentic aim of American democracy is to give all of its children an equal start.

A decent home for every American.

Fair and adequate compensation for an adjustable cost of living differential for civil servants.

More information

- Hentoff, Nat. *A Political Life: The Education of John V. Lindsay.* New York: Knopf, 1969.
- Klein, Woody. *Lindsay's Promise: The Dream That Failed.* New York: Macmillan, 1970.
- Niebuhr, Reinhold. *Faith and History.* New York: Scribner's, 1949.

On the Web

- Liberal Party of New York. Nationmaster.com. *http://www.nationmaster.com/encyclopedia/Liberal-Party-(New-York-State).*
- Liberal Party of New York State. *http://www.liberalparty.org/.*
- New York's Liberal Party. *http://www.msys.net/cress/ballots2/liberal.htm.*

Progressive Party, 1948–52

FlashFocus: Progressive Party, 1948

Origins

Frustration with President Harry Truman's foreign policy caused liberal Democrats to reconstitute the Progressive Party after World War II. Disenchanted Democrats, represented by former Truman cabinet secretary Henry Wallace, launched the new party at a convention in July 1948. Wallace, who had been fired from Truman's cabinet for publicly advocating peaceful relations with the Soviet Union after World War II, was nominated for president, and Senator Glen Taylor, a Democrat from Idaho, was nominated for vice president.

Issues

Foreign policy. The central theme of the Progressive Party was opposition to President Harry Truman's foreign policy, including rebuilding war-torn Europe with the Marshall Plan and viewing the Soviet Union as a threat. The Truman Doctrine, which called for containing the spread of communism, ran counter to Wallace's theory of peaceful coexistence with the Soviets, including acceptance that Eastern Europe was a Soviet sphere of influence.
United Nations. The Progressive Party strongly supported the United Nations as a world legislative body that would prevent a repetition of World War II.
Civil rights. The Progressive Party called for new civil rights legislation to end racial segregation and discrimination, especially in the South. Such laws would protect the voting rights of African Americans, the right to an equal and fair education, and an end to discriminatory hiring practices. Progressives also advocated a constitutional amendment to give women equal rights.
Welfare. The Progressive Party supported the expansion of federal welfare programs such as social security and unemployment insurance.

Impact

The Progressive Party's presidential ticket of Wallace and Taylor appeared on the presidential ballot in 45 states in 1948. It received 1,157,326 votes (2.4 percent) but failed to carry any electoral votes. Nor did the Progressives elect a single representative or senator. After the disappointing results in 1948, the Progressive Party tried to regroup, but its opposition to the Korean War in 1950, which was launched to combat the Communist-led invasion of South Korea, repelled many of its members, including Wallace himself. The party ran a presidential ticket in 1952 but won just over 140,000 votes. Thereafter it dismantled entirely.

See also: States' Rights Democrats, Vol. 4, p. 87; Democratic Party, 1932–68, p. 141; Progressive (Bull Moose) Party, p. 121; Progressive Party, 1924, p. 132.

The name of the Progressive Party has been shared by four different parties—in the presidential elections of 1892 (see Vol. 1, p. 102); in 1912, when it was nicknamed the Bull Moose Party (see p. 121); in 1924 (see p. 132); and in 1948. The common theme of these four parties has been moving to counter the power and influence of the economic elite through federal government action in favor of the rights and welfare of people at the bottom of the economic pecking order. Unable to achieve power as an independent party, all four Progressive Parties soon folded, usually into the ranks of the Democratic Party.

The Election of 1948

In 1946, the Democratic Party developed an ideological rift. Liberal members of the party became disenchanted with the policies of President Harry Truman (see Vol. 1, p. 155), who had become president after the death of Franklin Roosevelt (see Vol. 1, p. 141) the previous year. After the Allied victory in World War II, attention focused on Truman's foreign policy, which had thrust the United States into a struggle with the Soviet Union for political influence in Europe. In this developing Cold War, the Soviets backed communists in Eastern Europe, and the United States backed anticommunists. Many within the Democratic Party believed that Truman's emphasis on containing the spread of communism had reversed Roosevelt's goal of peaceful relations with the Soviet Union. They also thought the Truman Doctrine ran counter to the goals of the newly organized United Nations.

Truman's opponents thought that the United States could not act as the "world's policeman." Instead, they advocated working within the United Nations to maintain world peace. One of the more prominent critics of Truman was a former member of his cabinet and former vice president, Henry Wallace (see p. 161). Wallace had served with distinction as vice president, secretary of agriculture, and secretary of commerce under Roosevelt. Wallace had been one of the most liberal members of Roosevelt's administration, a position that made some Democrats nervous. Roosevelt was persuaded to keep Wallace off the national ticket in 1944; he chose Truman as his running mate instead. The choice became significant after Roosevelt's death in office. Wallace remained in his post as secretary of commerce, but in 1946, Wallace delivered a speech in which he called for the United States to recognize Soviet interests in eastern Europe and warned against British influence over American foreign policy. This was in almost direct opposition to the newly proclaimed "Truman Doctrine" of containing Russian influence in Europe, including letting European communists seize control of governments. Truman dismissed Wallace from his cabinet.

Wallace began to flirt with the idea of a third-party candidacy for the White House after a successful tour of the nation in which he spoke out against the policies of the Truman administration. He found support for this notion from the American Labor Party (see p. 152), the Progressive Citizens of America, and similar groups in Illinois and California. As his support grew, Wallace formally announced his candidacy in December 1947. The latest version of the Progressive Party convened in July 1948 and nominated Wallace for president and Democratic Senator Glen Taylor of Idaho for vice president.

The Progressives attracted support from minorities such as African Americans, Jews, and Latinos, as well as from women. The party was also endorsed by the Communist Party (see p. 128), which put Wallace and the new Progressive Party on the defensive for much of the 1948 campaign.

The End of the Progressive Party

While many of the domestic issues that the Progressive Party supported may have been ahead of their time, its foreign policy seemed wrong for the beginning of the Cold War era that pitted the United States against the Soviet Union. Peaceful coexistence with the Soviets struck the wrong chord with the American electorate at a time when both the United States and the Soviet Union perceived themselves to be on a collision course. Moreover, most voters believed that the Truman administration sincerely wanted peace and that it was the Soviets who stood in the way. Political candidates opposed to American foreign policy were looked upon with suspicion.

Establishing a national organization proved to be a difficult task, made even harder by internal disagreements over strategy and a slim pool of qualified political veterans to staff state and local Progressive offices. Communication between national party leaders and local leaders was inefficient; and while the party did manage to get on the ballot in 45 states, the lack of organization hurt the campaign. Some municipalities refused to rent auditoriums, and the mayor of Asheville, North Carolina, wrote Wallace to tell the candidate that his presence was not welcome. In addition, the party charged admission to most of its political rallies, which discouraged attendance.

Wallace himself proved to be ineffective as a campaigner, striking many as being distant and aloof, and a poor speaker. Eventually, Wallace was unable to draw crowds to his rallies, and he canceled public appearances to concentrate on radio addresses after October 17, 1948.

In the election, over half of Wallace's votes came from the state of New York alone, and the party did not win a majority in any state.

Despite its weak showing, the Progressive Party tried to continue, but its opposition to the Korean War in 1950 caused many moderate members of the party to leave, including Wallace himself. A national ticket was nominated in 1952 but won only 140,023 votes. The party was dismantled following the 1952 election.

FlashFocus: Henry Agard Wallace

Born: October 7, 1888, Orient, Iowa
Died: November 18, 1965, Danbury, Connecticut
Political Career: Secretary of agriculture, 1933–41; vice president, 1941–45; secreatary of commerce, 1945; Progressive candidate for president, 1948.

Henry Wallace grew up on his father's farm. He attended Iowa State College, where he studied plant genetics, graduating in 1910. He continued his work with plant genetics and developed a species of hybrid corn that proved highly profitable. He worked on his own small farm in Des Moines, Iowa, and did writing and editing for his father's newspaper, *Wallace's Farmer*. He became editor of the news-paper in 1921.

The 1920s were a difficult time for farmers, when massive overproduction led to a depression in the Midwest. Wallace encouraged cutbacks in production, but his suggestions were not popular with farmers. He was a strong supporter of President Roosevelt and the New Deal, and in return for his support, Roosevelt appointed Wallace secretary of agriculture. Here, Wallace continued his work on behalf of farmers, implementing policies such as the Agriculture Adjustment Act, which paid farmers to decrease their output and tried to establish markets abroad where farmers could export their goods.

In 1940, Roosevelt insisted that the Democratic Party nominate Wallace as their vice-presidential candidate, threatening to refuse his own nomination for president if the party did not comply. As vice president, Wallace kept a high profile and was outspoken in his support of a cooperative foreign policy, which at the time meant cooperation with Russia. However, these views did not sit well with a public that was increasingly anticommunist, and in 1944, Wallace was dropped from the Democratic ticket, replaced by Harry Truman. Wallace continued to support Roosevelt and was rewarded with the secretary of commerce post. When Truman became president after Roosevelt's death, he developed a "firm" policy toward Russia. Wallace continued to voice his opposition to this policy, leading Truman to ask Wallace for his resignation, which he offered in 1946. He became editor of *The New Republic* and used that publication to urge cooperation in foreign affairs.

The Progressive Party, formed in 1947, nominated Wallace as their candidate for president, but Wallace alienated many voters by accepting the support of communists. After his unsuccessful campaign, he retired from public life and returned to his farm in South Salem, New York. He died in 1965.

The Progressive Party Platform

Excerpts from the 1948 Progressive Party platform:

Three years after the end of the second world war, the drums are beating for a third. Civil liberties are being destroyed. Millions cry out for relief from unbearably high prices. The American way of life is in danger.

The root cause of this crisis is Big Business control of our economy and government.

With toil and enterprise the American people have created from their rich resources the world's greatest productive machine. This machine no longer belongs to the people. Its ownership is concentrated in the hands of a few and its product used for their enrichment.

Never before have so few owned so much at the expense of so many....

The Progressive Party...demands negotiation and discussion with the Soviet Union to find areas of agreement to win the peace.

The Progressive Party believes that enduring peace among the peoples of the world is possible only through world law. Continued anarchy among nations in the atomic age threatens our civilization and humanity itself with annihilation. The only ultimate alternative to war is the abandonment of the principle of the coercion of sovereignties by sovereignties, and the adoption of the principle of the just enforcement upon individuals of world federal law, enacted by a world federal legislature with limited but adequate powers to safeguard the common defense and the general welfare of all mankind.

The Progressive Party will work through the United Nations for a world disarmament agreement to outlaw the atomic bomb, bacteriological warfare, and all other instruments of mass destruction; to destroy existing stockpiles of atomic bombs and to establish United Nations controls, including inspection, over the production of atomic energy; and to reduce conventional armaments drastically in accordance with resolutions already passed by the United Nations General Assembly....

The Progressive Party calls for the repeal of the peacetime draft and the rejection of Universal Military Training....

We demand amnesty for conscientious objectors imprisoned in World War II....

We denounce anti-Soviet hysteria as a mask for monopoly, militarism, and reaction....

The Progressive Party will fight for the constitutional rights of Communists and all other political groups to express their views as the first line in the defense of the liberties of a democratic people....

We demand the repudiation of the Truman Doctrine and an end to military and economic intervention in support of reactionary and fascist regimes in China, Greece, Turkey, the Middle East, and Latin America.

We demand that the United States completely sever diplomatic and economic relations with Franco Spain....

We call for the abandonment of military bases designed to encircle and intimidate other nations.

The Progressive Party will work to realize Franklin Roosevelt's ideal of the United Nations as a world family of nations, by defending its Charter and seeking to prevent its transformation into the diplomatic or military instrument of any one group of powers.

The Progressive Party condemns segregation and discrimination in all places....

We call for a Presidential proclamation ending segregation and all forms of discrimination in the armed services and Federal employment.

We demand Federal anti-lynch, anti-discrimination, and fair-employment-practices legislation and legislation abolishing segregation in interstate travel.

We call for immediate passage of anti-poll tax legislation, enactment of a universal suffrage law to permit all citizens to vote in Federal elections, and the full use of Federal enforcement powers to assure free exercise of the right to franchise....

We demand that Indians, the earliest Americans, be given full citizenship rights without loss of reservation rights and be permitted to administer their own affairs....

We will initiate a Federal program of education, in cooperation with state, local, and private agencies to combat racial and religious prejudice....

We call for a Constitutional amendment which will effectively prohibit every form of discrimination against women— economic, educational, legal, and political.

We also call for assistance to low-income consumers through such programs as the food stamp plan and the school hot-lunch program....

We pledge an attack on the chronic housing shortage and the slums through a long-range program to build 25 million new homes during the next ten years. This program will include public subsidized housing for low-income families....

As a first step, the largest banks, the railroads, the merchant marine, the electric power and gas industry, and industries primarily dependent on government funds or government purchases such as the aircraft, synthetic rubber and synthetic oil industries might be placed under public ownership....

We call for the right to vote at eighteen.

More Information

▶ Culver, John C. *American Dreamer: The Life and Times of Henry A. Wallace.* New York: Norton, 2000.

▶ MacDonald, Dwight. *Henry Wallace: The Man and the Myth.* New York: Garland, 1979.

▶ Markowitz, Norman D. *The Rise and Fall of the People's Century: Henry A. Wallace and American Liberalism, 1941–1948.* New York: Free Press, 1973.

▶ White, Graham and John Maze. *Henry A. Wallace: His Search for a New World Order.* Chapel Hill: University of North Carolina Press, 1995.

On the Web:

▶ Progressive Party of 1948. *http://www.lib.uiowa.edu/spec-coll/Bai/epstein.htm.*

▶ Epstein, Marc J. "The Progressive Party of 1948." Books at Iowa 16. *http://www.lib.uiowa.edu/spec-coll/Bai/epstein.htm.*

▶ "Democrats' Last Chance," The New Republic, July 12, 1948. *http://www.tnr.com/doc.mhtml%3Fi=redux&s=editors071248.*

Democratic Party, 1968–2004

FlashFocus: Democratic Party, 1968–2004

Origins

The Democratic Party was severely split in 1968 over the Vietnam War and civil rights. Conservative white-collar workers, especially in the South, were attracted by former Alabama Governor George Wallace's independent presidential campaign, while liberals were repelled by the Vietnam War and the influence of urban political "machines." After a chaotic 1968 convention, the party introduced changes that gave more influence to African Americans and women. By 1992, Democrats introduced a new platform drafted by the Democratic Leadership Council, a group of conservative and moderate Democrats who were persuaded the party needed to counter the conservative appeals of the Republicans with a more conservative, probusiness platform.

Issues

Vietnam War. By 1968, public opinion was turning against the Vietnam War, and voters were willing to give the Republicans a chance to end a conflict that appeared to many to be a quagmire.

Civil unrest. Widespread antiwar demonstrations and race riots in the late 1960s alienated many white working-class voters who were eager for a return to tranquility in 1968.

Iran Hostage Crisis. The presidency of Jimmy Carter became a virtual hostage of conservative, fundamentalist Islamic leaders in Iran after American hostages were seized at the U.S. embassy in Tehran.

Fiscal conservatism. After 12 years of conservative Republican administrations, a group of younger Democratic politicians pushed through a new Democratic platform in 1992 that put much more emphasis on using private enterprise as a means of solving social problems and deemphasized the role of government.

Terrorism and war in Iraq. Attacks on September 11, 2001, by fundamentalist Islamic terrorists put Democrats on the defensive as incumbent Republican President George W. Bush claimed the mantle of "war president."

Impact

In nine presidential elections starting in 1968, Democrats won the White House only three times (1976, 1992, 1996), compared to Republican victories in six elections. After the midterm elections of 1994, Republicans took over both houses of Congress, effectively thwarting virtually all of President Bill Clinton's initiatives.

See also: Democratic Party, 1932–68, p. 141; Republican Party, 1932–68, p. 135; Republican Party, 1968–2004, p. 169; Green Party, p. 190.

The election of 1968 marked a turning point for the Democratic Party. Its presidential candidate, Vice President Hubert Humphrey (see Vol. 1, p. 175), lost to Republican candidate Richard Nixon (see Vol. 1, p. 174) by just 510,315 popular votes. But it was a sharp turnaround from four years earlier, when Democrat Lyndon Johnson (see Vol. 1, p. 170) was elected with 61.1 percent of the popular vote. More significantly, Humphrey was the last Democrat from the New Deal tradition of Franklin Roosevelt (see Vol. 1, p. 141) to run for president. In the next 36 years, Democrats would occupy the White House for just 12. In Congress, Democrats continued their majorities in both houses until 1981, when Republicans won control of the Senate, after which followed a seesaw battle for control of the legislative branch.

Origins of Change

The surprise in 1968 was that Hubert Humphrey, who as mayor of Minneapolis in 1944 had arranged a merger of Minnesota's weak Democratic Party with the radical but fading Farmer-Labor Party (see p. 125), came as close to victory as he did. Indeed, had it not been for the 9.9 million votes collected by American Independent candidate George Wallace (see p. 180), Humphrey might well have won. As it was, however, Wallace attracted a significant vote from the traditional Democratic base of white voters in the South, carrying five states in Dixie—his native Alabama, Georgia, Mississippi, Louisiana, and Arkansas, worth a total of 46 electoral votes. Wallace had appealed to many lower- and middle-class voters who felt threatened by the social chaos that marked American society in 1968, ranging from the assassinations of civil rights leader Martin Luther King, Jr. (see Vol. 4, p. 97), and Senator Robert F. Kennedy, to rioting at the Democratic National Convention in Chicago. The disorder on the streets seemed to reflect a sense of disorder in a society wracked by a decade of change in civil rights for African Americans, a controversial war in Vietnam, successive summers of rioting in large cities, and an apparent breakdown of what Wallace called "law and order."

Humphrey led a party deeply divided over American participation in Vietnam. Johnson had declined to run for reelection, partly because he feared that antiwar protests would follow his every move on the campaign trail. Years of escalating U.S. military action in Vietnam had seemed to make little dent in the campaign by Vietnamese communists to seize control of the southern half of the country.

More significant than Humphrey's loss to Nixon—it took the Republicans over a decade before they successfully challenged the Democrats' strength in congressional districts—was the response of the Democratic Party to the chaos of their convention. Senator George McGovern (see Vol. 1, p. 179) of

South Dakota was named to head a special committee to revise the party's rules for selecting delegates—changes that would have an even more profound impact on the party than the loss of the White House.

The McGovern Reforms

The McGovern Commission, as the committee was known, introduced wide-ranging reforms that profoundly changed the way the Democratic Party chose delegates to its national conventions starting in 1972.

The essence of the reforms was to emphasize the role of primary elections in delegate selection and to minimize the role of state-level party committees. The committee also instituted national standards for delegate selection, replacing a variety of state rules. The result was twofold. First, the reforms opened the process of selecting party candidates for president and vice president to a much wider variety of voters—especially women and minority voters—and took the decisions out of the hands of party professionals. Second, the new rules resulted in a party that largely operated on one national standard, changing the Democratic Party from an alliance of autonomous state parties to a single national organization. The primary beneficiaries of the new rules, as measured in party influence, were African Americans, women, younger voters, and Latinos. Symbolic of the impact of the new rules was a challenge at the 1972 national convention to the delegation headed by Chicago's Mayor Richard Daley. The convention ruled that Daley's set of delegates were not properly chosen, and the mayor was denied a seat as a delegate. The man who had presided over what was later labeled a "police riot" attacking protesters in Chicago in 1968 was no longer a delegate at the party's convention four years later.

In early 1972, McGovern announced that he would be a candidate for the Democratic presidential nomination. McGovern's signature issue had long been his opposition to the war in Vietnam. He soon became the favored candidate of Democrats who four years earlier had supported Senators McCarthy and Kennedy.

The Wallace Revolt

The most threatening challenger to McGovern was Governor George Wallace of Alabama, who in 1968 had run as an independent and siphoned off enough Democratic votes to put Republican Richard Nixon into the White House. In 1972, Wallace challenged McGovern for the Democratic nomination. Wallace was favored by many voters in the South and also appealed to many traditional Democratic white-collar voters in the North. Wallace's campaign was cut short, however, when he was wounded and paralyzed in an assassination attempt. In the aftermath of the shooting, many Wallace voters switched to President Nixon, who was pursuing his "southern strategy" to capture the former Democratic stronghold in Dixie for the Republicans. The strategy included emphasizing states' rights—taken by most people to mean deemphasizing federal enforcement of civil rights—and emphasizing both law and order and national security. The result was to drive a wedge between the national Democratic Party and its traditional base of southern white voters. After 1968, the "solid South" no longer existed for the Democrats.

The changes in how the Democrats chose delegates led, somewhat unexpectedly, to changes in the way the party's national ticket campaigned. As a result of bypassing the traditional local party structures in choosing delegates, McGovern discovered that he could not count on the traditional party organization to boost his campaign. His solution was to replace the party with the media, particularly television. In order to deliver his appeal to local voters, McGovern took to making a series of campaign stops at local airports, where local television stations could send a camera crew to videotape the event. McGovern's campaign became a series of airport appearances, where he stayed just long enough to make a few remarks for the evening local news show, then fly off to another airport in order to appear on another local television news show. The strategy did not serve McGovern well. He was largely "out of touch" with voters, both physically and symbolically, and by ignoring local Democratic organizations, McGovern left himself without key support in getting voters to the polls on election day.

McGovern won the nomination on the strength of a series of primary election victories and at the convention chose Missouri Senator Thomas Eagleton as his vice presidential running mate. Shortly after the convention, Eagleton confirmed reports that he had once received electric shock therapy for what he called "nervous exhaustion." At first, McGovern said he supported Eagleton "one thousand percent," but after conducting research into voter attitudes, McGovern asked his running mate to resign. The incident plagued the rest of the McGovern campaign.

False Peace Hopes

A final blow to McGovern's campaign came on October 26, just days before the election, when Nixon's national security advisor, Henry Kissinger, announced that "peace is at hand" in Vietnam. Kissinger confidently asserted that a breakthrough in peace negotiations with the North Vietnamese meant that the end to the controversial war—McGovern's signature issue—would take place in a matter of days. The announcement robbed McGovern of what little wind he had left in his sails.

On election day, Nixon won over 60 percent of the popular vote and won the electoral college vote in every state except Massachusetts and the District of Columbia. The Wallace vote—white working-class voters who once went for Democrats overwhelmingly—went largely to Nixon. What was termed as the ethnic vote—descendants of immigrants from southern and eastern Europe—also went to Nixon in 1972, reflecting continuing conflicts between lower- and middle-class whites living in cities and African Americans (African Americans voted overwhelmingly for McGovern in 1972). Significantly, however, these defections from the presidential ticket by members of the traditional Roosevelt coalition of the Democratic Party did not extend to congressional races. Democrats continued to control both houses of Congress.

Watergate Scandal

Halfway through Nixon's second term as president, the Watergate scandal began to emerge. Watergate was the name of a Washington office building where the Democratic Party had its national headquarters. In 1972, burglars had been arrested in the offices of the Democrats. By 1973, a series of newspaper reports began emerging suggesting that the Watergate burglars were acting at the behest of CREEP—the Committee for the Reelection of the President. Nixon strenuously denied any connection with the burglars, declaring at one point: "I am not a crook." In the summer of 1974, however, the nation was transfixed by televised Congressional hearings that clearly showed senior White House officials were linked to the burglary aimed at the Democrats. Faced with almost certain impeachment, Nixon resigned, handing the White House to his vice president, Gerald Ford, who had taken office in the wake of the earlier resignation of Nixon's 1972 running mate, Vice President Spiro Agnew, who was accused of tax fraud. Ford, the former Republican leader in the House, issued a presidential pardon to Nixon, foreclosing any possible criminal proceedings against the former president but also indirectly staining Ford's administration with the Watergate scandal.

A former one-term governor of Georgia, Jimmy Carter, used the McGovern reforms to win the Democratic presidential nomination in 1976 by entering 30 primaries and winning 17. Carter was a moderate southern Democrat who had appointed many African Americans to state offices while governor. A virtual unknown outside of Georgia when he started campaigning in 1975, Carter appealed to many Democrats as a new face in a field crowded with Democratic veterans. Carter promised promised to restore a sense of morality to the federal government, emphasizing his devout Christianity and his role as a Baptist Sunday school teacher. Carter narrowly defeated the incumbent Ford in a campaign largely defined by his personality.

Carter was challenged for the 1980 Democratic nomination by Senator Edward Kennedy of Massachusetts, younger brother of President John Kennedy (see Vol. 1, p. 166). Carter easily defeated Kennedy, but the Massachusetts senator won primaries in such key states as California and New York, forcing Carter to accept many of Kennedy's proposals for the party platform. Of more importance, however, was the Iran hostage crisis, which saw 53 Americans held hostage by radical Islamists in Tehran, Iran, for more than 400 days. Despite diplomatic efforts and one failed military rescue mission, the long drama weakened Carter and opened the way for Republican charges in 1980 that Carter had allowed the United States to be humiliated. Carter's Republican opponent in 1980, California Governor Ronald Reagan, came across on television

FlashFocus: Terry McAuliffe

Born: February 1947, Syracuse, New York
Political Career: Chair, Democratic National Committee, 2001–.

Terry McAuliffe began his political career while he was still in elementary school, accompanying his father, a real estate agent and treasurer of the local Democratic Party, at party events and selling tickets to fundraisers door-to-door. He began his own driveway-sealing business at age 14 and became a millionaire within 10 years by investing his profits. He attended Catholic University in Washington, D.C., and went on to earn a law degree from Georgetown University.

McAuliffe continued his political career with President Carter's campaign in 1976. Due to his unusual dedication to his job—during one campaign he wrestled an alligator to elicit a donation—he became an important fundraiser for the Democratic Party in the 1980s, serving as Democratic National Committee finance director and a fundraiser for the Democratic Congressional Campaign Committee. He worked closely with Repre-sentative Richard Gephardt of Missouri and served as his finance director when Gephardt ran for president in 1988.

McAuliffe worked as a lobbyist until the Democratic Party officially hired him to do fundraising in 1994. He worked as the finance chair of President Clinton's reelection campaign in 1996, then became national cochair of the entire campaign.

By 2000, McAuliffe estimated that he had raised about $300 million during his career, making him the most successful political fundraiser in history. In 2000, the Democratic Party chose McAuliffe to chair the Democratic National Convention in Los Angeles. He was elected chair of the Democratic National Committee in 2001.

as self-assured and confident, not unlike the image of Franklin Roosevelt (see Vol. 1, p. 141) running in 1932. Reagan won 50.7 percent of the popular vote to Carter's 41 percent, and the electoral college vote 489 to 49.

Democrats in the Reagan era

The election of 1980 resulted in Democrats losing both the White House and control of the Senate for the first time since 1953, although they maintained a majority in the House of Representatives. More significantly, 1980 showed unmistakably that a new conservative era had replaced the liberal Roosevelt era. In the next two presidential races, in 1984 and 1988 (see Vol. 1, pp. 189 and 192), Democrats nominated traditional Roosevelt liberals to run, Walter Mondale (see Vol. 1, p. 191) of Minnesota and Governor Michael Dukakis (see Vol. 1, p. 194) of Massachusetts. Mondale lost to Reagan, drawing 40.6 percent of the popular vote to Reagan's 58.8 percent, and Dukakis lost to Reagan's vice president, George H. W. Bush (see Vol. 1, p. 193), with 45.6 percent of the vote to Bush's 53.4 percent.

Midway through Reagan's term, a group of conservative Democrats from the South organized the Democratic

The Democratic Party was shaken by allegations of sexual misconduct by President Clinton, allegations that he first denied but then later admitted. This cartoon from the *Baltimore Sun* in 1998 illustrates the issue that became the focus of Clinton's second administration.

Leadership Council (DLC), dedicated to reforming the Democratic Party along more conservative lines. Early figures in the DLC were Senators Sam Nunn of Georgia and Charles Robb of Virginia, and Governor Bill Clinton (see Vol. 1, p. 197) of Arkansas. In essence, the DLC tried to reorient the Democratic Party toward the middle class, rather than persist with identifying with the Roosevelt era working class. Mondale's crashing defeat in 1984 gave impetus to organization of the DLC the following year. In 1988, the presidential hopeful preferred by the more conservative DLC was Senator Gary Hart of Colorado, running against Dukakis of Massachusetts. Hart's campaign was derailed by revelations of a sexual indiscretion, rather than by issues of philosophy.

Four years later, in 1992, Clinton, a former chairman of the DLC, waged a campaign as a "new Democrat," focused on such issues as welfare reform (emphasizing the need to get jobs for welfare recipients) and building a new sense of community within the party. Clinton spoke of a "third way" between the traditional liberalism of Roosevelt and the traditional conservatism of the Republicans, represented in 1992 by the incumbent Bush.

Characteristically of presidential elections, the contest in 1992 (see Vol. 1, p. 196) did not hinge solely on political philosophy. An economic recession had cast a pall over Bush's oversight of the Persian Gulf War, during which the United States led a coalition of forces to expel the Iraqi Army from occupied Kuwait. Moreover, soaring federal deficits had marked the 12 years of Republican administrations, a marked turnaround from the previous generation in which Democrats were accused of having irresponsible fiscal programs. And Clinton's personal charisma contrasted with the patrician, out-of-touch image projected by Bush.

Two years after Clinton's election, the Democratic Party lost control of both houses of Congress. For the first time since 1952, Republicans won a majority in the House of Representatives. The change in power reflected two basic trends. One was a shift of population away from urban areas to suburbs, and from the North to the South. The other was the continuing Republican ideological shift to the right. Although Clinton was reelected in 1996, Republicans maintained control of Congress.

In 2000, the incumbent vice president, Albert Gore (see Vol. 1, p. 206), lost to Republican George W. Bush (see Vol. 1, p. 205), son of the former president, in the most controversial presidential election since 1876 (see Vol. 1, p. 86). Gore narrowly won the popular vote, but lost the electoral college vote when the U.S. Supreme Court ordered a halt to vote recounting in Florida when Bush was narrowly ahead, thereby giving Florida's electoral votes—and the election—to the Republican candidate. Control of the Senate was evenly divided during the first two years of Bush's first administration. A 50-50 tie between Democrats and Republicans was broken by the votes of the vice president (Democrat Vice President Al Gore until George W. Bush was inaugurated, after which it was Republican Richard Cheney). The shift from Republican to Independent by Vermont Senator James Jeffords gave Democrats a one-vote majority until the autumn of 2002, when Democrat Paul Wellstone of Minnesota died in a plane crash and was replaced by an Independent, and when a special election replaced a Democrat from Missouri, Jean Carnahan, with a Republican, James Talent. After the 2002 elections, Republicans regained power in the Senate, 51-48 (plus one Independent, Jeffords, voting with the Democrats).

Democrats were energized for the 2004 elections by two factors: the U.S. invasion of Iraq, initiated by Bush, and a series of controversial and conservative reforms that showed Bush to be a much more conservative politician than many voters had been led to believe in 2000. Bush pushed through income tax reductions that the Congressional Budget Office concluded had favored wealthy tax payers and presided over the largest government deficits in history. A sluggish recovery from an economic recession that started in 2001 also invigorated Democrats. On the other hand, attacks on the World Trade Center office building in New York and the Pentagon near Washington on September 11, 2001, provided Bush with a campaign issue as an effective fighter against Islamic fundamentalist terrorism.

Democratic Party Platform, 1992

The Democratic Party platform of 1992 reflected a newly emerged conservative group of Democrats who were convinced that regaining the White House required modifying the traditional New Deal assumptions about government's role in economic and social affairs. The 1992 platform put new emphasis on the role of private enterprise in helping solve social problems and called for a reduced role for government, even while guaranteeing equal opportunities for all citizens. Some critics called the program developed by the Democratic Leadership Council "Republican Lite." Excerpts from the platform on which Governor Bill Clinton of Arkansas successfully ran for the presidency:

A New Covenant with the American People

...We vow to make government more decentralized, more flexible, and more accountable—to reform public institutions and replace public officials who aren't leading with ones who will....

An expanding, entrepreneurial economy of high-skill, high-wage jobs is the most important family policy, urban policy, labor policy, minority policy and foreign policy America can have.

The Revolution of 1992 is about putting government back on the side of working men and women—to help those who work hard, pay their bills, play by the rules, don't lobby for tax breaks, do their best to give their kids a good education and to keep them away from drugs, who want a safe neighborhood for their families, the security of decent, productive jobs for themselves, and a dignified life for their parents.

The Revolution of 1992 is about a radical change in the way government operates—not the Republican proposition that government has no role, nor the old notion that there's a program for every problem, but a shift to a more efficient, flexible and results-oriented government that improves services, expands choices, and empowers citizens and communities to change our country from the bottom up. We believe in an activist government, but it must work in a different, more responsive way....

Above all the Revolution of 1992 is about restoring the basic American values that built this country and will always make it great: personal responsibility, individual liberty, tolerance, faith, family and hard work. We offer the American people not only new ideas, a new course, and a new President, but a return to the enduring principles that set our nation apart: the promise of opportunity, the strength of community, the dignity of work, and a decent life for senior citizens.

To make this revolution, we seek a New Covenant to repair the damaged bond between the American people and their government, that will expand opportunity, insist upon greater individual responsibility in return, restore community, and ensure national security in a profoundly new era....

We reject both the do-nothing government of the last twelve years and the big government theory that says we can hamstring business and tax and spend our way to prosperity. Instead we offer a third way.... [W]e honor business as a noble endeavor, and vow to create a far better climate for firms and independent contractors of all sizes that empower their workers, revolutionize their workplaces, respect the environment, and serve their communities well....

In place of the Republican supply-side disaster, the Democratic investment, economic conversion, and growth strategy will generate more revenues from a growing economy. We must also tackle spending by putting everything on the table; eliminate nonproductive programs; achieve defense savings; reform entitlement programs to control soaring health care costs; cut federal administrative costs by 3 percent annually for four years...; apply a strict "pay as you go" rule to new non-investment spending; and make the rich pay their fair share in taxes....

We will create jobs by investing significant resources to put people back to work, beginning with a summer jobs initiative and training programs for inner-city youth.... A national public works investment and infrastructure program will provide jobs and strengthen our cities, suburbs, rural communities and country....

It is time to reestablish the private/public partnership to ensure that family farmers get a fair return for their labor and in-

vestment, so that consumers receive safe and nutritious foods, and that needed investments are made in basic research, education, rural business development, market development and infrastructure to sustain rural communities....

We will reform the job safety laws to empower workers with greater rights and to hold employers accountable for dangers on the job. We will act against sexual harassment in the workplace. We will honor the work ethic—by expanding the earned income tax credit so no one with children at home who works full-time is still in poverty....

All Americans should have universal access to quality, affordable health care—not as a privilege, but as a right....

We reject the Republican myth that energy efficiency and environmental protection are enemies of economic growth. We will make our economy more efficient, by using less energy, reducing our dependence on foreign oil, and producing less solid and toxic waste....

Democrats will continue to lead the fight to ensure that no Americans suffer discrimination or deprivation of rights on the basis of race, gender, language, national origin, religion, age, disability, sexual orientation, or other characteristics irrelevant to ability. We support the ratification of the Equal Rights Amendment; affirmative action; stronger protection of voting rights for racial and ethnic minorities, including language access to voting; and continued resistance to discriminatory English-only pressure groups..., provide civil rights protection for gay men and lesbians and an end to Defense Department discrimination....

Sixty years ago, Franklin Roosevelt gave hope to a nation mired in the Great Depression. While government should promise every American the opportunity to get ahead, it was the people's responsibility, he said, to make the most of that opportunity.... [W]e offer a new social contract based neither on callous, do-nothing Republican neglect, nor on an outdated faith in programs as the solution to every problem. We favor a third way beyond the old approaches—to put government back on the side of citizens who play by the rules. We believe that by what it says and how it conducts its business, government must once again make responsibility an instrument of national purpose. Our future as a nation depends upon the daily assumption of personal responsibility by millions of Americans from all walks of life—for the religious faiths they follow, the ethics they practice, the values they instill, and the pride they take in their work....

Welfare should be a second chance, not a way of life. We want to break the cycle of welfare by adhering to two simple principles: no one who is able to work can stay on welfare forever, and no one who works should live in poverty. We will continue to help those who cannot help themselves. We will offer people on welfare a new social contract. We'll invest in education and job training, and provide the child care and health care they need to go to work and achieve long-term self-sufficiency. We will give them the help they need to make the transition from welfare to work, and require people who can work to go to work within two years in available jobs either in the private sector or in community service to meet unmet needs. This will restore the covenant that welfare was meant to be: a promise of temporary help for people who have fallen on hard times....

Workers must also accept added responsibilities in the new economy. In return for an increased voice and a greater stake in the success of their enterprises, workers should be prepared to join in cooperative efforts to increase productivity, flexibility and quality....

Democrats in 1992 intend to lead a revolution in government, challenging it to act responsibly and be accountable, starting with the hardest and most urgent problems of the deficit and economic growth. Rather than throw money at obsolete programs, we will eliminate unnecessary layers of management, cut administrative costs, give people more choices in the service they get, and empower them to make those choices. To foster greater responsibility in government at every level, we support giving greater flexibility to our cities, counties and states in achieving Federal mandates and carrying out existing programs....

More Information

▶ Baer, Kenneth S. *Reinventing Democrats: The Politics of Liberalism from Reagan to Clinton.* Lawrence: University Press of Kansas, 2000.

▶ Clinton, Bill and Al Gore. *Putting People First: How We Can All Change America.* New York: Times Books, 1992.

▶ Dodd, Lawrence C. and Calvin Jillson (eds.). *New Perspectives on American Politics.* Washington: CQ Press, 1994.

▶ Judis, John B. and Ruy Teixeira. *The Emerging Democratic Majority.* New York: Scribner, 2002.

▶ Menefee-Libey, David. *The Triumph of Campaign-Centered Politics.* New York: Chatham House Publishers, Seven Bridges Press, 2000.

▶ Radosh, Ronald. *Divided They Fell: The Demise of the Democratic Party, 1964–1996.* New York: Free Press, 1996.

▶ Witcover, Jules. *Party of the People: A History of the Democrats.* New York: Random House, 2003.

On the Web

▶ Democratic Party Platforms, 1968–2000. The American Presidency Project, University of California at Santa Barbara. *http://www.presidency.ucsb.edu/site/docs/platforms.php.*

▶ Democratic Party. Reader's Companion to American History, Houghton Mifflin. *http://college.hmco.com/history/readerscomp/rcah/html/ah_024300_democraticpa.htm.*

▶ History of the Democratic Party, Democratic National Committee. *http://www.democrats.org/about/history.html.*

▶ Inaugural Addresses of Jimmy Carter (1977) and Bill Clinton (1993 and 1997). The American Presidency Project, University of California at Santa Barbara. *http://www.presidency.ucsb.edu/site/docs/inaugurals.php.*

▶ Public Papers of President Jimmy Carter, 1977. The American Presidency Project, University of California at Santa Barbara. *http://www.presidency.ucsb.edu/site/docs/pppusyear.php?yearindex=1977.*

Republican Party, 1968–2004

FlashFocus: Republican Party, 1968–2004

Origins
Following the 1964 presidential nomination of Senator Barry Goldwater, the Republican Party began a long transformation into a much more ideological organization dedicated to rolling back the reforms of the New Deal of the 1930s. The party shifted its electoral base to the South, where Democrats once reigned, and adopted a string of social issues, rather than economic issues, aimed at attracting not only wealthy business interests, but also conservative blue-collar workers who felt alienated by the cultural changes of the 1960s.

Issues
Conservative ideology. From 1964 forward, the Republican Party was gradually transformed from an alliance of related interests to an ideologically driven organization dedicated to limiting the size of government and rolling back many of the reforms of the New Deal. In many cases, this took the form of privatization—turning over to private enterprise functions formerly carried out by the federal government.

States' rights. As part of its "southern strategy," the party emphasized the primacy of the states over the federal government. Many critics charged this position was racism in disguise, meant to appeal to southern resistance to civil rights legislation of the 1960s.

Tax cuts. As part of its conservative bent, Republicans consistently advocated reducing federal taxes, even if this meant running up huge government debts when spending outstripped reduced tax revenues.

Terrorism. In September 2001, radical Islamic fundamentalists attacked the World Trade Center in New York City and the Pentagon (U.S. military headquarters) in Washington, D.C. The deadly attacks focused the nation's attention on terrorism and led to U.S. attacks on Afghanistan and Iraq, as well as Republican-sponsored legislation to curtail civil liberties in the United States, on grounds that this was necessary to prevent future terrorist attacks.

Impact
From 1969 to 2005, Republicans controlled the White House for 24 years, and Democrats controlled it for 12 years. In the 18 Congresses since the 1968 elections, Republicans had a majority in the Senate for eight sessions and a majority in the House for five starting in 1995. Republicans successfully ended the Democrats' exclusive claim on power in the South and challenged the assumption, prevalent since the New Deal, that the federal government should provide a solution to many social problems. The Republicans gradually became an ideologically driven party intent on reversing much of the New Deal. The party moved away from the model of a pragmatic alliance of conservatives who were willing to work with conservative Democrats.

The devastating Republican loss in the 1964 presidential election (see Vol. 1, p. 169) temporarily masked a deeper trend toward becoming an ideological party dedicated to rolling back the reforms of the New Deal and restoring a social system in which the federal government played a diminished role in addressing economic and social issues. Although the Republican Party had long been more conservative and business oriented than the Democratic Party, it had nevertheless functioned as an alliance of regional and economic interests capable of working with Democrats to reach a consensus on most issues. Beginning with the 1964 presidential election, the party came under the influence of theorists who concentrated on ideology, even at the expense of traditional political horse-trading within Congress or between Congress and the White House. One result was an increased polarization in national political life.

The Turning Point

Major political institutions do not change overnight. For the Republican Party (also called the Grand Old Party, or GOP), its conversion from an alliance of regional and class interests into a more ideological organization occurred gradually. As early as the Eisenhower administration in the mid-1950s, a group of younger Republicans dissatisfied with the traditional Midwestern conservatism of Ohio Senator Robert Taft (see p. 138) began pressing for a more vigorous challenge to the Democratic Party. The new Republican conservatives did not come from the ranks of elected officials, but rather from a group of conservative intellectuals whose initial home was *The National Review,* a magazine that reflected the views of Taft, long known as "Mr. Republican." Taft was willing to cooperate with Democrats while arguing over the size and scope of federal programs. He did not question the legitimacy of the New Deal programs that provided such benefits as Social Security pensions and unemployment benefits.

After Taft's death in 1953, there was no immediate successor to fill the gap. But a group of younger Republicans emerged, determined to question the underlying assumptions behind the New Deal and, whenever possible, to undo the reforms sponsored by President Franklin Roosevelt (see Vol. 1, p. 141). Unlike the older generation of Republicans, the new conservatives were largely intolerant of the party's relatively liberal eastern wing.

In 1964, this new strain of conservative Republicans nominated Arizona Senator Barry Goldwater (see Vol. 1, p. 171) for president. Goldwater had won a total of about 2.3 million votes

See also: Republican Party, 1900–32, p. 105; Republican Party, 1932–68, p. 135; Democratic Party, 1968–2004, p. 163; American Independent Party, p. 179.

(38.2 percent of the total) in Republican primary elections earlier in the year, compared to 1.3 million votes (22 percent) for his next closest rival, New York Governor Nelson Rockefeller, who represented the party's more liberal eastern wing. At the party's national convention in San Francisco that year, Rockefeller was loudly booed—a symbol of the ideological intolerance of the new conservatives who backed Goldwater.

Goldwater lost the general election against Democrat Lyndon Johnson (see Vol. 1, p. 170) by a wide margin—43 million votes for Johnson versus 27 million for Goldwater. But what some commentators viewed as a huge loss was construed as a good start by the party's conservative wing. Goldwater, who had been a somewhat reluctant presidential candidate, was unwilling to continue as the standard-bearer of the new conservatives. Instead, they discovered a new hero at the convention—actor and corporate spokesman Ronald Reagan (see Vol. 1, p. 186). Reagan had delivered a stirring speech on Goldwater's behalf and seemed willing to carry the banner for the new conservative movement.

1968 Campaign

In 1968, Reagan made a bid for the Republican nomination. He collected over 1.5 million votes in the California primary, held on June 4, where he was the only candidate. Going into the convention, Reagan had collected 1,696,270 primary votes, or 37.9 percent of the total, narrowly edging Richard Nixon (see Vol. 1, p. 174), the former vice president and Republican presidential nominee in 1960, who had 1,679,443 primary votes (37.5 percent). Nixon positioned himself as the centrist candidate between Reagan on the right and Rockefeller on the left. Most party leaders, including many elected officials, wanted more than anything to win the White House and detected a good opportunity in 1968 amid national dissatisfaction with the conduct of the Vietnam war, antiwar demonstrations, and urban unrest. Despite Reagan's popularity, Nixon and his designated running mate, Spiro Agnew of Maryland, were nominated on the first ballot at the Republican convention held in Miami Beach in August 1968.

In his successful campaign, Nixon carefully threaded a path between the Democrat, Hubert Humphrey (see Vol. 1, p. 175), on his left and former Alabama Governor George Wallace, running as the American Independent candidate (see p. 180), on his right. Nixon's "southern strategy" was designed to emphasize states' rights and a "new" Supreme Court (both euphemisms for reducing emphasis on vigorous enforcement of civil rights for African Americans), law and order, and a strong national defense. On the subject of the Vietnam War, Nixon promised that he would be able to end the conflict on honorable terms.

Despite the chaos of the Democratic National Convention in 1968 and widespread dissatisfaction with the Vietnam War, Humphrey almost closed the gap by election day. Final returns gave Nixon 31.8 million votes (43.5 percent) to Humphrey's 31.4 million (42.9 percent) and Wallace's 9.9 million (13.6 percent). Nixon won 301 electoral college votes to Humphrey's 191 and Wallace's 46. Wallace's electoral votes came from the formerly Democratic "solid South," and his popular votes in some northern states helped contribute to Nixon's electoral college total. Although many Wallace voters, especially in the South, were former Democratic voters, the 1968 election also showed the growing strength of conservatism—not just economic conservatism, but also conservative attitudes on social issues, such as civil rights—that was beginning to cut into Democratic strength among working- and middle-class voters.

As the incumbent, Nixon had no trouble gaining the Republican nomination in 1972 against nominal opposition from the conservative John Ashbrook of Ohio and the liberal Paul McCloskey of California. In the popular vote, Nixon won an overwhelming 60.7 percent of the popular vote to Democrat George McGovern's (see Vol. 1, p. 179) 37.5 percent and American Independent John Schmitz's 1.4 percent. Nixon carried every state except Massachusetts and the District of Columbia (see Vol. 1, p. 177).

Less than three years later, however, Nixon was forced to resign from office in the face of likely impeachment over the issue of Watergate, a scandal named after the site of the Democratic Party's national headquarters in Washington, D.C. During the runup to the 1972 election, burglars were caught inside the Democrats' campaign offices; eventually, the investigation into the burglary led to Nixon and the Committee to Reelect the President (CREEP). Weeks of televised hearings into the affair in the summer of 1975 developed evidence that Nixon had been aware of the wrongdoing and had tried to cover it up.

Nixon's resignation from office in August 1975 led to Vice President Gerald Ford becoming president. Ford had been appointed to the office after the resignation of Spiro Agnew on charges of tax fraud. Ford, a former Republican minority leader in the House of Representatives, was representative of traditional midwestern Republican conservatives. Ford ran as the Republican nominee in 1976 (see Vol. 1, p. 182), but lost to Democrat Jimmy Carter (see Vol. 1, p. 183), largely on the strength of Carter's promise to restore morality to government.

The Reagan Era

In 1980, the evolution of the Republican Party became evident with the nomination and election of Ronald Reagan (see Vol. 1, p. 186), governor of California and a leading spokesman for the conservative wing of the party since 1964. Reagan's campaign was based on twin pillars of neoconservative thought: a much smaller role for the federal government in national life and tax reductions designed to stimulate economic growth. Regan's economic program was dubbed "supply-side economics," suggesting that providing stimulus to the "supply" side, i.e., corporations and investors, rather than the "demand side," i.e., consumers, was the most efficient means of stimulating economic growth. In the view of supply-side economists, government spending had effectively robbed the economy of sufficient money for new investment and thereby stunted economic growth. Although Reagan argued that economic stimulation on

This cartoon, which appeared in the *Washington Post* in 1988, shows George H.W. Bush riding the Republican elephant, which strongly resembles Ronald Reagan. Bush won the presidency due in part to the popularity of Reagan.

the supply side would eventually generate higher government revenues, he acknowledged that to avoid runaway budget deficits, reductions would have to be made in expenditures.

Along with other neoconservatives, Reagan particularly targeted federal welfare programs. He denounced "welfare queens," whom he depicted as welfare recipients driving around in Cadillacs while refusing to get jobs to earn a living. It was a line that was widely appreciated by the same audience of white working-class voters targeted by George Wallace's American Independent Party (see p. 179).

Reagan also campaigned as a cold warrior who would restore U.S. military strength as a means of facing down the Soviet Union. Reagan opposed signing a new treaty with the Soviet Union to limit strategic (nuclear) weapons and instead advocated actions to compete more vigorously with the Russians.

Reagan won the nomination by competing successfully in a long string of Republican primaries. Although he lost the vote in the Iowa caucuses to Republican moderate Representative John Anderson (who later dropped out of the Republican race and ran for president as an independent), Reagan won a convincing victory in the first primary election, in New Hampshire, and had enough delegate votes to win the nomination before the Republican convention opened.

After Anderson, Reagan's strongest opponent was George H. W. Bush (see Vol. 1, p. 193), a former director of the Central Intelligence Agency and the chairman of the Republican National Committee. Bush ridiculed Reagan's plans as "voodoo economics," but this did not prevent him from accepting Reagan's invitation to run on the Republican ticket as the vice presidential nominee in 1980.

As with many presidential elections, the outcome in 1980 was a combination of personality and ideology. Reagan won a convincing victory over both Carter and independent John Anderson (see Vol. 1, p. 185), partly by appealing to voters who became known as "Reagan Democrats"—members of the traditional Democratic working-class constituency who liked Reagan's optimistic presentation of what seemed like "common sense" American values. Reagan's personality was such that voters were willing to forgive or ignore errors or even scandals during his administration—such as the discovery that from 1984 to 1986 members of his administration illegally sold arms to Iran and used the proceeds to help finance anticommunist "contras" in Nicaragua, also against U.S. law. In 1984, Reagan was reelected by an even larger margin than in his 1980 victory (see Vol. 1, p. 189).

Contract with America

Reagan's vice president, George H. W. Bush, easily won the Republican nomination in 1988 and faced Democratic Governor Michael Dukakis of Massachusetts (see Vol. 1, p.

194) in the general election. Bush characterized Dukakis as a "Massachusetts liberal" who favored government solutions to social problems, would be soft on crime, and would reverse the past eight years of the Reagan conservative revolution. Although Bush was not originally part of the Reagan Republican conservative revolution, his 1988 campaign promised to continue Reagan's policies—despite the fact that Bush's 1980 characterization of "voodoo economics" appeared to have been borne out by rising government deficits over the period 1981–88. Bush easily defeated Dukakis, winning 53.4 percent of the vote to 45.6 percent for Dukakis and 426 electoral votes to 111 for the Democrat (see Vol. 1, p. 192). As a measure of the influence of the Republican conservative revolution, a group of conservative southern Democrats, working as the Democratic Leadership Council, nominated Arkansas Governor Bill Clinton (see Vol. 1, p. 197) in 1992 on a platform that promised to replace the Roosevelt liberal tradition with a more conservative program of smaller government.

Clinton's defeat of Bush in 1992 (see Vol. 1, p. 196) did not mark an end to the Reagan revolution by any means. Two years later, in 1994, Republicans recaptured control of both houses of Congress for the first time since 1955. The victory in the House was largely engineered by Representative Newt Gingrich of Georgia, who devised the "Contract with America," a 10-point agenda for Republicans in Congress (see p. 173). The laws that the Republicans promised to pass neatly summarized the conservative ideological evolution of the party. They ranged from curbing government spending to reducing welfare, controlling crime, cutting taxes, and rebuilding military strength.

Gingrich was chosen as the first Republican Speaker in 40 years. He introduced a new style of politics, aggressively combating Clinton at every opportunity. In 1995, Gingrich refused to compromise with Clinton in passing a new federal budget and effectively shut down the federal government over the Thanksgiving holiday.

Gingrich's tactics alienated many Americans, who just three years earlier had elected Bill Clinton and would reelect him the following November. The size of the Republican majority in the House declined in both 1996 and again in 1998, and Gingrich himself resigned as Speaker, and from Congress, in November 1998 following the poor Republican showing and allegations of wrongdoing in a deal to write a book and in raising political funds. Gingrich was fined $300,000 for violating House rules that barred using tax-exempt foundations for political purposes.

Although Gingrich was removed from the scene, he was replaced by other conservative Republicans, largely from the South, who were intent on fighting the Clinton administration.

The Election of 2000

In 2000, two-term Texas Governor George W. Bush (see Vol. 1, p. 205), son of George H. W. Bush, won the Republican presidential nomination as a result of a series of primary election victories. The other two leading contenders were Senator

FlashFocus: Karl Christian Rove

Born: December 25, 1950, Denver, Colorado

Karl Rove spent his childhood in Colorado, Utah, and Nevada. His father, a geologist, was not at home very often, and his somewhat unstable mother, who eventually committed suicide, relocated the family several times. Rove attended high school in Salt Lake City. A self-described "nerd," he participated on the debate team and read in his spare time. His family was not religious or political, but in high school Rove discovered conservative politics and began his career volunteering for Utah Senator Wallace Bennett's campaign.

Rove entered the University of Utah in 1969, where he deepened his involvement in politics. In a time of increasing negative sentiments about the Vietnam War and frequent anti-war demonstrations, Rove found himself on the opposite end of the political spectrum from most college students. He never finished his degree, choosing instead to serve as chairman of the College Republicans and travel throughout the country recruiting student supporters. While working with the College Republicans, Rove became friends with George H.W. Bush. When Bush ran for president in 1980, Rove moved to Texas to work on fundraising for the campaign.

After the campaign, Rove decided to open his own political consulting firm. He served several important Republican clients and soon became a leading consultant for the Republican Party. He was especially successful in Texas, where he helped Republicans capture every statewide office, including the governorship, which went to George W. Bush (son of George H.W. Bush) when he defeated Democrat Ann Richards in 1994.

Throughout his career, Rove attracted many critics who question his tactics. Despite this criticism, Rove remained a key consultant for the Republican Party and served as President George W. Bush's top adviser, exerting significant influence over the actions and decisions of the administration.

John McCain of Arizona and magazine publisher Steve Forbes. Bush positioned himself as a moderate, describing himself as "a uniter, not a divider." He was not explicitly ideological and largely campaigned on a platform of restoring honor to the White House following the admission by Clinton of an extramarital affair carried out with a young intern and an abortive effort by House Republicans to impeach the president. Bush promised to institute tax cuts in the face of rising government surpluses (in which tax revenues exceeded spending for the first time in many years) under Clinton.

On September 11, 2001, Islamic fundamentalists attacked the World Trade Center skyscrapers in New York City and the U.S. military headquarters at the Pentagon, just outside Washington, D.C. The deadly attacks transformed the Bush presidency and became the focal point, not only for Bush but

The Contract with America (1994)

The Contract with America is rooted in three core principles:

Accountability: The government is too big and spends too much, and Congress and unelected bureaucrats have become so entrenched to be unresponsive to the public they are supposed to serve. The GOP contract restores accountability to government.
Responsibility: Bigger government and more federal programs usurp personal responsibility from families and individuals. The GOP contract restores a proper balance between govern-ment and personal responsibility.
Opportunity: The American Dream is out of the reach of too many families because of burdensome government regulations and harsh tax laws. The GOP contract restores the American dream.

The Contract

As Republican Members of the House of Representatives and as citizens seeking to join that body we propose not just to change its policies, but even more important, to restore the bonds of trust between the people and their elected representatives. That is why, in this era of official evasion and posturing, we offer instead a detailed agenda for national renewal, a written commitment with no fine print. This year's election offers the chance, after four decades of one-party control, to bring to the House a new majority that will transform the way Congress works. That historic change would be the end of government that is too big, too intrusive, and too easy with the public's money. It can be the beginning of a Congress that respects the values and shares the faith of the American family. Like Lincoln, our first Republican president, we intend to act "with firmness in the right, as God gives us to see the right." To restore accountability to Congress. To end its cycle of scandal and disgrace. To make us all proud again of the way free people govern themselves.

On the first day of the 104th Congress, the new Republican majority will immediately pass the following major reforms, aimed at restoring the faith and trust of the American people in their government:
First, require all laws that apply to the rest of the country also apply equally to the Congress;
Second, select a major, independent auditing firm to conduct a comprehensive audit of Congress for waste, fraud or abuse;
Third, cut the number of House committees, and cut committee staff by one-third;
Fourth, limit the terms of all committee chairs;
Fifth, ban the casting of proxy votes in committee;
Sixth, require committee meetings to be open to the public;
Seventh, require a three-fifths majority vote to pass a tax increase;
Eighth, guarantee an honest accounting of our Federal Budget by implementing zero base-line budgeting.

Thereafter, within the first 100 days of the 104th Congress, we shall bring to the House Floor the following bills, each to be given full and open debate, each to be given a clear and fair vote and each to be immediately available this day for public inspection and scrutiny.

1. The Fiscal Responsibility Act. A balanced budget/tax limitation amendment and a legislative line-item veto to restore fiscal responsibility to an out-of-control Congress, requiring them to live under the same budget constraints as families and businesses.

2. The Taking Back Our Streets Act. An anti-crime package including stronger truth-in-sentencing, "good faith" exclusionary rule exemptions, effective death penalty provisions, and cuts in social spending from this summer's "crime" bill to fund prison construction and additional law enforcement to keep people secure in their neighborhoods and kids safe in their schools.

3. The Personal Responsibility Act. Discourage illegitimacy and teen pregnancy by prohibiting welfare to minor mothers and denying increased AFDC for additional children while on welfare, cut spending for welfare programs, and enact a tough two-years-and-out provision with work requirements to promote individual responsibility.

4. The Family Reinforcement Act. Child support enforcement, tax incentives for adoption, strengthening rights of parents in their children's education, stronger child pornography laws, and an elderly dependent care tax credit to reinforce the central role of families in American society.

5. The American Dream Restoration Act. A $500 per child tax credit, begin repeal of the marriage tax penalty, and creation of American Dream Savings Accounts to provide middle class tax relief.

6. The National Security Restoration Act. No U.S. troops under U.N. command and restoration of the essential parts of our national security funding to strengthen our national defense and maintain our credibility around the world.

7. The Senior Citizens' Fairness Act. Raise the Social Security earnings limit which currently forces seniors out of the work force, repeal the 1993 tax hikes on Social Security benefits and provide tax incentives for private long-term care insurance to let Older Americans keep more of what they have earned over the years.

8. The Job Creation and Wage Enhancement Act. Small business incentives, capital gains cut and indexation, neutral cost recovery, risk assessment/cost-benefit analysis, strengthening the Regulatory Flexibility Act and unfunded mandate reform to create jobs and raise worker wages.

9. The Common Sense Legal Reform Act. "Loser pays" laws, reasonable limits on punitive damages and reform of product liability laws to stem the endless tide of litigation.

10. The Citizen Legislature Act. A first-ever vote on term limits to replace career politicians with citizen legislators.

Further, we will instruct the House Budget Committee to report to the floor and we will work to enact additional budget savings, beyond the budget cuts specifically included in the legislation described above, to ensure that the Federal budget deficit will be less than it would have been without the enactment of these bills.

for the nation as a whole. Declaring himself to be a "war president," Bush attacked the headquarters of Al Qaeda, the Islamic group responsible for the attacks, in Afghanistan. In 2003, he also attacked Iraq, on grounds that the country had weapons of mass destruction (such as chemical, biological, and nuclear weapons) that posed a threat to the United States. After the invasion, no such weapons were found and the war became a point of sharp debate in the runup to the 2004 presidential elections.

Bush made good on his promise of tax cuts, although these too became highly controversial. A nonpartisan Congressional Budget Office study concluded in 2004 that the wealthiest individuals enjoyed the greatest benefit from the tax cuts, which also led to unprecedented federal deficits as Bush continued to finance the war in Iraq and avoided large cuts in other government spending. In addition, Bush pushed through regulatory changes that tended to favor businesses, an action in line with the "supply-side" economics of Ronald Reagan.

Republican Party Platform, 1980

Excerpts from the domestic policy portion of the 1980 Republican Platform follow. The platform emphasized the importance of cutting taxes to stimulate economic activity and expressed confidence that a stronger economy would lead to solutions for many social woes.

> Our foremost goal here at home is simple: economic growth and full employment without inflation. Sweeping change in economic policy in America is needed so that ... hard times and austerity ... can be replaced with ... economic growth and job creation.... Overseas, our goal is equally simple and direct: to preserve a world at peace by keeping America strong....
>
> For too many years, the political debate in America has been conducted in terms set by the Democrats. They believe that every time new problems arise beyond the power of men and women as individuals to solve, it becomes the duty of government to solve them, as if there were never any alternative. Republicans disagree and have always taken the side of the individual, whose freedoms are threatened by the big government that Democratic idea has spawned. Our case for the individual is stronger than ever. A defense of the individual against government was never more needed. And we will continue to mount it....
>
> We will reemphasize those vital communities like the family, the neighborhood, the workplace, and others which are found at the center of society, between government and the individual. We will restore and strengthen their ability to solve problems in the places where people spend their daily lives and can turn to each other for support and help.
>
> We seek energy independence through economic policies that free up our energy production and encourage conservation. We seek improvements in health care, education, housing, and opportunities for youth. We seek new avenues for the needy to break out of the tragic cycle of dependency. All of these goals ... we confidently expect to achieve through a rebirth of liberty and resurgence of private initiatives, for we believe that at the root of most of our troubles today is the misguided and discredited philosophy of an all-powerful government, ceaselessly striving to subsidize, manipulate, and control individuals. But it is the individual, not the government, who reigns at the center of our Republican philosophy....
>
> To those who, with Mr. Carter, say the American people suffer from a national "malaise," we respond: The only malaise in this country is found in the leadership of the Democratic Party, in the White House and in Congress. Its symptoms are an incompetence to lead, a refusal to change, and a reluctance to act. This malaise has become epidemic in Washington. Its cure is government led by Republicans who share the values of the majority of Americans....
>
> [W]e believe it is essential to cut personal tax rates out of fairness to the individual.... The Republican Party believes balancing the budget is essential but opposes the Democrats' attempt to do so through higher taxes. We believe that an essential aspect of balancing the budget is spending restraint by the federal government and higher economic growth, not higher tax burdens on working men and women....
>
> Improving the welfare system....For two generations, especially since the mid-1960s, the Democrats have deliberately perpetuated a status of federally subsidized poverty and manipulated dependency for millions of Americans.... Our nation's welfare problems will not be solved merely by providing increased benefits.... We categorically reject the notion of a guaranteed annual income, no matter how it may be disguised.... We pledge a system that will: provide adequate living standards for the truly needy; end welfare fraud by removing ineligibles from the welfare rolls, tightening food stamp eligibility requirements, and ending aid to illegal aliens and the voluntarily unemployed; strengthen work incentives, particularly directed at the productive involvement of able-bodied persons in useful community work projects; provide educational and vocational incentives to allow recipients to become self-supporting; and better coordinate federal efforts with local and state social welfare agencies and strengthen local and state administrative functions....
>
> Black Americans. Our fundamental answer to the economic problems of black Americans is the same answer we make to all Americans—full employment without inflation through economic growth. First and foremost, we are committed to a policy of economic expansion through tax-rate reductions, spending restraint, regulatory reform, and other incentives....
>
> Women's rights.... We support equal rights and equal opportunities for women, without taking away traditional rights of women such as exemption from the military draft. We support the enforcement of all equal opportunity laws and urge the elimination of discrimination against women. We oppose any move which would give the federal government more power over families.
>
> Ratification of the Equal Rights Amendment is now in the hands of state legislatures.... The states have a constitutional right to accept or reject a constitutional amendment without federal interference or pressure....

Equal rights.... Millions of Americans who trace their heritage to the nations of Eastern, Central, and Southern Europe have for too long seen their values neglected. The time has come to go beyond the ritual election year praise given to Ethnic Americans. We must make them an integral part of government. We must make recognition of their values an integral part of government policy. The Republican Party will take positive steps to see to it that these Americans, along with others too long neglected, have the opportunity to share the power, as well as the burdens of our society. The came holds true of our Asian-American citizens from the cultures of the Orient.

Abortion.... [W]e affirm our support of a constitutional amendment to restore protection of the right to life for unborn children. We also support the Congressional efforts to restrict the use of taxpayers' dollars for abortion....

Education.... [W]e condemn the forced busing of school children to achieve arbitrary racial quotas.... We must halt forced busing and get on with the education of all our children .... [W]e reaffirm our support for a system of educational assistance based on tax credits that will in part compensate parents for their financial sacrifices in paying tuition at the elementary, secondary, and post-secondary level....

Health.... Republicans unequivocally oppose socialized medicine, in whatever guise it is presented by the Democratic Party. We reject the creation of a national health service and all proposals for compulsory national health insurance....

Small business ... is the backbone of the American economy, with unique strengths and problems which must be recognized and addressed.... Republicans realize the immediate necessity of reducing the regulatory burden to give small business a fighting chance against the federal agencies. We believe that wherever feasible, small business should be exempt from regulations and, where exemption is not feasible, small business should be subject to a less onerous tier of regulation.... Republicans believe the number one priority for small business in America is the achievement of lower business and personal tax rates for small businessmen and women and we intend to work to secure them.....

The Nation.... Under the guise of providing for the common good, Democratic Party domination of the body politic over the last 47 years [since 1932] has produced a central government of vastly expanded size, scope, and rigidity. Confidence in government, especially big government, has been the chief casualty of too many promises made and broken, too many commitments unkept. It is time for change— time to de-emphasize big bureaucracies—time to shift the focus of national politics from expanding government's power to that of restoring the strength of smaller communities such as the family, the neighborhood, and the workplace.....

The Republican Party believes that it is important to develop a growing constituency which recognizes its direct relationship to the health and success of free enterprise, and realizes the negative impact of excessive regulation. Education and involvement in the system are the best means to accomplish this. To this end, we will actively pursue new and expanding opportunities for all Americans to become more directly involved in our free enterprise system.... The Republican Party reaffirms its belief in the decentralization of the federal government and in the traditional American principle that the best government is the one closest to the people.... We pledge to continue and redouble our efforts to return power to the state and local governments.... When we mistakenly rely on government to solve all our problems we ignore the abilities of people to solve their own problems. We pledge to renew the dispersion of power from the federal government to the states and localities. But this will not be enough. We pledge to extend the process so that power can be transferred as well to non-governmental institutions.

More Information

- Easton, Nina J. *Gang of Five: Leaders at the Center of the Conservative Crusade.* New York: Simon & Schuster, 2000.
- Gould, Lewis L. *Grand Old Party: A History of the Republicans.* New York: Random House, 2003.
- Green, John C., Mark J. Rozell, and Clyde Wilcox (eds.). *The Christian Right in American Politics: Marching to the Millennium.* Washington: Georgetown University Press, 2003.
- Kayden, Xandra and Eddie Mahe, Jr. *The Party Goes On: The Persistence of the Two-Party System in the United States.* New York: Basic Books, 1985.
- Kristol, Irving. *Neoconservatism: The Autobiography of an Idea.* New York: Free Press, 1995.
- Schoenwald, Jonathan M. *A Time for Choosing: The Rise of Modern American Conservatism.* New York: Oxford University Press, 2001.
- Williams, Dick. *Newt!: Leader of the Second American Revolution.* Marietta, Ga: Longstreet Press, 1995.

On the Web

- Gayner, Jeffrey. "The Contract with America: Implementing New Ideas in the U.S." The Heritage Foundation. *http://www.heritage.org/Research/PoliticalPhilosophy/HL549.cfm.*
- Inaugural Addresses of Ronald Reagan (1981, 1985), George H. W. Bush (1989); and George W. Bush (2001). The American Presidency Project, University of California at Santa Barbara. *http://www.presidency.ucsb.edu/site/docs/inaugurals.php.*
- Public Papers of President George H. W. Bush. The American Presidency Project, University of California at Santa Barbara. *http://www.presidency.ucsb.edu/site/docs/index_pppus.php.*
- Republican Party Platforms, 1968–2000. The American Presidency Project, University of California at Santa Barbara. *http://www.presidency.ucsb.edu/site/docs/platforms.php.*
- The Republican Party—GOP History. Republican National Committee. *http://www.gop.com/About/GOPHistory/Default.aspx.*

National Socialist White People's Party, 1967–

FlashFocus: National Socialist White People's Party

Origins
The National Socialist White People's Party was a direct outgrowth of the American Nazi Party, an extreme right-wing organization espousing the essential principles of World War II German dictator Adolf Hitler. At the core of the party's beliefs is a conviction that "Aryan" people—loosely defined as whites—should form a racially pure society, combat an alleged Jewish conspiracy to impose an international government, and form a communitarian society in which people would be guaranteed an annual wage and given inexpensive loans to buy houses.

Issues
Racial purity. The range of American Nazi parties, like their German predecessors, advocate forming a society comprised solely of racially pure "Aryans," or whites.
Social welfare. The socialist aspects of the National Socialist White People's Party have included calls for a guaranteed annual wage for white people living in the proposed Aryan nation, interest-free mortgages to enable young couples to buy houses, and universal free health care.
Christian nation. Arm in arm with the party's racial purity platform is its call for a Christian nation, comprised of white people. Some neo-Nazis have suggested that Jesus was not a Jew, but rather a blond, blue-eyed Aryan living in biblical times.
Anti-Semitism. Neo-Nazis preach virulent hatred of Jews and blame Jews for most of the world's ills.
Holocaust denial. As part of its anti-Semitic teachings, the National Socialist White People's Party denies that German Nazis slaughtered six million European Jews during the early 1940s, an event known as the Holocaust. Despite plentiful evidence of the Holocaust, neo-Nazis claim that the Holocaust is a Jewish fabrication designed to build sympathy for the Jewish state of Israel.

Impact
The National Socialist White People's Party, and numerous spin-offs using similar names and adopting similar political philosophies, have never had a significant impact on electoral politics. Occasionally, former members of such groups, such as Louisiana politician David Duke, have been elected to state-level offices. More often, such groups have received attention from television coverage during demonstrations calculated to outrage most people by emulating the costumes and antics of 1930s-era German Nazis. While party membership has remained low—fewer than 500 by most estimates—contemporary American Nazis have attracted the support of some individuals, many of whom are thought to be unbalanced or socially and economically disadvantaged.

The National Socialist White People's Party (NSWPP) does not fit the mold of political parties intent on gaining political power through elections. The party has a small handful of members, around 500 by most accounts, and has never elected a candidate to office, although some former members have run successfully as candidates for the Republican Party in state-level elections.

Origins

In 1958, a former World War II Navy aviator, George Lincoln Rockwell, formed the American Nazi Party, a conscious effort to replicate and imitate the National Socialist Party of Germany of the 1930s and 1940s. Rockwell's followers respected his Navy rank and called him commander in imitation of the German term *Führer* (leader) used to describe dictator Adolf Hitler. Rockwell had been a longtime supporter of Wisconsin Senator Joseph McCarthy, who claimed to have detected communists in the federal government, and of U.S. Army General Douglas McArthur, commander of U.S. forces in the Pacific during World War II. After reading Hitler's autobiography, *Mein Kampf,* Rockwell founded an American imitation with himself as *Führer*.

Describing Rockwell's group as a political party is somewhat misleading; the term fringe group would be more accurate. The party only had about two dozen members operating out of headquarters established in Alexandria, Virginia, near Washington, D.C. But by donning Nazi-style uniforms and giving the Nazi salute while shouting, in German, *sieg heil!* (hail victory), the American Nazis were able to attract the attention of television cameras and thereby seem to be larger and more significant than their actual influence merited.

Rockwell, hard pressed for finances, hoped he could build a domestic Nazi movement by generating publicity, largely by public demonstrations against Jews and African Americans. Despite his dislike of black people, Rockwell once created an alliance with black nationalist Elijah Muhammad and the Nation of Islam (see Vol. 4, p. 142). In 1964, Rockwell envisioned running for president, but he could not obtain the 100 signatures needed to enter the New Hampshire presidential primary in 1964. The next year, Rockwell ran for governor of Virginia without attracting significant support. Nevertheless, he began developing plans to run for president in 1972.

In 1967, Rockwell was murdered by an unbalanced former member of his group. A member of the American Nazi Party, Mathias Koehl, took over leadership and renamed the party the National Socialist White People's Party. Still later, in the early 1980s, Koehl adopted yet another name, New Order. All three groups—American Nazi Party, National Socialist White

A poster advertising a campaign event for George Lincoln Rockwell when he was running for governor of Virginia.

People's Party, and New Order—were essentially the same organization operating under a succession of names. To further confuse the issue, other breakaway groups with similar teachings and inclinations have also adopted similar names.

Under Koehl's Leadership

Koehl, as Rockwell's successor, moved the party headquarters to a suburb of Milwaukee, Wisconsin, in the upper Midwest, which he considered a "more Aryan" atmosphere since many residents there are descendants of German immigrants. Koehl also launched efforts to capture local offices for party members, including one who ran for mayor of Milwaukee and others who ran for the Milwaukee Board of Education. None of the Nazis' electoral attempts were successful. Koehl traveled to Germany to contact surviving members of the original German Nazi Party.

Although Koehl's party did not achieve success in elections, it did develop a political platform based on three major pillars: white supremacy, socialism, and Christian identity. The goal of the group was to establish a new "National Socialist Aryan Republic" in North America and to attract a racially pure population from all over the world.

In this new republic, only "Aryans," or whites, would be welcome. Jews and African Americans particularly would be driven out, as would anyone with "mixed" or "impure" racial heritage. The society envisioned by the NSWPP would em-

> ### FlashFocus: George Lincoln Rockwell
>
>
>
> **Born:** March 9, 1918, Bloomington, Illinois
> **Died:** August 25, 1967, Arlington, Virginia
> **Political Career:** National Socialist White People's candidate for president, 1968.
>
> As a young boy, George Lincoln Rockwell toured the country with his parents, who were vaudeville performers. He attended Atlantic City High School in New Jersey and then Central High School in Providence, Rhode Island. He entered Brown University in 1938, where he received the lowest grades of any student in the history of the school. The paranoia Rockwell had felt about Jewish and black students while in high school became more intense in college. He left Brown to serve in World War II as a Navy pilot and upon his return entered the Pratt Institute in New York on the G.I. Bill but never graduated. He founded a small advertising agency in Portland, Maine, before being called back to Navy service, this time in the Korean War. During this time, he discovered anti-Semitic and racist writings and became a disciple of the German Nazi leader Adolf Hitler. In 1958, while still serving in the Navy, Rockwell founded the American Nazi Party in Arlington, Virginia. Due to his political views and activities, the Navy discharged him in 1960.
>
> Through the party, Rockwell developed and delivered his message of anti-Semitism, anticommunism, and racism. The party staged many controversial demonstrations, including a counterdemonstration at the civil rights March on Washington in 1963, but it never developed a substantial following and was criticized, even by other right-wing extremists.
>
> Rockwell ran for governor of Virginia in 1965 and announced his intention to run for president. In an effort to identify with the white backlash to the civil rights movement, Rockwell renamed the party the National Socialist White People's party and changed its slogan to "white power" in response to the "black power" slogan of civil rights groups such as the Black Panthers. Despite these efforts, Rockwell never captured any significant support. He was shot to death in 1967 by an expelled former member of the American Nazi Party.

brace principles of socialism and agrarian populism long associated with left-wing parties, including such policies as a right to decent housing, interest-free loans to help young families buy a house, and free medical care. On social issues, the NSWPP envisioned families comprising a working father and a mother at home caring for the children. Divorce would be made difficult, and abortions would be limited to cases in which the fetus was shown to be deformed or mentally retarded. More important, in the view of the NSWPP, was the notion of "Christian identity." The party's envisioned country would be explicitly and officially Christian.

The NSWPP economic program was based around family farms and an "honest and efficient" economy carried out without speculation or monetary manipulation.

Running Outside the Party

Some former members of the NSWPP were able to achieve a measure of success running for office under different labels. Of these, the best known was David Duke of Louisiana, who left the NSWPP and was elected as a Republican to the Louisiana state legislature in 1989. Duke was the Republican candidate for the U.S. Senate in 1990 (he lost) and for governor of Louisiana in 1991 (he lost to Edwards). In the govenro's race, Duke claimed that he no longer believed in white supremacy, a claim disputed by the newly named New Order Party led by Koehl.

Also in 1990, a former associate of Rockwell, Ralph Forbes, won the Republican primary election for lieutenant governor, gathering 46 percent of the vote, but losing the run-off election to an African American. Forbes ran for president in 1996 as the candidate of the America First Party (namesake of the World War II-era party of the same name; see p. 155).

As with many third parties, the NSWPP has long lacked funding to finance serious election efforts. Most likely contributors are loath to contribute to a party that holds Hitler in high esteem, and the party has not attracted either members or potential candidates who can finance their own election efforts.

Nor has Koehl been able to retain the loyalty of like-minded extremists. Several other organizations, such as the Nationalist Socialist Party of America and the National Alliance, have sprung from members of the original American Nazi Party. None have achieved significant success in terms of recruiting members, although several have managed to attract media attention.

What Is the New Order?

Statement of principles from the New Order, successor to the National Socialist White People's Party:

The New Order is a National Socialist religious community representing a revolutionary, new faith and a great historic movement.

We are comprised of white men and women of all ages and social backgrounds who are committed to building a better world for future generations of their race.

Our program is in our name: We stand for a revolutionary New Order here on Earth.

Today we live under an Old Order which is corrupt, decadent and diseased—a mad, psychotic system of mindless materialism, self-indulgence, drugs, pollution, pornography, race-mixing, filth, chaos and alienation. It is the way of Death, and more people are coming to recognize it as such.

But there is a better way, a way of Life. That way calls for the elimination of the egocentric/materialistic outlook. It calls for a new awareness and understanding. It involves a spiritual awakening, and calls for a rebirth of idealism and natural values.

It begins with the realization that we are part of something much bigger than our individual selves; that man is part of a great natural order; that to be healthy and whole, he must act in accordance with its laws; and that among its ordinances are the laws of Race and racial conservation.

As National Socialists, we see ourselves as part of a world Aryan community and a new folk in formation. No multiracial society can be viable in the long run. That is why we want to build a separate, all-white society, with its own unique culture and way of life.

Toward that end, it is the function of the NEW ORDER to provide a focus for the moral and spiritual mobilization of our race. Our task is to give it a sense of common identity, common purpose and common direction, and to furnish it with a set of common values and ideals essential for survival in an increasingly chaotic and disoriented world.

Ours is more than just another organization. We represent a cause—the most sacred cause of all time.

We are the Movement of Adolf Hitler. We are His heirs. He has given us a commission, which it is our duty to discharge.

For it was Adolf Hitler who came into the world to remind modern man of Nature's eternal laws, and to make them the basis for a miraculous regeneration in human affairs. That is why we proudly recognize Him as the greatest figure of the age, and why we regard His cause as the one great hope of Aryan mankind on this Earth.

More information

▶ Bingham, Richard D. and James L. Gibson. *Civil Liberties and Nazis: The Skokie Free-Speech Controversy.* New York: Praeger, 1985.

▶ Dobratz, Betty A. and Stephanie L. Shanks-Melie. *The White Separatist Movement in the United States: "White Power, White Pride!"* New York: Twayne, 1997.

▶ Gillespie, J. David. *Politics at the Periphery: Third Parties in Two-Party America.* Columbia: University of South Carolina Press, 1993.

▶ Schmaltz, William H. *Hate: George Lincoln Rockwell and the American Nazi Party.* Washington: Brassey's, 1999.

▶ Simonelli, Frederick J. *American Fuehrer: George Lincoln Rockwell and the American Nazi Party.* Urbana: University of Illinois Press, 1999.

▶ Williams, Mary E. (ed.). *The White Separatist Movement.* San Diego, CA: Greenhaven Press, 2002.

On the Web

▶ Hate On Display: A Visual Database of Extremist Symbols, Logos and Tattoos. Anti-Defamation League. *http://www.adl.org/hate_symbols/groups_am_nazi.asp.*

▶ New Order Web site. *http://www.theneworder.org/.*

▶ Rockwell, George Lincoln. "This Time the World." *http://www.skrewdriver.org.uk/tttwcont.html.*

American Independent Party, 1968
American Party, 1972

FlashFocus: American hdependent Party, American Party

Origins
The American Independent Party began as the vehicle for the third-party presidential candidacy of Alabama Governor George C. Wallace, an outspoken defender of racial segregation during the civil rights movement, in 1968. The party attracted whites, concentrated in the South, who were disturbed by the success of the civil rights movement and by demonstrations against the Vietnam War. Southerners who were drawn to Wallace resented the fact that the entire social order of the country seemed to be under assault.

Issues
Law and order. Wallace used the term "law and order" in reference to chaotic civil rights and antiwar demonstrations that had marked the mid-1960s. But the phrase also stood for an unspoken desire to return to the status quo before passage of civil rights legislation gave African Americans a much greater political voice in the South.

Federal judiciary. The American Independent Party objected to the role of federal judges in enforcing civil rights laws and in striking down local practices as being contrary to the Constitution or federal law. The party blamed "legislation from the judicial bench" as a fundamental cause of the social and political difficulties the nation faced in the 1960s and advocated subjecting federal judges to a popular vote.

United Nations. The parties opposed U.S. membership in the United Nations, arguing that it hurt the sovereignty of the United States.

End to trade with communist nations. Conservatives opposed economic partnerships with communist nations, arguing that it was immoral to help support oppressive communist governments.

Welfare. Both parties opposed the expansion of government benefits as an unnecessary and dangerous growth of the federal government's role in individual lives.

Impact
Wallace was on the presidential ballot in all 50 states in 1968 and won close to 10 million votes, nearly sending the election to the House of Representatives. In the next election, Representative John Schmitz won over a million votes. After 1972, the party broke into two factions and began to decline. The party consistently drew fewer votes in each successive presidential election, and by 1992 neither the American Independent Party nor the American Party had a significant impact. Most followers had returned to the two major parties.

The United States was a nation in turmoil in 1968. Protests against the Vietnam War escalated on college campuses and outside federal buildings, African American ghettos in northern cities erupted in riots, civil rights leader Martin Luther King, Jr. (see Vol. 4, p. 97), and Democratic presidential contender Senator Robert F. Kennedy were both assassinated, and President Lyndon Johnson (see Vol. 1, p. 170) announced he would not run for another term as president.

For many conservative Americans, the entire social order seemed to be under attack from within. In the South, African Americans had gained a political role for the first time, challenging the monopoly long held by whites. Throughout the country, college students denounced American involvement in Vietnam and some went so far as to wave enemy flags at demonstrations on the steps of the Pentagon. Despite significant new welfare programs and civil rights legislation, rioting and looting broke out in large cities such as Los Angeles and Detroit. Circumstances invited a massive reaction.

Origins of the American Independent Party

In Alabama, former governor George Wallace had achieved national fame by resisting the integration of the University of Alabama. In a famous scene, Wallace "stood in the schoolhouse door," symbolically blocking the entrance of the university's first African American students, who had obtained a federal court order for their admission. His stand had symbolized two strains in American conservative thought: resistance to civil rights for African Americans (including the end to racial segregation in public transportation, restaurants, and schools) and opposition to the role of the judicial branch in opening the door to civil rights, starting with the 1954 Supreme Court decision *Brown v. Board of Education* (see Vol. 3, p. 141) that ruled racial segregation in schools was unconstitutional.

Wallace launched a third-party candidacy for the presidency in 1967 under the banner of the American Independent Party. Initially, the party and Wallace's candidacy were one and the same. Later, the American Independent Party split, with dissidents forming the American Party in 1972. Despite their differences, however, the two parties continued to represent the same political strains in American life.

Wallace first showed his presidential ambitions in 1964, when he challenged President Lyndon Johnson for the Democratic nomination. Wallace hoped to unite the Democratic Party's solid southern bloc behind him in reaction to civil rights legislation backed by Johnson. Wallace also challenged Johnson's Great Society social welfare programs. His campaign in the Wisconsin, Indiana, and Maryland pri-

FlashFocus: George Corley Wallace

Born: August 25, 1919, Clio, Alabama
Died: September 13, 1998, Montgomery, Alabama
Political Career: Alabama state house of representatives, 1947–53; judge, Alabama Third Judicial Court, 1953–58; governor of Alabama, 1963–67, 1971–79, 1983–87; American Independent candidate for president, 1972.

Wallace first ran for governor of Alabama in 1958, declining the support of the Ku Klux Klan and receiving the endorsement of the National Association for the Advancement of Colored People (NAACP). After he lost in the Democratic primary, Wallace realized he would have to court segregationist voters and organizations to be a successful gubernatorial candidate.

Wallace ran for governor again in 1962 and won. He soon found himself at the center of national attention, as the civil rights movement led by Dr. Martin Luther King confronted police in Birmingham, where police used fire hoses to quell nonviolent demonstrations for equal rights. Wallace, facing federal court orders to desegregate the University of Alabama, made a highly publicized "stand in the schoolhouse door" in a failed effort to defy the federal court order. In doing so, he became a national symbol of resistance to racial integration.

Wallace lobbied the Alabama legislature to overturn a state law that barred a sitting governor from running for a second consecutive term. Failing to overturn the law, Wallace's wife Lurleen ran successfully in his place. In the meantime, Wallace ran for the Democratic presidential nomination in 1968 in an unsuccessful challenge to Lyndon Johnson. Wallace again ran for governor in 1970 and was elected. He returned to presidential politics in 1972. He was shot and severely injured in an assassination attempt that left his legs paralyzed. He was reelected governor in 1974 (the legislature having overturned the ban on running again) and again in 1982 after a brief retirement, remarkably relying on a successful appeal to black voters. Wallace died in 1998.

maries that year gained surprisingly strong support, winning no less than 31 percent of the vote in Indiana and as high as 43 percent in Maryland, but ultimately losing to Johnson (see Vol. 1, p. 169).

Four years later, Wallace left the Democratic Party and announced he would run for president as the candidate of the American Independent Party. The party and the campaign were largely sustained by the magnetism of Wallace's personality rather than by a well-organized political operation. Wallace managed to get onto the ballot in all 50 states, thanks in part to television coverage rather than the dogged collection of petitions from party workers.

In his 1968 campaign, Wallace offered basic solutions to underlying social problems by promoting slogans such as "law and order" and "Get the federal government out of people's lives." Wallace proposed restoring power to state and local governments and providing more support for law enforcement. He also argued that the existing system of appointment of federal judges should be replaced by election of judges.

Wallace's party did not hold a formal convention in 1968, but it did adopt a platform. Wallace chose for his running mate retired Air Force General Curtis LeMay, known for his hawkish stance on the Vietnam War. In November, Wallace and LeMay won 9,906,473 votes (13.5 percent), five states, and 46 electoral votes. If Wallace had won 55,000 more votes in Missouri, he would have eliminated Richard Nixon's majority in the electoral college and forced the election into the House of Representatives (see Vol. 1, p. 173). Wallace's electoral vote count was more than mainstream Republican candidate Barry Goldwater won in the 1964 election.

Wallace decided to run in the 1972 presidential primaries as a Democrat, but he was severely injured and left paralyzed in a shooting by a would-be assassin. With Wallace unable to campaign, the American Independent Party shortened its name to the American Party and united behind U.S. Representative John Schmitz of California, a member of the ultraconservative John Birch Society, and vice presidential candidate Thomas Anderson, publisher of a farm magazine. The American Party won just over a million votes (see Vol. 1, p. 177), largely emphasizing the same themes as in the campaign of 1968.

After the election, Anderson gained control of the party after a factional dispute with William K. Shearer, who decided in turn to expand his base in California under the name American Independent Party. As a result, the once united party had split into two entities by 1976, basically along conservative and less conservative lines.

Anderson was nominated for president by the American Party in 1976 after its failure to lure a better known conservative to head the campaign. Anderson campaigned on the basic principles of the party, which included opposition to giving foreign aid, opposition to U.S. participation in the United Nations, and a call for cutting off economic relations between the United States and Communist nations. The party supported a limited federal government. It gained positions on the ballot of only 18 states in 1976.

Simultaneously, the American Independent Party convened in Chicago and nominated former Georgia governor Lester Maddox, a Democrat who had first won fame as a restaurant owner who refused to serve African Americans. Former Madison, Wisconsin, mayor William Dyke was chosen as Maddox's running mate after a group of nationally prominent conservatives made a failed attempt to gain control of the party. The leadership, which included William Rusher of *The National Review* and former Wallace fundraiser Richard Viguerie, contended that the party needed to transform into a philosophical haven for supporters of free enterprise and moral values. Attempts to attract conservative Republican officeholders did not succeed, and Maddox ended up with only five percent of the national vote in the election (see Vol. 1, p. 181).

Shrinking Parties

As the 1980 presidential campaign began, neither the American Independent Party nor the American Party wielded much influence. Both rolled out similar platforms and managed to get themselves on the ballots in only a few states. The American Independent Party did not run a candidate in 1984. In 1988, James Griffin ran for the presidency under the American Independent label and received only 27,818 votes. By 1992, the American Party candidate for president appeared only on the Utah ballot, winning only 292 votes. The American Independent Party did not appear on any state ballots in the 1990s or in 2000.

American Independent Platform, 1968

The American Independent Party presented a detailed critique of federal policies and issues confronting the nation and offered a long list of specific actions to resolve those problems. But its emphasis was on domestic affairs and on the seeming social chaos that gripped the country in 1968. Excerpts from the platform:

> *A sense of destiny pervades the creation and adoption of this first Platform of the American Independent Party, a Platform personifying the ideals, hopes, aspirations and proposals for action of the Party and its candidates for the Presidency and Vice Presidency of the United States, George C. Wallace and Curtis E. LeMay.*
>
> *As this great nation searched vainly for leadership while beset by riots, minority group rebellions, domestic disorders, student protests, spiraling living costs, soaring interest rates, a frightening increase in the crime rate, war abroad and loss of personal liberty at home; while our national political parties and their leaders paid homage to the legions of dissent and disorder and worshipped at the shrine of political expediency, only this Party, the American Independent Party, and its candidates, George C. Wallace and Curtis E. LeMay, possessed the courage and fortitude to openly propose and advocate to the nation those actions which are necessary to return this country to its accustomed and deserved position of leadership among the community of nations and to offer hope to our people of some relief from the continued turmoil, frustration and confusion brought about through the fearful and inept leadership of our national political parties....*
>
> *Clearly, our citizens are deeply concerned over the domestic plight of this nation. Its cities are in decay and turmoil; its local schools and other institutions stand stripped of their rightful authority; law enforcement agencies and officers are hampered by arbitrary and unreasonable restrictions imposed by a beguiled judiciary; crime runs rampant through the nation; our farmers exist only through unrealistic government subsidies; welfare rolls and costs soar to astronomical heights; our great American institutions of learning are in chaos; living costs rise ever higher as do taxes; interest rates are reaching new heights; disciples of dissent and disorder are rewarded for their disruptive actions at the expense of our law-abiding, God fearing, hard working citizenry.*
>
> *America is alarmed that these conditions have come to exist and that our national leadership takes no corrective action. We feel that the programs and policies of our Party offer this leadership and provide constructive proposals of action for the elimination of the conditions now existing....*
>
> *The Federal Government ... has in the past three decades seized and usurped many powers not delegated to it, such as, among others: the operation and control of the public school system of the several states; the power to prescribe the eligibility and qualifications of those who would vote in our state and local elections; the power to intrude upon and control the farmer in the operation of his farm; the power to tell the property owner to whom he can and cannot sell or rent his property; and, many other rights and privileges of the individual citizen, which are properly subject to state or local control, as distinguished from federal control. The Federal Government has forced the states to reapportion their legislatures, a prerogative of the states alone. The Federal Government has attempted to take over and control the seniority and apprenticeship lists of the labor unions; the Federal Government has adopted so-called "Civil Rights Acts," particularly the one adopted in 1964, which have set race against race and class against class, all of which we condemn. It shall be our purpose to take such steps and pursue such courses as may be necessary and required to restore to the states the powers and authority which rightfully belong to the state and local governments, so that each state shall govern and control its internal affairs without interference or domination of the Federal Government. We feel that the people of a given state are in better position to operate its internal affairs, such as its public schools, than is the Federal Government in Washington; and, we pledge our best efforts to restore to state governments those powers which rightfully belong to the respective states, and which have been illegally and unlawfully seized by the Federal Government, in direct violation of Article X of the Bill of Rights....*
>
> *[W]e have seen the Federal judiciary, primarily the Supreme Court, transgress repeatedly upon the prerogatives of the Congress and exceed its authority by enacting judicial legislation, in the form of decisions based upon political and sociological considerations, which would never have been enacted by the Congress.... It shall be our policy and our purpose, at the earliest possible time, to propose and advocate and urge the adoption of an amendment to the United States Constitution whereby members of the Federal judiciary at District level be required to face the electorate on his record at periodical intervals; and, in the event he receives a negative vote upon such election, his office shall thereupon become vacant, and a successor shall be appointed to succeed him....*
>
> *We object to a federal policy which has poured billions of dollars into our cities over the past decades but which has not been able to prevent their stagnation and decay and has resulted in the flight of millions to the suburbs. We reject the notion that the solution is untold additional billions to be poured into the cities in the same manner.... Specifically, there must be a restoration and maintenance of law and order before any program, no matter how well conceived, will succeed....*

Our foreign policy will be one designed to secure a just and lasting peace.... Foreign aid and assistance, both of an economic and military nature, will be granted on a basis of what is in the best interest of our own nation as well as the receiving nation. We will deny aid and assistance to those nations who oppose us militarily in Vietnam and elsewhere....

It is too late to engage in debate as to why we are so deeply involved and committed in Vietnam.... The prime consideration at this time is the honorable conclusion of hostilities in Vietnam. This must be accomplished at the earliest possible moment.

More Information

- Carter, Dan T. *The Politics of Rage: George Wallace, the Origins of the New Conservatism, and the Transformation of American Politics.* New York: Simon & Schuster, 1995.
- Kurland, Gerald. *George Wallace, Southern Governor and Presidential Candidate.* Charlotteville, NY: SamHar Press, 1972.
- Lesher, Stephan. *George Wallace: American Populist.* Reading, MA: Addison-Wesley, 1993.
- Schlesinger, Arthur M. Jr. *History of U.S. Political Parties.* New York: Chelsea House, 1981.
- Wallace, George C. *Stand Up for America.* Garden City, NY: Doubleday, 1976.

On the Web

- American Independent Party. Reader's Companion to American History. *http://college.hmco.com/history/readerscomp/rcah/html/ah_003500_americaninde.htm.*
- George Wallace, American Independent Party. *http://www.geocities.com/dave_enrich/ctd/3p.wallace.html.*

La Raza Unida Party, 1970–81

FlashFocus: La Raza Unida Party

Origins

La Raza Unida ("United People" in Spanish) Party was organized in Crystal City, Texas, in 1970, as a means of acquiring political power for the majority Mexican American population on a local level. Branches of the party were formed in California, Texas, Colorado, New Mexico, and Arizona—states formed from territory acquired by the United States after the Mexican War of 1846–48. La Raza Unida was part of a larger concept of Aztlan, a term used to refer to the portion of Mexico ceded to the United States after the Mexican War and implying political control by Spanish-speaking inhabitants, including the ethnic heirs of the Aztec population conquered by the Spanish conquistadors. La Raza Unida never had aspirations to become a majority party in the United States.

Issues

Hispanic political power. At the heart of La Raza Unida was political control by majority Hispanics in the southwestern United States. The party focused on towns or small cities where the overwhelming Hispanic majority had little or no representation in local government.

Bilingual Education and Government. La Raza Unida initially targeted school board elections with a program to institute bilingual education, greater emphasis on Hispanic culture, and community control of public schools, as well as bilingual government employees.

Economic control. La Raza Unida campaigned on greater economic control for poor Hispanics, including many migrant workers. The party blamed the dominant Anglo (or English-speaking) political and economic structure for exploiting Hispanics and vowed to "drive out" the "economic exploiters"

Impact

La Raza Unida was the first political party formed around the concept of ethnicity: political power for a particular group based on race, language, or national origin. The party scored initial successes by capturing control of local school boards and mayor's offices in towns with a clear majority of Spanish-speaking inhabitants, almost all of whom traced their ancestry to Mexico. In most cases, La Raza Unida took control from Democrats. In 1978, for the first time in over a century, a Republican was elected governor of Texas. Some historians blamed La Raza Unida for siphoning off votes from the Democratic Party in the election, although there was also a trend toward conservatism in Texas that aided the Republicans. Internal squabbling resulted in the loss of power for La Raza Unida even in its initial redoubts, and the party ceased functioning in 1981, although other groups by the same name continue to exist on a small scale.

In the small town of Crystal City, Texas (population 7,900 in 2000), a slate of candidates from the newly formed La Raza Unida Party defeated Democratic Party candidates for the school board on April 4, 1970. It was the first election contested by a new party formed the previous autumn for purposes of exerting political control on behalf of Mexican Americans (officially, the elections were nonpartisan, but the party affiliations of the candidates were widely known in the small community). About 85 percent of Crystal City's population was *chicano,* or Mexican American, including a large number of migrant workers whose annual income was under $1,700. The Democratic Party had long controlled the city's municipal government, but many Mexican Americans felt taken for granted, if not ignored altogether. La Raza Unida called the Democratic power structure *vendidos,* or sell-outs—Hispanics who represented the interests of the city's minority white population (or *gringos* as they were called by La Raza Unida).

Three days after La Raza Unida's first showing in Crystal City, the party's candidates won mayor's races in Carrizo Springs and Cotulla, Texas, and a city council seat in Crystal City.

Origins of La Raza Unida

La Raza Unida was the first political party formed strictly along ethnic lines, designed to gain political power for the Spanish-speaking population of the American Southwest—roughly the area ceded to the United States by Mexico after the Mexican War of 1846–48. The Spanish term *la raza* refers to "the race" or "the people." But in a political context, *la raza* is used to refer to people whose ancestry is from the broad area of Mexico (sometimes called *Aztlán*), including portions of Mexico ceded to the United States in 1848 (the term *la raza* is also often used by other groups of Hispanics who are unrelated to the La Raza Unida Party of the 1970s).

La Raza Unida Party emerged about five years after the African American civil rights movement had achieved major political success with passage of the Civil Rights Act of 1964 (see Vol. 4, p. 128). Although the party achieved its initial electoral success in Texas, branches also quickly sprang up in California, Arizona, and New Mexico, all areas with significant Spanish-speaking populations that traced their origins to Mexico.

In addition to the model of the African American civil rights movement, La Raza Unida incorporated the idea of Aztlán, a term that describes the unified territory of Mexico and the states formed after the Mexican War of 1846–48, including Texas, New Mexico, Arizona, Colorado, Utah, and California. The Mexican War opened up this territory for settlement by European Americans at the expense of the existing

FlashFocus: José Angel Gutiérrez

Born: October 25, 1944, Crystal City, Texas
Political career: Organized a series of Mexican American political and cultural organizations, including the Mexican American Youth Organization (MAYO), La Raza Unida Party, the Winter Garden Project, the Oregon Council for Hispanic Advancement, and *Grupo de Apoyo para Immigrantes Latin Americanos* (GAILA).

José Angel Gutiérrez was born in the small town of Crystal City, in southwestern Texas, a town populated by poor migrant workers. He first rose to prominence shortly after graduating from Texas A&M University and St. Mary's University in San Antonio, Texas, as the founder of the Mexican American Youth Organization (MAYO) and La Raza Unida Party. Both groups were aimed at giving Mexican Americans (or *chicanos*) political influence.

In 1970, Gutiérrez was elected to the Crystal City school board (along with two other La Raza Unida candidates) at age 26 in the new party's first electoral challenge to the dominant gringos (light skinned European Americans). Gutiérrez was also elected Urban Renewal Commissioner for Crystal City. Four years later, he was elected a county judge in Zavala County and reelected in 1978. It was not until 1988, however, that Gutiérrez earned his law degree from the University of Houston.

Gutiérrez became a leading spokesman and strategist for the burgeoning *chicano* political movement in the 1970s. In an interview in 1999, Gutiérrez described his activities in the 1970s this way: "We built an empowerment movement that took control of our political and social and economic destiny. We built a political party, *El Partido La Raza Unida,* and proceeded to become the governors, established political sovereignty, creating Aztlán" (the term Aztlán is used to describe a virtual country, comprised of Mexican Americans, living inside the borders of the United States, primarily in territories acquired from Mexico after the Mexican War of 1846–48).

La Raza Unida lost power in the late 1970s when many of its elected officials joined the Democratic Party. Gutiérrez himself left Texas for Oregon, then returned to Dallas as an attorney. Nevertheless, in his 1999 interview, he declared: "Our numbers [of *chicanos*] now are such that we are critical mass throughout the nation. Depending on what state you're in, we're on the verge of already being a majority minority. In some places, a majority.... We will exercise our rights, which include political sovereignty. So Aztlán will become a reality."

Mexican population, including descendants of the Aztec empire and the Spanish conquistadors. Following the Mexican War, the Spanish-speaking population of the newly acquired territory was largely shut out of political power and participation by the new English-speaking settlers from the United States.

La Raza Unida did not spring from a single group. Rather, it represented an effort to collect under one roof several local political movements spread across Aztlán in the late 1960s, all of which aimed at achieving greater political influence for Mexican Americans. Most prominent among these groups was the Crusade for Justice (*La Crusada por Justicia*) in Colorado, led by Corky Gonzales and focused on Mexican American nationalism; the Mexican American Youth Organization (MAYO) in Texas, led by José Angel Gutiérrez, a native of Crystal City, Texas, and one of the first La Raza Unida candidates elected to office in April 1970, who focused on political control of local communities with a majority of Mexican Americans; and La Raza Unida, formed in northern California and focused on organizing Mexican-American agricultural and industrial workers. Eventually, the diversity of La Raza Unida's founders would sew discord in the party and result in its decline.

In 1972, La Raza Unida Party held its first national convention. Gutiérrez was elected national chairman, having actually achieved electoral success in Crystal City. However, despite the party's name, the group was far from united on its goals and strategy. Whereas Gutiérrez was bent on winning elections in cities and towns with a *chicano* majority, other party leaders had different goals. César Chávez, leader of the United Farmworkers, a union of migrant workers, concentrated on the economic well-being of his constituents, while other leaders advocated working with youth groups and emphasized the concept of *chicano* nationalism. For much of the rest of the decade, La Raza Unida reorganized itself several times but never achieved a clear consensus, nor did a single national leader emerge who might have been able to hammer out a series of compromises.

The same year, the party ran its first candidate for governor of Texas, nominating Ramsey Muñiz, a lawyer from Waco, Texas. The party also ran candidates for nine other statewide offices, as well as candidates for local positions. The party made a minor impact— Muñiz won 214,000 votes, or six percent—but it was enough to deprive the eventual victor, Democrat Dolph Briscoe, a majority of the popular vote. The Raza Unida support came from mainly rural areas; the party was far less successful among Hispanic voters living in cities. In 1974, Raza Unida ran candidates for statewide offices again, with Muñiz at the head of the ticket. He received fewer votes than in his previous race and posed no threat to Briscoe's reelection. Nor did any other Raza Unida candidate win state office. The party's base of support remained in Crystal City.

Demise of La Raza Unida

Even in southwest Texas, where the party achieved its initial electoral successes, La Raza Unida lost political power in the second half of the 1970s. Texas Democrats had long nominated Mexican American candidates for office; and although these politicians were denounced as *vendidos* or coconuts (brown on the outside, white inside) by La Raza Unida, Democrats were effective at incorporating the appeals of La Raza Unida into their own platforms, including on the local level.

By the end of the 1970s, a decade after its initial successes, many La Raza Unida candidates joined the Democratic Party, effectively signaling the end of La Raza Unida as a political force in their local communities.

In 1978, party gubernatorial candidate Mario Compean won just 15,000 votes, which resulted in a state cutoff of funding for the party's primary. It was the last election contested by La Raza Unida in Texas.

Ideas of turning La Raza Unida into even a regional party to help consolidate *chicano* political strength had also faded, and by 1981 the original La Raza Unida had disappeared as a political force.

El Plan Espiritual de Aztlán, 1969

In March 1969, the National Chicano Youth Liberation Conference in Denver, Colorado, adopted *El Plan Espiritual de Aztlán* [the Spiritual Plan of Aztlán], a statement of its aspirations for a Mexican American nation within the United States (Aztlán). The next year, La Raza Unida was founded in Texas as a *chicano* (Mexican American) party to contest local elections in Crystal City, Texas, and later in statewide races. *El Plan de Aztlán* was the underlying platform of the party. Excerpts:

> *In the spirit of a new people that is conscious not only of its proud historical heritage but also of the brutal 'gringo' invasion of our territories, we, the Chicano inhabitants and civilizers of the northern land of Aztlan from whence came our forefathers, reclaiming the land of their birth and consecrating the determination of our people of the sun, declare that the call of our blood is our power, our responsibility, and our inevitable destiny….*
>
> *Brotherhood unites us, and love for our brothers makes us a people whose time has come and who struggles against the foreigner 'gabacho' [white man] who exploits our riches and destroys our culture. With our heart in our hands and our hands in the soil, we declare the independence of our mestizo nation. We are a bronze people with a bronze culture. Before the world, before all of North America, before all our brothers in the bronze continent, we are a nation, we are a union of free pueblos, we are Aztlan….*
>
> *El Plan Espiritual de Aztlán sets the theme that the Chicanos (La Raza de Bronze) must use their nationalism as the key or common denominator for mass mobilization and organization. Once we are committed to the idea and philosophy of El Plan de Aztlan, we can only conclude that social, economic, cultural, and political independence is the only road to total liberation from oppression, exploitation, and racism. Our struggle then must be for the control of our barrios, campos, pueblos, lands, our economy, our culture, and our political life. El Plan commits all levels of Chicano society— the barrio, the campo, the ranchero, the writer, the teacher, the worker, the professional— to La Causa….*

Organizational Goals

> *1. UNITY in the thinking of our people concerning the barrios, the pueblo, the campo, the land, the poor, the middle class, the professional—all committed to the liberation of La Raza.*
>
> *2. ECONOMY: Economic control of our lives and our communities can only come about by driving the exploiter out of our communities, our pueblos, and our lands and by controlling and developing our own talents, sweat, and resources…. Lands rightfully ours will be fought for and defended. Land and realty ownership will be acquired by the community for the people's welfare. Economic ties of responsibility must be secured by nationalism and the chicano defense units.*
>
> *3. EDUCATION must be relative to our people, i.e., history, culture, bilingual education, contributions, etc. Community control of our schools, our teachers, our administrators, our counselors, and our programs.*
>
> *4. INSTITUTIONS shall serve our people by providing the service necessary for a full life and their welfare on the basis of restitution, not handouts or beggar's crumbs. Restitution for past economic slavery, political exploitation, ethnic and cultural psychological destruction and denial of civil and human rights. Institutions in our community which do not serve the people have no place in the community. The institutions belong to the people.*
>
> *5. SELF-DEFENSE of the community must rely on the combined strength of the people. The front line defense will come from the barrios, the campos, the pueblos, and the ranchitos. Their involvement as protectors of their people will be given respect and dignity. They in turn offer their responsibility and their lives for their people…. Those institutions which are fattened by our brothers to provide employment and political pork barrels for the gringo will do so only as acts of liberation and for La Causa. For the very young there will no longer be acts of juvenile delinquency, but revolutionary acts.*
>
> *6. CULTURAL values of our people strengthen our identity and the moral backbone of the movement. Our culture unites and educates the family of La Raza towards liberation with one heart and one mind. We must insure that our writers, poets, musicians, and artists produce literature and art that is appealing to our people and relates to our revolutionary culture. Our cultural values of life, family, and home will serve as a powerful weapon to defeat the gringo dollar value system and encourage the process of love and brotherhood.*
>
> *7. POLITICAL LIBERATION can only come through independent action on our part, since the two-party system is the same animal with two heads that feed from the same trough. Where we are a majority, we will control; where we are a minority, we will represent a pressure group; nationally, we will represent one party: La Familia de La Raza!*

More Information

▶ Corona, Bert. *Bert Corona Speaks on La Raza Unida Party and the "Illegal Alien" Scare.* New York: Pathfinder Press, 1972.

▶ Gutiérrez, José Angel. *The Making of a Chicano Militant: Lessons from Cristal.* Madison: University of Wisconsin Press, 1998.

▶ Navarro, Armando. *La Raza Unida Party: A Chicano Challenge to the U.S. Two-Party Dictatorship.* Philadelphia: Temple University Press, 2000.

- Ochoa, George. *Atlas of Hispanic-American History.* New York: Facts on File, 2001.
- Piñon, Fernando. *Of Myths and Realities: Dynamics of Ethnic Politics.* New York: Vantage Press, 1978.

On the Web

- In Search of Aztlán. José Angel Gutiérrez Interview, August 8, 1999. *http://www.insearchofaztlan.com/gutierrez.html.*
- Interview with Jose Angel Gutierrez, founder of La Raza Unida. October 18, 2000. *http://aztlan.net/jaginter.htm.*
- Mexican American Voices: La Raza Unida Party. Digital History. *http://www.digitalhistory.uh.edu/mexican_voices/voices_display.cfm?id=114.*
- Raza Unida Party. The Handbook of Texas Online. *http://www.tsha.utexas.edu/handbook/online/articles/view/RR/war1.html.*

Libertarian Party, 1971–

FlashFocus: Libertarian Party

Origins
Organized in 1971, the Libertarian Party reflects a view of strict individual responsibility and minimizing the size and involvement of government at all levels and in all aspects of social life. The party defends an individual's decision whether to use narcotic drugs, such as heroin or cocaine, as well as a company's decision on what to pay its workers, how to make its products, and how to operate its factories. Equally, the party defends customers' decisions on whether to patronize companies that pollute the atmosphere or pay employees very low wages. To virtually every question, the Libertarian answer is the same: reduce the size and role of government. They oppose federal police agencies and advocate United States withdrawal from a broad range of organizations and treaty commitments that bind the country to involvement with international institutions.

Issues
Government regulation. The Libertarian Party advocates the repeal of laws that interfere with corporate or individual business operations, insisting that individuals should be able to freely trade with each other in a free market system.
"Victimless" crimes. Libertarians advocate repeal of crimes that criminalize drug use, pornography, and homosexual activity, on grounds that such acts have no victims.
Welfare. Libertarians regard social programs such as welfare, Social Security, government-sponsored medical care, and poverty relief as unconstitutional.
Gun control. The party opposes federal gun-control laws, relying on individual responsibility for citizens to police themselves in not abusing guns.
Foreign policy. Libertarians advocate bringing home American troops stationed overseas and cutting defense spending, as well as pulling out of international treaty obligations such as the North American Treaty Organization and the United Nations.

Impact
The Libertarian candidates for president in 1996 and 2000 each won fewer than 500,000 votes. The Libertarians have always been a party of ideology, rather than a party of alliances (like the Democrats and Republicans). The Libertarian aversion to government control has been reflected in the Republican Party's platforms as well, creating a dilemma for many voters who share this fundamental idea: whether to vote for the ideologically "pure" Libertarian Party, or whether to vote for the Republicans who seem to share the underlying suspicion of government alongside positions that the Libertarians might find distasteful.

The idea that the federal government threatened individual freedom was not new in 1971 when a group of individuals in Colorado organized the Libertarian Party. The party's organizers were motivated by a combination of President Lyndon Johnson's (see Vol. 1, p. 170) Great Society social welfare program and the simultaneous conduct of the Vietnam War, nominally to prevent communists from seizing control of Vietnam, which caused the federal budget to grow rapidly. The founders of the Libertarian Party were concerned that the size of the federal government was growing out of control and could threaten individual freedoms.

Among the founders of the Libertarians were intellectuals such as Dr. John Hospers, a professor of philosophy at the University of Southern California; Manuel Klausner, the editor of *Reason* magazine; Murray Rothbard, an economics professor from New York; and Jim Dean of California's *Santa Ana Register* newspaper. Their political philosophy was rooted in personal liberty, which they felt was put in jeopardy by expanding social and economic welfare programs. Rather, the founders believed that the founding principles of the United States called for leaving individuals to their own devices without government restrictions, except in cases of criminal conduct that harms other people.

Entering Politics

In 1972, the party nominated Hospers for president and Theodore Nathan of Oregon for vice president. Because the party was so new, the Libertarian ticket appeared on the ballot only in Colorado and Washington State, winning only 3,673 votes. However, Hospers and the party received their first exposure to national attention when one Republican presidential elector from Virginia, Roger MacBride, cast his electoral college vote for Hospers, who had not even appeared on the ballot in Virginia.

MacBride, cocreator of the television series *Little House on the Prairie,* had served in the Vermont legislature in the 1960s and had since devoted his time to writing and public affairs in Virginia. His electoral vote for the Libertarian ticket in 1972 endeared him to the leadership of the fledgling party, and the delegates to the 1975 Libertarian convention nominated MacBride for president.

The party's newfound publicity also motivated its leadership to make a major effort in the 1976 election. It established the Young Libertarian Alliance to try and recruit members on college campuses and founded the Center for Libertarian Studies in New York City, from which the party published journals and papers advocating free market principles.

Politically, the party managed to gain access to the presidential ballot in 32 states in 1976. MacBride won 173,011 votes, only 0.2 percent of the popular vote. However, the party was encouraged by its showing in states such as Alaska, Arizona, California, Hawaii, and Nevada.

FlashFocus: Harry Browne

Born: June 17, 1933, New York, New York
Political Career: Harry Browne was an investment advisor and author before turning to politics under the banner of the Libertarian Party.

Browne grew up in Los Angeles. He dropped out of college after two weeks and educated himself on subjects including economics and finance. While working as an investment advisor, he wrote and published his first book, *How You Can Profit from the Coming Devaluation* in 1970. The book offered investment advice that contradicted the prevailing theories of the time. It was a bestseller and brought Browne national fame, especially in the world of investment. He published a financial newsletter, spoke on numerous radio and television shows, and published several other books, two of which also became bestsellers.

In 1994, Browne began his campaign for the presidency. He was the nominee of the Libertarian Party, and he made campaign appearances throughout the country, as well as on television and radio shows. His campaign emphasized the Libertarian Party principles of small government and abolishment of all laws that interfere with personal freedom, such as taxes, abortion laws, and gun-control laws. Browne earned the support of many college students and several journalists.

After winning 485,759 votes in the 1996 election, he was determined to run again in 2000, with a goal of winning 1 million votes. The Libertarian Party nominated Browne as their candidate again in 2000, but he won less than 387,000 votes in that election. Although his small-government message was compelling to those disenchanted with big government, ultimately the message did not seem to hold enough mainstream appeal.

The Libertarian Party continued to gain strength as its message of personal freedom and smaller government reached a wider audience. In the 1980 presidential election, Libertarian candidate Edward Clark, a California attorney, received over 921,000 votes. Again, the major support for the party came from western states. In 1984, the Libertarian ticket of David Bergland and Jim Lewis appeared on the ballot in 38 states.

In 1988, U.S. Congressman Ron Paul of Texas won the Libertarian nomination for president. Paul had supported Ronald Reagan (see Vol. 1, p. 186), a fellow Republican, in 1980 and 1984. However, Paul indicated that he was dissatisfied with the Republican Party and the increasing federal budget deficit, as well as the inability of the Republicans to eliminate the cabinet departments of energy and education. Paul's candidacy, which advocated the abolition of social security, income tax, and farm support, won 432,179 votes.

The party finished fourth in the 1992 presidential voting results behind Democrat Bill Clinton (see Vol. 1, p. 197), Republican incumbent George H. W. Bush (see Vol. 1, p. 193), and independent Ross Perot (see Vol. 1, p. 198). The Libertarian candidate, Andre Marrou, won 291,627 votes.

By 1995, the party's membership and voter registration had reached an all-time high, and the party was able to move into national offices in Washington, D.C. The next year, the Libertarian Party became the only third party in American history to gain ballot access in all 50 states for two presidential elections in a row. The party's message of limited federal government, the repeal of laws against "victimless" crimes such as drug use, and opposition to gun control appealed to voters tired of what they perceived as an ever-expanding federal government. However, the Libertarian presidential candidate, Harry Browne, managed only a fifth-place finish, behind Ralph Nader of the new Green Party (see p. 190) and Perot.

Twenty-first Century

The party brought together its philosophy and political activism in 1999, when it began an Internet-based campaign against the Federal Deposit Insurance Corporation (FDIC) "know your customer" proposal. The proposal would have kept electronic tabs on all banking transactions to monitor illegal transfers and money laundering. The Libertarians protested that this was an outrageous invasion of privacy and brought enough pressure on the FDIC to effect the withdrawal of the proposal.

By 2000, the party claimed over 224,000 registered members and also scored a victory in the Supreme Court when Libertarian attorneys persuaded the Court to end random drug-searching roadblocks conducted by police along Indiana roads.

The presidential candidate in 2000 was again Harry Browne, though he managed to win just 386,024 votes. Thirty-four Libertarians were elected to office in all that year.

Libertarian Platform, 1976

Excerpts from the 1976 Libertarian Party platform:.

No conflict exists between civil order and individual rights. Both concepts are based on the same fundamental principle: that no individual, group, or government may initiate force against any other individual, group, or government.

Governmental violations of rights undermine the people's sense of justice with regard to crime. Impartial and consistent law enforcement protecting individual rights is the appropriate way to suppress crime....

The individual's privacy, property, and right to speak or not to speak should not be infringed by the government. The government should not use electronic or other means of covert surveillance of an individual's actions on private property without the consent of the owner or occupant. Correspondence, bank and other transactions and records, doctors' and lawyers' communications, employment records, and the like, should not be open to review by government without the consent of the parties involved in those actions. So long as the National Census and all federal, state, and other government agency compilations of data on an individual continue to exist, they should be conducted only with the consent of the persons from whom the data are sought....

We call for the abolition of all federal secret police agencies...we seek the abolition of the Central Intelligence Agency and the Federal Bureau of Investigation, and we call for a return to the American tradition of local law enforcement....

Maintaining our belief in the inviolability of the right to keep and bear arms, we oppose all laws at any level of government requiring registration of, or restricting, the ownership, manufacture, or transfer or sale of firearms ammunition...We favor the repeal of laws banning the concealment of weapons or prohibiting pocket weapons....

We...hold that the owners of property have the full right to control, use, dispose of, or in any manner enjoy their property without interference, until and unless the exercise of their control infringes the valid rights of others....

No individual rights should be denied or abridged by the laws of the United States or any state or locality on account of sex, race, color, creed, age, national origin, or sexual preference... Nonetheless, we oppose any governmental attempts to regulate private discrimination, including discrimination in employment, housing, and privately owned so-called "public" accommodations. The right to trade includes the right not to trade – for any reasons whatsoever....

We call for the repeal of all legal tender laws and reaffirm the right to private ownership of, and contracts for, gold....We favor the use of a free market commodity standard, such as gold coin denominated by units of weight.

We oppose all government activity which consists of the forcible collection of money or goods from individuals in violation of their individual rights...We support the eventual repeal of all taxation...we oppose as involuntary servitude any legal requirements forcing employers or business owners to serve as tax collectors for federal, state, or local tax agencies....

We support the repeal of all compulsory education laws, and an end to government operation, regulation, and subsidy of schools and colleges...We support both a tax-credit system and a steady reduction of tax support for schools...We further support immediate relief from the burden of school taxes for those not responsible for the education of children....

We oppose all government welfare, relief projects, and "aid to the poor" programs. All aid to the poor should come from private sources....

We favor the repeal of the fraudulent, virtually bankrupt, and increasingly oppressive Social Security system. Pending that repeal, participation in Social Security should be made voluntary. Victims of the Social Security tax should have a claim against government property....

We recognize the necessity for maintaining a sufficient military force to defend the United States against aggression. We should reduce the overall cost and size of our total governmental defense establishment....

We call for the withdrawal of all American troops from abroad....

We call for withdrawal from multilateral and bilateral commitments to military intervention (such as to NATO and to South Korea) and for abandonment of interventionist doctrines (such as the Monroe Doctrine).

We support immediate withdrawal of the United States from the United Nations. We also call for the United Nations to withdraw itself from the United States. We oppose any treaty that the United States may enter into or any existing treaty under which individual rights would be violated....

The United States should grant immediate independence to its colonial dependencies, including Samoa, Guam, Micronesia, the Virgin Islands, and Puerto Rico....

Our silence about any other particular government law, regulation, ordinance, directive, edict, control, regulatory agency, activity, or machination should not be construed to imply approval.

More Information

- Bering, P.H. *Libertarianism: The Economy of Freedom.* New York: Berne, 1995.
- Hazlett, Joseph M. *The Libertarian Party and Other Minor Political Parties.* Jefferson, NC: McFarland & Co., 1992.
- Kelley, John L. *Bringing the Market Back In: The Public Revitalization of Market Liberalism.* New York: New York University Press, 1997.
- Machan, Tibor R. and Douglas B. Rasmussen. *Liberty for the 21st Century: Contemporary Libertarian Thought.* Lanham, MD: Rowman and Littlefield, 1995.

On the Web:

- Libertarian Party. *http://www.lp.org/issues/platform/sop.html.*
- Libertarianism. *http://www.libertarian.org/.*

Green Party, 1989–

FlashFocus: Green Party

Origins
The Green Party in the United States was formed as a confederation of state Green parties in 1996 with the primary goal of building and maintaining state organizations.

Issues
Globalization. The Green Party opposes the globalization of domestic corporations, including the ability of companies to export jobs to lower-cost areas outside the United States.
Campaign finance reform. The Green Party campaigns against corporate influence over elections as exercised through campaign contributions.
Environmental protection. Strict environmental protection to maintain clean air and water was the first signature issue of the Green Party.
Tax reform. The Green Party advocated reforming federal tax policy to close tax loopholes and incentives that the party argues favor large corporations at the expense of higher taxes on the middle class.
Education. The Greens support free choice of schools within public education and development of magnet schools. On the state level, the Green Party campaigns for states to fund local schools in a way to redistribute money to schools in poor districts.
Foreign policy. Reducing arms by cutting the defense budget by half over 10 years (with savings redirected to social welfare programs) is a key element of the Green Party's foreign policy platform, as is the complete elimination of nuclear weapons. The party supports a boycott of U.S. funding for repressive regimes.
Health care. The party supports a single-payer national insurance program financed nationally but administered locally and privately. It also supports federal price controls on prescription drugs.

Impact
Consumer advocate Ralph Nader helped the Greens make an impressive debut in presidential politics in 1996. In 2000, Nader won nearly three million votes in the presidential race. The Greens have also had several candidates win local office throughout the nation. Nader's impact on the 2000 campaign was significant and injected the Greens with enthusiasm. The

See also: People's Party (Populists), p. 98; Progressive ("Bull Moose") Party, p. 121; Progressive Party, 1924, p. 132; Progressive Party, 1948, p. 160.

The Green Party, organized in 1996, became the latest in a long string of parties under the label "progressive," including four earlier Progressive parties (in the 1890s, 1912, 1924, and 1948; see pp. 98, 121, 132, and 160). Like those earlier parties, the Greens focused on ways to limit the powers of private corporations. Two particular issues stood out for the Greens: extensive water and air pollution caused by industrial plants and political influence gained through large contributions to candidates of the Democrats and Republicans.

Like earlier efforts to marshal progressives under the banner of an independent party, the Greens split off a small but significant percentage of the popular vote for its presidential candidate in 1996 and 2000, Ralph Nader. While the Green vote did not change the outcome in 1996 (see Vol. 1, p. 200), many Democrats argued that Nader received enough votes in the very close 2000 presidential election (see Vol. 1, p. 204) to swing the electoral college vote to Republican George W. Bush (see Vol. 1, p. 205).

Origins and Philosophy

The national Green Party was organized in 1996 in an attempt to coordinate the efforts and successes of state-level Green parties. The party reflected a decentralized worldwide movement advocating environmental protection, social justice, and the end of military conflicts. Before the collapse of communism in eastern Europe, the Green Party was most successful in Germany but lost ground when it opposed reunification of the two halves of Germany.

The Green Party in the United States was dedicated to similar principles, with a particular emphasis on the corporate influence in politics and the so-called "duopoly" of the two major parties. The party argued that the contemporary Republican and Democratic parties had both been compromised by enormous amounts of campaign money contributed by large corporations. These contributions were vital in an era marked by expensive television advertising, but they also carried an implicit (if not explicit) promise to support corporate interests, or at least moderate policies such as environmental controls, product regulation, and corporate taxation. In the view of the Green Party, such contributions overwhelmed the ability of individuals to influence government policies.

Consequently, the Green Party made campaign finance reform a leading issue. The party had advocated eliminating "soft" money contributions (unlimited contributions to a political party without designating a particular candidate). The Green Party also supported abolishing the electoral college in presidential elections, which has enabled a candidate to take office with fewer popular votes than his opponent (as happened in 2000; see Vol. 1, p. 204). Instead, the party favors a system it calls an "instant runoff," in which voters rank their top three choices for chief executive positions (such as president or governor) so if one candidate fails to win a majority of first-choice ballots, the "instant runoff" can produce a candidate who takes office with a majority.

The Green Party of the United States also committed itself to peaceful resolutions of international conflicts, reflecting a partnership with other Green parties outside the United States. The party vigorously opposed United States military action in Afghanistan and Iraq in 2001 and 2003 respectively.

On the Ballot

Nader first ran for the presidency on the Green ticket in 1996. He finished fourth with 685,040 votes (0.7 percent), well behind another third-party candidate, Ross Perot of the Reform Party (see p. 196). The results in 2000 were quite different. Nader won 2.9 million votes (2.7 percent) in an extremely close contest between Republican George W. Bush and Democrat Al Gore. Nader was not content to present a mere protest candidacy, but instead campaigned aggressively at rallies, union meetings, and on numerous cable television programs. The addition of all-news cable channels made it much easier for smaller parties to gain access to the public than in the past, and Nader's anticorporate campaign resonated with many voters.

Nader's presence in the campaign agitated many Democrats, who became convinced that Nader and the Green Party took votes away from Gore in closely contested states, none more so than in Florida. There, after a controversy over vote totals, Bush won the state's electoral college votes with a popular margin of 525 votes—well below the 97,500 votes that Nader collected. Many Democrats believed that without Nader on the ballot, Gore would have received many of the votes cast for Nader.

The Future

While the 2000 presidential vote was the focus of most journalistic attention, the Green Party achieved notable successes in state and local offices, running 550 candidates throughout the United States in 2002. In 2004, the party did not endorse Nader's independent campaign for president, but continued to mount candidates for local offices.

The Green Party Platform, 2000

In 2000, the Green Party identified 10 key components that defined their purpose and their party.

1. Grassroots democracy. Every human being deserves a say in the decisions that affect their lives and should not be subject to the will of another. Therefore, we will work to increase public participation at every level of government and to ensure that our public representatives are fully accountable to the people who elect them. We will also work to create new types of political organizations which expand the process of participatory democracy by directly including citizens in the decision-making process.

2. Social justice and equal opportunity. All persons should have the rights and opportunity to benefit equally from the resources afforded us by society and the environment. We must consciously confront in ourselves, our organizations, and society at large, barriers such as racism and class oppression, sexism and homophobia, ageism and disability, which act to deny fair treatment and equal justice under the law.

3. Ecological wisdom. Human societies must operate with the understanding that we are part of nature, not separate from nature. We must maintain an ecological balance and live within the ecological and resource limits of our communities and our planet. We support a sustainable society which utilizes resources in such a way that future generations will benefit and not suffer from the practices of our generation. To this end we must practice agriculture which replenishes the soil; move to an energy ef-

FlashFocus: Ralph Nader

Born: February 27, 1934, Winstead, Connecticut
Political career: Green candidate for president, 1996, 2000; independent candidate for president, 2004.

Ralph Nader is the son of immigrant parents from Lebanon. He graduated from Harvard Law School in 1958 and in 1963 joined the staff of Assistant Labor Secretary Daniel Patrick Moynihan. Following his service there, Nader was an adviser to a Senate subcommittee on auto safety.

Nader came to national prominence with the publication of *Unsafe at Any Speed* in 1965. The work was a study revealing how American automobiles—particularly those manufactured by General Motors (GM)—were structurally flawed. GM unsuccessfully attempted to discredit Nader and his findings.

In 1971 Nader founded Public Citizen, an organization dedicated to investigating and prosecuting consumer fraud, and monitoring corporate excess and congressional activity.

Nader resigned as director of Public Citizen in 1980 to study the impact of the growing political influence of multinational corporations. He also began to speak out against what he termed the "two-party duopoly" of American politics. Nader argued that neither the Democratic nor Republican party served the interests of the people, but instead served the interests of large corporations that donated large sums of campaign money to the parties. Nader's outspokenness on the issue led the Green Party to nominate him for the presidency in 1996. The party was unable to gain ballot access in many states, and Nader refused to raise more than $5,000 for the campaign; he won less than one percent of the vote.

The Green Party again nominated Nader in 2000. He drew considerable criticism from Democrats in the wake of the close and controversial election between Vice President Al Gore and Texas Governor George W. Bush. Gore supporters contended Nader, who won three percent of the vote, took away votes from their candidate, but Nader responded by saying the differences between Gore and Bush were too negligible to warrant support for Gore. Despite harsh criticism from Democrats, Nader announced that he would run again in 2004, receiving strong support from Republicans who hoped he would once again take votes away from the Democratic nominee, John Kerry.

ficient economy; and live in ways that respect the integrity of natural systems.

4. *Nonviolence.* It is essential that we develop effective alternatives to society's current patterns of violence. We will work to demilitarize, and eliminate weapons of mass destruction, without being naive about the intentions of other governments. We recognize the need for self-defense and the defense of others who are in helpless situations. We promote non-violent methods to oppose practices and policies with which we disagree, and will guide our actions toward lasting personal, community and global peace.

5. *Decentralization.* Centralization of wealth and power contributes to social and economic injustice, environmental destruction, and militarization. Therefore, we support a restructuring of social, political and economic institutions away from a system which is controlled by and mostly benefits the powerful few, to a democratic, less bureaucratic system. Decision-making should, as much as possible, remain at the individual and local level, while assuring that civil rights are protected for all citizens.

6. *Community-based economics and economic justice.* We recognize it is essential to create a vibrant and sustainable economic system, one that can create jobs and provide a decent standard of living for all people while maintaining a healthy ecological balance. A successful economic system will offer meaningful work with dignity, while paying a "living wage" which reflects the real value of a person's work.

7. *Feminism and gender equity.* We have inherited a social system based on male domination of politics and economics. We call for the replacement of the cultural ethics of domination and control with more cooperative ways of interacting that respect differences of opinion and gender. Human values such as equity between the sexes, interpersonal responsibility, and honesty must be developed with moral conscience. We should remember that the process that determines our decisions and actions is just as important as achieving the outcome we want.

8. *Respect for diversity.* We believe it is important to value cultural, ethnic, racial, sexual, religious and spiritual diversity, and to promote the development of respectful relationships across these lines. We believe that the many diverse elements of society should be reflected in our organizations and decision-making bodies, and we support the leadership of people who have been traditionally closed out of leadership roles. We acknowledge and encourage respect for other life forms than our own and the preservation of biodiversity.

9. *Personal and global responsibility.* We encourage individuals to act to improve their personal well-being and, at the same time, to enhance ecological balance and social harmony. We seek to join with people and organizations around the world to foster peace, economic justice, and the health of the planet.

10. *Future focus and sustainability.* Our actions and policies should be motivated by long-term goals. We seek to protect valuable natural resources, safely disposing of or "unmaking" all waste we create, while developing a sustainable economics that does not depend on continual expansion for survival. We must counterbalance the drive for short-term profits by assuring that economic development, new technologies, and fiscal policies are responsible to future generations who will inherit the results of our actions.

More Information

▶ Graham, Kevin. *Ralph Nader: Battling for Democracy.* Denver, CO: Windom, 2000.

▶ Martin, Justin. *Nader: Crusader, Spoiler, Icon.* Cambridge: Harvard University Press, 2002.

▶ Nader, Ralph. *Crashing the Party: Taking on the Corporate Government in the Age of Surrender.* New York: St. Martin's Press, 2002.

On the Web:

▶ Green Party of the United States. *http://www.gp.org/.*
▶ The Greens/Green Party USA. *http://www.greenparty.org/.*

Natural Law Party, 1992–

FlashFocus: Natural Law Party

Origins
The Natural Law Party was founded in 1992 by a group of lawyers, businessmen, and educators who advocated a 50-point plan incorporating what the founders believed were proven solutions for a variety of problems. The party founders were convinced that these solutions were being ignored by politicians because of the influence of special interests. The party emphasized the role of preventing problems, rather than waiting until problems grew into crises to take action.

Issues
Balanced budget. The party claimed it could reduce spending while retaining traditional social programs. Cost-effective solutions to crime and health care would propel the economy.
Health care. Prevention-oriented educational programs would reduce "self-inflicted" health problems and thereby reduce overall health care costs. The party advocated special individual tax incentives for medical savings accounts for Medicare and Medicaid recipients and vouchers enabling recipients to choose any insurance plan.
Education. The party supported Head Start prekindergarten classes, school vouchers that could be used to pay for private schools, establishment of national education standards, computer-aided instruction, and rigorous teacher training.
Environment. The Natural Law Party endorsed removing federal subsidies for nuclear energy and fossil fuels and taxing fossil fuels.
Campaign finance reform. The party advocated equal access to the ballot for third parties and elimination of excessive political donations to political action committees.

Impact
In 1992, the Natural Law Party qualified for the presidential ballot in 32 states and became the first party after the Democrats and Republicans to qualify for "national party" status by the Federal Election Commission. Party candidates won 1.4 million votes in the 2000 election. In 2003, the party announced the formation of a "complementary" peace government, made up of scientific leaders and educators to bring a scientific basis to governance.

See also: Reform Party, p. 196.

The Natural Law Party might be described as the scientific approach to government. Formed by a group of scientists, educators, and businessmen, the Natural Law Party believes in "prevention-oriented government, conflict-free politics, and proven solutions to America's problems designed to bring the life of the nation into harmony with natural law." In this context, the party is referring to natural laws that govern the universe—laws that scientists are intent on discovering. Rather than using a "crisis management" approach to social issues, the party emphasizes the role of prevention. In effect, the Natural Law Party believes political conflicts over fundamental differences between various economic groups (workers and owners, for example) can be overcome scientifically. Special interest groups in the existing system blind politicians and government officials to "natural" solutions that have already been shown to work.

The Natural Law Party founders also have expressed confidence that the widespread practice of Transcendental Meditation®, a meditation technique developed by Maharishi Mahesh Yogi, can reduce personal stress and thus lead to fewer social problems as well as greater economic productivity.

Prevention vs. Squabbling

The focus of the Natural Law Party is prevention—in government squabbling, health care, and virtually every other issue. The psychological health of individuals, which the party contends is enhanced through Transcendental Meditation, lies at the heart of many of the party's solutions to social problems.

The Natural Law Party is difficult to position on the traditional scale of right-wing, left-wing parties. On crime, for example, the party opposes the conservative emphasis on punishment, but it also opposes drug treatment and education. It supports cutting taxes, partly on grounds that a happier, healthier population will require fewer government services. On the sensitive issue of abortion, the Natural Law Party urges a substantial reduction in the number of abortions through education rather than legislation.

Agricultural issues have played a large role in the party's growth. In particular, the party has campaigned against genetic engineering of foods on grounds that such engineering violates the natural order and could do serious damage to the ecosystem.

Rapid Growth from Small Beginnings

Quickly making an impact after its founding, the Natural Law Party qualified to appear on the ballot in 32 states for the 1992 election and ran 128 candidates in state and local contests. One of the party's founders, physicist John Hagelin of Iowa, was the party's nominee for president in 1992; he won nearly 40,000 votes. In 1996, Hagelin ran again, collecting 83,520 votes. Most of his strength came from his home state of Iowa and from Ohio, Michigan, New York, and California.

Hagelin was again the nominee in 2000. He finished in seventh place. Hagelin had also tried to win the nomination of the Reform Party (see p. 196), but lost to Patrick Buchanan (see p. 197). Afterwards, Hagelin organized a separate Reform Party that aligned itself with the Natural Law Party and in the process created a confusion over the "real" Reform Party.

FlashFocus: John Hagelin

Born: June 9, 1954, Pittsburgh, Pennsylvania
Political career: Natural Law candidate for president, 1992, 1996, 2000.

John Hagelin was born in Pennsylvania but grew up in Connecticut and attended Dartmouth College and Harvard University, where he received a Ph.D. in physics. Considered a highly qualified physicist, Hagelin worked for the prestigious European Center for Particle Physics (CERN) in Switzerland and at Stanford University's Linear Accelerator Center.

In 1984, Hagelin moved to Fairfield, Iowa, and became a professor of physics at Maharishi University of Management, founded by Maharishi Mahesh Yogi, an Indian-born advocate of Transcendental Meditation and once a spiritual advisor to the Beatles. Hagelin's political philosophy combines his scientific training—which he regards as a study of "natural law," or the forces of nature—and the psychological effects of meditation.

In 1992, Hagelin established the Institute of Science, Technology, and Public Policy, and also cofounded the Natural Law Party, a political group dedicated to the proposition that nonpolitical solutions exist for most social problems, and that government should focus on preventing problems before they develop into crises.

Despite his impressive scientific credentials, Hagelin had trouble being taken seriously in three presidential campaigns—in 1992, 1996, and 2000—for the Natural Law Party. A widely quoted remark in a magazine interview, that a thousand "yogic flyers" (a form of meditation) could solve the ethnic conflicts in Bosnia, had the effect of labeling Hagelin as a marginal player in politics.

Hagelin's Natural Law Party managed to get onto the presidential ballot in 38 states in 2000 and fulfilled the requirements of the Federal Election Commission to appear on the ballot in at least ten states for the 2004 presidential race.

The U.S. Peace Government

Perhaps as a simultaneous measure of the Natural Law Party's approach to problems and its detachment from practical reality, the party announced in 2003 that it was organizing a "U.S. Peace Government," a "complementary" government made up of scientific scholars who would advise the federal government on how to achieve world peace and improve the organization of the government in the United States. This initiative had no discernible impact.

In 2004, the Natural Law Party formally endorsed Representative Dennis Kucinich of Ohio, a Democrat, for the presidency. Kucinich advocates a complete withdrawal of U.S. troops from Iraq and has proposed legislation to institute a cabinet-level Department of Peace. The Natural Law Party based its endorsement on Kucinich's peace proposals.

The Natural Law Party in the United States is but one of several such parties registered around the world. The parties share a belief that Transcendental Meditation can lead political leaders to "natural" solutions to social problems, free of political conflict between competing interest groups. Some former members of the Transcendental Meditation movement are outspoken in their criticism of both the effects of such meditation and of the political aims of its leader and founder.

Platform of the Natural Law Party

The Natural Law Party platform is based on a 50-point plan to revitalize America. Excerpts from the plan:

Prevention-oriented government. End crisis management through prevention-oriented programs that will both solve existing problems and prevent future ones from arising.

Conflict-free politics. The Natural Law Party supports "all-party government"—bringing together the best ideas, programs, and leaders from all political parties and the private sector to solve and prevent problems. The Natural Law Party advocates an end to negative campaigning and partisan politics, and supports essential campaign finance reform to eliminate special interest control of government.

Proven solutions. Government should be based on what works—not what is politically expedient or bought and paid for by special interest groups. There are simple, humane, cost-effective, scientifically proven solutions to all of America's problems....

Government in accord with natural law. Solve problems at their basis by bringing individual life, and our national policies, into greater harmony with natural law through proven educational programs; natural, preventive health care; renewable energy; sustainable agriculture; and other forward-looking, prevention-oriented programs....

Fully harness America's most precious resource—the unlimited intelligence and creativity of America's 270 million citizens. In today's information-based economy, intelligence and creativity, innovation and ideas, drive economic growth. The Natural Law Party strongly supports proven educational, job training, and apprenticeship programs that develop intelligence and creativity and prevent school dropouts. Only the full utilization of our human resource through the Natural Law Party's fundamental commitment to education will ensure America's competitiveness and future leadership in the family of nations....

Support health strategies that focus on prevention and strengthen the general health of the nation, thereby shifting our national focus from disease care to health care. Recent research shows that at least 50% of deaths and 70% of disease in America are "self-inflicted"—caused by an epidemic of unhealthy habits. The vast majority of disease is therefore preventable.

Support the introduction of financial incentives that will help prevent abuse of the health care system and ensure high-quality care, including (1) medical savings accounts for Medicare and Medicaid subscribers, which will provide financial rewards for good health; and (2) vouchers enabling Medicare and Medicaid enrollees to choose any insurance plan or health care provider they desire, thereby promoting competitive costs and quality of care among medical providers....

Support systematic, scientifically proven programs to reduce stress in the individual and throughout society—thus eliminating the root cause of crime.

Target individuals who are at highest risk for crime—the current prison inmate population—through proven rehabilitation programs and advanced scientific methods to assess rehabilitation and eligibility for parole....

Create an immediate shift in U.S. foreign policy away from military aid towards a more life-supporting policy based on the exportation of U.S. know-how—American expertise and technical assistance in business administration, entrepreneurship, education, sustainable agriculture, energy conservation, and emerging environmental technologies, supplemented where necessary with economic support....

Ensure that our foreign aid resources are applied effectively — not wasted through inefficiency, mishandling, or inappropriate allocation— by making foreign aid decisions in consultation with the government and citizens of recipient countries.

More Information

- Hagelin, John. *Manual for a Perfect Government.* Fairfield, Iowa: Maharishi University of Management Press,1998.
- Ness, Immanuel and James Ciment. *The Encyclopedia of Third Parties in America.* Armonk, NY: Sharpe Reference, 2000.
- Roth, Robert. *The Natural Law Party: A Reason to Vote.* New York: St. Martin's Press, 1998.

On the Web

- The Natural Law Party. *http://www.natural-law.org/.*
- John Hagelin, Ph.D. *http://www.hagelin.org/.*
- An independent and critical resource on the Natural Law Party. *http://www.trancenet.org/nlp/index.shtml.*

Reform Party, 1992–

FlashFocus: Reform Party

Origins
The Reform Party, though not a full-fledged political organization until 1995, had its roots in the 1992 self-financed presidential campaign of billionaire Ross Perot, who ran his campaign based on his desire to eliminate the federal deficit. Perot ran again in 1996, after which the Reform Party nominated Patrick Buchanan in 2000, who ran on a more conservative platform to the right of both the Republicans and the Democrats.

Issues
Balanced federal budget. The party advocates a constitutional amendment requiring Congress to pass an annual balanced budget each year and supports a line-item veto for the president (allowing the president to reject certain provisions of a bill without vetoing the entire legislation).
Campaign reform. The Reform Party supports limiting candidates for Congress to financial contributions from their own district or state and replacing the electoral college with a direct vote for president. It also advocates a shorter campaign cycle to reduce the need to raise funds for campaigns.
Lobbying restrictions. The Reform Party advocates prohibiting former members of Congress and elected officials from lobbying for foreign interests for five years after leaving office.
American jobs. Perot had been vehemently opposed to the North American Free Trade Agreement, which was seen by him and his supporters as being detrimental to American workers. The Reform Party supports trade agreements that benefit American workers and advocates measures to foster the success of small businesses.

Impact
Perot collected 19,741,657 votes, or 18.9 percent of the total, in 1992, the strongest third-party bid since Theodore Roosevelt's Progressive ("Bull Moose") Party in 1912. Four years later, however, Perot's support sagged to 8.4 percent. Former wrestler Jesse Ventura won the governorship of Minnesota in 1998 on the Reform Party ticket. In the absence of Perot in 2000, the Reform Party went through infighting that made the party's 2000 presidential campaign seem disorganized and ineffective, and conservative Patrick Buchanan made a poor showing in the popular vote.

Ross Perot (see Vol. 1, p. 198) was a slightly eccentric billionaire businessman who became highly critical of President George H. W. Bush (see Vol. 1, p. 193) in the months preceding the 1992 election. In particular, Perot criticized Bush for raising taxes after having promised not to do so. He and his supporters expressed concern about large government deficits that had marked the Reagan and Bush administrations. Perot made a public promise on television to run for the White House if there were signs of popular support for such a move in the form of citizens organizing a campaign to get Perot's name on the ballot in every state.

Origins of the Reform Party

In response to Perot's announcement, a grassroots movement developed that succeeded in getting Perot's name on the ballot in all 50 states as an individual, rather than as a party candidate. Perot dived headfirst into the campaign, using his personal wealth to purchase television time that he used to explain his plan to rein in government spending.

From the 1992 campaign emerged an organization named United We Stand America, comprised of people who had backed Perot. The group hoped Perot would align with it, but instead Perot devoted himself to organizing a campaign in Congress to oppose the North American Free Trade Agreement, a tariff-free zone including Canada, the United States, and Mexico. Many people thought the treaty would lead to lost jobs in the United States, and Perot shrewdly used his followers' outrage to keep himself in the political spotlight. In 1995, he formally created the Reform Party, which in turn nominated him for president in 1996. Rather than spend his own fortune for a second race, Perot accepted federal campaign funds.

Perot's 1992 campaign was predicated largely on his promise to eliminate the federal deficit. In addition, the Reform Party became associated with related issues, all along a similar theme: bringing about a drastic change in the way government functions in Washington.

Perot proved to be an erratic candidate. In July 1992, he withdrew from the race, then resumed campaigning in October. Perot's populist appeal generated 19,741,657 votes (18.9 percent), enough to help give Clinton the edge in the popular vote (43 percent) against Bush (37 percent) and in the electoral college (Clinton 370, Bush 168; see Vol. 1, p. 196).

The 1996 campaign was an exercise in frustration. Perot had been challenged within his new party for the nomination by former Colorado Governor Richard Lamm, who called for deep cuts in the popular Medicare program. After a complex process of electronic voting and mail ballots sent in by registered party members, Perot won the party's nomination.

But in four years, Perot's appeal had faded. Public opinion polls conducted shortly before the 1996 presidential debates resulted in Perot being denied the chance to participate. Instead, he bought time on television to make his case, calling for higher ethical standards in the White House and Congress, along with other issues. In the election, incumbent President Clinton again failed to get a majority of the vote, but Perot fell to 8.4 percent, less than half his previous total (see Vol. 1, p. 200).

After Perot

Despite the fading of Perot, the Reform Party carried on. In 1998 a former professional wrestler, Jesse Ventura, was elected governor of Minnesota on the Reform ticket. In 2000, several well-known politicians and personalities (such as real estate magnate Donald Trump) considered running for the 2000 Reform presidential nomination. A conservative former Republican and political commentator, Patrick Buchanan, eventually won the party's endorsement. Buchanan's nomination resulted in a split in the Reform Party between his supporters and those of Perot, who saw the former Republican as an insurgent determined to give the party a conservative image. Ventura pronounced the Reform Party "dysfunctional" and left it in February 2000. Even Perot distanced himself from the party he had created.

Buchanan eventually gained control and convinced a federal court to award him full use of the $12.6 million in federal campaign funds that the party was qualified to receive as a result of Perot's 1996 showing. To some observers, gaining access to those funds, and the automatic right to appear on many state ballots, seemed to be the principal reason Buchanan had fought for the party's nomination.

For the second straight presidential election, the Reform candidate was shut out of the televised debates, as the bipartisan Commission on Presidential Debates decided that Buchanan's public support, as judged in public opinion polls, fell short of the 15 percent required for inclusion.

The 2000 election turned out to be one of the most controversial in history (see Vol. 1, p. 204). Buchanan and his running mate, California educator Ezola Foster, won only 448,868 votes, or 0.43 percent of the total cast. But the race between Republican George Bush (see Vol. 1, p. 205) and Democrat Al Gore (see Vol. 1, p. 206) was so close that even Buchanan's votes may have swung the final result in four states to Gore, giving him 30 electoral votes that might otherwise have gone to Bush.

Reform Party Platform, 2002

The Reform Party platform is a document that evolved over time, with the original platform of 1996 revised or amended in 2000 and again in 2002. The party's platform was long on generalities and relatively short on specifics in many cases. Following are excerpts from the platform as it was revised in 2002:

Budget: *We shall enact economic and fiscal policies that require fiscal responsibility and accountability from our government. The Federal government shall be managed within its means, and will not continually run budget deficits.*

Pass a Balanced Budget Amendment.

Pay down the Federal Debt until the principal balance is zero and American taxpayers no longer have to pay interest on the debt.

Use any budget surpluses generated to pay down the debt; they should not be used to fund tax reductions nor to fund new programs....

Manage mandatory spending programs and government-sponsored enterprises so that they are self-funding....

A ten-year plan to disband the Department of Housing and Urban Development should be adopted that is linked to a revenue guarantee program for municipalities. The plan should require a binding commitment on the part of cities to restructure local systems of revenue raising to promote employment creation and the construction and rehabilitation of the city's housing and business infrastructure....

The Tennessee Valley Authority should be privatized, after which consideration should be given as to the most efficient way to privatize the regional Power Marketing Administrations.

FlashFocus: Patrick Joseph Buchanan

Born: November 2, 1938, Washington, D.C.
Political Career: Reform candidate for president, 2000.

Pat Buchanan was born in Washington, D.C., the son of an accountant and a nurse. Along with his eight brothers and sisters, he attended Catholic schools. He enrolled at Georgetown University in 1956 and studied English until he was suspended for one year after assaulting two police officers during an argument over a parking ticket. During his year off, he worked for his father's accounting firm and became acquainted with right-wing political writings. He returned to Georgetown, graduated in 1961, and entered the Columbia University School of Journalism, earning his Masters degree in 1962. He then moved to St. Louis, Missouri, to begin a career in journalism.

In 1966, Buchanan met with former Vice President Richard Nixon, who was impressed by Buchanan's conservative views and hired Buchanan as the press spokesman for his 1968 presidential campaign. After Nixon's election, Buchanan became a member of Nixon's staff as a speechwriter and worked many of his own conservative ideas into Nixon's speeches. After Nixon's resignation in 1974 over the Watergate scandal, Buchanan returned to St. Louis to pursue journalism.

Buchanan returned to Washington in 1985 to work as director of communications for President Reagan's administration, where he worked for two years before returning again to journalism in 1987. He gained national prominence through radio and television as an outspoken conservative, and in 1992 he announced his candidacy for the Republican Party's presidential nomination. While he lost the race for the nomination to incumbent President George H. W. Bush, his campaign earned him more national attention. Buchanan sought the Republican nomination again in 1996, but again lost, this time to Kansas Senator Bob Dole. He intended to seek the nomination yet again in 2000; but when polls showed him far behind all the other Republican candidates, Buchanan left the Republican Party and instead sought the nomination of the Reform Party. However, the party split over the issue of Buchanan's candidacy, and Buchanan earned less than one percent of the popular vote in 2000.

The Corporation for Public Broadcasting should be subsidized at a rate equal to 25% of its budget for the previous fiscal year, so that it does not become too reliant on corporate sponsorship and in turn compromise its news coverage.

Entitlements.

We shall return fiscal integrity to trust funds such as Social Security, Medicare, government retirements and all programs dealing with future obligations to individual citizens.

Social Security

Fulfill the promises and obligations of the old system and ensure that current retirees' benefits are not reduced....

Phase out the old pay-as-you-go system and create a new system of private accounts using federally-supervised, individually-controlled investment options.

Maintain a safety net which insures a minimum pension to those who have met the requirements.

Require all new entrants to the labor force to join the new system. Those under the current system may join voluntarily.

Insure the long term solvency of the social security program by forbidding the use of FICA tax revenues for discretionary spending. Social Security Trust Fund surpluses maybe used to establish individually controlled savings accounts....

Medicare/Medicaid

Reduce medical care inflation through pilot-testing of market-based reforms including managed care, medical savings accounts and creation and regulation of private insurance.

End subsidies for the health care of the wealthy....

Tax Reform

We shall create a new tax system.

The new system shall be fair and simple.

The new system shall raise the money needed to pay the nation's constitutionally legitimate bills.

Analyze, model, and publicly debate the best options. All options should be considered, including tariffs, value-added taxes, and taxes on income, sales, assets, gasoline, and financial transactions.

Allow voters to provide input on the new system.

Any future tax increases under the new system must be approved by the people in the next federal election, in order to impose discipline on spending

Any tax law that benefits a discrete minority shall be subject to strict scrutiny and shall become law only if a compelling interest can be demonstrated.

Campaign Finance Reform

We shall reform our electoral, lobbying and campaign practices to ensure that our elected officials owe their allegiance to the people whom they are elected to serve.

Vigorously enforce all present campaign finance laws.

We will work with Congress to change the composition of the Federal Elections Commission to include independent and non-partisan representation.

Campaigns should include free and equal access to the media resources for all qualified candidates.

TV and radio stations will allocate sufficient time for candidate forums which includes all qualified candidates, or presidential candidates that qualify for matching funds.

Political Action Committees (PACS) should be outlawed....

Foreign-Policy

The Reform Party of the United States is committed to a foreign policy based on the principles of consistency, decisiveness, and accountability. We insist on a foreign policy that is proactive rather than reactive, and whose primary purpose is to enhance our country's national security.

Education

We shall promote an independent, non partisan dialogue to carefully examine and take action on the crucial educational issues that have become dangerously politicized and bureaucratized in the hands of government and the two party system.

While federal, state and local governments may each have an appropriate role to play in the education system, for instance to ensure equal access to education for all children, the control over education must be returned to the people.

Convene a panel of experts to produce a 'statement of impact' of various options (for example, vouchers, educational savings accounts and charter schools) on the public school system.

Americans must have accurate information on these options before changes are made to the public school system that educates 90% of our children....

More Information:

- Black, Gordon S. *The Politics of American Discontent: How a New Party Can Make Democracy Work Again.* New York: Wiley, 1994.
- Buchanan, Patrick. *Right from the Beginning.* Boston: Little, Brown, 1988.
- Chiu, Tony. *Ross Perot in His Own Words.* New York: Warner Books, 1992.
- Jelen, Ted G. *Ross for Boss: the Perot Phenomenon and Beyond.* Albany: State University of New York Press, 2001.
- Perot, H. Ross. *United We Stand: How We Can Take Back Our Country.* New York: Hyperion, 1992.

On the Web:

- 2003 Reform Party USA. *http://www.reformparty.org/.*
- American Reform Party. *http://www.americanreform.org/.*
- The Reform Party. *http://www.americanreform.org/.*

Set Index

Volume numbers are in bold. Page numbers in italics refer to pictures or their captions. (SC) at the end of an entry refers to Supreme Court case(s).

527 committees **2**:8
1812, War of **1**:22, 26, 28; **2**:11
1820, Compromise of **1**:62–63; **3**:31; **4**:21
1833, Compromise of **1**:46
1837, Panic of **1**:48; **2**:33
1850, Compromise of **1**:60, 62–63; **2**:43, 44; **4**:22
    Fugitive Slave Act (1850) **1**:62; **2**:52; **4**:22, 38–39
1873, Panic of **2**:88, 92; **4**:187, 188
1893, Panic of **1**:117
1907, Panic of **1**:117

A

AASS (American Anti-Slavery Society) **2**:34; **4**:21, 25–26
Abernathy, Ralph **4**:96, 137
    biography **4**:*138*
abolitionism **1**:56; **4**:21–22
    American Anti-Slavery Society **2**:34; **4**:21, 25–26
    Amistad case and **4**:29–*30*
    freed/escaped slaves as abolitionists
        Frederick Douglass **2**:72; **4**:*33*–34
        Sojourner Truth **4**:*40*–41
    John Brown's raids **1**:66, 68, 71–72; **4**:22, 31–*32*, 38
    The Liberator (Garrison) **4**:21, 23–*24*
    National Negro Convention Movement **4**:28
    political parties and
        Democratic Party (1828–60) **2**:4, 17, 19–20
        Democratic Party (1860–76) **2**:61
        Liberty Party **1**:58; **2**:34–37
        Republican Party (1854–76) **1**:66, 68; **2**:55–56
        Southern Democratic Party **2**:52–54
        Whig Party **2**:28, 29
        see also Free Soil Party
    Scott v. Sanford (*Dred Scott* case; 1857) and **4**:22
    Underground Railroad **4**:38–39
    women abolitionists **4**:22, 25, 27
        Sarah and Angelina Grimké **4**:27, *35*–36
        Sarah Mapps Douglass **4**:*37*
        Sojourner Truth **4**:*40*–41
    see also 1850, Compromise of; slavery; Wilmot Proviso
Abolition Society (Pennsylvania Abolition Society) **4**:4, 21
abortion
    and presidential elections
        of 1976 **1**:183–184
        of 1980 **1**:187
        of 1992 **1**:198
    Prohibition Party and **2**:66

    right to, *Roe v. Wade* (1973) **1**:187; **3**:154, 163–164
Abrams v. United States (1919) **3**:84, 92–93
Act to Repeal the Chinese Exclusion Acts, to Establish Quotas, and for Other Purposes (1943) **4**:205
Adams, Abigail **4**:153
Adams, Charles Francis **2**:43
Adams, John
    biography **1**:*10*
    and the election of 1789 **1**:5
    and the election of 1792 **1**:7, 8
    presidential candidate (1796) **1**:9–*11*
    presidential candidate (1800) **1**:12–15
Adams, John Quincy **1**:29
    and the *Amistad* case **4**:29–30
    biography **1**:*33*
    marriage **1**:39
    presidential candidate (1824) **1**:32–*35*; **2**:15, 17, 21, 27
    presidential candidate (1828) **1**:36–39; **2**:21
Adamson Act (1916) **1**:126, 127
Addams, Jane **1**:123
Address to the Free People of Color of these United States (Allen) **4**:28
affirmative action, violates the rights of whites? (SC) **3**:155, 166–167
Africa
    African American colonization of **4**:11–*12*, 13
    "homeland" for African Americans **4**:140
African Americans
    colonization in Africa **4**:11–*12*, 13
    Jim Crow laws and **4**:74, 75
    NAACP Legal Defense Fund and **4**:74–78
    northern migration **4**:71
        African American Women's Associations and **4**:59
        National Urban League and **4**:70–71
    postponement of civil rights *see Atlanta Compromise*
    Supreme Court cases involving
        exclusion from juries **3**:110, 111
        interracial marriage **3**:152–153
        murder of, and voting rights **3**:56, 62–63
        property "covenants" and **3**:127, 129–130
        voting in primaries **3**:119, 126
    union, Brotherhood of Sleeping Car Porters **4**:72–73
    voting
        Civil Rights Act (1960) **4**:110
        literacy tests **4**:132
        Mississippi Summer Project **4**:125–126
        rights *see* Fifteenth Amendment; Voting Rights Act (1965); Voting Rights Acts (1870–71)
        Selma marches (1965) and **4**:130–131, 132
    see also black nationalism; civil rights; racial discrimination;

segregation; slavery
African American Women's Associations **4**:59
African Methodist Episcopal (AME) Church **4**:6, 7, 9–10
Agnew, Spiro **1**:3, 180, 181; **2**:165
agriculture
    and the election of 1928 **1**:138
    farm foreclosures, Farmer-Labor Party and **2**:125
    and high freight charges (late 1800s) **2**:98; **3**:56
Ain't I a Woman? (speech) **4**:40, 41
Alabama, University of, integration **4**:119–120
Albany Evening Journal **2**:24
Albany Movement (1961) **4**:96, 111
Albermarle v. Moody (1975) **4**:76
alcohol, opposition to **2**:66
    by the Republican Party (1900–32) **2**:107
    Women's Christian Temperance Union **4**:166
    see also Prohibition
Alien and Sedition Acts (1798) **1**:12–13, 16; **2**:10
    legitimacy challenged **2**:11, 14, 15
Allegheny County v. Greater Pittsburgh ACLU (1989) **3**:168, 174–175
Allen, Charles **2**:46
Allen, Richard **4**:6, 7, 9, 28
    biography **4**:*10*
Allegiance, Pledge of *see* flag, saluting the
AME (African Methodist Episcopal) Church **4**:6, 7, 9–10
Amendments, to the Constitution **3**:xiii–xvi
    see also Rights, Bill of; various amendments e.g: Fourteenth Amendment
America First Party **2**:155–156
American Anti-Slavery Society (AASS) **2**:34; **4**:21, 25–26
    Declaration of Sentiments **4**:25–26
American Colonization Society **4**:11–12
American Dream Restoration Act **2**:173
American Federation of Labor (AFL) **4**:73
American Independent Party (1968); American Party (1972) **1**:175; **2**:179–182
    platform (1968) **2**:181–182
American Labor Party **2**:152–154
American Muslim Mission **4**:142
American Nazi Party **2**:176–177
American (Know-Nothing) Party (1849–57) **2**:46–49
    and the election of 1856 **1**:64, 65, 66–67
    platform (1856) **2**:48–49
American Party (1972) **2**:180, 181
American Railway Union (ARU) **1**:105, 107, 110
American Sugar Refining Company **3**:75
"American System" **1**:32, 33, 41, 44, 49; **2**:21

American Woman Suffrage Association (AWSA) **2**:72; **4**:153, 161–162
Amistad case (1841) **3**:31, 42–43; **4**:29–*30*
Anderson, John, presidential candidate (1980) **1**:185–188; **2**:171
Anderson, Thomas **2**:180
Anderson, W.G. **4**:111
Anthony, Susan B. **1**:56, 84–85; **2**:72; **4**:153, 158, 161, 176
    biography **4**:*159*
anticommunism
    American Independent Party and **2**:179
    Liberal Party and **2**:157
    see also Communism; Red Scare
Antifederalists *see* Democratic-Republican Party
Anti-Masonic Party **1**:40–41, 44, 46; **2**:22, 23–26
    platform (1891) **2**:25–26
Anti-Saloon League **2**:66, 67
anti-Semitism
    America First Party and **2**:155
    National Socialist White People's Party and **2**:176
Anti-Slavery Convention of American Women **4**:27
Appeal (David Walker) **4**:16–17
armed forces *see* military, the
arms race
    and the election of 1984 **1**:190
    see also nuclear weapons
Arthur, Chester **1**:93
    biography **1**:*93*
    and the election of 1884 **1**:95
ARU (American Railway Union) **1**:105, 107, 110
Asian Exclusion Zone **4**:183
Asiatic Barred Zone **4**:199
    replacement **4**:205
Asiatic Exclusion League **4**:190, 192
Atlanta Compromise **4**:60–61, 63
AWSA (American Woman Suffrage Association) **2**:72; **4**:153, 161–162
Aztlán **2**:183
    El Plan Espiritual de Aztlán **2**:185

B

Baker, Ella **4**:106, *107*
Baker v. Carr (1962) **3**:135, 144–145
Baldwin, Henry **3**:*19*
Baldwin, Ruth Standish **4**:70
banknotes **2**:30
bank(s)
    First Bank of the United States **1**:7, 9; **2**:9, 13
    and the Panic of 1837 **1**:48
    Second Bank of the United States (Second National Bank) **1**:28, 32, 40, 41, 42, 44, 45–46; **2**:29–30
        establishment constitutional? (SC) **3**:24–25
        reestablishment opposed **1**:52, 54; **2**:17, 21, 27, 30
    see also Federal Reserve System

199

Barbary pirates 1:16, 17
Barbour, Philip 3:33
Barnburners 1:58; 2:42, 43
Barnett, Ross 4:112, 113
Barron v. Baltimore (1833) 3:13, 29–30
Bates, Daisy 4:*103*
Bayard, Thomas 1:91, 94
Beecher, Henry Ward 2:73
Beirut, U.S. Marines bombed near 1:189
Bell, John
 biography 1:*73*
 presidential candidate (1860) 1:68–73; 2:50, 62
Benson, A.L., presidential candidate (1916) 1:125–127
Benson, Elmer 2:127
Berger, Victor Louis, biography 2:*103*
Bevel, James 4:116, 117
Biddle, Nicholas 1:46
Bidwell, John
 biography 2:*67*
 presidential candidate (1892) 1:102–104; 2:66
Bilalian Community 4:142
Bill of Rights *see* Rights, Bill of
Bipartisan Campaign Reform Act (2002) 2:8
Birmingham, Alabama
 bombing of Sixteenth Street Baptist Church 4:90, 124
 civil rights campaign (1963) 4:90, 96, 116–118
Birney, James 2:34
 biography 2:*36*
 presidential candidate (1840) 2:34
 presidential candidate (1844) 1:52–55; 2:34, 35
birth control, Supreme Court case 3:135, 149–150
black codes 4:49
Black, Hugo 3:*106*–107, 119
Black, James 2:66
Blackman, Harry 3:*156*
black nationalism 4:139
 Abernathy, Ralph 4:96, 137, *138*
 Black Panther Party 1:173; 4:107, 136, 146–148
 Carmichael, Stokeley 1:173; 4:90, 107, *133*, 134, 135–136
 Cleaver, Eldridge 4:146, *148*
 Elijah Muhammad 4:142, *143*–144
 Farrakhan, Louis 4:144, *145*, 149, *150*
 Garvey, Marcus 4:139, 140, *141*
 Malcolm X 4:143–*144*, 146
 Million Man March 4:144, *145*, 149–151
 Nation of Islam 4:142–*145*
 Newton, Huey 4:146, *147*
 Universal Negro Improvement Association (UNIA) 4:140–*141*
 see also black power
Black Panther Party 1:173; 4:107, 136, 146–148
black power 1:173; 4:107, 108, 126, 133, 135–*136*, 139
Black Star Line 4:140
Blackwell, Henry 4:153, 161
Blaine, James 1:86
 biography 1:*96*
 and the election of 1880 1:90, 91
 and the election of 1892 1:102

presidential candidate (1884) 1:94–97
scandal surrounding 1:96
Blair, Frank 1:80
Blair, John, Jr. 3:*3*–4
Blatchford, Samuel 3:*60*
"bloody shirt, waving the" 2:57
Bloody Sunday (Selma–Montgomery march) 4:106–107, *129*–131, 132
Bob Jones University v. U.S. (1982) 4:76
Boston, police strike (1919) 1:132, 133
Bradley, Joseph 3:*50*; 4:58
Bradwell v. Illinois (1873) 3:54–55
Brandeis, Louis 3:*88*
 on freedom of speech 3:101
 on wiretapping 3:102–103
Breadbasket, Operation 4:96
Breckinridge, John
 biography 1:*72*
 presidential candidate (1860) 1:68–73; 2:52, 61
Brennan, William, Jr. 3:*137*–138
Brewer, David 3:*67*–68
Breyer, Stephen 3:*172*–173
Bristow, Benjamin 1:86
Britain, trade embargo with (1807) 1:19, 20–21, 22; 2:11
Brotherhood of Sleeping Car Porters 4:72–73
Browder, Earl 2:129, 130
 biography 2:*130*
Browne, Harry, biography 2:*188*
Brown, Henry 3:*68*
Brown, H. Rap 4:107, *136*
 biography 4:135
Brown, John 4:22, *31*
 biography 4:*31*
 and the Kansas-Nebraska Act 4:31–32
 raids 1:66, 68, 71–72; 4:22, 31–32, 38
Brownson, Orestes 2:39–41
Brown v. Board of Education of Topeka (1954) 3:ii, 127, 135, 136, 141–142, 158; 4:75, 89, 91
 NAACP and 4:66
 Southern Manifesto and 4:99
Brown v. Maryland (1827) 3:13, 26–27
Bryan, Charles 2:114
Bryan, William
 biography 1:*107*
 and currency 2:111–112
 "cross of gold" speech 1:107–108, 110; 2:82–84
 and the election of 1904 1:114
 presidential candidate (1896) 1:105–108; 2:78, 81–82, 93, 99
 presidential candidate (1900) 1:109–112; 2:111–112
 presidential candidate (1908) 1:117–120; 2:112
 and the Scopes trial 1:107
Buchanan, James
 biography 1:*65*
 and the election of 1852 1:61
 presidential candidate (1856) 1:64–67
 and slavery 2:19–20
Buchanan, Pat 1:196
 biography 2:197
 presidential candidate (2000) 1:206, 207; 2:196, 197

Buck v. Bell (1927) 3:94, 99–100
Buckley v. Valeo (1976) 2:8; 3:154, 164–165
Bull Moose Party *see* Progressive Party (1912–16)
Burger Court 3:154–167
Burger, Warren 3:154, *155*
Burlingame Treaty (1868) 1:92; 4:187, 188
Burns, Lucy 4:173, 175
Burr, Aaron 1:8, 10
 biography 1:*14*
 gun duel with Hamilton 1:14, 17; 2:10
 presidential candidate (1796) 1:9, 11
 and the presidential election (1800) 1:1, 12, 14–15
Burstyn v. Wilson (1952) 3:127, 133–134
Burton, Harold 3:*122*
Bush, George H.W.
 biography 1:*193*
 and the election of 1980 1:186, 187
 as president 1:196
 presidential candidate (1988) 1:192–195; 2:165, *171*–172
 presidential candidate (1992) 1:196–199
Bush, George W.
 biography 1:*205*
 as president 2:167
 and the September 11 terrorist attacks 2:172–174
 presidential candidate (2000) 1:204–208; 2:166–167, 172
 Florida ballot-counting halted (SC) 3:168, 179–180
businesses
 racial discrimination in (SC) 3:63–64
 regulation
  by the state (SC) 3:56, 61–62
  and the election of 1904 1:113
 see also workers' rights
busing, school
 and the election of 1976 1:183–184
 to end segregation of public schools (SC) 3:158–159
Butler, Andrew 1:66
Butler, Benjamin, presidential candidate (1884) 1:94–97; 2:89
Butler, Pierce 3:*96*
Byrnes, James 3:*120*–121

C

Calhoun, John 2:28
 presidential candidate (1824) 1:32–35
California
 and Chinese immigrants 2:85–86
 state constitution (1879) 2:85–86, 87
 Workingmen's Party of California 2:85–87
Campbell, John 3:*37*–38
capitalism, anticapitalistic Social Democrats 2:102
capital punishment, Supreme Court cases 3:154, 162–163, 165–166
Cardozo, Benjamin 3:*106*
Carmichael, Stokeley 1:173; 4:90, 107, *133*, 134, 135–136
 see also black power

Carnegie, Andrew 1:109
Carter, James "Jimmy"
 biography 1:*183*
 presidential candidate (1976) 1:181–184; 2:165
 presidential candidate (1980) 1:185–188; 2:165
Cass, Lewis
 biography 1:*58*
 and the election of 1844 1:53–54
 and the election of 1848 1:56–59; 2:43
 and the election of 1852 1:61
 presidential candidate (1848) 1:56–59
Catholics *see* Roman Catholics
Catron, John 3:*33*–34
Catt, Carrie Chapman 4:154, 168, 176
 biography 4:*180*
Celler, Emanuel 4:110
Chafin, Eugene
 presidential candidate (1908) 1:117–120
 presidential candidate (1912) 1:121–124
Chambers, Whittaker 2:137
Chaney, James 4:125
Chaplinsky v. New Hampshire (1942) 3:119, 122–123
Chapman, Maria Weston 4:27
Chase Court 3:48–55
Chase, Salmon 1:70, 74; 3:48, *49*
Chase, Samuel 3:*7*–8
Chávez, César 2:184
"checks and balances" 3:41, 52
Cheney, Richard 1:205
Cherokee Nation v. State of Georgia (1831) 3:13, 17, 28–29
Chicago
 civil rights struggle (1966–67) 4:96
 Haymarket Square bombings (1886) 2:95
 race riots (1919) 1:130
Chicago B.& Q. RY. v. Chicago (1897) 3:77–78
Chicago, Milwaukee and St. Paul RY v. Minnesota (1890) 3:73
child labor, Supreme Court case involving 3:84, 90–91
Chinese Exclusion Act (1882) 2:87; 4:183, 187, 188–189, *189*
Chinese immigrants *see* immigration and immigrants, Chinese
Chisholm v. Georgia (1793) 3:1, 3, 4, 5–6
Christensen, P.P., presidential candidate (1920) 1:128–131
church and state, separation of
 American (Know-Nothing) Party and 2:46
 and prayers at graduation ceremonies (SC) 3:177
 and public funds for religious schools (SC) 3:161
 and religious displays (SC) 3:168, 174–175
Citizen Legislature Act 2:173
Citizens Committee to Repeal Chinese Exclusion and Place Immigration on a Quota Basis 4:205
citizenship
 American-born children of noncitizen immigrants (SC) 3:78

immigrant, American (Know-Nothing) Party and **2**:46
of a native of India (SC) **4**:184, 197–198
Naturalization Act (1790) and **2**:10; **4**:183, 185
of people born in Japan (SC) **4**:195–196
see also Fourteenth Amendment
civil disobedience, Martin Luther King and **4**:97
civil liberties, and the election of 1864 **1**:74, 76–77
Civil Liberties Act (1988) **4**:204
civil rights
  Albany Movement (1961) **4**:96, 111
  assassination of Medgar Evers and **4**:90, *121*
  black power **1**:173; **4**:107, 108, 126, 133, 135–*136*, 139
  Bloody Sunday (Selma–Montgomery march) **4**:106–107, *129*–131, 132
  bombing of Sixteenth Street Baptist Church **4**:90, 124
  Civil Rights Act (1866) **1**:78; **4**:49–50
  Civil Rights Act (1875) **3**:63; **4**:58
  Civil Rights Act (1957) **2**:144; **4**:104
  Civil Rights Act (1960) **4**:110
  Civil Rights Act (1964) **1**:169; **4**:67, 128
    and discrimination in hotels (SC) **3**:148–149
  civil rights movement (1954–70) **4**:89–90
  Congress of Racial Equality (CORE) **4**:80–81, 82
  freedom rides and riders **4**:80, 81, *82*, 109, 111
  Japanese American Citizens League and **4**:201–202
  March Against Fear (1966) **4**:90, *133–134*
  March on Washington (1963) **4**:96, 97, 122–*123*
  Mississippi Freedom Democratic Party **4**:106, 127
  Mississippi Summer Project (1964) **4**:125–126
  NAACP and **4**:60, 63, 64, 66–69
  Niagara Movement and **4**:63–65
  opposition to
    Ku Klux Klan **4**:54
    States' Rights Democrats (Dixiecrats) **2**:144; **4**:87
  political parties and
    American Labor Party **2**:152
    Communist Party **2**:128
    Democratic Party (1932–68) **2**:144
    Democratic platform (1948) **4**:85–86
    Liberal Party and **2**:157
    People's Party (Populists) **2**:98
    Progressive Party (1948–52) and **2**:160
    Socialist Party **2**:116
  Poor People's Campaign (1968) **4**:96, 137–*138*
  and presidential elections
    of 1948 **1**:156
    of 1952 **1**:160–161
    of 1956 **1**:162, 164
    of 1960 **1**:167

of 1964 **1**:169, 171
of 1968 **1**:175–176
Project C, Birmingham, Alabama **4**:116–118
Southern Christian Leadership Conference (SCLC) **4**:89, 95, 96–98
Southern Manifesto (1956) **4**:99–100
Student Nonviolent Coordinating Committee (SNCC 1960–68) **4**:106–108
Voting Rights Act (1965) **2**:139, 145; **3**:178; **4**:67, 132
see also Brown v. Board of Education; integration; King, Martin Luther; racial discrimination; segregation; women's rights
Civil Rights Act (1866) **1**:78; **4**:49–50
Civil Rights Act (1875) **3**:63; **4**:58
Civil Rights Act (1957) **2**:144; **4**:104
Civil Rights Act (1960) **4**:110
Civil Rights Act (1964) **1**:169; **4**:67, 128
  and discrimination in hotels (SC) **3**:148–149
Civil Rights Cases (1883) **3**:56, 63–64; **4**:48
civil service reform
  and the election of 1880 **1**:90
  and the election of 1884 **2**:81
  and the election of 1888 **1**:100
  Liberal Republican Party and **2**:69
Civil Service Reform Act (1883) **2**:6
Civil War **1**:70; **4**:22
  Democrats and **2**:61, 62
  postwar **2**:62–64
  and the election of 1864 **1**:74, 76, 77
  paper money (greenbacks) issued during **2**:77, 88, 92
  pensions for veterans **1**:100
  Reconstruction after *see* Reconstruction
  Republicans and **2**:55, 56
  Supreme Court and *see Ex Parte Milligan; Prize Cases*
Clancy, Robert H. **4**:200
Clark, Edward **2**:188
Clarke, John **3**:88–89
Clark, Tom **3**:*128*–129
class warfare, Democratic Party (1932–68) and **2**:141
Clay, Henry **1**:30, 36
  biography **1**:*41*
  presidential candidate (1824) **1**:32–*35*; **2**:15, 17, 21, 27
  presidential candidate (1832) **1**:40–43; **2**:21, 22
  presidential candidate (1844) **1**:52–55; **2**:29
Clayton Antitrust Act (1914) **1**:122
Cleaver, Eldridge **4**:146, *148*
Cleveland, Grover
  biography **1**:*95*
  as president **1**:98; **2**:81
  presidential candidate (1884) **1**:94–97; **2**:76–77, 81
  presidential candidate (1888) **1**:98–101; **2**:81
  presidential candidate (1892) **1**:102–104
  scandal surrounding **1**:96–97
Clifford, Nathan **3**:*38*, 39

Clinton, DeWitt
  biography **1**:*23*
  presidential candidate (1812) **1**:22–25
Clinton, George **1**:8, 17, 19, *21*, 23
Clinton, Hillary Rodham **2**:158
Clinton v. Jones (1997) **3**:178–179
Clinton, William "Bill"
  biography **1**:*197*
  as president **1**:200
    could be sued for private conduct? (SC) **3**:178–179
    impeachment **1**:197, 202, 204
    sexual misconduct **2**:166
  presidential candidate (1992) **1**:196–*199*; **2**:166
  presidential candidate (1996) **1**:200–203
Cohens v. Virginia (1821) **3**:25
Cohen v. California (1971) **3**:154, 159–160
coinage, silver versus gold **1**:105, 106–108, 109, 110–111, 115
Coinage Act (1873) **2**:92
Coker v. Georgia (1977) **4**:77
Cold War
  and the election of 1948 **1**:154–155, 156, 160
  and the election of 1960 **1**:165, 167
  Republican Party (1932–68) and **2**:136–137
Colfax Massacre **3**:62
colonies, acquisition *see* territorial expansion
Colorado, and women's suffrage **4**:168
Colored Women's League **4**:59
commerce
  interstate
    Congress and (SC) **3**:13, 25–26
    and imported-goods licenses (SC) **3**:26–27
Common Sense Legal Reform Act **2**:173
communism
  and the election of 1944 **1**:151
  and the election of 1948 **1**:154, 156
  and the election of 1952 **1**:158, 160
  see also anticommunism; Communist Party
Communist Party **2**:128–131, 137
  platform (1924) **2**:130–131
  see also communism
Compean, Mario **2**:185
Compensation Act (1816) **1**:26, 27
Compromise of 1820 **1**:62–63; **3**:31; **4**:21
Compromise of 1833 **1**:46
Compromise of 1850 **1**:60, 62–63; **2**:43, 44; **4**:22
  Fugitive Slave Act (1850) **1**:62; **2**:52; **4**:22, 38–39
Confederate States of America **1**:74; **2**:53
  slaves declared free in *see* Emancipation Proclamation
  Supreme Court and **3**:53
  see also Reconstruction
Conference for Progressive Political Action (CPPA) **2**:132
Confessions of Nat Turner, The **4**:19–20
Congress
  power over the executive branch (SC) **3**:41–42

and the president ordering acts of war (SC) **3**:31, 46–47
Congress of Industrial Organizations (CIO) **2**:142; **4**:73
Congressional Union for Woman Suffrage *see* National Woman's Party
Congress of Racial Equality (CORE) **4**:80–81, 82
Conkling, Roscoe **1**:86, 90
Connor, Eugene "Bull" **4**:96, 116, 117
conspiracy theories, America First Party and **2**:155–156
Constitution **3**:ix–xiii
  Amendments **3**:xiii–xvi
  see also Rights, Bill of; various amendments e.g: Fourteenth Amendment
  Constitutional Union Party and **2**:50
  Democratic-Republicans and **2**:13–14
  and the president **1**:1–3
  three-fifths clause **2**:34; **4**:3
Constitutional Convention **1**:5
  slavery issue **4**:21
Constitutional Union Party **1**:69; **2**:50–51
Contract with America (1994) **2**:173
Coolidge, Calvin
  biography **1**:*133*
  not to run for a second term **1**:136
  as president **1**:132; **2**:105
  presidential candidate (1924) **1**:132–135; **2**:133
"coolie" trade **4**:187, 188
Cooper, Peter **2**:88–89
Copperheads (Peace Democrats) **1**:76; **2**:56, 62
corporations
  and the election of 1912 **1**:121, 123
  see also trusts
Corrupt Practices Act (1925) **2**:7
cotton gins **4**:3, 170
Cotton Whigs **2**:28
Coughlin, Charles **1**:144–145; **2**:149, 150
"court-packing" plan **3**:104
Coxey, Jacob **1**:105
Cox, James
  biography **1**:*130*
  presidential candidate (1920) **1**:128–131; **2**:114
crash, the *see* stock market crash (1929)
Crawford, William **1**:26, 27
  presidential candidate (1824) **1**:32–*35*; **2**:21
Crédit Mobilier **1**:85, 92
crime, victimless, Libertarian Party and **2**:187
criminal suspects
  advised of their rights (SC) **3**:135, 150–151
  charges filed against, before seeing a lawyer (SC) **3**:147–148
  and evidence seized without a warrant (SC) **3**:143
  juvenile, rights (SC) **3**:151–152
  right to have a lawyer (SC) **3**:135, 145–146
  stomach pumping (SC) **3**:132–133
  see also murder trials
Crisis, The (magazine) **4**:66
Croly, Jane **4**:172

"cross of gold" speech **1**:107–108, 110; **2**:82–84
Crusade for Justice **2**:184
Cruzan v. Director, Missouri Department of Health (1990) **3**:175–176
Cuba, and the election of 1900 **1**:109
Cuffe, Paul **4**:11, 13
Cumming v. Richmond County Board of Ed. (1899) **3**:78–79
Curley, James, biography **2**:*112*
currency
 paper
  banknotes **2**:30
  greenbacks **2**:77, 88, 92
 political parties and
  Democratic Party (1900–32) **2**:111
  see also Greenback Party; National Silver Party; Silver Republicans
 silver **1**:106–107; **2**:77–78, 80, 81–82, 92, 98, 111–112
 see also gold standard
Curtis, Benjamin **3**:*37*
Curtis, George **1**:70
Cushing, William **3**:*2–3*

D

Daley, Richard J., biography **2**:*146*
Dallas, George **1**:54
Daniel, Peter **3**:*34–35*
Dartmouth College v. Woodward (1819) **3**:13, 23–24
Daugherty, Harry **1**:132
Davis, Benjamin **2**:*129*
Davis, David **3**:*39–40*
Davis, John
 biography **1**:*134*
 presidential candidate (1924) **1**:132–135; **2**:114, 133
Dawes, Charles **1**:133
Day, William **3**:*71–72*
Dean, Jim **2**:187
death penalty *see* capital punishment
Debs, Eugene V. **2**:116
 biography **1**:*110*
 presidential candidate
  in 1900 **1**:109–112; **2**:102
  in 1904 **1**:113–116; **2**:*118*
  in 1908 **1**:117–120
  in 1912 **1**:121–124; **2**:117
  in 1920 **1**:128–131; **2**:102, 117
 see also In re Debs
debts, Union Party (1936–39) and **2**:149
Declaration of Rights for Women **4**:158–160
Declaration of Sentiments and Resolutions **4**:155–157
defense, Union Party (1936–39) and **2**:149
De Jonge, Dirk **3**:113
De Jonge v. Oregon (1937) **3**:113–114
DeLeon, Daniel **2**:95, 96
Democratic-Farmer-Labor (DFL) Party **2**:127
Democratic Leadership Council (DLC) **2**:165–166
Democratic Party (1828–60) **1**:44; **2**:17–20
 funded, by Customs employees **2**:6
 National Convention (1860), and the breakaway Southern Democrats **2**:20, 52
 presidents *see* Buchanan, James; Jackson, Andrew; Pierce, Franklin; Polk, James; Van Buren, Martin
 and slavery **2**:4, 17, 19–20
Democratic Party (1860–76) **2**:61–65
 Copperheads (Peace Democrats) **1**:76; **2**:56, 62
 during the Civil War **2**:62
 and the election of 1864 **1**:76
 platform (1864) **2**:64–65
 post-Civil War **2**:62–64
Democratic Party (1876–1900) **2**:80–84
 convention (1896), Bryan's "cross of gold" speech **1**:107–108, 110; **2**:82–84
 election (1876) **2**:80
 platform (1876) **2**:82
 presidents *see* Cleveland, Grover
Democratic Party (1900–32) **2**:111–115
 platform (1912) **2**:114–115
 presidents *see* Roosevelt, Franklin; Wilson, Woodrow
Democratic Party (1932–68) **2**:3, 137, 141–148
 platform (1932) **2**:145–146
 platform (1948) **4**:85–86
 presidents *see* Johnson, Lyndon; Kennedy, John; Roosevelt, Franklin; Truman, Harry
 see also States' Rights Democrats (Dixiecrats)
Democratic Party (1968–2004) **2**:163–168
 platform (1992) **2**:167–168
 presidents *see* Carter, James "Jimmy"; Clinton, William "Bill"
Democratic-Republican Party (Antifederalists) **1**:7, 9, 10–11, 12, 17; **2**:3–4, 9, 13–16
 and the election of 1820 **1**:30
 and foreign affairs **2**:14
 presidents *see* Adams, John Quincy; Jefferson, Thomas; Madison, James; Monroe, James
Dennis, Eugene **2**:*129*
depression, economic
 and the election of 1896 **1**:105, 106
 see also Great Depression
Dewey, Thomas
 biography **1**:*152*
 and the election of 1940 **1**:147
 presidential candidate (1944) **1**:151–153; **2**:158
 presidential candidate (1948) **1**:154–157; **2**:137
"direct democracy" **1**:121, 123–124
Dixiecrats *see* States' Rights Democrats
Dole, Robert "Bob"
 biography **1**:*202*
 presidential candidate (1996) **1**:200–203
Dorr's Rebellion **2**:38
Dorr, Thomas **2**:38, *40*
 biography **2**:*39*
"double jeopardy" **3**:114
Douglass, Frederick **2**:72; **4**:33–34
 biography **4**:*33*
Douglass, Sarah Mapps **4**:*37*

Douglas, Stephen
 biography **1**:*71*
 and the election of 1852 **1**:61
 presidential candidate (1860) **1**:68–73; **2**:61
 and slavery **2**:19
Douglas, William **3**:*108*–109, 119
Dow, Neal **1**:92
Dred Scott case *see Scott v. Sanford*
Drew, Timothy **4**:142
Dubinsky, David **2**:152, 153, *158*
Duane, William **1**:46
Dubois, W.E.B. **1**:135; **4**:6, 60, 63–64
 biography **4**:*64*
 quoted on Marcus Garvey **4**:140
Dukakis, Michael
 biography **1**:194
 presidential candidate (1988) **1**:192–195; **2**:165, 171–172
Duke, David **2**:178
Duvall, Gabriel **3**:*16*

E

Eagleton incident **1**:177, 178
Eagleton, Thomas **1**:177, 178; **2**:164
Eastland, James **4**:110
economics
 depression
  and the election of 1896 **1**:105, 106
  see also Great Depression
 laissez-faire **2**:107
 supply-side **2**:170–171
Edmunds, George **1**:95
Edmund v. Florida (1982) **4**:77–78
education
 affirmative action in, violates the rights of whites? (SC) **3**:155, 166–167
 censorship of student newspaper (SC) **3**:168, 173–174
 and the election of 1876 **1**:86
 and the election of 1996 **1**:201
 Green Party and **2**:190
 Liberal Party and **2**:157
 Natural Law Party and **2**:193
 segregation in *see* segregation, in education
 see also schools
Edwards v. California (1941) **3**:117–118
Eighteenth Amendment **1**:128; **3**:xiv
 Prohibition Party and **2**:66
Eighth Amendment **3**:xiii
Eisenhower, Dwight
 biography **1**:*159*
 health **1**:162, 163, 164
 as president **2**:138, 144
  and the Civil Rights Act (1957) **4**:104
  and the Civil Rights Act (1960) **4**:110
  and Little Rock High School **4**:101, 102
 presidential candidate (1952) **1**:158–161; **2**:137, 138, 144
 presidential candidate (1956) **1**:162–164; **2**:144
election campaigns, paying for **2**:6–8
Electoral College **1**:1
Eleventh Amendment **3**:xiii, 1, 3, 6
Ellsworth Court **3**:9–12
Ellsworth, Oliver **3**:9–10

Emancipation Proclamation (1863) **1**:70, 74; **2**:36, 55, 56, 58; **4**:42–44
Embargo Act (1807) **1**:19
employment
 hours worked by women (SC) **3**:66, 82–83, 88
 see also child labor
energy, and the election of 2000 **1**:206
Enforcement Act (1870) **3**:56, 62, 63; **4**:56
Engel v. Vitale (1962) **3**:143–144
environment
 and the election of 1992 **1**:198
 and the election of 2000 **1**:206
 Green Party and **2**:190
 Natural Law Party and **2**:193
 Progressive Party (1912–16) and **2**:121
Equal Opportunity Act (1964) **1**:171
Equal Rights Amendment **4**:178, 179, 181
Equal Rights Party **2**:72–74; **4**:163–165
 platform (1872) **2**:73
Esch-Cummins Act (1920) **2**:113
Escobedo v. Illinois (1964) **3**:147–148
Espionage Act (1917) **3**:84, 91
Essex Junto **1**:17
Everett, Edward **2**:50
Evers, Medgar, assassination **4**:90, *121*
Everson v. Board of Education (1947) **3**:122
Executive Order 8802 **4**:73, 79
Executive Orders 9980 and 9981 **4**:83–84, 184
Ex Parte Milligan (1866) **3**:48
extradition, interstate (SC) **3**:31, 45–46

F

Fall, Albert **1**:132
Family Reinforcement Act **2**:173
Fard, Wallace Dodd **4**:142
Farmer, James **4**:80, *81*
Farmer-Labor Association **2**:125–126
Farmer-Labor Party **2**:4, 125–127
Farmers' Alliance **2**:90, 98–99
Farmer's Non-Partisan League **2**:125
farming *see* agriculture
Farrakhan, Louis **4**:144, *145*, 149
 biography **4**:*150*
Faubus, Orval **4**:101–102
 biography **4**:*102*
Featherstone, Ralph **4**:*136*
federal budget, Reform Party and **2**:196
Federal Corrupt Practices Act (1910) **2**:7
Federal Election Campaign Act (1971) **2**:7–8
federal government
 Executive Order ending racial discrimination in **4**:83
 and river navigation (SC) **3**:27–28
 supremacy over states? (SC)
  see Brown v. Maryland; Gibbons v. Ogden; McCulloch v. Maryland; Ware v. Hylton
 versus state powers **2**:10, 11–12
Federalist Party **1**:8, 9; **2**:9–12
 attacks on Jefferson **1**:11
 and the election of 1804 **1**:17–18
 and the election of 1816 **1**:27–28
 and the election of 1820 **1**:30

and the French Revolution **1**:10
Hartford Convention (1814) **1**:26, 28; **2**:11
Federal Reserve System **1**:122
Federal Trade Commission (FTC), William Humphreys fired from **3**:112
Federal Trade Commission Act (1914) **1**:122
federal treaties, and state laws (SC) **3**:11–12
Feminine Mystique, The (Friedan) **4**:182
Ferraro, Geraldine **1**:189
Field, Stephen **3**:*40*–41
Fifteenth Amendment **1**:78; **3**:xiv; **4**:55
  political parties and **2**:63–64
  Voting Rights Acts (1870–71) and **4**:56–57
Fifth Amendment **3**:xiii, 29–30, 94, 102, 113
  and protection against "double jeopardy" **3**:114
Fillmore, Millard **2**:29
  biography **1**:*67*
  presidential candidate (1856) **1**:64–67; **2**:48
films, protected under the First Amendment **3**:133–134
Finley, Robert **4**:11
firearms, Supreme Court case involving **3**:115–116
First Amendment **3**:xiii
  burning the American flag and (SC) **3**:168, 175
  establishment clause **3**:143
  movies protected under (SC) **3**:133–134
  and prayers at graduation ceremonies (SC) **3**:177
  and prayers recited in schools (SC) **3**:143–144
  and religion **3**:161
  versus the advocacy of violent revolution (SC) **3**:94, 97–98
  see also freedom of speech
First Bank of the United States **1**:7, 9; **2**:9, 13
Fiscal Responsibility Act (1994) **2**:173
Fisk, Clinton, presidential candidate (1888) **1**:98–101
flag
  burning the (SC) **3**:168, 175, 176–177
  saluting the (and Pledge of Allegiance) **3**:116–117, 119, 123–124
Fletcher v. Peck (1810) **3**:17, 21–22
Florida, and the election of 2000 **1**:204, 207
Forbes, Ralph **2**:178
Force Act (1871) **1**:102, 103; **4**:56
Ford, Model T **1**:132
Ford, Gerald **2**:165, 170
  biography **1**:*182*
  as president **1**:182
  presidential candidate (1976) **1**:181–184
  as vice president **1**:3
Fortas, Abe **3**:*140*
Foster, Ezola **2**:197
Foster, William **2**:*129*
Four Horsemen **2**:136, 142; **3**:104
Fourteenth Amendment **1**:2, 78, 85; **3**:vii, xiv, 48; **4**:51–52

and the Bill of Rights (SC) **3**:79–80
Civil Rights Act (1875) and **4**:58
due process clause **3**:77, 132
  and noncitizens (SC) **3**:64–65
Supreme Court cases and **3**:53–55, 56, 61–62, 64–65, 77, 115
Fourth Amendment **3**:xiii
France, trade embargo with (1807) **1**:19, 20; **2**:11
Frankfurter, Felix **3**:*108*, 119
Free African Society **4**:6–7, 10
Freedom Rides and Riders **4**:80, 81, *82*, 109, 111
Freedom Schools **4**:125
freedom of speech
  advocating violent revolution (SC) **3**:94, 97–98, 101–102, 113–114
  during war (SC) **3**:84, 91–93
  federal limits on campaign spending and (SC) **3**:154, 164–165
  fighting words and (SC) **3**:119, 122–123
  four-letter words on a jacket (SC) **3**:154, 159–160
  in the movies (SC) **3**:133
  of students (SC) **3**:153
  see also First Amendment
Freedom Summer **4**:106
Freemasons *see* Masons
free soil debate
  Republicans and **2**:55–56, 58
  see also Free Soil Party
Free Soil Party **1**:56, 58–59, 60–61, 62; **2**:*35*, 42–45
  platform (1848) **2**:44–45
Frémont, John **1**:*66*, 75
  presidential candidate (1856) **1**:64–67; **2**:48, 56
French Revolution **1**:9, 10
Friedan, Betty **4**:181, *182*
Friends of Equal Rights **2**:32
Friends, Society of *see* Quakers
Fugitive Slave Act and Law (1850) **1**:62; **2**:52; **4**:22, 38–39
Fuller Court **3**:66–83
Fuller, Melville **3**:66–67
Furman v. Georgia (1972) **3**:154, 162–163

G

Gage, Matilda Joslyn **4**:166, 170
  biography **4**:*171*
Gaines, Lloyd **3**:115
Gardner, Henry **2**:48
Garfield, James **1**:74
  biography **1**:*91*
  presidential candidate (1880) **1**:90–93; **2**:76
Garrison, William Lloyd **2**:34; **4**:21–22, *24*
  and the American Anti-Slavery Society **2**:34; **4**:21–22, 25
  biography **4**:*24*
  quoted on Richard Allen **4**:10
  and *The Liberator* **4**:21, 23–24
Garvey, Marcus **4**:139, 140
  biography **4**:*141*
General Federation of Women's Clubs **4**:172
Gentlemen's Agreement (1907–08) **4**:183, 190, 192, 193–194
George W. Bush et al. v. Albert Gore Jr., et al. (2000) **3**:168, 179–180
Gerry, Elbridge **1**:23

Ghent, Treaty of (1814) **1**:26
Gibbons v. Ogden (1824) **3**:13, 25–26
Giddings, Joshua **1**:70
Gideon v. Wainwright (1963) **3**:135, 145–146
Gilded Age **2**:75
Gingrich, Newt **1**:200; **2**:172
Ginsburg, Ruth Bader **3**:*172*
Gitlow v. State of New York (1925) **3**:94, 97–98
globalization, Green Party and **2**:190
Goldberg, Arthur **3**:*139*–140
Goldbugs and Silverbugs **1**:106
Gold Rush (1848), and immigrants **4**:183, 186, 188
gold standard **2**:64, 77, *93*
  and the election of 1896 **1**:105, 106, 107–108
  and the election of 1900 **1**:110–111
  and the election of 1904 **1**:115
Goldwater, Barry
  biography **1**:*171*
  presidential candidate (1964) **1**:169–172; **2**:138–139, 145, 169–170
Gompers, Samuel **1**:119
Gonzales, Corky **2**:184
Good Feeling, Era of **1**:26, 29; **2**:13, 14–15
Goodman, Andrew **4**:125
Gorbachev, Mikhail **1**:192, 194
Gore, Albert, Jr.
  biography **1**:*206*
  and the election of 1988 **1**:193
  presidential candidate (2000) **1**:204–208; **2**:166–167
  Florida ballot-counting halted (SC) **3**:168, 179–180
government
  federal *see* federal government
  reform, Democrats (1876–1900) and **2**:80
Grange, the (Patrons of Husbandry) **2**:98
Grant, Ulysses **1**:70, 75, 86; **2**:56
  biography **1**:*79*
  and the election of 1876 **1**:86
  and the election of 1880 **1**:90, 91
  as president (1869–73) **1**:82–83
  Liberal Republican opposition to **2**:69, 70
  as president (1873–77) **1**:90
  presidential candidate (1868) **1**:78–81
  presidential candidate (1872) **1**:82–85
Gray, Horace **3**:59–60
Great Awakening **4**:25
Great Britain *see* Britain
Great Depression **1**:140, 142; **2**:141, 149
  Communist Party and **2**:129
  Democratic Party (1932–68) and **2**:141–142
  see also New Deal
  Republican Party (1900–32) and **2**:105, 108
  Republican Party (1932–68) and **2**:135–136
Great Migration **4**:71
  African American Women's Associations and **4**:59
Great Society **2**:141
Greeley, Horace
  biography **1**:*83*

presidential candidate (1872) **1**:82–85; **2**:57, 64, 69, *70*
Greenback (Greenback-Labor; National Independent) Party **1**:92, 96; **2**:88–91
  platform (1884) **2**:90–91
greenbacks (money) **2**:77, 88, 92
Greene, Catherine Littlefield **4**:170
Green Party **1**:203; **2**:190–192
Gregg v. Georgia (1976) **3**:154, 165–166
Gregory, Dick **4**:*136*
Grier, Robert **3**:36–37
Griffin, James **2**:181
Griggs v. Duke Power Company (1971) **4**:76
Grimké, Sarah and Angelina **4**:25, 27, *35*–36
Griswold v. Connecticut (1965) **3**:135, 149–150
Grow, Galusha **2**:56
Guadalupe Hidalgo, Treaty of (1848) **1**:56
gun control, Libertarian Party and **2**:187
Gutiérrez, José Angel, biography **2**:184

H

habeas corpus, suspension by Lincoln's administration **1**:74, 76; **3**:32
Hagelin, John **2**:193, 194
Hale, John, presidential candidate (1852) **1**:60–63; **2**:44
Half-Breeds **1**:90, 96
Hallinan, Vincent **2**:153
Hall, Prince **4**:*5*
Hamilton, Alexander **1**:7, 9, 11
  biography **2**:*10*
  death **1**:16, 17; **2**:10
Hammer v. Dagenhart (1918) **3**:66, 84, 90–91
Hancock, Winfield
  biography **1**:*92*
  presidential candidate (1880) **1**:90–93
Hanford, Ben **2**:118
Hanly, J. Frank, presidential candidate (1916) **1**:125–127
Hanna, Mark **1**:113
  biography **2**:*76*
  influence over McKinley (William) **1**:*111*; **2**:6, *76*, 106
Harding, Warren
  biography **1**:*129*
  presidential candidate (1920) **1**:128–131
"hard money" **1**:86, 90; **2**:64
Harlan, John Marshall **3**:57–58
  biography **3**:*137*
Harper's Ferry, raid on **1**:68, 71–72; **4**:31, *32*
Harrington, Michael **2**:118–119
Harrison, Benjamin
  biography **1**:*99*
  presidency **1**:102
  and the spoils system **2**:*7*
  presidential candidate (1888) **1**:98–101
  presidential candidate (1892) **1**:102–104
Harrison, William
  biography **1**:*49*

death **1**:49, 52
  presidential candidate (1836)
    1:44–47; **2**:28
  presidential candidate (1840)
    1:48–51; **2**:28
Hartford Convention (1814) **1**:26, 28;
  2:11
Hart, Gary **1**:189
Haskell, Charles **1**:117
Hastie, William **4**:78
Hatch Act (1940) **2**:7
Hawaii, annexation of **1**:109
Hayes, Rutherford, presidential
  candidate (1876) **1**:86–89; **2**:57,
  80
Haynes, George Edmund **4**:70
*Hazelwood School District v.
  Kuhlmeier* (1988) **3**:168, 173–174
health care
  and the election of 1992 **1**:198
  Green Party and **2**:190
  Natural Law Party and **2**:193
Heart of Atlanta Motel v. United States
  (1964) **3**:148–149
Hemings, Sally **1**:16, 18
Hendricks, Thomas **1**:91
Hepburn Act (1906) **2**:106
Hill, James J. **3**:80
Hiss, Alger **2**:137
Holmes, Oliver Wendell, Jr. **3**:*70–71*
Holocaust denial **2**:176
homesteads
  Free Soil Party and **2**:42, 43
  Republican Party (1854–76) and
    2:55, 58–59
Homestead strike (1892) **1**:102, 103
Hoover, Herbert
  biography **1**:*137*
  as president **1**:140; **2**:141
    and the Great Depression **2**:108,
      114
    inaugural address (1929)
      2:108–109
  presidential candidate (1928)
    1:136–139; **2**:108
  presidential candidate (1932)
    1:140–143; **2**:108, 135
Hoover, J. Edgar **1**:128
Hoovervilles **2**:108
Horton, William ("Willie") **1**:194
Hospers, John **2**:187
hotels, racial discrimination in (SC)
  3:148–149
Houston, Charles **4**:76
Howe, Julia Ward **4**:153
Hughes, Charles
  biography **1**:*126*
  as a justice of the Supreme Court
    3:*104–105*
  presidential candidate (1916)
    1:125–*127*; **2**:107
Hughes Court **3**:104–118
Humphrey, Hubert **2**:127
  at the Democratic Party
    convention (1948) **4**:85, 86
  biography **1**:*175*
  presidential candidate (1968)
    1:173–176; **2**:163, 170
Humphrey's Executor v. United States
  (1935) **3**:104, 112
Hungarian revolt (1956) **1**:162, 164
Hunkers **1**:58; **2**:42
Hunt, Ward **3**:*51–52*

I

Idaho, and women's suffrage **4**:168
Immigration Act (1924) **2**:107;
  4:199–*200*
Immigration Act (1965) **4**:184, 206
immigration and immigrants **2**:107,
  111; **4**:183–184
  Chinese (1848–1882) **3**:64;
    4:186–187, *189*
    Burlingame Treaty and **1**:92;
      4:187, 188
    Chinese Exclusion Act (1882)
      2:87; **4**:183, 187, 188–189, 189
    "coolie" trade **4**:187, 188
    total ban lifted **4**:184
    Workingmen's Party of
      California and **2**:85–*86*, 87
  Immigration Act (1924) **2**:107;
    4:199–*200*
  Immigration Act (1965) **4**:184, 206
  Immigration and Nationality Act
    (McCarran-Walter Act; 1952)
    4:184, 201, 205
  Indian, citizenship (SC) **4**:197–198
  Japanese **4**:183, 190–191, *194*
    between 1869–1942 **4**:190–191
    Gentlemen's Agreement
      (1907–08) **4**:183, 190, 192,
      193–194
    internment (1942–45) **3**:119,
      124–125; **4**:184, 191, 201,
      203–*204*
    Japanese American Citizens
      League **4**:184, 201–202
    Japanese Exclusion League
      4:183, 192
    "picture brides" **4**:190–191
    Takao Ozawa v. United States
      (1922) **4**:184, 191, 195–196
    see also Japanese Americans
  opposition to
    American (Know-Nothing)
      Party **1**:66; **2**:46–47, 48
    Republican Party (1900–32)
      2:107
    see also Ku Klux Klan
  and presidential elections
    of 1852 **1**:60
    of 1856 **1**:64, 66
    of 1876 **1**:86
    of 1880 **1**:92–93
  quotas **4**:184, 199
  and religion **1**:137
  to Rhode Island, and male suffrage
    2:38
  see also citizenship
Immigration and Nationality Act
  (McCarran-Walter Act; 1952)
  4:184, 201, 205
imperialism *see* territorial expansion
imports, interstate, licenses to sell
  (SC) **3**:26–27
income limits, Union Party
  (1936–39) and **2**:149
Independence, Declaration of **4**:3,
  183
Independent Socialist League **2**:118
Independent Treasury Act (1840)
  2:33
India, a native of, citizenship (SC)
  4:197–198
Industrial Revolution **2**:102
In re Debs (1895) **3**:66, 73–74
In re Gault (1967) **3**:151–152
"instant runoff" **2**:190
integration
  Little Rock High School **4**:89,
    101–103
  University of Alabama **4**:119–120
  University of Mississippi
    4:112–115
Iran Hostage Crisis (1979) **1**:185;
  2:163
Iraq, invasion of (2003) **2**:174
Iredell, James **3**:*4*
Islam, Nation of **4**:142–*145*
  see also Farrakhan, Louis; Million
    Man March
isolationism, America First Party and
  2:155
Israel, and the election of 1996 **1**:201

J

Jackson, Andrew **1**:26; **2**:6
  biography **1**:*37*; **2**:*18*
  marriage **1**:39
  as president **2**:18–19
  presidential candidate (1824)
    1:32–*35*; **2**:14–15, 17, 21
  presidential candidate (1828)
    1:36–39; **2**:17–18, 21
  presidential candidate (1832)
    1:40–43
  Whig Party and **1**:50; **2**:28, *29*
Jackson, Howell **3**:69
Jackson, Jesse **1**:190, 193
Jackson, Robert **3**:119, 121
JACL (Japanese American Citizens
  League) **4**:184, 191, 201–202, 205
Japanese Americans
  internment (1942–45) **4**:184, 191,
    201, 203–*204*
    Supreme Court case **3**:119,
      124–125
  Japanese American Citizens League
    (JACL) **4**:184, 191, 201–202, 205
  see also immigration and
    immigrants, Japanese
Japanese Exclusion League **4**:183, 192
Jay Court **3**:1–6
Jay, John **1**:8, 10; **2**:9–10; **3**:1, *2*
Jay's Treaty (1794) **1**:9, 10, 12; **2**:9–10
Jefferson, Thomas
  an Antifederalist (Democratic-
    Republican) **1**:7, 9; **2**:11
  biography **1**:*13*; **2**:*15*
  and the French Revolution **1**:10
  presidential candidate
    in 1796 **1**:9–*11*; **2**:14
    in 1800 **1**:1, 12–*15*; **2**:10–11
    in 1804 **1**:16–*18*
Jehovah's Witnesses, and the Pledge
  of Allegiance **3**:116–117, 119,
  123–124
Jim Crow laws **4**:74, 75
Job Creation and Wage Enhancement
  Act **2**:173
Johnson, Andrew **1**:70, 75, 78–79
  biography **1**:*75*
  as president
    Civil Rights Act (1866) vetoed
      4:49
    impeachment **1**:78–79; **3**:48
    and Reconstruction laws (SC)
      3:52–53
Johnson, Hiram **1**:132; **2**:*122*
Johnson, Lyndon
  biography **1**:*170*
  as president **2**:139, 144–*145*
    and the Selma marches (1965)
      4:129, 130, 132
  presidential candidate (1964)
    1:169–172; **2**:145
Johnson, Thomas **3**:*4–5*
Johnson, William **3**:*15*
Jones, Absalom **4**:6, 9, 10
  biography **4**:*7*
Jones, Paula **3**:178–179
Journey of Reconciliation (1947) **4**:82
judicial reform, Progressive Party
  (1912–16) and **2**:121
judiciary
  American Independent Party and
    2:179
  Progressive Party (1924) and **2**:132
Judiciary Act (1789) **3**:1, 14
Jungle, The (Sinclair) **1**:116, 117;
  2:106
juries, African Americans excluded
  from (SC) **3**:110, 111
"just compensation" **3**:77

K

Kalloch, Isaac **2**:86; **4**:189
Kansas-Nebraska Act (1854) **1**:65–66;
  2:29, 44; **4**:31
Karenga, Maulana Ron **4**:*136*
Kearney, Denis **2**:85, 86; **4**:187,
  188–189
  biography **2**:*87*
Keating-Owen bill **1**:126
Keating-Owen Child Labor Act
  (1916), overturned by *Hammer
  v. Dagenhart* **3**:84, 90–91
Kefauver, Estes **1**:159, 163
Kendall v. United States (1838) **3**:31,
  41–42
Kennedy, Anthony **3**:*170–171*
Kennedy, Edward **1**:185–186; **2**:165
Kennedy, John
  biography **1**:*166*; **4**:*114*
  inaugural address (1961)
    2:146–148
  as president
    assassination **1**:166, 173
    and the Civil Rights Act (1964)
      4:128
    speech on civil rights (1963)
      4:119–120
    speech on the integration of the
      University of Mississippi
      4:114–115
  presidential candidate (1960)
    1:165–168; **2**:138, 144
Kennedy, Robert **1**:170–171, 174;
  4:109
Kentucky v. Dennison (1860) **3**:31,
  45–46
King, Martin Luther, Jr. **1**:162, 164,
  173; **2**:139; **4**:89, 90
  assassination **4**:98
  biography **4**:*97–98*
  "Letter From a Birmingham Jail"
    4:116
  and the March on Washington
    4:97, 122, 123
    "I have a dream" speech **4**:90,
      122, 123
  and the Montgomery bus boycott
    4:93–94
  and nonviolent civil disobedience
    4:97
  and Project C **4**:116

and the SCLC **4**:96, 97
and the Vietnam War **4**:97–98
King, Rufus **1**:23, *28*
   presidential candidate (1816) **1**:26–28
Kissinger, Henry **1**:179, *180*; **2**:164
Klausner, Manuel **2**:187
Know-Nothing Party *see* American Party
Koehl, Mathias **2**:176, 177, 178
Korean War, election of 1952 and **1**:158, 160; **2**:137
Korematsu v. United States (1943) **3**:119, 124–125
Kucinich, Dennis **2**:194
Ku Klux Klan **1**:132, 134–135; **2**:107, 111, 113; **4**:53–*54*, 57
   first Klan **4**:53
   Ku Klux Klan Act (1871) **4**:56–57
   second Klan **4**:53–54
   third Klan **4**:54

L

Labor, Department of **1**:95
labor reform, Greenback Party and **2**:88
labor unions
   Brotherhood of Sleeping Car Porters **4**:72–73
   and the election of 1908 **1**:119
   and the election of 1948 **1**:156
   Farmer-Labor Party and **2**:125
   New Deal and **2**:142
   see also strikes
La Follette, Robert **1**:135; **2**:132
   biography **2**:*133*
   and the election of 1912 **1**:123
   and the election of 1916 **2**:107
   presidential candidate (1924) **1**:132–135; **2**:132
La Guardia, Fiorello **2**:152
   biography **2**:*153*
Lamar, Joseph **3**:*86*
Lamar, Lucius **3**:*60*–61
Landon, Alfred "Alf"
   biography **1**:*145*
   presidential candidate (1936) **1**:144–146; **2**:136
La Raza Unida Party **2**:183–186
law and order, American Independent Party and **2**:179
Law and Order Party of Rhode Island **2**:4, 38–41
League of Nations **1**:122, 128, 130, 131, 146
League of Women Voters **4**:179–180
Lecompton Constitution **2**:50
Lee v. Weisman (1992) **3**:177
Legal Defense Fund (LDF), NAACP **4**:74–78
Leggett, William **2**:32
legislative districts, state, equal size (SC) **3**:135, 144–145
Lemke, William **2**:*150*, *151*
   presidential candidate (1936) **1**:144–146; **2**:149
Lemon v. Kurtzman (1971) **3**:161
Lend Lease **2**:142–143
liberalism, and the election of 1988 **1**:192, 193
Liberal Party **2**:4, 157–159
   platform (1944) **2**:158–159
Liberal Republican Party **1**:*84*; **2**:57, 64, 69–71

platform (1872) **2**:71
Liberals (Reformers) **1**:90
Liberator, The **4**:21, 23–*24*
Liberia **4**:11, 12
Libertarian Party **2**:4, 187–189
   platform (1976) **2**:187–188
Liberty League **1**:146
Liberty Party **1**:58; **2**:34–37
   platform (1840) **2**:36
   platform (1844) **2**:36–37
life-support equipment, and the terminally-ill (SC) **3**:175–176
Lincoln, Abraham **2**:*53*
   biography **1**:69–70
   as president **1**:69–70; **2**:56
   and the Emancipation Proclamation **1**:70, 74; **2**:36, 56, 58; **4**:*42*–44
   meeting with Sojourner Truth **4**:40, *41*
   presidential candidate (1860) **1**:68–73; **2**:52–53, 62
   presidential candidate (1864) **1**:74–77; **2**:56
Little Rock High School, integration of **4**:89, 101–103
Liuzzo, Viola **4**:131
Livingston, Henry **3**:*15*–16
Lochner v. New York (1905) **3**:66, 81–82
Lockwood, Belva Ann **2**:72, 73; **4**:165
Locofocos **2**:32–33
Lodge, Henry Cabot **1**:125; **2**:*108*
Logan, John **1**:90, 95
Long, Huey **2**:155
lotteries **3**:25
Louisiana Purchase **1**:16, 17; **4**:183
Loving v. Virginia (1967) **3**:152–153
Lowden, Frank **1**:133
Luevano v. Campbell (1980) **4**:76
lunch-counter sit-ins **4**:67, 80, 89, 105, 106, 116
Lurton, Horace **3**:*72*–73
Luther v. Borden (1849) **3**:31, 43–44
lynching **4**:66

M

McAdoo, William **1**:128, 133–134, 136–137; **2**:114
McAuliffe, Terry **2**:165
MacBride, Roger **2**:187
McCain-Feingold Bill **2**:8
McCarran-Walter Act (Immigration and Nationality Act; 1952) **4**:184, 201, 205
   vetoed by Truman **4**:205
McCarthy, Eugene **2**:145
McCarthy, Joseph **1**:158, 160, 162; **2**:137
McClellan, George
   biography **1**:*76*
   presidential candidate (1864) **1**:70, 74–77; **2**:56, 62
McCulloch v. Maryland (1819) **3**:24–25
McDonnell Douglas Corp. v. Green (1973) **4**:76
McGovern Commission **2**:164
McGovern, George **2**:163–164
   biography **1**:*179*
   presidential candidate (1972) **1**:177–180
McKenna, Joseph **3**:*70*
McKinley, John **3**:*34*

McKinley, William
   biography **1**:*106*
   and the election of 1892 **1**:102
   Hanna's influence over **1**:*111*; **2**:6, 76, 106
   presidential candidate (1896) **1**:105–108; **2**:6, 78, 93
   presidential candidate (1900) **1**:109–112; **2**:106, 112
McKissick, Floyd **4**:80
McLaurin v. Oklahoma State Regents (1950) **3**:127, 131–132; **4**:74–75
McLean, John **1**:65; **3**:*18*–19
McReynolds, James **3**:*87*
Macune, Charles William, biography **2**:99
Maddox, Lester **2**:180
Madison, James
   biography **1**:*20*
   presidential candidate (1808) **1**:*19*–*21*
   presidential candidate (1812) **1**:22–25
Magnus Act (1943) **4**:184
Maine (battleship) **1**:109
Malcolm X **4**:*143*–144, 146
Malloney, Joseph, presidential candidate (1900) **2**:96
Manifest Destiny **1**:52, 54, 111
Mapp v. Ohio (1961) **3**:143
Marbury v. Madison (1803) **3**:13, 20–21
Marcantonio, Vito **2**:152
March Against Fear (1966) **4**:90, 133–*134*
March on Washington (1963) **4**:96, 97, 122–*123*
   "I have a dream" speech **4**:90, 122, 123
Marcy, William, and the election of 1852 **1**:61
marriage, interracial (SC) **3**:152–153
Marrou, Andre **2**:187
Marshall Court **3**:13–30
Marshall, John **1**:23; **3**:v, 13, *14*–15
Marshall, Thurgood **3**:*140*–141; **4**:66
   biography **4**:*77*
Martin v. Hunter's Lessee (1816) **3**:13, 22–23
Marxism, Socialist Labor Party and **2**:95
Masons (Freemasons) **1**:41, 46; **2**:23
Massachusetts, slavery in **4**:5
Matchett, Charles, presidential candidate (1896) **2**:96
Matthews, Stanley **3**:*59*
Maxwell v. Dow (1900) **3**:79–80
meat-packing industry, Theodore Roosevelt and **1**:*116*, 117
Meredith, James **4**:90, *112*–114, 133–*134*
   biography **4**:*113*
Mexican Americans, and La Raza Unida Party **2**:183–186
Mexican American Youth Organization (MAYO) **2**:184
Mexican Revolution (1910–20), U.S. intervention in **1**:125, 126
Mexican War **2**:43
   land acquired after and immigration **4**:183
   La Raza Unida Party and **2**:183–184
   and slavery **1**:56, 57–58; **2**:17, 28, 42, 43

   see also free soil debate; Kansas-Nebraska Act
MFDP (Mississippi Freedom Democratic Party) **4**:106, 125, 127
Mfume, Kweisi **4**:69
military, the
   Executive Order ending discrimination in **4**:83
   military courts, power over civilians (SC) **3**:48, 51–52
   military spending, and the election of 1988 **1**:194
Miller, Samuel **3**:*39*
Million Man March **4**:144, *145*, 149–151
Mills, Roger **1**:101
Minersville School District v. Gobitis (1940) **3**:116–117, 120
Minor v. Happersett (1874) **3**:56, 61
Minton, Sherman **3**:*129*
Miracle, The (movie) **3**:133
Miranda v. Arizona (1966) **3**:135, 136, 150–151
"missile gap" **1**:166–167
Mississippi Council of Confederated Organizations (COFO) **4**:125
Mississippi Freedom Democratic Party (MFDP) **4**:106, 125, 127
Mississippi Summer Project (1964) **4**:125–126
Mississippi, University of, integration **4**:112–115
Mississippi v. Johnson (1867) **3**:52–53
Missouri Compromise (1820) **1**:27, 30; **3**:44; **4**:21
Missouri ex rel. Gaines v. Canada (1938) **3**:115; **4**:74
Mondale, Walter
   biography **1**:191
   presidential candidate (1984) **1**:189–191; **2**:165
monopolies *see* trusts
Monroe Doctrine **1**:27
Monroe, James **1**:19
   biography **1**:*27*
   presidential candidate (1816) **1**:26–28
   presidential candidate (1820) **1**:29–31
Montgomery bus boycott **1**:164; **4**:89, 92–95
Montgomery City Code **4**:92
Montgomery Improvement Association **4**:93, 94–95
Moody, William **3**:*72*
Moore, Alfred **3**:*11*
Morgan, J.P. **3**:80
Morgan, William **1**:38, 40–41; **2**:23, 24
Mormon Church, polygamy **1**:90
Morton, Oliver **1**:86
Moses, Robert **4**:*126*
movies, protected under the First Amendment **3**:133–134
muckraking and muckrakers **1**:113, *116*; **3**:84
Mugwumps **1**:96, 100
Muhammad, Elijah **4**:142, *143*
   Malcolm X and **4**:143–144
Muhammad, Wallace **4**:142–143
Muller v. Oregon (1908) **3**:66, 82–83, 88
Mulligan Letters **1**:96
Muñiz, Ramsey **2**:184

Set Index

Munn v. Illinois (1877) **3:**56, 61–62
murder trials, state, Supreme Court cases involving **3:**110–112
Murphy, Frank **3:***109*
Muslim Mission **4:**142
My Escape from Slavery (Frederick Douglass) **4:**33–34

N

NAACP (National Association for the Advancement of Colored People) **4:**60, 63, 64, 66–69
Legal Defense Fund (LDF) **4:**74–78
Nader, Ralph
biography **2:***191*
presidential candidate (1996) **1:**200–203; **2:**191
presidential candidate (2000) **1:**204–208; **2:**190, 191
NAFTA, Reform Party and **2:**196
Napoleonic Wars **1:**22
Nasser, Abdel **1:**162
National American Woman Suffrage Association (NAWSA) **4:**154, 168–169
constitution **4:**169
National Association for the Advancement of Colored People *see* NAACP
National Association Opposed to Woman Suffrage **4:**154
National Bank *see* bank(s)
National Convention of Friends of Immediate Emancipation **2:**34
national debt, Jefferson and **1:**16
National Farmers' Alliance *see* Farmers' Alliance
National Independent Party *see* Greenback Party
National Labor Relations Act (1935) **3:**104
National Negro Convention Movement **4:**28
National Organization for Women (NOW) **4:**181–182
National Prohibition Party *see* Prohibition Party
National Republican Party **2:**15, 21–22
National Security Restoration Act **2:**173
National Silver Party **1:**106; **2:**4, 92–94
platform (1896) **2:**93–94
National Socialist White People's Party **2:**176–178
National Union Republican Party **1:**79
National Urban League **4:**70–71
National Woman's Party (NWP) **4:**154, *173*–175
National Woman Suffrage Association (NWSA) **3:**61; **4:**153, 158–160
Nation of Islam **4:**142–*145*
see also Farrakhan, Louis; Million Man March
Nations, League of **1:**122, 128, 130, 131, 146
Native Americans, Cherokees as a foreign nation? (SC) **3:**28–29
Naturalization Act (1790) **2:**10; **4:**183, 185
Natural Law Party **2:**193–195

Naval Appropriations Bill (1867) **2:**6
NAWSA (National American Woman Suffrage Association) **4:**154, 168–169
Near v. Minnesota (1931) **3:**109–110
Nelson, Samuel **3:***35*
Nevada, statehood **2:**92
New Deal **1:**144, 145, 147, 149, 152–153, 156; **2:**141–142
American Labor Party support for **2:**152
Supreme Court justices and **2:**136; **3:**104
New Freedom **1:**123
New Nationalism **1:**123; **2:**122, 123
New Order **2:**176–177, 178
news media, can be sued for libel? (SC) **3:**146–147
newspapers
banning of (SC) **3:**109–110
and government control over the printing of documents (SC) **3:**154, 160–161
student, censorship of (SC) **3:**168, 173–174
Newton, Huey **4:**146, *147*, 148
New York, and national politics **2:**158
New York Times Company v. Sullivan (1964) **3:**146–147
New York Times v. United States (1971) **3:**160–161
Niagara Movement **4:**60, 63–65
Niebuhr, Reinhold **2:**158
Nineteenth Amendment **1:**130; **3:**xv; **4:**154, 175, 176–*177*, 180
Ninth Amendment **3:**xiii
Nixon, E.D. **4:**93, 94
Nixon, Richard **2:**137
biography **1:***174*
and the election of 1952 **1:**161; **2:**137
and the election of 1956 **1:**163
as president **1:**177
above the law? (SC) **3:**154, 164
resignation **1:**181; **2:**170
Watergate scandal **1:**181; **2:**165, 170; **3:**154
presidential candidate (1960) **1:**165–168; **2:**138
presidential candidate (1968) **1:**173–176; **2:**139, 170
presidential candidate (1972) **1:**177–180; **2:**164, 170
Nixon v. Fitzgerald (1982) **3:***179*
Non-Intercourse Act (1809) **1:**19, 21
"normalcy" **1:**128, 130, 136
Norris v. Alabama (1935) **3:**111
North American Free Trade Agreement (NAFTA), Reform Party and **2:**196
Northern Securities Co. **1:**113; **2:**106
Northern Securities Co. v. United States (1904) **3:**80–81
NOW (National Organization for Women) **4:**181–182
nuclear weapons
and the election of 1956 **1:**162, 164
and the election of 1980 **1:**187
see also arms race
nullification, of tariffs **1:**40, 44, 46
NWP (National Woman's Party) **4:**154, *173*–175
NWSA (National Woman Suffrage Association) **3:**61; **4:**153, 158–160

O

Oakland, California, and the Black Panther Party **4:**146, 147
O'Brien, Thomas **2:**149
O'Connor, Sandra Day **3:***157*–158
oil prices
and the election of 1976 **1:**181
and the election of 1980 **1:**185, 187
Olmstead v. United States (1928) **3:**94, 102–103
Olson, Floyd Bjerstjerne **2:***126*, 127
"Omaha Platform" **2:**100–101
"one man, one vote" **3:**135
OPEC **1:**181, 185, 187
Ovington, Mary White **4:**66, 67

P

Palko v. Connecticut (1937) **3:**114
Palmer, A. Mitchell **1:**128, 130; **2:**128
raids, on communists and "subversives" **1:**130; **2:**128
Pan-Africanism **4:**64
Panama Canal **1:**111, 113
Panic of 1837 **1:**48; **2:**33
Panic of 1873 **2:**88, 92; **4:**187, 188
Panic of 1893 **1:**117
Panic of 1907 **1:**117
Paris, Treaty of (1783) **3:**9
Paris, Treaty of (1898) **1:**109
Parker, Alton
biography **1:***115*
presidential candidate (1904) **1:**113–116; **2:**6, 112
Parks, Rosa **4:**66, 89, 92, *93*, 95
Paterson, William **3:***5*
Patrons of Husbandry (the Grange) **2:**98
Paul, Alice **4:**173, 175, 176, *177*, 179
biography **4:***174*
and the Equal Rights Amendment **4:**178
and the League of Women Voters **4:**179–180
Paul, Ron **2:**188
Peace Democrats *see* Copperheads
Peace and Freedom Party **4:**148
Pearl Harbor, Japanese attack on **4:**203
Peckham, Rufus **3:**69–70
Pendergast, Thomas, biography **2:***113*
Pendleton Civil Service Act (1883) **1:**93; **2:**6
Pendleton, George **1:**79
Pennsylvania Abolition Society (Abolition Society) **4:**4, 21
"Pentagon papers" **3:**154, 160–161
peonage **4:**48
People's Party (Populists) **1:**103, 104; **2:**98–101
platform (1892) "The Omaha Platform" **2:**100–101
Perot, Ross
biography **1:***198*
presidential candidate (1992) **1:**196–199; **2:**196
presidential candidate (1996) **1:**200–203; **2:**196
Perry, Matthew **1:**64
Personal Responsibility Act (1996) **2:**173
Philippines, and the election of 1900 **1:**109, 111, 112
"picture brides" **4:**183, 190–191

Pierce, Franklin
biography **1:***61*
presidential candidate (1852) **1:**60–63
Pinckney, Charles **1:**10
biography **1:***17*
presidential candidate
in 1796 **1:**9, 11
in 1804 **1:**16–*18*
in 1808 **1:**19–*21*; **2:**11
Pitney, Mahlon **3:**86–87
Plessy v. Ferguson (1896) **3:**vi, 76–77; **4:**48, 62
Plumer, William **1:**29, 30
"police riot", at the 1968 convention in Chicago **1:**175
political action committees (PACs) **2:**7, 8
political parties **2:**3–5
passing legislation **2:**3
and paying for election campaigns **2:**6–8
Polk, James
biography **1:***53*
presidential candidate (1844) **1:**52–55
Pollock v. Farmer's Loan and Trust Co. (1895) **3:**74–75
polygamy **1:**90
Pomeroy Circular **1:**74
Pomeroy, Samuel **1:**74
Poor People's Campaign (1968) **4:**96, *137*–138
"popular sovereignty" **1:**57, 58, 59
Populists *see* People's Party
Post Office, Supreme Court and **3:**31, 41–42
Pottawatomie Creek, raid on **4:**32
Powell, Lewis, Jr. **3:***156*–157
Powell v. Alabama (1932) **3:**111
Powell v. State of Alabama (1932; 1935) **3:**110–112
prayers
at graduation ceremonies (SC) **3:**177
recited in schools (SC) **3:**143–144
precedents, American law and **3:**vi
president(s)
are above the law? (SC) **3:**154, 164
being incapacitated **1:**2–3
can be sued to prevent him enforcing laws? (SC) **3:**52–53
candidates **1:**1–2, 121
date of taking office **1:**2
election, Progressive Party (1924) and **2:**132
impeachment **3:**8
ordering acts of war (SC) **3:**31, 46–47
presidential primaries **1:**165
sued for private conduct while still in office? (SC) **3:**178–179
terms in office **1:**2
Franklin Roosevelt and **1:**141, 147, 148–*149*, 151, 153
press *see* news media
Pritchett, Laurie **4:**111
privacy, right to **3:**135
Prize Cases (1862) **3:**31, 46–47
Progressive (Bull Moose) Party (1912–16) **1:**135; **2:**112, 121–124
and the election of 1912 **1:**123, 124
platform (1912) **2:**123–124
and women's suffrage **4:**154

206

Progressive Party (1924) **1**:135; **2**:132–134
    platform (1924) **2**:133–134
Progressive Party (1948–52) **2**:160–162
    and the election of 1948 **1**:156; **2**:160–161
    end **2**:161
    platform (1948) **2**:161–162
Progressive Political Action, Conference for (CPPA) **2**:132
progressivism
    and the election of 1916 **1**:126
    Woodrow Wilson and **1**:125
Prohibition **1**:128; **4**:166
    Democratic Party (1900–32) and **2**:111
    and the election of 1928 **1**:137–138
    and the election of 1932 **1**:142
    Prohibition Party **1**:92, 94, 96; **2**:4, 66–68
    see also Women's Christian Temperance Union
Prohibition of Coolie Trade Act (1862) **4**:187
Prohibition Party **1**:92, 94, 96; **2**:4, 66–68
    platform (1892) **2**:67–68
Project C, Birmingham, Alabama **4**:116–118
property
    "covenants" (SC) **3**:127, 129–130; **4**:74
    rights (SC) **3**:31, 41, 77–78, 94, 98–99
Proprietors of the Charles River Bridge v. Warren Bridge (1837) **3**:31, 41
Prosser, Gabriel, revolt **4**:8
protectionism, Union Party (1936–39) and **2**:149
Puerto Rico, and the election of 1900 **1**:109
Pullman Company **4**:72
Pullman railroad strike **1**:105, 107, 110; **2**:116; **3**:66
Pure Food and Drug Act (1906) **2**:106

Q

Quakers, opposition to slavery **4**:4, 21, 38
Quayle, Danforth **1**:193, 197

R

racial discrimination
    barred by Executive Order 8802 **4**:73, 79
    barred by Executive Orders 9980 and 9981 **4**:83–84, 184
    in businesses (SC) **3**:63–64
    Congress of Racial Equality and **4**:80–81, 82
    in hotels (SC) **3**:148–149
    see also African Americans; Ku Klux Klan; segregation
racial superiority
    black **4**:143
    white *see* white supremacy
Radical Democracy group **1**:74, 75
Radical Republicans **1**:75–76, 78; **4**:51
radio
    and the election of 1924 **1**:132, 135
    and the election of 1940 **1**:150

railroads
    Chinese labor **4**:186, 187
    government ownership, advocated by the Populists **2**:98
    high freight charges (1880s) **2**:98; **3**:56
    monopolies (SC) **3**:80–81
    rates (SC) **3**:73
    strikes
        and the election of 1896 **1**:105, 107
        in July 1877 **2**:85
        Pullman railroad strike **1**:105, 107, 110; **2**:116; **3**:66
        Supreme Court case **3**:66
Randall, Samuel **1**:91, 94
Randolph, A. Philip **4**:72, 122
    biography **4**:73
Raskob, John **1**:138; **2**:114
Reagan, Cordell **4**:111
Reagan, Ronald
    biography **1**:*186*
    and the election of 1968 **1**:174; **2**:170
    and the election of 1976 **1**:183
    presidential candidate (1980) **1**:185–188; **2**:165, 170–171
    presidential candidate (1984) **1**:189–191; **2**:165
Reconciliation, Journey of (1947) **4**:82
Reconstruction **1**:78, 80, 82, 86, 90; **2**:56–57, 58; **4**:45–46
    political parties and
        Democrats (1860–76) **2**:61, 62–64
        Democrats (1876–1900) **2**:80
        Liberal Republicans **2**:69
        Republicans after Reconstruction **2**:57–58, 75
    Supreme Court and **3**:52–53
Red Scare **1**:130
    Palmer raids **1**:130; **2**:128
Reed, Stanley **3**:*107*–108
Reformers (Liberals) **1**:90
Reform Party (1992–) **1**:201; **2**:196–198
    platform (2002) **2**:197–198
Regents of the University of California v. Bakke (1978) **3**:154–155, 166–167
Rehnquist Court **3**:168–180
Rehnquist, William **3**:168, *169*
religion
    African Methodist Episcopal (AME) Church **4**:6, 7, 9–10
    Christian
        America First Party and **2**:155
        National Socialist White People's Party and **2**:176
    and the election of 1908 **1**:119
    and the election of 1928 **1**:136
    and the election of 1960 **1**:165, 166
    First Amendment and **3**:161
    of immigrants **1**:137
    Mormon Church and polygamy **1**:90
    religious displays, and separation of church and state (SC) **3**:168, 174–175
    and saluting the flag (SC) **3**:116–117, 119, 123–124
    see also anti-Semitism; church and state, separation of; Roman Catholics

Republican Party (1854–76) **1**:65; **2**:44, 55–60
    African Americans and **4**:45
    after Reconstruction **2**:57–58
    anti-slavery stance **1**:68; **2**:55–56, 58
    philosophy **2**:58–59
    platform (1860) **2**:59
    presidents *see* Grant, Ulysses; Hayes, Rutherford; Lincoln, Abraham
    and women's suffrage **4**:176
Republican Party (1876–1900) **2**:75–79
    platform (1876) **2**:78–79
    presidents *see* Arthur, Chester; Garfield, James; Harrison, Benjamin; McKinley, William
    Silver Republicans **2**:77
Republican Party (1900–32) **2**:105–110
    depression and **2**:105, 108
    philosophy (1928) **2**:108–109
    presidents *see* Coolidge, Calvin; Harding, Warren; Hoover, Herbert; Roosevelt, Theodore; Taft, William
Republican Party (1932–68) **2**:135–140
    in the 1960s **2**:138–139
    Cold War and **2**:136–137
    platform (1940) **2**:139–140
    presidents *see* Eisenhower, Dwight; Nixon, Richard
Republican Party (1968–2004) **2**:169–175
    Contract with America (1994) **2**:173
    election of 2000 **2**:172–174
    platform (1980) **2**:174–175
    presidents *see* Bush, George H.W.; Bush, George W.; Ford, Gerald; Reagan, Ronald
Resurrection City **4**:96, 137
Revenue Act (1971) **2**:8
Rhode Island
    Law and Order Party of **2**:4, 38–41
    Supreme Court and **3**:31, 43–44
Richmond Junto **1**:30; **3**:34
Rieve, Emil **2**:152
Rights, Bill of **2**:13–14; **3**:iii
    Fourteenth Amendment and (SC) **3**:79–80
    states and **3**:29–30
riots
    in the 1960s **1**:176
    "police riot" at the 1968 convention in Chicago **1**:175
    Chicago race riots (1919) **1**:130
river navigation, federal government and (SC) **3**:27–28
Roaring Twenties **2**:107–108, 113–114
Robber Barons **1**:109, 113
Robertson, Pat **1**:192
Roberts, Owen **3**:*105*–106
Robinson, Jo Ann **4**:94
Rochin v. California (1952) **3**:127, 132–133
Rockefeller, John D. **1**:109
Rockefeller, Nelson **1**:3, 165, 174; **2**:170
Rockwell, George Lincoln **2**:176, *177*
Roe v. Wade (1973) **1**:187; **3**:154, 163–164

Roman Catholics
    Al Smith and the election of 1928 **1**:136, 137
    American (Know-Nothing) Party and **2**:46, *47*
    immigrants **1**:64
    John Kennedy and the election of 1960 **1**:165, 166
Romney, George **1**:174
Roosevelt, Franklin
    biography **1**:*141*
    detested by Gerald L.K. Smith **2**:155
    dog **1**:153
    and the election of 1920 **1**:129
    as president **2**:141–142, 149
        during World War II **1**:141; **2**:142–143
    plan for more Supreme Court justices **2**:142; **3**:104
    terms in office **1**:2
    see also New Deal
    presidential candidate
        in 1932 **1**:140–*143*; **2**:108, 135–136
        in 1936 **1**:141, 144–146; **2**:136, 142, 152
        in 1940 **1**:141, 147–150; **2**:143, 152, 153
        in 1944 **1**:141, 151–153; **2**:152, 153
Roosevelt, Theodore
    biography **1**:*114*
    and the election of 1900 **1**:110, *111*–112; **2**:106
    and the election of 1908 **1**:117–118
    and the election of 1912 **1**:121–123; **2**:106–107, 122–*123*
    and the election of 1916 **1**:125–126
    as president **1**:113, 114, 115, 117; **2**:105, 106, 121
        against corruption in federal elections **2**:6–7
        antitrust stance **3**:80
        and the Gentlemen's Agreement **4**:193
    presidential candidate (1904) **1**:113–*116*; **2**:6–7, 106
    presidential candidate (1912) **1**:121–124; **2**:122
    and the Progressive (Bull Moose) Party **2**:112, 121
Rosenberg, Julius and Ethel **1**:160
Rothbard, Murray **2**:187
Rove, Karl Christian, biography **2**:*172*
Rutledge Court **3**:7–8
Rutledge, John **3**:*7*
Rutledge, Wiley **3**:*121*–122

S

St. Augustine, Florida, civil rights campaign (1963) **4**:96
St. John, John
    biography **1**:*97*
    presidential candidate (1884) **1**:94–97
    scandal surrounding **1**:96
Sakamoto, Yoshinori "Jimmie" **4**:201, 202
Sanders, Bernie **2**:116
Sanford, Edward **3**:*97*
Scalia, Antonin **3**:*170*
Schenck v. United States (1919) **3**:84, 91–92

Schmitz, John, presidential candidate (1972) **1:**177–180
schools
 prayers recited in (SC) **3:**143–144
 religious, funding (SC) **3:**161
 saluting the flag and Pledge of Allegiance (SC) **3:**116–117, 119, 123–124
 school busing
  and the election of 1976 **1:**183–184
  to end segregation of public schools (SC) **3:**158–159
 see also education
Schurz, Carl **1:**84, 90, 96
Schwerner, Michael **4:**125
SCLC *see* Southern Christian Leadership Conference
Scopes, John **1:**107
Scotsboro Boys Cases (1932; 1935) **3:**110–112
Scott, Dred **1:**71; **3:**31, 32; **4:**22
Scott v. Sanford (*Dred Scott* case; 1857) **1:**71; **3:**18, 31, 32, 44–45; **4:**22
Scott, Winfield **1:**48, 79
 biography **1:***62*
 presidential candidate (1852) **1:**60–63
Seale, Bobby **4:**146
secession, from the Union **2:**61
Second Amendment **3:**xiii, 115–116
Second Bank of the United States (Second National Bank) **1:**28, 32, 40, 41, 42, 44, 45–46; **2:**29–30
 establishment constitutional? (SC) **3:**24–25
 reestablishment opposed **1:**52, 54; **2:**17, 21, 27, 30
sectionalism **1:**32
Sedition Act (1918) **2:**116
segregation **4:**74
 in education
  for Asians in California **4:**190, 193
  busing used to end (SC) **3:**158–159
  and the Missouri state law school (SC) **3:**115
  state university graduate schools (SC) **3:**127, 131–132
  see also Brown v. Board of Education; integration
 and the "equal" half of "separate but equal" (SC) **3:**78–79
 and lunch-counter sit-ins **4:**67, 80, 105, 106
 in public facilities (SC) **3:**76–77; **4:**48, 62
 on transportation
  Freedom Rides and Riders **4:**80, 81, *82*, 109, 111
  Plessy v. Ferguson **3:**76–77; **4:**48, 62
  Rosa Parks and the Montgomery bus boycott **1:**164; **4:**66, 92–*95*
 see also African Americans; integration; racial discrimination
Selma, Alabama, Selma–Montgomery march (Bloody Sunday) **4:**106–107, *129*–131, 132
Senior Citizens' Fairness Act **2:**173
"separate but equal" notion **3:**76, 115; **4:**52, 62

"separation of powers" **3:**52
September 11 terrorist attacks **2:**169, 172–173
Sergeant, John **1:**42
Seventeenth Amendment **3:**xiv
Seventh Amendment **3:**xiii
Seward, William H. **1:**69–70
Seymour, Horatio
 biography **1:***80*
 presidential candidate (1868) **1:**78–81
Shaw v. Reno (1993) **3:**178
Shelley v. Kraemer (1948) **3:**127, 129–130; **4:**74
Sheppard-Towner Act (1921) **4:**179
Sherman Antitrust Act (1890) **3:**66, 75, 80, 81, 84, 89
Sherman, James **1:**118, 123
Sherman, John **1:**74, 99
Sherman Silver Purchase Act (1890) **1:**105
Sherman, William **1:**77
Sherrod, Charles **4:**111
Shiras, George, Jr. **3:**68–69
Shuttlesworth, Fred **4:**116, *118*
silver
 as currency **1:**106–107; **2:**77–78, 80, 81–82, 92, 98, 111–112
 versus gold coinage **1:**105, 106–108, 109, 110–111
Silver Republicans **2:**77
Sinclair, Upton *The Jungle* **1:**116, 117; **2:**106
sit-ins **4:**80
 lunch-counter **4:**67, 80, 89, 105, 106, 116
Sixteenth Amendment **3:**xiv
Sixteenth Street Baptist Church, bombed **4:**90, 124
Sixth Amendment **3:**xiii
 and right to counsel **3:**147, 148
Slaughterhouse Cases (1872) **3:**48, 53–54; **4:**48
slavery
 emancipated slaves, Civil Right Act (1866) and **4:**49–50
 end
  in the Confederacy *see* Emancipation Proclamation
  see also Thirteenth Amendment
 escaped slaves helped to freedom (Underground Railroad) **4:**38–*39*
 expansion into land acquired after the Mexican War? **1:**56, 57–58; **2:**17, 28, 42, 43
 fight against **4:**3
  African Methodist Episcopal Church **4:**6, 7, 9–10
  Appeal (David Walker) **4:**16–17
  emigration of slaves to Africa **4:**11–12, 13
  Free African Society **4:**6–7, 10
  Pennsylvania Abolition Society **4:**4, 21
  political movement *see* abolitionism
  Prince Hall and **4:***5*
 slave revolts **4:**8, *14–15*, 18–20
 Fugitive Slave Act and Law (1850) **1:**62; **2:**52; **4:**22, 38–39
 Missouri Compromise and **1:**27, 30; **3:**44; **4:**21
 and presidential elections
  of 1828 **1:**38

 of 1840 **1:**48, 50
 of 1844 **1:**52, 54, 56
 of 1848 **1:**56, 57–59
 of 1852 **1:**60, 62
 of 1856 **1:**64, 65–66
 of 1860 **1:**68–69, 70, 71–72
 of 1864 **1:**74, 76
 slave codes **1:**68–69
 Southern Democrats and **2:**52
 Supreme Court cases *see Amistad* case; *Kentucky v. Dennison*; *Scott v. Sanford*
 and the three-fifths clause **2:**34; **4:**3, 21
 see also Kansas-Nebraska Act
Smith Act (1940), communists arrested for violation of **2:***129*, 130
Smith, Alfred "Al" **2:**111
 biography **1:**138
 and the election of 1924 **1:**133, 134; **2:**114
 presidential candidate (1928) **1:**136–139; **2:**114
Smith-Connally Act (1943) **2:**7
Smith, Gerald L.K. **2:**149, *151*, 155
 biography **2:***156*
Smith v. Allwright (1944) **3:**119, 126; **4:**74
SNCC (Student Nonviolent Coordinating Committee) **4:**106–108
Social Democratic Federation **2:**118
Social Democratic Party **2:**102–104
Socialist Labor Party **2:**95–97
 platform **2:**96–97
Socialist Party **2:**116–120
 and the election of 1908 **1:**119
 Left Wing Section **3:**97
 national platform (1912) **2:**119
 platform (1912) **2:**119
 World War I and **2:**117
Social Security, and the election of 2000 **1:**206–207
Social Security Act (1935) **3:**104
social welfare
 Democratic Party (1932–68) and **2:**141
 National Socialist White People's Party and **2:**176
"soft money" **1:**78, 79, 206; **2:**64
Souter, David **3:***171*
South Carolina
 nullification of tariffs **1:**40, 44, 46
 secession from the Union **1:**68
 Vesey's Revolt **4:***14–15*
Southern Christian Leadership Conference (SCLC) **4:**89, 95, 96–98
 campaign highlights **4:**96
Southern Democratic Party **2:**20, 52–54, 61–62
 end **2:**53
 platform (1860) **2:**53–54
Southern Manifesto (1956) **4:**99–100
Soviet Union
 American Labor Party and **2:**152
 Communist Party and **2:**128
 Republican Party (1968–2004) and **2:**171
Spanish-American War **1:**109
Specie Resumption Act (1875) **2:**88, 89
Spingarn, Joel Elias **4:**67
spoils system **2:**7
Square Deal **2:**106, 121

Stachel, Jack **2:***129*
Stalwarts **1:**90
Standard Oil Company and Trust **1:**116, 117
Standard Oil Company of New Jersey v. United States (1911) **3:**84, 89–90
Stanton, Edwin **1:**75, 77
Stanton, Elizabeth Cady **1:**56; **2:**72; **4:**153, *156*, 158, 161, 176
 Declaration of Sentiments and Resolutions **4:**155–157
Stanton, Henry **2:**34
Star-Spangled Banner, Order of the **2:**46
Star Wars program **1:**190, 201
states
 banning entry to the poor and unemployed (SC) **3:**117–118
 Bill of Rights and (SC) **3:**29–30
 and business regulation (SC) **3:**56, 61–62
 can tax federal institutions? (SC) **3:**24–25
 citizen of one state may sue the government of another? (SC) **3:**5–6
 federal government and *see* federal government
 grants, as contracts (SC) **3:**21–22
 legislatures, and private contracts (SC) **3:**13, 23–24
 legislative districts, equal size (SC) **3:**135, 144–145
 redrawing congressional voting districts (SC) **3:**178
 rights **1:**171
  Republican Party (1968–2004) and **2:**169
  Southern Manifesto (1956) and **4:**99
States' Rights Democrats (Dixiecrats) **1:**154, 156; **2:**137, 144; **4:**85, 87–88
sterilization, of the mentally handicapped (SC) **3:**94, 99–100
Stevens, John **3:***157*
Stevenson, Adlai (1835–1914) **2:***81*
Stevenson, Adlai, II
 biography **1:***160*
 presidential candidate (1952) **1:**158–161; **2:**144
 presidential candidate (1956) **1:**162–164
Stewart, Potter **3:***138*–139
stock market crash (1929) **2:**108
stomach pumping of criminal suspects (SC) **3:**132–133
Stone Court **3:**119–126
Stone, Harlan **3:**97, 119, *120*
Stone, Lucy **4:**153, 161
 biography **4:***162*
Story, Joseph **3:***17*
Stow, Marietta L.B. **2:**73
Strategic Arms Limitation Treaty (SALT) **1:**177
Streeter, Anson, presidential candidate (1888) **1:**98–101
strikes
 injunctions against, and the election of 1908 **1:**117, 119
 police (1919) **1:**132, 133
 the power of courts to prevent (SC) **3:**66, 73–74
 Pullman railroad strike **1:**105, 107,

208

110; **2:**116; **3:**66
truckers' (1934) **2:**127
Strong, William **3:***50*
Stuart v. Laird (1803) **3:**14
Student Nonviolent Coordinating
  Committee (SNCC; 1960–68)
  4:106–108
Suez Canal **1:**162, 164
suffrage (voting), women's
  American Woman Suffrage
    Association **2:**72; **4:**153, 161–162
  Equal Rights Party and **2:**72
  Greenback Party and **2:**88
  National American Woman
    Suffrage Association **4:**154, 168–169
  National Woman's Party and
    4:*173–175*
  National Woman Suffrage
    Association (NWSA) **3:**61; **4:**153, 158–160
  and opposition to the Fourteenth
    Amendment **4:**52
  suffragists
    Carrie Chapman Catt **4:**154, 168, 176, *180*
    Lucy Stone **4:**153, 161, *162*
    Matilda Joslyn Gage **4:**166, 170, *171*
    see also Anthony, Susan B.; Paul, Alice; Stanton, Elizabeth Cady
  Supreme Court case **3:**61
  Women's Christian Temperance
    Union and **4:**153
  Women's National Liberal Union
    4:170–171
  Wyoming and **4:**153
  see also Nineteenth Amendment;
    voting
Sumner, Charles **1:**66; **2:**58
Supreme Court **3:**v–vi
  arbiter of laws passed by Congress
    (SC) **3:**13, 20–21
  "court-packing" **3:**104
  first session **3:**1
  and "political" issues (SC) **3:**31, 43–44
  and state courts (SC) **3:**22–23, 25
Sutherland, George **3:***95–96*;
  4:197–198
Swallow, Silas, presidential candidate
  (1904) **1:**113–116
*Swann v. Charlotte-Mecklenburg
  Board of Education* (1971)
  3:158–159; **4:**75
Swayne, Noah **3:***38–39*
Sweatt v. Painter (1950) **3:**127, 130–131; **4:**75

T

Taft Court **3:**94–103
Taft-Hartley Act (1947) **1:**156, 157; **2:**7
Taft, Robert **1:**158; **2:**136, 169; **3:**94
  biography **2:***138*
Taft, William
  biography **1:***118*
  as chief justice **3:**94, *95*
  as president **1:**118, 122; **2:**106, 121–122
  presidential candidate (1908)
    1:117–120; **2:**106
  presidential candidate (1912)
    1:121–124; **2:**112

Takao Ozawa v. United States (1922)
  4:184, 191, 195–196
Taking Back Our Streets Act (1995)
  2:173
Tammany Democrats **2:**32
Taney Court **3:**31–47
Taney, Roger **1:**46; **3:***32–33*
Tariff Act (1883) **1:**93
tariffs
  and the election of 1844 **1:**52, 54–55
  nullification of **1:**40, 44, 46
  political parties and
    Democrats (1876–1900) **2:**80
    Republican Party (1854–76) and
      2:59
    Republican Party (1876–1900)
      and **2:**75–76
  and presidential elections
    of 1848 **1:**56
    of 1880 **1:**90
    of 1888 **1:**98, 99–*100*, 101
    of 1896 **1:**105, 107
    of 1928 **1:**136
taxes
  and the election of 1984 **1:**189, 190
  and the election of 1988 **1:**193
  Green Party and **2:**190
  income
    federal income tax (SC) **3:**74–75
    Greenback Party and **2:**88
    People's Party (Populists) and
      2:98
  Progressive Party (1912–16) and
    2:121
  Progressive Party (1924) and **2:**132
  Republican Party (1932–68) and
    2:135
  Republican Party (1968–2004) and
    2:169
Taylor, Zachary **1:**60
  biography **1:***57*
  presidential candidate (1848)
    1:56–59, 67; **2:**28, 29, 42, 43
Teamster's Union **2:**126–127
Teapot Dome scandal **1:**132
telephone, tapping, Supreme Court
  ruling **3:**94, 102–103
television
  and presidential elections
    of 1960 **1:**165, 167
    of 1964 **1:**172
    of 1984 **1:**190–191
    of 1988 **1:**194
Teller, Henry **2:**77
Tennessee, and women's suffrage
  4:176–177
Tennessee Valley Authority **2:**142
Tenth Amendment **3:**xiii, 90
terminally ill patients, life-support
  equipment and (SC) **3:**175–176
territorial expansion, and the election
  of 1900 **1:**109, 111, 112;
  2:112
terrorism, Republican Party
  (1968–2004) and **2:**169
Texas, application for statehood
  1:52–53, 54, 56
Texas v. Johnson (1989) **3:**168, 175
Texas v. White (1869) **3:**48, 53
Thind, Bhagat Singh **4:**197–198
Third Amendment **3:**ix
Thirteenth Amendment **1:**70, 78; **3:**x;
  4:47–48
Thomas, Clarence **3:***171–172*

Thomas, Norman
  biography **2:***117*
  and the election of 1960 **2:**118
  presidential candidate
    in 1928 **2:**117
    in 1932 **1:**140–143; **2:**116, 117–118
    in 1948 **2:**118
Thompson, Smith **3:***17*
three-fifths clause, of the
  Constitution **2:**34; **4:**3
Thurman, Allen **1:**99
Thurmond, Strom
  biography **4:***87*
  presidential candidate (1948)
    1:154–157; **4:**85, 87–88
Tilden, Samuel
  biography **1:***88*
  and the election of 1880 **1:**91, 93
  presidential candidate (1876)
    1:86–89; **2:**57, 80
Tillman Act (1907) **2:**7
*Tinker v. Des Moines Independent
  Community School District*
  (1969) **3:**153
Todd, Thomas **3:***16*
Tompkins, Daniel **1:**30
Townsend, Francis E. **2:**149, *151*
Transcendental Meditation **2:**193, 194
treasury, independent **1:**48, 49–50
Trimble, Robert **3:***18*
Trotter, William Monroe **4:**60, 63
  biography **4:***65*
Truman, Harry S.
  biography **1:***155*
  and the election of 1944 **1:**151–152
  and the election of 1952 **1:**159
  president **1:**154; **2:**143–144; **4:**83, 85
  veto of the McCarran-Walter Act
    4:205
  presidential candidate (1948)
    1:154–157; **2:**137, 158
trusts (monopolies)
  and the election of 1896 **1:**107
  and the election of 1900 **1:***111*
  and the election of 1904 **1:**113, 115
  and the election of 1912 **1:**121
  Progressive Party (1924) and **2:**132
  Supreme Court cases **3:**66, 75–76, 80–81, 84, 89–90
  Union Party (1936–39) and **2:**149
Truth, Sojourner **4:***40–41*
Tsongas, Paul **1:**197
Tubman, Harriet **4:**38
Turner, Nat, revolt **4:**18–20
Tweed, William "Boss" **2:***63*, *64*
Twelfth Amendment **1:**1, 12, 18;
  3:xiii–xiv
Twentieth Amendment **1:**2; **3:**xv
Twenty-fifth Amendment **1:**2–3;
  3:xiv–xvi
Twenty-first Amendment **3:**xv
Twenty-fourth Amendment **3:**xv
Twenty-second Amendment **1:**2; **3:**xv
Twenty-sixth Amendment **3:**xvi
Twenty-third Amendment **3:**xv
"two-party system" **2:**4
Tyler, John **1:**52, 54; **2:**28–29

U

Underground Railroad **4:**38–*39*
UNIA (Universal Negro
  Improvement Association)
  4:140–*141*

Union, preservation of the,
  Constitutional Union Party and
  2:50
Union Party (1864) **2:**56, 62
Union Party (1936–39) **1:**75, 145;
  2:149–151
  platform (1936) **2:**150–151
unions *see* labor unions
United Nations
  American Independent Party and
    2:179
  Liberal Party and **2:**157
  Progressive Party (1948–52) and
    2:160
"United States of Africa" **4:**140
United States, Bank of *see* bank(s)
United States v. Bhagat Singh Thind
  (1923) **4:**184, 197–198
United States v. Cruikshank (1876)
  3:56, 62–63
United States v. E.C. Knight Company
  (1895) **3:**66, 75–76, 89
United States v. Eichman (1990)
  3:168, 176–177
*United States v. Libellants and
  Claimants of the Schooner
  Amistad* (1841) **3:**31, 42–43
United States v. Miller (1939)
  3:115–116
United States v. Nixon (1974) **3:**154, 164
United States v. Wong Kim Ark (1898)
  3:78
United We Stand America **2:**196
"unit rule" **1:**49
Universal Negro Improvement Asso-
  ciation (UNIA) **4:**140–*141*
Urban Conditions Among Negroes,
  Committee on **4:**70
"U.S. Peace Government" **2:**194
Utah, and women's suffrage **4:**168

V

Vallandigham, Clement **2:**62
Van Buren, Martin **1:**24, 34, 42, 43;
  2:*35*, *44*
  biography **1:***45*
  and the election of 1844 **1:**53–54
  as president, and the Independent
    Treasury Act **2:**33
  presidential candidate
    in 1836 **1:**44–47; **2:**28
    in 1840 **1:**48–51
    in 1848 **1:**56–59; **2:**42
Vandenberg, Arthur **1:**147
Van Devanter, Willis **3:***85–86*
Ventura, Jesse **2:**197
Vesey, Denmark, revolt **4:**14–15
vice president(s), vacancy for **1:**2
Vietnam War
  Democratic Party and **2:**163, 164
  and the election of 1964 **1:**169, 171
  and the election of 1968 **1:**173, 175, 176
  and the election of 1972 **1:**177, 179;
    2:164
  end **1:**181
  Martin Luther King's opposition to
    4:97–98
  protest against **2:**139
  and freedom of speech (SC)
    3:153
*Village of Euclid v. Ambler Realty
  Company* ((1926) **3:**94, 98–99

209

Villa, Pancho **1**:126
Vinson Court **3**:127–134
Vinson, Frederick **3**:*127*–128
Virginia, slavery, Gabriel Prosser's Revolt **4**:8
"Virginia dynasty" **1**:22, 23
Virginia and Kentucky Resolutions (1798 and 1799) **2**:14
  Virginia Resolution (1798) **2**:11, 15
Volstead Act (1919) **2**:107
voting
  by African Americans
    Civil Rights Act (1960) **4**:110
    literacy tests **4**:132
    Mississippi Summer Project **4**:125–126
    Selma marches (1965) and **4**:130–131, 132
    see also Fifteenth Amendment; Voting Rights Act (1965); Voting Rights Acts (1870–71)
  by women
    in the election of 1920 **1**:130
    in the election of 1924 **1**:135
    League of Women Voters **4**:179–180
    Social Democratic Party and **2**:102
    see also suffrage
voting districts, congressional, redrawn (SC) **3**:178
Voting Rights Act (1965) **2**:139, 145; **3**:178; **4**:67, 132
Voting Rights Acts (1870–71) **4**:56–57
  Enforcement Act (1870) **3**:56, 62, 63; **4**:56
  Force Act (1871) **1**:102, 103; **4**:56
  Ku Klux Klan Act (1871) **4**:56–57

W

Waite Court **3**:56–65
Waite, Morrison **3**:56, *57*
Walker, David
  Appeal **4**:16–17
  biography **4**:16
Wallace, George **2**:163, 164, 179–180
  biography **2**:*180*
  opposing racial integration **2**:179, 180; **4**:119, 129, 130
  presidential candidate (1968) **1**:173–176; **2**:170, 180
Wallace, Henry
  biography **2**:*161*
  and the election of 1944 **1**:151–152
  presidential candidate (1948) **1**:154–157; **2**:127, 144, 152, 153, 160–161
War of 1812 **1**:22, 26, 28; **2**:11
war
  criticism involving (SC) **3**:84, 91–93
  opposition to, Socialist Party and **2**:116, 118
  presidents ordering acts of war (SC) **3**:31, 46–47
Ware v. Hylton (1796) **3**:11–12
War on Poverty **1**:171
Warren Court **3**:135–153
Warren, Earl **3**:v, 135, *136*–137
Washington, D.C.
  March on (1963) **4**:96, 97, 122–*123*
  Million Man March **4**:144, *145*, 149–151
  Poor People's Campaign **4**:96, 137–*138*

Washington, Booker T. **4**:60, *61*, 63
  biography **4**:*61*
Washington, Bushrod **3**:*10*–11
Washington, George
  biography **1**:*6*
  candidate for the Virginia House of Burgesses **2**:6
  presidential candidate (1789) **1**:5–6
  presidential candidate (1792) **1**:*7*–*8*
  and the Supreme Court **3**:1
Watergate scandal **1**:181; **2**:165, 170; **3**:154
"waving the bloody shirt" **2**:57
Wayne, James **3**:19
WCTU (Women's Christian Temperance Union) **2**:66, 67; **4**:153, 166–167
Weaver, James
  biography **2**:*90*
  presidential candidate (1880) **1**:90–93; **2**:89
  presidential candidate (1892) **1**:102–104; **2**:99
Webster, Daniel
  biography **1**:*46*
  presidential candidate (1836) **1**:44–47; **2**:28
Weed, Thurlow **2**:23–24, 29
welfare, Libertarian Party and **2**:187
welfare reform
  Progressive Party (1948–52) and **2**:160
  Republican Party (1932–68) and **2**:135
West Virginia State Board of Education v. Barnette (1943) **3**:123–124
West Virginia v. Barnette (1942) **3**:119
Wheeler, Burton **4**:132
Whig Party **1**:50; **2**:4, 21, 27–31
  Conscience Whigs **2**:28, 42
  Cotton Whigs **2**:28
  Daniel Webster and **1**:46
  platform (1848) **2**:30–31
  presidents *see* Fillmore, Millard; Harrison, William; Taylor, Zachary
  and slavery **2**:28, 29
Whiskey Rebellion **1**:9–10
White, Byron **3**:139
White Camellia, Knights of the **4**:53, 56
White Citizens Council **4**:54
White Court **3**:84–93
White, Edward **3**:69, 84–85
White, Hugh **2**:28
  biography **1**:*47*
  presidential candidate (1836) **1**:44–47; **2**:28
White League **3**:62
white supremacy
  Ku Klux Klan and **4**:53
  National Socialist White People's Party and **2**:176, 177
White, Walter **4**:82
  biography **4**:*68*
Whitney, Eli **4**:170
Whitney v. California (1927) **3**:94, 100–102
Whittaker, Charles **3**:*138*
"Wide Awake" clubs **1**:72
Wilkins, Roy **4**:68–69
Willard, Frances **4**:166, *167*
Williams, Hosea **4**:*130*
Williamson, John **2**:*129*
Willkie, Wendell

biography **1**:*148*
  and the election of 1944 **1**:151
  presidential candidate (1940) **1**:147–150; **2**:*137*
Willson v. Blackbird Creek Marsh Company (1829) **3**:27–28
Wilmot Proviso **1**:56, 57–58; **2**:28, 34, 42, 43
Wilson, James **3**:*3*
Wilson, Woodrow **2**:111
  biography **1**:*122*
  and the election of 1920 **1**:128; **2**:111
  presidency **1**:128
    and women's suffrage **4**:175, 176
    and World War I **1**:122, 125; **2**:107, 113
  presidential candidate (1912) **1**:121–124; **2**:107, 112–113, 122–123
  presidential candidate (1916) **1**:125–*127*; **2**:113
  stroke **1**:2, 128
Wing, Simon, presidential candidate (1892) **2**:95
Winston, Henry **2**:*129*
wiretapping, Supreme Court ruling **3**:94, 102–103
Wirt, William
  biography **2**:*24*
  presidential candidate (1832) **1**:40–43; **2**:23
"Woman a Mystery" **4**:170
women
  antialcohol campaign **4**:166
  clubs, General Federation of Women's Clubs **4**:172
  hours worked by (SC) **3**:66, 82–83, 88
  see also women's rights
Women's Christian Temperance Union (WCTU) **2**:66, 67; **4**:153, 166–167
Women's Journal **4**:162
Women's National Liberal Union **4**:170–171
women's rights **1**:56, 84–85; **4**:153–154
  Declaration of Sentiments and Resolutions **4**:155–157
  and the election of 1916 **1**:125, 126–127
  and the election of 1920 **1**:130
  in employment (SC) **3**:54–55
  Equal Rights Amendment **4**:178
  Equal Rights Party and **2**:72–73
  General Federation of Women's Clubs **4**:172
  National Organization for Women (NOW) and **4**:181–182
  Prohibition Party and **2**:66
  right to abortion, *Roe v. Wade* (1973) **1**:187; **3**:154, 163–164
  voting *see* suffrage
Women Voters, League of **4**:179–180
Woodbury, Levi **1**:61; **3**:35–36
Woodhull, Victoria **2**:72–73; **4**:163
  biography **4**:*164*
  lecture on constitutional equality **4**:163–164
Woods, William **3**:*58*
Wooley, John, presidential candidate (1900) **1**:109–112
Workers' Party **2**:129

workers' rights
  Communist Party and **2**:128
  eight-hour working day **2**:85
  Progressive Party (1912–16) and **2**:121
  Progressive Party (1924) and **2**:132
  Social Democratic Party and **2**:102
  Socialist Party and **2**:116
  Supreme Court Case **3**:66, 81–83
Workingmen's Party of California **2**:85–87; **4**:187
World Community of Al-Islam in the West **4**:142
World War I (Great War)
  criticism involving (SC) **3**:84, 91–93
  and the election of 1916 **1**:126; **2**:107
  Socialist Party and **2**:117
  Woodrow Wilson and **1**:122, 125, 126; **2**:107, 111, 113
World War II
  internment of Japanese Americans **4**:184, 191, 201, 203–*204*
  Supreme Court case **3**:119, 124–125
  Pearl Harbor, Japanese attack on **4**:203
  and presidential elections **1**:141, 147, 149, 151, 153
  Republican Party (1932–68) and **2**:135, 136
  Roosevelt (Franklin) as president during **1**:141; **2**:142–143
  Socialist Party and **2**:116
  Truman as president during **1**:154, 155
Wyoming, and women's suffrage **4**:153, 168

X

XYZ Affair **1**:10, 13

Y

Yick Wo v. Hopkins (1886) **3**:56, 64–65
Young Libertarian Alliance **2**:187
Young, Whitney **4**:70, 71

Z

Zahnd, John **2**:89